Child Welfare Leaders Guidebook

Positioning Human Service Programs to Help Abused and Neglect Children Become Effective Adults

David Gilgoff

Dedication

For Betsy,
the love of my life

Chapter 1 Overview

Abbreviations
CCS –   Caring Children's Services.
BOD -   board of directors
GCWA – government child welfare agency
IRS –   Internal Revenue Service
PCWA – private child welfare agency
VYH -   Valley Youth House

The President Assures the Infrastructure

This book aims to help aspiring and experienced staff leaders to transform the lives of   troubled children. The PCWA leader helps very few children. They assure that the organization's infrastructure supports the helping and healing experiences that direct service staff, children, and families have that result in improved lives. The goal is to have the reader acquire the knowledge that will enable their organization to achieve excellent service, financial, and organizational results.

Overview of the Chapters

Chapter 1 – Overview The remainder of this chapter briefly describes the other chapters. This chapter also includes the rationale for the selection of subjects in the book. In addition, I discuss the key components of private child welfare agencies (PCWA) along with the important external events that shape them.

Chapter 2 - Successful Leader's Actions and Character I describe the actions and behaviors of leaders that result in high regard and relate them to important American beliefs. Next is a discussion of the ideal character of the executive.

Chapter 3 - Hiring the Top Tier Staff that are Essential to Organizational Success There is an emphasis on having great staff and how to get them. The interview process functions to determine if candidates possess the background, attitudes, and characteristics to make a difference for children. Following there is a portrayal of staff compensation including salary, benefits, and leave time along with some beliefs about what the staff thinks is important

Chapter 4 - Management Collaborates with Staff to Achieve Great Outcomes There is an analysis of the duties of the front-line supervisor and the direct service staff. A discussion of training direct service staff, first line supervisors, and administrative support personnel follows. There is advice on staff evaluation, staff discipline and staff personal development. Taken together this information will help the reader arrive at a way to have the staff focused, accountable and supported. There is an analysis of the relationship between the supervisee and the supervisor. Using this information results in good client engagement and risk management, and an outcome-oriented case process.

Chapter 5 -Avoiding a Monstrous Kerfuffle by Knowing Federal Employment Law In this chapter I concentrate on the key civil rights regulations, the operation of the Equal Employment Opportunity Commission (EEOC), the complaint investigation process along with the actions PCWAs take to avoid complaints. There is instruction on training staff to be agency ambassadors.

Chapter 6 - Succession Planning There is an investigation of several executive search alternatives including promotion, use of an executive search firm, and a BOD led search, to complete this irregular but crucial task. I write about membership in, and the many activities of The BOD leadership recruitment committee, executive compensation and employment contracts.

Chapter 7 - Prevention of a Pain in the Neck – The Effective and Successful Board of Directors The main topics of interest are the recruitment, and functioning of the BOD. I cover the preparation for and the conduct of meetings. I emphasize the role of the president in engaging the BOD members, and working with them to make the committee and board meetings satisfying for the members. There is a discussion of the similarities and differences between the values of the (BOD) members and staff. An appendix has charters for board, finance, fundraising, personnel, information technology, executive compensation, 401kl committees.

Chapter 8 - Four Powerful Ideas to Use as a Policy Smell Test
This chapter describes the criteria to meet in policy formulation. The key is the four principles that underpin the many policies that govern PCWA operations. These are child safety, professional operations, sound business practices and the prudent person standard. There is a case example illustrating the importance of the prudent person principle.

Chapter 9 - Tactical Policies that Reduce Migraines The chapter begins with a review of criteria for starting programs. I review different tools used in program development – mixed environmental scanning, the case-based method, and service selection style. Also, I cover business plans and criteria for closing programs.

Chapter 10 - Policy Making, Bylaws, and Conflict of Interest Policies I mull over the mechanics of policy consideration and adoption. The chapter addresses the articles of incorporation, by-laws, the mission statement, conflict of interest policy and whistleblower policy

Chapter 11 - Sixteen Child Welfare Specific Policies This chapter discusses 16 policies that PCWAs ought to consider. Both administrative and clinical polices are in included.

Chapter 12 - The Rightfully Feared and Deservedly Avoided Strategic Planning Process This chapter instructs readers on how to construct a strategic plan. It discusses the planning committee composition and tasks. Methods for obtaining, reviewing, and analyzing community data and obtaining inputs from key agency constituencies are detailed. There is a plan outline.

Chapter 13 - The Big Money - Public Child Welfare Contracts This chapter delves into the most important funding source for PCWAs. It is essential to develop and maintain a positive relationship with the public child welfare agency's lead administrator. Acquiring knowledge of the GCWA (Government Child Welfare Agency) structure and understanding the challenges (such as funding, licensure reviews, program initiatives, etc.) facing the administrator is integral to decision making for the PCWA. Understanding the structure of the GCWA, and the administrator's focus and how to begin a relationship with them is essential. There is a review of legal and regulatory subjects as well as the contracting process and the contents of contracts.

Chapter 14 - The Yellow Brick Road to Grant Writing Proficiency
This chapter spells out how to add a grant writing component to the organization and deciding on whether to pursue a grant. There is scrutiny of needed data, project selection, the written proposal pro forma, the division of grant writing responsibilities and key community contacts. The discussion includes using the grants.gov web site, and meeting federal administrative requirements. Information on the federal grant application process and information on how to respond to a specific funding opportunity announcement concludes the chapter.

Chapter 15 - The Other Big Money - Winning Large Federal Grants This chapter gives specific instructions on writing the federal grant narrative. The PCWA delineates their proposed project's objectives, outcomes, and documents the need for the project using community statistics. The purpose of the approach section is to detail how the agency will implement the project idea. Next, applicants provide a profile of their PCWA emphasizing the organization's specific experience that enables it to do an effective job in providing the services described as well as a general description of the PCWA including its auspices and structure. The last subject in the chapter is the construction of the budget and budget narrative.

Chapter - 16 Money for Program, Endowment, and Buildings – Private Fund Raising This chapter begins with an assessment of an organization's readiness to engage in private fund raising. The formulation of a development plan, development reports, and funding tools follow. There is a consideration of staff roles and job descriptions, along with a brief discussion on marketing. Next, there is a demarcation of the role of events in organizational life, in raising money, making friends for the agency, and involving the BOD. The time, effort, and rewards of large donor cultivation, and the annual and capital campaigns receive attention.

Chapter - 17 Financial Statements, Schedules and Staff The focus of this chapter is the organizational financial statement. There is a review of the debate of speed versus accuracy in statement preparation. In addition, there is consideration of the basic decisions that affect reporting such as recording depreciation and the cash versus accrual method of accounting. The topic includes the components of the financial statement and its formatting. Several examples of financial report analysis inform leaders when action is necessary to improve results. There is a presentation of how to use the accounts receivable report to guide expansion of each customer's use of the PCWA. The next topic is the annual budget plan. The chapter ends with a discussion of activities leaders engage in to assure the financial policy and financial policy implementation are consistent.

Chapter – 18 Independent, and IRS Audits; Medicaid Fraud Policy This chapter starts with a discussion of a purchasing process that complements the conflict of interest policy, and reflects federal government standards. Next is a detailed discussion of the PCWA audit components including the engagement, fieldwork, audit report opinion letter and bidding out the audit. Other topics include the role of the audit committee, IRS audits, and Medicaid Fraud Waste and Abuse Policy.

Chapter 19 - Treasury, Investment and Related Financial Policies The formulation of two key money management tools, the treasury, and the investment policies form the basis of financial practices. The chapter also addresses related financial policies; the agency credit card program, spending authority limits, competitive bidding, and purchase approval requirements. The other topics include check signing practices and restricted fund purposes and rules. There is a review on managing endowment gifts and considering gifts of property.

Chapter 20 - The Mysterious 990 Tax Filing A detailed examination of the 990-tax filing is important because it embodies best practice in charitable BOD and management functioning, and is an excellent business intelligence tool. There is also a short section on state charitable commissions

Chapter -21 Untangling Insurance Policies and Purchasing Process There is an explanation about how obtaining insurance differs from making other agency purchases. In addition, the types of insurance policies and policy coverage receive scrutiny. A presentation of a fictional example of the claim processes lists and explains each step.

Assorted and Sundry The material following the chapters includes a citation of sources followed by a description of the composition, membership, and duties of each BOD committee. Next and the acknowledgements, and last is the index.

Strategy in Choosing Material Covered

Readers may question the level of detail given to some of the above topics in a book aimed at presidents, upper level managers, and candidates and students that aspire to hold these positions. Although senior people will not be organizing the personnel files, they will ultimately be accountable for the accuracy of this as well as the other human resource tasks. One of the important jobs of senior managers is to assure the organization has good protocols in place, and routinely check that they are operational. If protocols do not exist or are not functional, small problems can turn into big headaches if things go wrong.

A solid agency infrastructure is necessary so that the day to day business of the agency occurs in an orderly way and agency leaders can advance their agendas rather than dealing with low level problems. For instance, a lack of clear policies and procedures can result in difficulties including customers who are unhappy with the agency invoice format, audits with significant findings, investigations by regulatory bodies, or employee complaints.

I address government contracting and grant writing in depth because of their importance in funding the child welfare mission. Readers will be able to set up and implement a successful grant-writing program. They will have a clear idea of the nuances of public contracting in child welfare and know the strategies that lead to success in establishing agreements. I have taken care in the selection of topics, so that the reader ends up being more capable of doing an effective job.

I do not address every possible topic. The work of John Maxwell and Peter Drucker are excellent sources to consult on personal leadership development. The Council on Nonprofits, Board Source, Independent Sector, the Foundation Center, and state PANO websites has information and resources on many topics relevant to nonprofit leaders.

The Universe of the Human Service Agency

The universe has its planets and stars. Similarly, a PCWA has parts to its "universe", and I briefly describe them here. Human service leaders are "astronomers" who need to know the stars and planets in their solar system and how each part of their cosmos works.

The Mission

The purpose and driver of any PCWA is its mission. PCWA's aid abused, neglected, and emotionally troubled children and their families. Success is the ability to play a role in these youth becoming successful adults. The mission is the most basic statement of the rationale for the organization's existence; agreed to by all involved. The litmus test of any organizational decision is: Does it further the mission? Someone first learning about a social service organization should find the relationship between the services offered and the mission statement apparent.

Programs and Services

In most PCWAs, there is specialization in one or more residential services. These include foster care, group home care, congregate care, and independent living. In addition, specialty residential programs exist. These include runaway and homeless youth shelters, group homes for sexual offenders, and homes for youth with conduct disorders, and treatment foster care. The second major category, are non-residential services. These include a very broad range of services some of which are educational programs, office, home and school-based counseling programs, mentoring efforts, intensive day psychiatric services, as well as outpatient services. There are other services outside of these categories such as computer based or telephone-based crisis services, drug prevention services, parenting education services, and community crises response services such as sending counselors to schools following a school or student tragedy. Often PCWAs also provide services outside the field of child welfare services. These include day care or domestic violence services.

The mix of services offered by each PCWA relates to their history, or "mother ship programs", the agency's strategic plan, community need, and federal, state, and local priorities, large donor interests, and the agency mission. Two additional important factors are that funding sources sometimes identify agencies to implement new programs based on the similarity between the new program and the agency's current programs or their unique physical facilities. In addition, funding sources may request an agency to provide a program that has stringent reporting requirements because of the agency's superior administrative infrastructure.

Consumers - Their Circumstances, Characteristics, and the Service Relationship

Most children helped at PCWAs are abuse victims, neglected or experience emotional difficulties. There are "service characteristics" worth mentioning about them. These differ for children and teenagers.

Referral Process Younger children get help only if staff at a child welfare agency, school, police department, hospital or a parent, or neighbor, refers them or their family to a GCWA or PCWA. Younger children usually do not request services on their own. Hospital staff refers a newborn of a drug-addicted mother to a GCWA. Medical and school staff informs this agency about infants and young children with visible burn marks and scars. In addition, educators refer elementary and middle school youth with excessive truancy. Police officers who respond to a domestic violence call sometimes take emergency custody of children who are also in danger of being domestic violence victims.

However, the teenager compared with a younger child often-initiate help seeking behaviors. As a result, the parents are involved when their teenage child asks for help. This holds in the case of the runaway who seek help because of unhappy family situations. Several other types of older youth also self-refer. These include, youth whose parents eject from their homes. Also, there are the youth who fail in their attempts to live independently when they leave foster care. In this group of older teens, there are many GLBTQ youth, and teen mothers because parents will not permit them to continue to live at home. Generally, this is associated with shame and anger on the part of the parent.

Services There is specialized programming for each age group. With young children counselors use sand boxes, figurines, and other types of play therapy. Therapeutic childcare, nurseries, nurse home visitation programs and foster care are other programs that help infants. In very disorganized homes, homemakers assist parents. Help for teenagers include verbal counseling, role-playing, and adventure therapy. Some teenagers go to live in a foster home, a group home, or large residential program.

Help Seeking Patterns Another characteristic is the client's willingness to participate in services. There are three types of consumers, voluntary, semi-voluntary, and involuntary. The first situation is when the children and or parents recognize that things are not going well and seek out help on their own. The second group, which is significant in size, comes upon referral from a GCWA in connection with a finding of abuse, neglect, or the need for supervision of the child due to child behaviors (chronic runaway, or truant). The parents participate in services or they do not. Sometimes the GCWA ties service participation with the parent(s) keeping custody of their child.

Parents are often resistant to and resentful of help because it is associated with the idea that they are unsatisfactory caregivers. The involuntary consumer is a family in which the youth is under the supervision of the juvenile probation department due to delinquent behavior. Failure to participate in services may lead to incarceration for the delinquent child.

Internal Stakeholders

The Staff The most important organizational resource is the direct service staff. The staff's dedication to accomplishing the mission, their compassion, skill, knowledge, commitment to quality and hard work are the main contributors to agency success. Even though BOD members are unpaid, it is up to them and agency management to let the staff know they are valuable. If you have a superior set of policies, and a wonderful management team and BOD, but the staff is not talented and committed, you cannot achieve the mission. The other key internal parts of the staff are the managers and leaders. The president and vice president need to be good clinicians and business people, skilled at customer relationships and fund raising and possess the ability to inspire the staff and be excellent strategists. Middle managers are important to agency stability as turnover is often high among direct service staff at a PCWA due to poor salaries and working conditions, and the age of the direct service staff. Because they are at the beginning of their career paths direct service staff often return for graduate work, switch fields, and jobs. Middle Managers need to be excellent clinical teachers, assure the quality of the work, and interface well with their peers at customer agencies.

The Board of Directors (BOD) The BOD monitors the implementation of the mission and the financial integrity of the organization. BOD members act as a liaison between the organization and the community and arrange fundraising contacts. They create agency policy and the members provide expertise in the areas of finance, marketing and fundraising, human resources, and risk management.

External Stakeholders

Customers The most important of the customers are the city, county, state and federal child welfare agencies (GCWA). Although there are written contracts, I always regard the GCWA – PCWA relationship as one of being on the same team but playing different positions. Another important customer is the managed care company who is the government's agent in managing behavioral health service for the poor, and monitoring the expenditure of Medical Assistance dollars. The relationships with the child welfare and managed care organizations are different from the relationship with grantors. In the former GCWA, choose the specific consumers. In the latter, the agency selects the individuals using grant guidelines. Children who receive GCWA and public behavioral health services (funded by Medical Assistance) must meet service criteria, and these organizations are the gate keepers determining who gets help and the kind of help they get.

Donors Donors are individuals, foundations, corporations, small businesses, churches, and civic groups that make cash, and sometimes non-cash gift to support the agency's work. The gifts can support an event, or program, endow a project, support a capital campaign, or be in response to agency annual campaign activities. The range of gifts varies depending for the most part on the ability of the giver and the amount requested.

Private donations are unique compared to government support because often they are more flexible, and sometimes because they fund projects that are of interest to the donor. Among large donors, determination of the projects they support is more common than in the past. Private dollars also are unique in that they fund program activities not supported by public dollars. Donations can endow projects to ensure their long-term viability which government usually will not do. Private contributions usually supply most of funding for capital acquisitions such as buildings and property, although government also makes significant grants for these projects. Some government grants require matching funds, which often come from donors that wish their gifts to leverage other funding. Service payments made by government sometimes do not cover the full cost of services, or the full quantity of services needed. Undesignated private funds "subsidize' government payments in these situations.

The Impact of External Events

Events outside of the PCWA have important implications for the organization, and provide lessons on the values of constituents. In these situations, the old saw "when the clue phone rings pick it up" applies.

For the most part these events raise questions about risks, practices, and standards. One example of this happened near the middle of my career when the leader of Covenant House, (which then as now is the preeminent organization serving runaway and homeless youth internationally) Bruce Ritter, a Roman Catholic priest, was reported to be involved in sexual relationships with children and to have stolen money to finance family member businesses (Kelly, 1999). When this story broke in 1989, BOD members asked me how I knew that our staff was not molesting children. In addition to reviewing child abuse reporting procedures, staff supervision, and risk management strategies with the BOD it led me to think about the issue of transparency. Accordingly, if we are involved in any litigation, a child dies, if one of our staff commits child abuse, or there is any other serious situation I promptly report it to the BOD. Openness and accountability characterize communication by the president to the BOD.

Organizational Infrastructure

I think of the infrastructure as the activities that support implementation of agency programs. These include:

Human Resource staff sometimes hires staff, tracks the extensive paperwork associated with staff hiring, manages staff benefits, tracks paperwork associated with leaves of absence etc. However, the staff and processes involved in the hiring of the direct service staff is the core of the quality assurance program. It is important that the direct service staff supervisor make the final decision on whom to hire.

Customer Relations is a joint responsibility shared by management and direct service staff to assure that the agency satisfies the needs of the GCWA, behavioral health organization, United Way, and donors that fund the work

Grant Writing The grant writing staff is responsible for procuring and maintaining the grant income that comes from government and foundations.

Finance The finance director delivers monthly the good or bad news about the bottom line, the state of the cash flow, and cash assets. The finance staff keeps the financial records and assures compliance with legal and customer requirements related to organizational finances.

Information Technology assures human resource, consumer, business, and reporting technologies organization wide and coordinates hardware, software, and cloud-based applications.

Maintenance This staff makes repairs and completes renovations at agency buildings and properties, as well as, rental properties occupied by Independent Living Program consumers.

Private Fundraising and Marketing includes conducting events aimed at fund raising and friend making, individual donor relationships, annual campaign efforts as well as capital campaigns and planned giving.

Chapter 2 Successful Leader's Actions and Character

How do Child Welfare Leaders Become Successful?

The reasons private child welfare leaders get positive evaluations from BOD members and community leaders is that they demonstrate the following characteristics, which reflect important American values.

First, they repeatedly end the year in the black and others think of them as competent businesses managers. They demonstrate the important social value of prudence.

Second, they protect children in their program from harm. The rule "do no harm" in the Hippocratic Oath translates to "keep the child safe" in the field of child welfare.

Third, high quality services characterize the implementation of the mission. This reflects the American value of "do your best". They distinguish their organizations in a positive way from other agencies.

Fourth, people know they have a good character and demonstrate positive behaviors in their professional relationships.

The Ten Commandments and the Leader's Behaviors and Beliefs

There is a history dating back to the ten commandments (Bibleinfo, 2019) of correct moral behavior. The commandments and their applicability to leaders of a PCWA, as I interpret them are:

> ➤ *You shall have no other gods but me.* Put your belief in the organization's work first, above other interests.
>
> ➤ *You shall make no idols.* You do not waver from achieving the mission by unworthy ideas *or projects.*
>
> ➤ *You shall not take the name of the Lord God in vain.* Be respectful of your organization, and do not speak in a way that degrades it.

> *Keep the Sabbath day holy.* Do not sully the mission of helping children by allowing activities that detract from it.
> *Honor thy father and the mother.* Respect the knowledge and importance of the organizational predecessors. Respect legitimate authority.
> *You shall not murder.* Anger or bitterness does not characterize your professional behavior
> *You shall not commit adultery.* Your professional life does not include illicit sexual relationships.
> *You shall not steal.* Do not steal from your PCWA.
> *You shall not bear false Witness against the neighbor.* Do not slander competitors
> *You shall not covet.* Be content, and do not seek excessive compensation.

Fifth, they engage the BOD members and the staff in the urgency and importance of the mission. Good leaders are visionaries. They maintain good staff morale, and an involved, interested board. In this vein, they set the agenda for the BOD and staff through discussing their vision and sense of organizational direction. They create and uphold good agency business practices

Sixth, they get important things done. They have focus and do not squander their time. If you continually feel the number of things on your things to do list exceed your work capacity do what is important rather than what is urgent. Assign some of the tasks to other staff, and resign yourself to the fact that you will not get everything done. For those things you will not get to, email the person involved, and tell them to ask someone else to help instead of you, unless they are willing to wait a considerable amount of time. Apologize and let them know the workload is too high and you cannot get everything that is important done.

Check the email twice a day. You do not have to respond to the noise every time the computer beeps. Some people are now putting one email address on their business cards, and asking people who are essential to email them at a second email address.

Rules of the Road

Rule # 1 - The Agency Mission Guides Everything Else.
 If the connections between any program proposal and the mission is not apparent "fuggetaboutit".
Rule #2 - The Children Determine What to Do
Over the course of my first decade at VYH, I heard about the lives of thousands of runaway and homeless youth staying at the shelter during staff meetings. Listening and thinking about what I heard was a very important experience for me. The stories of these youth were an in-depth qualitative needs assessment. The stories about the lives of these youth shaped my thinking about what we should do to improve their lives and strengthened my resolve that many children would get a better deal in life than they had to date.

Most of the stories of these youth are very troubling. They are about teenagers who are the victims of physical and sexual assault. Other children live with the kind of neglect that occurs when parents are committed to drug and alcohol use, or have serious mental health problems.

There are stories about children, whose emotional scars result in alienation from their families and mainstream institutions, including their churches and schools because they are reluctant to trust anyone. Helping these children is the core mission. The experiences of traumatized children and the trauma's impact on children's personality and social functioning are important considerations in program design.

Rule # 3- Create an Agency Culture that Promotes Positive Youth Development
Be sensitive to each child's story but do not see them as a story but rather as an individual with skills, talents, strengths, ambitions and hopes. This is essential to a strength-based approach. Staff helps youth to utilize these attributes, through counseling, support, protection, housing, and encouragement. They create the circumstances and opportunities that will allow youth to turn things around for themselves.

It is essential to appreciate the resilience, effort, and struggle to succeed of many of these youngsters. It is inspirational. Integrate things that youth do to improve their own lives, into the agency practices.

Rule # 4 – Address Important Organizational Problems
The job includes the duties listed in a specific job description and several other important tasks. These latter items include: 1) strengthening areas of agency weakness, which are quickly revealed through organization self-assessment instruments, 2) addressing any "elephants in the room" such as BOD members or staff who have been allowed to remain affiliated with the PCWA but do not make much of a contribution, or worse create problems

that distract from a focus on the mission, and 3) knowing the specifics particular to the organization that will move it from being good to being great. This may include service elements not offered by other agencies, high quality services, or superior customer satisfaction.

Rule # 5 - Assure Decision Making is Inclusive

Create an inclusive organizational decision-making process. One in which everyone has a voice and the leaders actively seek out the ideas of the people who help the children. Talk with staff at all levels who are top performers. Periodically attend program level staff meetings. Have direct service staff serve on committees, and participate in agency strategic planning efforts. Use monthly leadership meetings to receive manager's input about decisions.

Rule # 6 - Develop an Ownership Culture

Create a culture in which you decentralize power, and the staff are owners rather than employees. Do this by matching authority with responsibility and accountability.

Rule # 7 - Have a Vision for the Agency's Development

The vision is simple, inspiring, and easily communicated. There needs to be a good match between agency activity and the vision. My personal vision is to provide the highest quality services to as many troubled children as possible that will improve their lives.

Rule # 8 - Respect Everyone.

There is a great deal of diversity in human service organizations. This includes a workforce that is primarily female, people of different races, and people with different sexual orientations using and providing services. Unless someone acts to hurt himself, herself, or someone else, or is violating the law or agency policy, it is important to respect their attitudes, and actions, even when you do not agree with them. For example, an important American value is hard work. In other cultures, loyalty and assistance to family members is more important than hard work.

Rule # 9 - Be Aware of the Environment

Be knowledgeable about community values and standards. Keep up with important community news. Know about developments in child welfare as well as funding trends. Pay attention to developments in the business world and political news.

Rule # 10 - **You Do Not Have to be Right; You Just Have to Get It Right**

It is not important to be right, but to do the right thing, no matter who has the right idea. Always give credit when a staff member comes up with a good solution. Even if it is not your idea, you will share in the credit.

Rule # -11 - Live Up to the Prudent Person Standard for Leaders

Use the prudent person standard to manage each situation. Rather than specific criteria, the prudent person standard relies on a normative model marked by the due diligence, and actions of a person, when compared to what a prudent person would do in the same situation. The prudent person who is a leader possesses knowledge, conducts research, analyzes information, and takes action that one would ordinarily expect of a person in the position of president. The professional leader has the responsibility of being knowledgeable about both the field of child welfare and good business practices and applying this knowledge to organizational operations and decisions.

Rule # 12 - Leaders Understand the Priorities and Values of the Five Major Stakeholders

The important agency stakeholders are the children and families, the staff, the BOD, large donors, and government Children and families want help and solutions that improve their lives. They have their own values, beliefs, and priorities. If they do not see the PCWA as helpful, receptive, and respectful, they resist participating in services

The BOD and staff are different from other stakeholders in that they are internal to the organization. Staff is interested in fairness, social justice, nurturing children, and making the world a better place to live. The bottom line for staff is to help children. Many of the BOD members have corporate affiliations. Other members are small businesses owners or professionals such as lawyers and accountants. BOD members, are likely to emphasize effectiveness and efficiency in implementing the mission.

GCWAs want the PCWA to help children, assure children attend school, stay out of trouble, and are safe. In addition, they want the PCWA to help improve the parenting skills of a child's caretaker. They value PCWAs that accept children upon referral and for the most part offer unconditional care.

Large donors are interested in the difference that their gift makes for the children and the organization. They want to be up to date on the utilization of their gifts. Knowing these different priorities is important and addressing the priorities of each stakeholder group in a way that they find satisfying keeps them engaged with the agency work.

Chapter 3 Hiring Top Tier Staff that are Essential to Organizational Success

Great Staff are Essential

The main way the agency changes a young life is through the staff who works with the children. **The ability to assemble, to retain, and appropriately deploy a caring and knowledgeable staff is the single most important factor in achieving the mission.**

Staffing the Human Resource Function

A small human resources department is superior to a large one. Program managers and supervisors are best able to handle the hiring and firing functions often performed by a human resources department. The program managers know the skill sets, experiences, and the personality types required for program implementation. Personnel requirements vary by program.

The human resources staff provides benefit enrollment information to new employees and responds to staff questions about compensation and the personnel policy. They ensure organizational conformance with non-financial personnel laws and regulations.

The program manager that will be the successful applicant's supervisor handles interviewing, reference checks, hiring, employee evaluations, and compensation recommendations. Automate timecards, calendars, and benefit management to bring efficiencies to personnel routines whenever feasible. With executive approval, usually given, managers have the authority to discharge their direct service staff. Executive approval authority assures adequate documentation exists, and that the manager's administration of employee discipline is fair. The time, cost, aggravation, and effort entailed in managing one sex discrimination, disability discrimination, or race discrimination case supplies the rationale to not make mistakes regarding protected class firings.

In addition to hiring, beyond what is in the personnel policies, program manuals, grant award agreements, prescribed by law or licensing regulations each manager uses their own discretion in managing the staff. As a result, there are some differences between programs in personnel administration.

Line supervisors and program directors have this kind of authority to encourage a culture of ownership. Each manager "owns" their program, much as if they are the owner of a small business. The idea is to delegate both the authority and responsibility for success.

Hiring the Direct Service Staff

Many years ago, VYH opened a small long-term group home. It was our first effort of this sort and an external expert in the field did a program review. When we met, the reviewer said, "I have very good news for you, the staff likes children". I was very surprised that this was even a question. The reviewer went on to explain that for some other PCWAs employees, the job was just for the paycheck.

Some readers will recall James Carville's famous remark used in Bill Clinton's 1992 campaign against George Bush "It is the economy, stupid". In private child welfare work, "It is the relationship". In dealing with traumatized and alienated children, a trusting relationship with the staff allows the child to consider positive actions on his or her own behalf rather than spending their energies defending against past and perceived current dangers. The staff needs to support each child. It is not easy to maintain a relationship with some of these children. The children's anger and sadness require a staff with emotional fortitude. While many people laud the talent and effort of successful business people, sports figures, and actors, know that many child welfare workers are the real heroes. Along with police, fire fighters, first responders and doctors and nurses these case workers salvage and save young people. For me this is much more important than getting a basketball through a hoop.

While good staff never supports bad youth behavior their acceptance of the children for who they are, and their belief that a child can succeed, often encourages children to grow and change. First, hire staff with the ability to have good relationships with youth and probe for this dimension during the interviewing process. This includes the qualities of enjoying people, accepting people for who they are, the desire to help others become autonomous, compassion for others, patience, being a good cheerleader for youth, and very importantly acting as an appropriate role model for youth.

Many people seek private child welfare work because they have these qualities. They are mission-oriented people and want to do this work. It is a mistake to think that we motivate our staff. Our staff is self-motivated. They are self-motivated for many different reasons. Some have experienced themselves as "natural helpers"- they are the ones others often seek out for help. Others are faith oriented. Still others have overcome their own family difficulties. People helped by a teacher, minister, social worker, etc. want to repay the favor. If a counselor has successfully overcome personal difficulties it is often a very powerful helping tool in working with troubled youth (i.e. If I can do it, so can you).

Next, discuss the applicant's educational credentials and their experience, to see what they have learned from school and work. This is important because it gives some idea of their potential for further personal and intellectual growth. An ability to learn on the job, as well as a commitment to do so is important, because there is specialized training. If the candidate has not benefitted from their academic experience even if they have a degree, it may mean they are a weak learner. The staff is often inexperienced and need to have the ability to gain from the internal training program, supervision, and staff meetings.

Assess the extent to which applicants have a professional identity. The existence of such an identity usually means that the staff has a bachelor's or master's degree in the field of psychology or social work, several years of experience, and a good sense of ethics and boundaries. The amount of time and level of effort required to supervise staff is usually inverse to their educational level and professional identity. Staff members who do not have much formal training are likely to rely more on personal experience and knowledge than professional standards and expectations.

Hire independent minded people. For the manager this characteristic of independence in the staff leads to the problem akin to herding cats, but also a staff of capable people who can use their own judgment in a line of work that requires this characteristic. Last, hire people who are committed to high quality work and to working hard. Quality work is often one of the main correlates with agency growth. The community begins to believe that if they entrust the agency to help children the agency will do a good job. Ask a candidate whom you wish to hire for the names of three people who will give them references. Also, have the candidate sign a form authorizing you to call the references. Most important have the candidate call the people and tell them you will be calling. Because of fear of reprisals sometimes, a candidate will not want you to contact their current employer. If this is the case, ask them to use a coworker as a reference. Do not accept the names of friends as references. If the person is a new graduate check references available from internships and jobs they worked while going through school. This will tell you something about their aptitude and work habits.

For more experienced applicants talk with their supervisor at their current (if possible) and past jobs. Ask the applicant if they want to tell you about the main positive and negative comments a reference will make. Tell the applicant that if there are any issues, you want to give them the chance to tell their sides of the story, before you speak to the reference giver. The responses you get from candidates to this question are often interesting. In some situations, they talk about positive supervisor comments. Other times they talk about a negative performance situation, such as their tendency to get into conflicts with coworkers. Some candidates make a balanced evaluation of their own work. Record reference checks results.

Hiring Requisition

The hiring process begins with the submission of a requisition to hire by the hiring manager to a senior manager. The requisition then goes to the administrative staff person placing the employment ad. In human services, personnel expenses are the largest cost, and good cost control in this area helps keep a balanced budget. The senior manager reviews and approves all new hires to contain costs. They assure that for new programs, hiring requests are consistent with business plans or grant funding, and that for current programs there are no serious financial deficits. On the other hand, sometimes, a program is losing money but hiring is necessary to meet state licensing requirements or not hiring staff takes away manager's potential to gain additional income.

You have a superior in-house candidate for a job. Go through the interviewing process with this person and if the results warrants, handle it as a promotion and do not advertise the position. Be careful that a promotion decision does not violate the business ethics policies around nepotism or personal relationships. Hiring internally will make most staff excited about their own potential for advancement.

Advertising and Selecting Candidates

In addition to paid advertising, other methods can yield good candidates. College placement offices will likely welcome hiring notices. Staff, BOD members, and their families will often help to get the word out. Students completing internships at the agency who did good work can be good hires.

Usually, there are few internal applicants. However, when you do not post a position notice at each location current staff may regard this as unfair and insulting. To increase staff diversity, contact organizations that have contacts with racial minorities, veterans, etc. Consider offering current employees a modest cash reward when you hire an external applicant they refer.

The resumes of applicants go to the hiring manager (not HR) who rates the resumes and interview as many candidates as they judge necessary, usually three to five candidates. Due to shortages of staff with selected needed characteristics give preferences to staff having characteristics important to your PCWA. These include applicants that reflect race, sex, and sexual preference characteristics of consumers. Internal candidates can interview, unless they are in their present position for lessthan a year or they are on probationary status due to performance problems.

To deal with disability issues give all applicants a copy of the job description, and ask them to acknowledge receiving it in writing. Then discuss the job duties with each applicant (disabled or not) and obtain their opinion on their ability to do the job. In the job description, include the counseling duties, required paperwork and mobility related duties such as climbing stairs, weight lifting responsibilities, and driving requirements. Indicate that the job can be stressful. Where there are concerns expressed by the candidate ask them if there are reasonable accommodations the organization can make so the candidate can perform the job. See chapter 5 for a discussion of disabilities and reasonable accommodations.

Driving and Criminal History Records

Many positions require staff to drive to appointments at consumer homes and to transport consumers. Applicants with poor driving records may not be able to perform this duty due to the risk of an accident. If a consumer is hurt or killed when their counselor or case manager is driving them somewhere, the agency can face negligence charges if they employ staff who have a drunken driving conviction, or have many citations for speeding or dangerous driving. See the annotated example at the beginning of chapter 21.

Check state regulations in your state, and do not hire staff with convictions that law or state regulations prohibit.

There are criminal convictions that you learn about when the required finger printing and criminal record review process is complete. With many crimes, the employer has the discretion on making the hire. In considering practice in this area, relevant factors are 1) safety risks for consumers. 2) negligence risks for the agency 3) type of crime, 4) classification of the crime – a misdemeanor or felony 5) the total number of crimes and arrests 6) time elapsed between the conviction date and hiring date, 7) The relatedness of the crime to the position duties 8) hiring prohibitions in grant conditions, government contracts, professional liability insurance policy, and the Directors and Officers liability policy.

Many middle managers will want to give a potential employee with a criminal history a chance, and that upper management may have to say no if they feel the risks are too high. These situations bring to light upper management's primary concern about risk management, and the hiring manager's desire to fill the position and their high sense of social justice as a value (give the persons who has had bad behavior in the past a chance to get back on the right track through employing them). The uncheck the box movement support this social justice position.

When you do not hire an applicant because they have a criminal record, inform them of this and tell them they can appeal the criminal record if they believe it is incorrect.

Creating an Applicant Tracking Record

Hiring managers keep a written record of the process for all applicants that the PCWA does not hire should they reapply for employment or if they make an EEOC complaint. The form includes standard demographics on the applicant, and important dates such as when the candidate applied, the timing of the EEOC questionnaire, (often a post card mailing asking the applicant to indicate their race) interview dates, and what the applicant revealed about their driving and criminal history. Write the reason you do not hire them. This could be that they are not the most qualified applicant, or they do not possess certain skills or characteristics. For candidates you interview but do not hire write an individualized letter that lets them know you enjoyed getting to know them and may contact them if another position becomes available. Do not send this letter until the person hired has worked for a month. If things do not go well with the new hire, one of the other people interviewed becomes a potential replacement.

Create a standard agency cover sheet that you attach to each resume. Write the applicant name, and the date you receive each resume. Use a resume review ranking system rating the candidates from 1 to 5 or A+ to F. Write the ranking of the resume on the cover sheet. Only interview candidates whose resumes rank high enough. Write the reason you did not interview the applicant on the cover sheet. This could be the lack of a certain credential, that their resume indicates that they go from job to job, or that they did not compare favorably to other applicants. Send the cover sheet and resume to HR for storage. Keep the materials for 18 months. HR sends a post card to the applicant thanking them for their interest in employment and letting them know that a review of their resume indicates that there they are not among the best qualified candidates. Let them know you are retaining their resume for eighteen months. After that time if they want to apply for employment again, they should submit an updated resume and brief cover letter. If you do not get any applications that rank b+ or above, try one or more of the following 1) pull the ad and place it again after two weeks, 2)consider offering a higher than usual starting salary 3) advertise in a different place and list the salary in the ad 4)Send a memo to staff saying the for this job only you are raising the reward for an applicant referred by a staff member by $50.00). Encourage agency staff to apply for the position.

For unsolicited resumes interview the person even if you are not hiring if a review of their resume indicates they are an excellent potential candidate. The interview is an applicant cultivation tool. For other resumes have HR send a postcard thanking the person for submitting their resume and letting them know there are no open positions at present.

Personnel File Startup

Human Resource staff review the results of the following documents and files them: the reference check, the driving record verification, the criminal record check, the physical exam and drug testing results, the employment application, interviewers' ratings and comments, and special certifications and training. Also, note the date of receipt of one or more pieces of information after the hiring date. Retention of the new employee is dependent on the nature of the information received. In the employment letter state the submission of material within 30 days is an employment requirement.

Staff Compensation and Benefits

The staff classifications are salaried (exempt) or paid hourly (nonexempt) employees. The classification matches the employee's duties and salary. Keep abreast of Fair Labor Standards Act rules to make classification decisions

After reviewing hundreds of written exit interview forms completed by employees who left VYH, I find that the theme is most people hold their supervisor and the agency mission in high regard but feel the compensation is not very good. When I have asked people about compensation priorities, I have usually gotten the same answer from the staff 1) salary and 2) health benefits with reasonable deductions. Other benefits particularly retirement plans, tuition reimbursement programs etc. are not as important to them.

Compensation for direct service staff and supervisors is often very low. When setting initial salary scales, and at least once every three years, thereafter, research current salaries. The agency can sometimes get compensation information from the local chapter of the Society of Human Resource Management. Use any existing human service salary surveys for the geographical market. Other inputs can include older salary data, with adjustments for Cost of Living (NASW Center for Workforce Studies and Social Work Practices (2011)) . In addition, as desired, the agency can purchase detailed nonprofit sector salary and benefit information from the Non-Profit Times. (Nonprofit Times, 2014) . The Watkins and Uberall survey results of 518 Tennessee nonprofits are worthwhile to review because of the detail provided (Watkins-Uberall, 2013). Additionally, you can call college placement offices and see if they know the range of offers for new graduates.

Review salary ranges listed in employment ads. Consider conducting a salary survey among agencies that are like yours, as well as others which are not, but will be organizations that staff you wish to employ work for or will apply to. Often in exchange for a copy of the completed salary study, organizations in the area will participate in the study, as they do not know any more than you do, and because personnel expenses are the largest part of their overall expenses. This can be a good project for a student intern with an interest in administration.

In the analysis of the survey results, eliminate organizations where the salaries are much higher because an organization is of a different type. Hospitals, school districts, and public agencies are examples. Once you have excluded these, make sure that your salaries are 10% above the median. If they are not, accomplishing this should be the first goal. Although the agency will probably get by in a down market, once the economy improves it is likely the salaries will not attract new staff and some current staff will seek other employment,

If the organization has a good reputation, it cuts both ways. Superior new graduates will prefer the agency to agencies with mediocre reputations because they will start their career in an environment where they will learn something and do good work. On the other hand, the agency's good reputation makes it is easy for the staff to find positions at other organizations. Just as no money no mission, no staff no mission.

Managers will quickly get an idea of actual salaries needed to attract quality candidates once they start the hiring process. There can be pressure to hire several people quickly because of a new program startup, and the agency needs to offer (and have the funding for) higher salaries. Existing staff are rankled if they see this as unfair. For instance, the agency gets a grant to provide counseling in the male wing of the local juvenile detention center. All the current detention center staff is males under 40 and the detention center director wants the agency to hire young male staff as therapists. The grant amount is generous and the agency succeeds in staffing the program. The next time human resources do a salary review they find the young men hired are earning as much or more than the more experienced female staff. The agency then has an unhappy veteran staff, and there is a risk of employees making an EEOC complaint, based on gender discrimination. The only option is to raise the salaries of the veterans. If the job requires a special skill this does not apply. For example, if the new program requires all staff to be bilingual or have Functional Family Therapy training, the credential justifies the higher salaries.

In addition, the agency will get situations in which current employees use salary offers received from other organizations as the basis for salary increase requests. Be careful about affirmative responses to these because once staff finds out that this tactic is successful, several others may try it.

There are four schools of thought on pay increases 1) give the same raise amount to everyone 2) give raises that recognize good performance 3) do not give raises but if the agency ends a year with a surplus give a bonus. 4) Give everyone a cost of living increase and give bonuses to outstanding performers. Human service workers find the first choice most closely aligned with social justice values (the same for all). Business people like the second alternative because it recognizes individual accomplishments and encourages hard work. This difference of opinion gives some insight into the different values of the BOD and the direct service staff members. Cautious people like the third alternative. The type of raises given should be a matter of BOD policy. I personally do not like bonuses because it gets too close to IRS distribution of surpluses and excess benefit transaction prohibitions. Yet I know several instances of bonuses given, and I suspect unless the agency or president has an enemy who makes an issue about this practice it will not attract anyone's attention. Another downside to bonus systems is that it causes unhappiness among most staff if word gets around that the executive staff receives large bonuses but the direct service staff does not.

The first step for annual staff salary increases is for the personnel committee of the BOD to make a recommendation on a salary pool amount based on available funds, their knowledge of the cost of living increase, salary trends in the field, the likely increase in employee health insurance premium copays, and the effectiveness of typical starting salaries in attracting new staff. The finance committee of the BOD usually agrees with the recommendation because they see the staff as deserving, but reviews it in light of a commitment to a balanced budget.

Health Care Insurance

Like salaries, an important issue is the competitiveness of the employee health plan. A challenge in determining the variety of plans to offer is the staff age divide. Often PCWAs have many young staff that is not as concerned about health insurance compared to salary. A second group of staff who are older, and may have many years of service, will be very concerned about having a high-quality health care plan. Another dimension is that health insurance companies are changing plan types year to year including premiums, deductibles, and copays. As health care premiums rise substantially, some employers choose a higher deductible plan and then make deposits to employee health savings accounts.

Another new consideration under the American Care Act (ACA) is that plan rates are age based. Also, there are penalties for "Cadillac plans" as well as for not offering plans. From my anecdotal observations, different organizations are doing different things. Some are staying the course with their present plans. Others are getting lower cost plans that have higher deductible amounts and higher copays when premiums for their present plan rises. Others are making increased use of health savings accounts, making deposits to employee accounts, and then purchasing lower priced plans. In this environment assure yourself of the knowledge base, expertise, and sophistication of your insurance agent. Meet with them to discuss emerging practices and innovations at other companies. Be attentive to the insurance broker's ability to answer questions, and make recommendations in line with agency goals. It could be a good time to explore with other insurance brokers what they have to offer, so the agency gets a good sense of the alternatives.

Retirement Plans

The design of retirement plans represents both philosophy and cost considerations. Many people think about these plans in terms of their competitiveness with offerings by peer agencies. Others believe that because salaries are often low at children's' charities a strong retirement plan is important. Some feel that as employment tenure, in general declines, the competitive perspective and portability are most important. There is some sentiment that strong retirement plans promote employee retention. My thinking is that there is a bimodal benefit. Young direct service staff has higher turnover rates than older management staff. Consequently, this then is a less important benefit to younger staff and a more important benefit to older staff. If there is no retirement program, though, applicants see the agency as having an uncompetitive compensation plan.

Agencies sometimes design plan contributions based on the money that is available after managers' budget for salary and health benefit costs. A retirement plan is usually available. At a minimum, the PCWA will adopt employee-funded programs. However, most PCWAs offer 403(b) or 401(k) plans. Fewer offer IRA plans or pensions. When the philosophy is that the salaries of the employees is too low for them to make any plan contributions, then the plan, provides for an annual employer contribution without requiring a match. Many plans, however, entail the agency matching employee contributions up to a maximum amount or percent. Some organizations do both, depositing x% a year for all qualifying employees and then offering to match employee contributions up to y%. An example: A PCWA budgets 4% of the salary of qualifying staff to fund the employee retirement plan in a particular year. The PCWA deposits 2% for all qualifying employees. The agency then offers up to an additional 2% to match employee's contribution to the plan. Leadership decides upon a plan participation-waiting period. It is common to allow employees to participate within the first year of employment.

A vestment policy is necessary to decide when employees are eligible to receive the full amount the agency has deposited for them. Vestment of employee deposits is immediate. The plan provider will be familiar with limits applicable to the plan the agency is considering. A mini "golden handcuffs" effect exists with a longer vestment period for deposits made by the PCWA. The agency saves more money with a longer vestment period because of employee turnover. Perhaps because the salaries are modest my observation is that employee participation in PCWA 401(k) plans requiring an employee matching contribution is lower than in the private for-profit sector. Participation rates improve when the product provider takes the time to attend staff meetings to educate employees and encourage people to participate. An automatic opt in policy on a 401(k) plan will also increase participation. This means that if employees do not complete and return enrollment materials then they are automatically plan participants. Many plan designs allow loans for mortgage, medical, and educational costs. An oversight committee with a charter and a written plan document reviews the annual plan audit, make decisions about the plan's mutual funds, and assure the plan meets ERISA requirements. Monitoring poorly performing mutual funds is an important committee task. Each plan participant selects from a predetermined list of funds. Participants make changes at their discretion about which mutual funds they want to invest in. See the401(k) committee description in the appendix for more detail about changing mutual fund choices. PCWA managers are usually not licensed investment professionals. They do not recommend specific mutual fund investments to staff.

Other Cash Benefits

Most agencies will offer mileage reimbursement payments for staff travel, which can become a considerable expense for programs that provide services in consumer homes. Many organizations tie their reimbursement rates to the IRS rates. I think this is a bit generous and I recommend a lower per mile reimbursement rate as a cost containment measure. In addition, many organizations cover the deductible on staff auto insurance policies when staff is on a home visit and their car sustains damages while parked. Other cash payments include training registration costs and associated per diem costs

Tax Shelter Benefits

The most common form of these allows employees to forgo federal income tax payments on the amounts they deposit, usually through payroll deductions. These include retirement plan contribution, health savings accounts, and flexible spending accounts.

Leave Policies

For many PCWAs, the most generous benefit is time off. Compared with the for-profit sector leave policies in the private nonprofit sector can be substantial. Many organizations offer vacation, sick, holiday and personal days. Others offer a total amount of annual leave. Sometimes policy allows for limited leave accumulation. Then an employee receives the cash equivalent for accrued leave when employment ends. Frequently an employee may accumulate sick leave but usually there is no cash compensation if employment ends. With the advent of hourly billing for services, organizations do not earn income when staff is not meeting with consumers. Organizational cost for leave time is much higher than when customer payment begins on the consumer program entry date and ends on the consumer exit date. A factor that affects decisions on whether to offer a total number of annual leave days instead of the more traditional vacation, holiday, personal and sick leave day scheme is the extent to which staff uses their sick leave days.

Most staff use sick leave appropriately. My perception is that perhaps 20% of staff use more sick leave than their state of health suggests is appropriate. The staff member that takes many days of leave loses earned income for the agency. Organizations may want to reduce leave or go to a fixed annual leave day scheme depending on how closely revenue relates to service provision. When there are fewer vacation and personal leave days, the increased number of working (billing) day's results in additional proceeds. There is usually not enough abuse of sick leave to make a big difference. Some agencies are using more part-time staff compared to full time positions to save money. However, many part-time staff also hold full time jobs to which they give a higher priority. The turnover rate appears to me to be higher among part time staff compared with full time staff. In addition, many part-time staff are unwilling to work more hours than their fixed schedule.

An associated issue is leave accumulation policy. Generous vacation leave accumulation policies can result in high balance sheet liabilities (monies owed to departing employees). In addition, accumulated vacation leave payments are at the employee's current salary so an incremental increase in the amount owed by the PCWA to the employee occurs as staff salaries increase. One solution is to limit the number of vacation days that staff can accumulate. A second is to pay days accumulated at the end of the fiscal year at a reduced rate such as 75% of salary.

Sick leave day accumulation limits sometimes cover days until the long-term disability insurance policy payment start date. If the agency also carries short-term disability insurance than the sick leave accumulation period can be shorter. If the philosophy is that, the risk of income loss is a joint employee and agency responsibility adopt a policy that the agency pays half of the ordinary compensation when a staff member uses more than a specified number of sick leave days. The amount paid to employees by disability insurance policies varies and many pays at 50%-60% of salary. Other circumstances regarding leave policy to consider are jury duty, and National Guard service.

The regulations around Family Medical Leave Act (FMLA) situations are straightforward in most cases. Employees take leaves in connection with childbirth, adoption, personal illness; o r care of an ill family member, provided; the employee has worked for 2000 hours during the prior twelve months and provides written substantiation of the request. The documentation is usually either a doctor's note regarding the employee or the family member needing care. Most agencies require a physician complete an FMLA form that indicates the reason for the leave and the probable length of the leave, needed. Leaves are for up to 12 weeks and used in increments at the employee's discretion.

Many agencies allow for the coordination of accumulated personal, vacation and sick leave with FMLA leaves, but varies the type of leave to the leave event. For example, there is a healthy birth of a newborn. The mother can take up to 6 weeks of sick leave to recover from the birth event and up to six weeks of vacation leave to care for the newborn. Note that the father's FMLA entitlement is the same as the mother's, excepting the father cannot take leave to recover from the birth event. The father though can use twelve weeks to care for the newborn.

The recent trend is for some states to mandate some form of paid parental leave (Miller 2019) If the employee does not request the leave and the employer does not put the employee on FMLA leave than for FMLA purposes the FMLA leave starts when either party initiates the leave. If neither act, even if there is a period of leave it does not count toward the 12-week FMLA time limit. The subject as to when the employer should initiate the leave is not always easy to determine. For example, an employee falls at home. Following the fall, they take a day or two a week sick leave for the next ten weeks due to back pain. The employee than informs their supervisor that they will be having back fusion surgery and will be out of work for three months. The employee has already taken fifteen days of sick leave. If the employer had initiated an FMLA after five days of leave than the employee would have 10 FMLA weeks of leave remaining instead of twelve. In this example, presuming good performance, the employer would probably grant an extra week or two for recovery. However, in other circumstances the employer would not want to do this.

Upon return from an FMLA leave, the employee is entitled to a comparable position meaning their job type and compensation remain the same, as well as the work hours and probably the location. However, they do not have the right to their present position. A different work location is also acceptable if the employees commute is no longer than it was before the leave.

Another issue is whetherto provide paid overtime to residential childcare workers who work holidays. This is an incentive for staff to take shifts so others can spend the holiday with families. Again, this is a judgment call about agency emphasis on cost containment versus kindness.

Use of Independent Contractors

In some situations, the use of contractors instead of employees, results in substantial cost savings. This is because contract terms include payment only for the time the contractor spends with the consumer. The determination of whether an employee must complete work or an independent contractor can do it depends on the facts and circumstances of each situation. The primary issue relates to the organization's degree of behavioral control of the contractor. The way to make the determination is to take each situation in which the agency wishes to establish an independent contractor's agreement, instead of establishing an employment relationship and review the work consideringthe Internal Revenue Service (IRS) criteria. The IRS prefers the private employer collect payroll taxes rather than have the individual make payments. IRS criteria limit the type of situations in which the agency can classify theperson as an independent contractor.

Independent contractors are self-employed individuals. They control the important aspects of their work. If the person is workingon PCWA premises, and the work schedule is at the discretion of the PCWA then generally, they are an employee rather than an independent contractor. On the other hand, the agency could have an independent contractor doing school-based counseling. If the contractor works directly with the school staff, has the freedom to determine the time and place of the work, and the type of counseling supplied, this suggests an independent contractor relationship. If the PCWA determines these things than this suggests an employment relationship.

Employer rights are also important. If the PCWA has the right to determine the above, - the work schedule, the counseling technique used, hours worked, even though it did not exercise it, then this suggests an employment relationship. The key is that the only real control that exists for the PCWA is the right to end the contract. In a private contractor relationship, there is no right to supervise, specify work procedures or the sequencing of work, evaluate, or give specific instructions or training on job completion methods. The contractor has the right to hire their own staff to do a job. Independent contractors' invoice for their work. They receive a 1099 tax form rather than a w-4 form. They do not receive reimbursement for their own business expenses such as travel expenses. Payment to the independent contractor is for the completion of a job. For example, compensation for a case aide working as an independent contractor is for the task of transporting a mother and child to medical appointment, not for the driving time or the time spent with the consumer. Risk of profit or loss is another factor in determining independent contractor status. If in the school counseling example, the number of appointments is variable and travel is involved then the contractor could face a loss if the travel and other costs exceed the number of appointments during a given week. In addition, independent contractors offer services to the public so if the contractor works at several schools or has contracts with more than one PCWA this suggests self-employment. Independent contractor agreements should be time limited, for example a school year, as permanency of relationship suggests an employment relationship. The IRS does a good job of listing the various aspects of the relationship with a person to determine employment or independent contractor status. (IRS, 2017)In addition, to the above summary take the time to review the information from the IRS at https://www.irs.gov/newsroom/understanding-employee-vs-contractor-designation

The IRS is likely to review independent contract legitimacy either because of a complaint or in the course of an audit. If the service rules that the agency contractor determination is not correct than the agency is liable for the employer share of payroll taxes, including Social Security and Medicare taxes, and can face fines. The independent contractor status is not a consideration when the contractor applies for unemployment benefits. My experience is that independent contractors have been successful in obtaining unemployment benefits when the agency chooses to end the contract. However, the favorable unemployment insurance benefit decisions have not led to any inquiries from state or federal officials regarding the classification of the person as an independent contractor.

The PCWA uses a document called an independent contractor's agreement, which serves as the agreement between the PCWA and the independent contractor. There can be variations regarding the content of this agreement; however generally they contain a background section, which includes the agency name, address and employer identification number as well as the contractor name address, and social security number. This section also includes the agency's purpose in entering into the agreement and that the individual is an independent contractor that provides, services.

The agreement lists the work that the contractor is to undertake in enough detail so that the work is discernable, but not in so much detail, that one could infer a set of instructions from the description. The rate of work payment, unit of work, and invoicing procedures are in the agreement. Specifically, state that contractor expenses, travel time etc. is not billable. Indicate that the contractor is responsible for all insurance including professional liability insurance and payment of all taxes as required by law. Codicils that are in law rather than agency practice and required by customer contracts are fine to specify in independent contractor agreements including child abuse reporting, discrimination, sexual harassment, HIPPA regulations, and Medicaid regulatory provisions. Do not include personnel or agency policy, and practice statements that a reader interprets as supporting an employment relationship between the independent contractor and the PCWA. After a PCWA staff member writes the first independent contractor agreement, the PCWA labor attorney reviews it. An example of an independent contract example can be viewed at https://nonprofitdocuments.law.stanford.edu/wp-content/uploads/ Independent-contractor-agreement-SLS-sample-06-21-18.pdf

Exit Interviews

A tool that provides leadership with employee perceptions of organizational strengths and weaknesses is a written exit interview form. In as much as employees complete this as part of ending their employment it is summative in nature. I recommend a questionnaire with fixed questions and a 1-5 Likert scale response format.

An introductory paragraph explains the purpose of the exit interview form is to obtain staff members' impression of their employment experience, any issues that the PCWA should address, and the employee's plan upon ending employment with the PCWA. Indicate the form goes to the president's office. To encourage frankness let the employee know the direct supervisor will not see it. The survey could cover the following areas, although again for your organization, other things could be more important - the employee's perception of 1) the hiring and orientation process. 2) the compensation package both the salary and each of the benefits including the various insurance programs, the retirement benefit and different types of time off - sick time, vacation leave etc.3) organizational policies and rules - particularly the evaluation process, and personnel policies 4) organizational culture related to employees including a) friendliness of the staff, b) flexibility of managers in meeting the employee's needs, c) the degree of freedom the worker had in doing their job, d) employee morale, e) opportunities for advancement, f) the training program and g) supervision.

End the form with four separate comment sections asking about 1) Why the employee is leaving their position 2) Agency strengths 3) Agency weaknesses 4) Other thoughts. Occasionally there are negative comments on specific supervisors or policies. If these are program related it is a good idea to let the vice president know about them. Vice president's act when several exit interview forms cite problems with a specific first line supervisor or policy. Compiling the reports every two years and discussing them with the personnel committee of the BOD is one tool to keep policies and practices current.

Chapter 4 Management Partners with Staff to Achieve Great Outcomes

Staff Supervision

This chapter delivers information about using clinical supervision and training to maximize consumer outcomes. Clinical supervision meeting discussions help the supervisee (the direct service worker) to establish intervention plans, and assist them in implementing them. In addition, the supervisor and supervise formulate ideas to deal with problems that arise in the task of engaging the consumers in the helping process and surmounting hurdles encountered in putting the implementation plan into action. Meetings between staff
helping youth and supervisors are case based.

The information below is specific, but it is not prescriptive. Clinical processes vary by program, customer requirements, and organizational traditions. Interventions awarded "model program" status; usually have program specific clinical processes and procedures. Each program has its own operating and procedural manual. Within these you find the PCWA mission, the program history, rules, all program specific paperwork and corresponding due dates.

The president and top managers will not perform clinical supervision work at a large or midsized PCWA. Leaders in small settings may have clinical supervision responsibilities. However, because in my experience the quality of the PCWA clinical work is so strongly associated with organizational success, all leaders are knowledgeable about their organization's clinical work processes. Leaders with a lot of clinical oversight experience may want to skim sections of this material. Leaders who primarily have a business, collegiate or ministerial background can get a good idea of the kinds of processes that are involved in getting good outcomes.

For many years, the tradition was for managers to meet individually with their reports on a weekly basis. With the rise of team provided service, and an emphasis on higher direct service rates this tradition appears to be changing. Individual meetings are less frequent and team and group meetings are more common

State licensing regulations determine staff qualifications, staffing patterns, program services, the characteristics of service sites and impose certain operational requirements. Grant programs can be prescriptive regarding program elements, and the target population components

Starting with a New Supervisee The supervisor is quality assurance agent, teacher, evaluator, support person, role model, and advocate for their supervisees. A high level of caring combined with high performance expectations is a winning combination. Bad supervisor behaviors include humiliating or otherwise disrespecting a supervisee, using supervisory meeting time to talk about the supervisor's problems, and allowing gossip and/or bad mouthing of other staff.

Supervisors develop tools that they use to manage performance. These include reviewing 1) monthly time sheets indicating days and hours worked and 2) staff day sheets to see how many appointments staff schedule and keep.

For home or community- based services administrative staff should call 10% of each direct service staff member's caseload quarterly too determine if staff make and keep appointments and if the consumer is satisfied with services. In residential settings, due to the in loco parentis status of the agency, a vice president has a monthly group meeting with the youth to learn their impression of the service. No other staff attends. At these meetings, the vice president asks the group if anyone is bothering them physically or sexually and if they are satisfied with the care, they receive. Also, in addition to the above all consumers receive verbal and written information on how to make a complaint soon after service begins.

The supervisor communicates performance expectations about caseload size, consumer face time, the case recording method, type, and frequency, as well as the frequency and types of customer communications. Due dates, caseload size, and engagement rates and case process will be program specific. The blanks in the orientation "talk" below will vary by program.

New Supervisee Orientation "Speech"

The supervisor says: "In program x direct service staff have a caseload of about ___ families, spend ___% of their time in face to face contact with their families, and ___% writing notes and reports, traveling to appointments, communicating with the referring caseworker and attending supervisory, staff and other meetings. The families are sometimes tough to engage but the standard is, you engage with ___ percentage of families on your caseload. If you make several efforts during the first three weeks after you begin the case, including phone calls, and unannounced home visits and you have not met with the family than put the family on the supervisory agenda for discussion.

Intakes are due ___ days after ____ meetings with the family. You write a brief case note after each session, as well as a (monthly, quarterly, or semiannual) summary. The format for each of these recordings is in the program operations manual. Please review the manual within the next week. You meet with the customer or otherwise communicate as indicated in the program manual. If there is a crisis or if you have serious concerns about a child's safety email the caseworker, and copy me. Follow up with the GCWA worker within 24 hours if there is no response. Plan to update me at our next meeting on the case status. In addition, if you need to talk anything through when you are dealing with an emergency call me. If you need information or a decision from the referring GCWA caseworker, also do this by email, following up as needed if there is no response. In the sent email box, organize all case related emails using the agency case # as the first characters on the subject line.

It is important for me to have a supportive attitude towards you. I know this a difficult job, and I do not expect perfection. I will be making either constructive comments about some situations in which I think you have done very well as well as situations in which the work needs improvement. You will get a good idea of my opinion of your performance from these. When things go badly, I tend not to focus on criticism but will verbalize what I want you to strive for in terms of performance.

We are jointly responsible for setting the agenda for supervisory meetings. When giving new assignments I will try to make deadlines mutually agreeable. If there are things, I can do for you so that you can get more out of our meetings or develop yourself professionally please tell me. If there is something going wrong for you here that you do not wish to discuss with me please contact the employee complaint officer. Similarly, if you think you have been the subject of discrimination or harassment, we can discuss it, but again feel free to discuss it with the employee complaint officer. I am glad that you have chosen to spend part of the career helping these children get a chance at a successful life"

Just as a supervisor has certain goals to achieve in running the program, they keep in mind that the worker's need to feel respected, safe, part of the team, and to have their aspirations known and supported.

In supervisory meetings cases involving suicidal or homicidal risk get priority. Second priority is cases where progress is difficult. Last are cases that are going well. It is the job of the supervisor to initiate a case review schedule with each worker, based on his or her review of the recordings in the child's clinical record. A written agenda shared in advance can facilitate productive meetings and keep people on track.

Upper management has supervisors determine agency record keeping requirements considering customer requirements and to minimize the time direct service staff spend on administrative duties and maximize face-to-face consumer contacts. Managed care organizations that fund agency behavioral health work regularly audit consumer records and will reclaim significant amounts of money if records indicate staff provide excess, unnecessary or undocumented services. It is essential for managed care cases that the supervisor's review of case records is prompt, regular, thorough, and that the review is attentive to Medical Assistance fraud, waste, and abuse standards, which I discuss in chapter 18.

There is a clear understanding of the presenting problem from the consumer and referral source perspective. These are often different and staff needs training in balancing consumer and referral source expectations. The supervisor monitors timely and thorough completion of assessments, releases of information, and safety plans. The supervisor assures the new worker knows the goals for each case.

Prior to a case review meeting the supervisor reviews consumer record entries, the case plan, and frequency of visits. Toward this end, the agency may have staff write intervention plans in a management by objective style. The supervisor reviews consumers' plans, the results of the quality assurance telephone contacts with the worker's consumers, and the results of any consumer satisfaction surveys. The supervisor's level of instruction and guidance of staff is inverse to the direct service worker's knowledge and experience. As the worker gains experience and knowledge there is a shift to having them assume more problem-solving responsibility.

There are five main areas of responsibility for the direct service worker. These are 1) consumer engagement 2) case assessment 3) problem solving and achieving outcomes 4) termination and follow up and 5) administrative duties. For several reasons, in child welfare work, consumer engagement is difficult. Start to help with something that is important to the consumer. Staff who personalize consumers rebuffing them and feels disliked and criticized by an initial lack of consumer acceptance will have trouble with consumer engagement and may be more suitable to work in settings where consumers are voluntary and seek help on their own. Supervisors monitor supervisee's performance in engaging consumers and the client engagement rate is part of their evaluation.

The information learned, the components of the diagnostic statement, and the treatment plan is sequential. Consumer functioning in key life areas, their history, and affect are all part of the assessment instrument. Crises issues require an immediate response and delay the assessment process. It is best for the supervisee to meet with the families a few times before writing the assessment. As part of the assessment process, the worker describes the program and gives the consumer a pamphlet that reiterates this information, and contains contact information for the worker and administrative staff.

Problem solving and achieving outcomes has some specific dimensions with GCWA consumers. Securing housing, food, and clothing are basic needs. Consumers will rarely be attentive to parenting until they meet their basic needs. This can mean linking families with emergency shelters, food banks, or rental assistance resources. It is often necessary to address emergency problems such as an illness of a family member or a mother involved in domestic violence that has recently left the family home. An important goal of the problem solving and achieving outcomes processes is having the consumer develop skills that they can use to deal with current and future issues.

The worker is responsible for changing personal attitudes and behaviors that negatively influence their work. Workers select their own methods of stress management, and dealing with personal issues such as anxiety, disorganization, or exhaustion. An employee assistance program can be an excellent resource.

Staff Evaluation

The personnel policy at many private agencies specifies a timetable for staff evaluation. Typically, the supervisor provides frequent evaluations during the initial year of employment and thereafter evaluates supervisees once a year. Each department uses a single evaluation format for all staff. Likert scale formats are the most common. The areas evaluated are consistent with the job description. These might include client engagement rate, client achievement of outcome goals, crisis management ability, and quality of case recordings. Some managers ask supervisees to evaluate their own performance to start, and then use a review of the self- evaluation to finalize the evaluation. This process helps focus areas of agreement and disagreement between the supervisor and supervisee. Some evaluation instruments measure only quality of performance and some evaluate the quantity of performance as well.

In programs where customers pay by the hour of service rendered, quantitativeperformance is a significant portion of the evaluation rating. The goal is the number of hours billed monthly that will support the program expenses. Quantitative performance consists of the number of supervisee billable hours each month compared to a goal. For example, the goal for billable hours is 50% of time worked. For an annual evaluation count the supervisee's 10 highest billing months. Eliminating the supervisee's two lowest months allows for poor weather, which affects staff providing home-based services, and personal situations that causes inefficiency such as illness. Divide billing goals and performance into monthly increments so the worker is cognizant of their quantitative performance each month. The supervisor regularly shares the monthly quantitative performance goal and achievement with each supervisee. In setting time worked goals managers use the following formula. Divide the total program expense budget by the per hour fee billed. Next, divide the result by the number of staff and then divide the result by 12. For example, a home-based counseling program has an annual budget of half a million dollars, eight full time staff and an hourly billing rate of $50. The calculation for a monthly billing goal is $500,000 / $50/8/12 = 104 billing hours per month for each staff member. Staff that consistently exceeds the goal percentage will achieve a superior rating on the quantitative portion of their evaluation. In the above example, managers may set the monthly hour goal somewhat higher than 104 hours to account for lower billings for the two months they do not use. In as much as a typical month, including leave days, will include 21 work days or 168 work hours, in the above example. This amounts to about 5 hours a day for client contacts, and three hour a day to complete paper work, attend meetings, and travel to home-based appointments

The comment section of the evaluation lists goals, completion dates and any disciplinary action during the evaluation period. Managers who are evaluating staff whose performance is below what is acceptable should document the areas of deficiency carefully. Also record areas of strength, projects undertaken that fall outside of the job description, and meritorious service. If the evaluation is sugar coated, and thereafter the manager proceeds with disciplinary action, especially termination of employment, then a person reviewing the situation will wonder why the evaluation did not give any indication of the problems. Evaluations are timely and signed by the supervisor and staff member. Some organizations give the employee the right to add an addendum to the evaluation. I do not favor doing this as the evaluation is the supervisor's evaluation of the supervisee. If the supervisor and worker cannot reconcile their differences about the evaluation, the worker may want to file a complaint. The contested evaluation may represent problem areas in the relationship between the worker and supervisor that need attention. Sometimes the employee complaint officer can play an ombudsman role and relieve the tension. Often the evaluation is fair and accurate and the worker has difficulty in getting negative feedback.

A second possibility for monitoring staff performance is abandoning evaluations all together and going with the presumption of good performance unless there is employee discipline. My repeated experience is that although the performance of all of my supervisees was most often in the very good to excellent range that the person remembered the critical comments and either did not agree with my assessment, or had hurt feelings about these comments or even comments that indicated good but not excellent performance. I have reviewed many "Lake Woebegone" evaluations where everything is perfect. On the other hand, evaluations that are very critical of direct staff work lead staff to become downtrodden or combative. Most people have a reasonable capacity to know when they are and are not doing a good job. Often due to their own discomfort, supervisors will not raise areas in which the supervisee is performing poorly. This situation results in a positive rather than an accurate evaluation.

When a job is well-done give positive verbal feedback. When work is unsatisfactory, the supervisor states the desired results and some good ways to achieve it. In cases of unsatisfactory work, the supervisor should be considering ideas that will position staff to do better quality work. If a supervisor is working with staff and the supervisor lacks expertise in the work, in general or in a specific area they need to make additional knowledge resources available to the staff member. This could include meetings with other staff, readings, and outside training. However, some staff lack either the aptitude or work ethic to do well, and when this is the situation the staff discipline process commences.

Staff Discipline

The type of discipline used matches the situation. 1) Informal counseling, which is a discussion that the supervisor documents and keeps the written summary of the discussion in their desk file 2) Verbal warning that includes the reason for discipline and the expectation of future performance (also documented in in the supervisor's desk file). 3) Written warning- the process is the same as for a verbal warning except the disciplinary memo states it is a written warning and indicates clearly the behavioral changes necessary and a timetable for performance improvements. The memo also indicates the consequence of future unsatisfactory performance. File a copy of the memo in the employee's personnel file. 4) Suspension from employment with or without pay. Finally, of course is termination.

The supervisor keeps a notebook summarizing what happened during disciplinary meetings. Each entry includes who attended the meeting, the meeting time and date. In dismissal situations the file contains the supervisor's notes, employment performance evaluations, disciplinary memos, and other relevant records which taken together clearly document the reason for termination of employment and the employee discipline that preceded it

Keep the following general points in mind: Always, have the supervisor meet with the employee prior to administering discipline and listen to the employee's story. This can avoid injustice, employee complaints, and costly litigation. If the situation involves several employees, get everyone in the room to discuss it and have each person tells their "side" or the story. Separate meetings with different employee's leads to a "he said, she said" situation where the stories conflict. Do not follow this process when a customer or consumer is involved in a complaint. Match disciplinary action to the seriousness of the infraction.

In implementing discipline, consider the potential damage, and risks. Ask the "so what?" question when administering discipline. Did the behavior have consequences for a child, particularly the child's safety? Did the behavior weaken the quality or outcome of a service? Did it result in harm to the agency, through payment disallowances or loss of business or property? Did the mistake cause difficulty with an important customer? If the agency has a great performer who is always very late in completing their paperwork, but the agency will not fire them because customers hold the worker in high regard and the worker does a terrific job in helping difficult people, deal with the paperwork issue in a way that this does not involve employee discipline. Whenever possible use logical consequences. For example, the employee does not take vacation or personal leave until they complete the paper work. Any days taken are without pay. The employee submits a doctor's note for each episode of sick leave.

If there is no or little harm done because of a worker's behavior, although the behavior is annoying it may be best not to call much attention to it. Try to differentiate between staff behavior that is harmful and behavior that you find to be a nuisance but has few consequences.

Consider situational mitigating personal and professional circumstances. Consider whether the infraction is part of an intolerable pattern or a onetime event. Discipline should be progressive if the behavior is not very serious. If it is very serious i.e. hitting a child than employment ends

Administer discipline equally. If you have reached the end of your rope with an employee with no children showing up late for work than it is not o.k. to discipline this person, but not someone who has two children to get off to school in the morning and is often late because of this.

New staff at most organizations go through a probationary period. If during the probationary period performance is not good employment ends. Beginners usually want to do their best and impress their boss, so if they do not do so during the first few months chances are their performance will not improve as time goes on. Because social service managers are kind people, they will often want to extend a new staff member's probationary period to give them time to improve - just as we give our consumers time to improve. Doing this usually results in up and down performance and supervisor's regret occurs.

The long-term employee whose performance falters returns to probationary employee status. The supervisor lists needed changes and a deadline for accomplishment. If they meet the criteria, they return to regular employee status. Consider writing the personnel policies so that an employee can only have one return to probation episode during their employment. If their work becomes deficient, again employment ends.

Good employee discipline policies begin with an effective section in the personnel policies. The section lists specific rule violations, and performance indicators, which trigger discipline or discharge. See figure 5-1 below. Poor performance includes an inability to engage youth and families, not seeing families regularly, poor outcomes, and low service levels.

Not completing required case recordings and other paperwork is often a reason for supervisor dissatisfaction with staff performance. The first step is a monthly review of each staff member's charts. When this does not happen and the worker is leaving employment with three or four months of incomplete case recordings, it is evident that neither the supervisor nor the worker did their job. Once a direct service worker submits a letter of resignation, the supervisor does a file check for completeness, and as needed, negotiate a date, no later than the last day of employment for final file entries. In dealing with these situations, be aware that under the Federal Fair Labor Standards Act that if the employee worked the hours, even if there is incomplete work, you must pay them. Tell the employee if the paperwork is not complete by their last date of employment then any bank credit check, employment or license application reference will have a negative component.

Executive staff should review every firing recommendation made. This review includes 1) a brief discussion with the manager on their thinking regarding the firing and the staff's explanation or position regarding the work problems 2) a review of the disciplinary materials in the employee's personnel file 3) a review of the personnel policy handbook to check if the behavior is included 4) a review of performance evaluations 6) a review of any reasonable accommodation request and 7) a review of the employee medical file for relevant information. After reviewing this information, keep several questions in mind. Did the employee performance evaluations and disciplinary communication make the case for firing? Is there clear documentation of poor performance in evaluations and disciplinary memos? Is a single act such as hitting a child at issue? Does the employee, if terminated, have a good case that sex, race or age discrimination was involved in the termination.

Is the termination the discipline used in similar situations with other employees? What are the risks of continuing to employ the person? Do you know the employee's side of the story? Did the supervisor, as appropriate give the employee a chance to improve?

Beware of the "angry supervisor syndrome". Sometimes bad employee performance has gone on for a long time yet the supervisor has not been forthcoming in the employee's performance evaluation nor have there been

Staff Disciplinary Items
*Child abuse *physical or verbal assault *sexual harassment* damaging or negligence of agency property *dishonesty *theft *coming to work high, drunk or hungover *falsification of time sheets, case notes, invoices or administrative approval forms *abuse of sick leave *possession of a weapon while working *inappropriate attire *inappropriate personal behavior, *criminal conviction *violation of program operating manual provision *license violation *illegal discrimination *repeated lateness arriving at work *sleeping on the job

any disciplinary actions. Then at some point, the manager becomes angry that the person has not improved despite the supervisor's support and effort. The supervisor then wants to dismiss the employee, because they feel the employee has taken advantage of the supervisor's kindness. In those kinds of situations, ask the manager to complete the steps and processes, which create the case for a firing. These could include a special interim performance evaluation or an employee discipline memo or both. Doing this usually does not change the outcome, but lets the rest of the staff know that people get a fair chance to succeed.

Do a good job of counseling people out. Termination with cause is a humiliating experience for the person losing their job. If an employee understands they are not doing well they will often leave of their own accord to avoid damage to their self-esteem and avoid the stigma of dismissal and poor employment references. Allow employment resignation rather than firing the person when this is possible. When the agency has long-term staff (7+ years of employment) who are poor performers tell them to look for another job, and give them some time and coaching to do this. This could include help with resume prep, time off to interview, and linkage with organizations specializing in helping with job searches. Do not give untruthful employee references. One choice is to confirm only the position and dates of employment. Whatever the circumstances surrounding an employee leaving do not give a reference until the departing person gives written permission to do so.

Training

An agency training program has three different audiences, direct service staff, administrative support staff, and middle managers. Later in the chapter, there is a discussion of training for upper management employees that are participating in a succession-planning program. In addition, there is a separate discussion of personal development planning and training which prepares direct service staff and middle managers for promotion opportunities.

Training has two general goals, first to assist the staff at becoming more skillful at their job and second, to complete specific new tasks related to new program, IT or financial procedures. Training has many components. In designing training programs, consider the variety of formal and informal training experiences the staff has. For clinical staff these include: 1) formal education culminating in an earned associate, bachelors, or master's degree in counseling, psychology, or social work. Administrative support staff holds a wide range of degrees including high school diplomas, and college degrees in business, accounting etc.

Both groups have some or all of the following: 1) professional experience at the agency, prior work experience, and student internships 2) what is taught and learned in individual supervision and staff meetings, 3) what is contained in program manuals and other materials 4) mentoring from one or more people who possess knowledge and wisdom, and 5) formal agency based training programs.

Management Training for Front Line Supervisors Since the charitable organization's product is an improved life for consumers, training for direct service staff is widely available in the community and often at the agency. However, training for front line managers is scarcer. Up to about a decade ago, supervisors were primarily responsible for arranging the case assessment process, assuring the quality of services and providing supervision and coaching to the direct service staff on implementation strategies. Now their responsibilities also include monitoring program income and expenses, conformance of program operations to grant or funder standards and maximizing staff productivity.

Management training for front line supervisors includes both didactic and open discussion components involving specific "live situations". The name of the supervisee is anonymous in open discussions. Group discussion is important because unlike direct service staff, supervisors are not in regular contact with their peers either because of geography or program differences. A function of supervisor training is to have them begin to form peer relationships that serve to promote mutual support and the sharing of program level materials. For instance, one supervisor might use a great staff evaluation instrument that others will find of use. Some group training topics to consider are:

- Hiring Processes, Procedures and Forms
- HR and the Law – Sexual Harassment, EEOC, ADA, FMLA etc.
- Employee Discipline and Termination
- Counseling Out Employees and Linking Employees to the EAP
- Staff Evaluation

> ➢ Weekly Supervision Process
> ➢ Staff Accountability Tools: Time sheets, billing logs, case note reviews, calendars, intervention plans

Direct Service Staff Training

The following forms the core of an internal training program. The sessions might last for two to three hours each, and all-new direct service staff completes all of them during thefirst year or two of employment.

1. Intake, Assessment, and Case Planning

This includes presenting problem(s) current functioning, family history, and probing in interviews. Client interview write up including, basic demographics, presenting problem, family background, health, social diagnosis and case plan

2. Client Safety (2-7 hours each)

CPR, First Aid, medication management, and fire safety

Crisis management and de-escalation

3. Child abuse reporting

Incident reporting requirements in residential programs, professional reporting responsibilities, review of child abuse and neglect legal definitions, review of the child abuse reporting legislation, using state reporting tools and methods

4. Ethics and Boundaries

Confidentiality, duty to warn, personal relationships with consumers, and dual relationships, review of National Association of Social Work and/or American Psychological Association Code of Ethics.

5. Professional Communication

Communication with child welfare caseworkers, case recordings, case presentations, court testimony

6. Marketing

Handling charitable contributions, working with the development department on solicitation, planning small program events, and marketing to GCWA caseworkers

7. Cultural Competency training

Knowledge about different cultures their history, and values. Racism. The importance of respect.

8. Consumer Behavioral Health

Diagnosis, mental health status exams, psychotropic medication, involuntary hospitalization procedures, managed care procedures.

Training Surveys What is important at your agency may be different from the above suggestions. To see what a direct service staff-training program at your agency should include do a survey. Form a committee that will meet once. The members are two leadership people, three direct service workers hired in the last year and two with three years' experience, two supervisors with less than three years' experience, and two employed more than three years. These people represent each of the agency's major programs. The work product of the meeting is a list of twenty-five training topics. An anonymous survey of all agency direct service staff and front-line supervisors listing each training suggestion and a blank line next to each, instructs the staff to rank the suggestions 1-25. It also includes a space for additional training suggestions. The administrative assistant of one of the leadership members of the committee collates the survey results for each group separately - supervisors and direct service workers. The leadership person presents the summaries at a management team meeting and the management team selects 10 -15 training topics. Add topics if the management team strongly believes that they should be part of the training course. Five staff who has management development plans (management development plan discussion to follow) writes the curriculum for the training sessions. The sessions are one to three hours in length. A person in clinical leadership approves the curriculum. The curriculum writer and a training partner provide the training to staff. Repeat each training session two or three times to accommodate various staff schedules and agency locations.

A phenomenon common to professionals in the helping professions is that they often have had personal difficulties themselves, and this is a double-edged sword. The person who has made the heroic journey of conquering an obstacle is usually courageous, resilient, persistent, and knowledgeable. These are all good personal characteristics for a counselor. Through their own victory over personal adversity, they act as an inspiration and role model for the youth and families. On the other hand, there are many who enter the profession as "wounded angels". They enter the work of helping in part to find solutions to their own continuing dilemmas, as well as, believing that having trouble, themselves, makes them empathetic to others and give them superior ability to bond with consumers.

The experiences and empathy offered by the "wounded angel" are valuable. Negative personal behaviors though result in work difficulties. For example, a staff member has a diagnosis of bipolar disorder and they are benefitting from a therapeutic regimen, involving medication and counseling. Job performance is good. These staff represent the consumer movement in behavioral health and the current trend is to have them participate in helping others because of the assets they have. However, if they have frequent relapses because they stop taking their medication or they find the work with the consumer population depressing things do not go well. The hunt for solutions to their own problems often limits the energy and attention they can give to consumers. Most front-line supervisors promoted internally were direct service workers prior to being managers. They are deeply committed to the helping process and because of this commitment; there is a risk that the manager relates to the staff member having difficulty as a consumer rather than a professional. It is sometimes difficult for them to remember that the mission is to assist the youth and families and not the staff. The best course is to hold these staff to the standards of performance that exist for all staff, while making personal assistance available to them through the employee assistance program and granting reasonable accommodations.

Training for Non-Clinical Administrative Staff

Before designing a training program for administrative staff, a needs assessment and /or survey of staff may be a good idea. A staff-training program for administrative support personnel can include the following segments.

- Owning referral source and consumer inquiries
- Advanced training in Microsoft Office Word, Excel, PowerPoint, etc.
- Training in the range of agency programs and program linking
- Using the IT capacity for organizing files and cross program file sharing.

Management Development Plans

Commitment to staff development begins with the establishment of a plan. The supervisor asks each staff member, annually, if they want to develop and implement a plan. Beyond this, there is no prodding. If the staff member does not take the initiative to submit a draft plan to their supervisor, this is the same as saying they are not interested. It is a poor idea for staff to get involved in personal development work principally to please the supervisor. Supervisors encourage but never leads in the personal development planning process. The implementation of a plan prepares staff for promotion. Some people like to hire from outside the organization because it brings in fresh thinking and avoids the potential conflicts that a newly promoted supervisor can experience with their former peers. Promoting from within shows confidence in the current staff, brings people who know and accept the organizational culture into management, and supports staff retention because people know if they are qualified, they have a chance to become a manager. The specific steps in creating a personal development plan are:

1. The interested staff member lets their supervisor know they are interested in personal development work on their own, or responds

positively to the supervisor's invitation. 2. They include their own ideas about what they should be doing and get input from the supervisor, peers, and other managers for their plan. 3. The plan includes obtaining a mentor who, if possible, is a manager not working in their program. 4. The plan specifies what activities the staff will undertake during the next twelve months in each of six areas: training, practice, mentoring, self-development, administrative knowledge, and skill development. Some potential activities follow. However, in different organizations other tasks might be preferable.

1. Training (choose one activity)
  - ➤ Take undergraduate/graduate work to meet basic degree requirements.
  - ➤ Take courses that are part of an MBA program
  - ➤ Take or audit a college level course in finance

2. Practice (choose 1 or 2 from the list)
  - ➤ Write a grant narrative and/or a grant budget
  - ➤ Lead a staff meeting; train your peers on a specific topic
  - ➤ Assist the program director in preparing the annual program report for the BOD
  - ➤ Serve as a member of an event fundraising committee
  - ➤ Supervise an intern
  - ➤ Write or help write a business plan

3. Mentoring
  - ➤ Start one or two relationships with knowledgeable and helpful managers other than your supervisor or
  - ➤ program director
  - ➤ Meet with the mentor(s) two times annually developing meaningful agenda items for each meeting

4. Self-Development
  - ➤ Deal with personal issues that impede your growth and performance
  - ➤ Choose as many as needed: reading, personal counseling, self-help groups, friendship, spirituality, physical activity, rest, meditation, church attendance and medication

5. Administrative Knowledge and Skill Development (choose three annually)
  - ➤ Understand and apply the agency mission to make decisions.
  - ➤ Knows the goals, objectives, and outcomes of existing programs.
  - ➤ Understands program requirements, licensing, grant or contract terms
  - ➤ Knows the actions listed in the long-range plan
  - ➤ Understands the components of the monthly financial statement.
  - ➤ Knows how to supervise a staff person.

> Can relate to people in a purposeful way to achieve objectives and outcomes
> Has a good working knowledge of managed care
> Understands the key principles of fundraising
> Understands key personnel law - wage and hours, EEOC, ADA, etc.

Chapter 5 Avoiding A Monstrous Kerfuffle by Knowing Federal Employment Law

Federal Legislation

Federal civil rights, sexual harassment, sex discrimination, age and disability discrimination legislation and regulations, cover employment applicants, employees and consumers if the PCWA has more than 15 employees. PCWA with fewer employees are exempt from compliance with the mandates that follow. Protection for consumers does not vary by staff size. In discrimination law, race, national origin and skin color are categories that often overlap but have differences as well. Race refers to people that are different from others based on a physical characteristic such as their hair type, and skin color. National origin refers to the country or region of the world that a person comes from. Color refers to skin color. People with the same skin color may be of different races, and have different national origins.

An important concept in this field of law is that of equal treatment. This means that the process of employment and employment policies are the same for all employees and that management administers them in a way that does not discriminate against anyone based on the criteria above. Equal opportunity means that employment opportunities are available to all qualified employees.

An employer may not discriminate against applicants or employees based on their sex, sexual orientation, race, skin color, religion, national origin, disability, or age if they are older than age 39. Sexual harassment in the workplace is also illegal and is a type of sex discrimination, as is discrimination against lesbian, gay, bisexual or transgender people. All federal anti-discrimination legislation directs employers not to discriminate in any facet of employment. This includes hiring, firing, compensation, job assignments, promotions, layoffs, training, or fringe benefits. It is also a violation in all the anti-discrimination laws listed in figure 5-1 to harass someone. Harassment include derisive comments, jokes, name calling, derogatory wall posters directed at any employees that are members of a protected class. Harassment includes repeatedly calling a person restricted to wheel chair derogatory names related to their appliance. Sexual harassment includes unwelcome sexual advances or, requests for sexual favors. It is also illegal to consider an employee's genetic information in making employment decisions. Verbal harassment is illegal when it happens so often that it creates a hostile or offensive work environment or when it results in a negative employment decision most usually demotion or firing. Casual infrequent teasing however is not discrimination. The person who is the perpetrator of harassment can be a supervisor, a peer, or from outside the agency such as a customer. A first line tactic for the person who is the victim of verbal or sexual harassment that is not egregious is to tell the perpetrator that their behavior is offensive and they need to stop the behavior. Figure 5-1 is a narrative version of the civil rights legislation summary, presented in table format. Only sections of the legislation applicable to employment are

presented. Other forms of prohibited behaviors, such as discrimination in housing may be part of the laws cited, but are not included in Figure 5-1

Figure 5-1 Civil Rights Legislation Summary

Title II of the Genetic Information Nondiscrimination Act of 2008

The title prohibits the use of genetic information in making employment decisions. Genetic information includes information about a person's genetic tests and the genetic tests of a person's family members, as well as about diseases or conditions that are part of the family medical history. Medical personal performing preemployment or fitness for duty examination may not ask about family medical history or any genetic testing results, except in limited circumstances such as FMLA leave requests.

Americans with Disabilities Act of 1990

The purpose of the act is to prohibit employment discrimination against qualified individuals with disabilities. A disability is a physical or mental impairment that substantially limits one or more major life activities. A qualified employee is a disabled person who, with or without a reasonable accommodation can perform the essential functions of the job. Reasonable accommodations include special devices, altered work schedules, and modifications to the work place. Employers may not ask job applicants about the existence, nature or severity of a disability. Ask applicants about their ability to perform specific job functions. Former drug users may qualify as disabled if they meet the other criteria for a disability. ADA does not protect applicants currently engaging in the abuse of alcohol or illegal drugs. The basis of discipline with these employees is their job performance.

Pregnancy Discrimination Act of 1978

It is unlawful to discriminate against or harass a woman because of pregnancy, childbirth or a medical condition related to pregnancy or childbirth. The employer must treat the pregnant woman in the same way as it treats any other temporarily disabled employee.

Equal Pay Act of 1963

This law makes it illegal to pay different wages to men and women if they perform equal work in the same workplace.

The Age Discrimination in Employment Act of 1967

This law protects people who are 40 or older from discrimination because of age.

Title 7 of the Civil Rights Act of 1964

It is unlawful for an employer to discriminate against any employee or applicant because of their race, color, religion, sex, sexual identity (lesbian, gay, bisexual, transgender) or to allow sexual harassment in the workplace

Title VII also prohibits discrimination based on a condition predominantly affecting one race. For Afro-Americans this include sickle cell anemia, or the wearing of beards among men suffering from severe shaving bumps. Color discrimination occurs when a person is the subject of discrimination based on the lightness, darkness or other color characteristic of the person.

Religious discrimination law contains language regarding restricting the job placement because of a customer objection to the employee's religious practice. The law requires employers to make reasonable accommodations such as holiday switching in order for employees to take time to observe religious holidays.

Sexual harassment includes unwelcome sexual advances, requests for sexual favors and other verbal or physical sexual harassment.

(EEOC, 2019)

Equal Employment Opportunity Commission (EEOC)

The EEOC receives employment discrimination complaints related to the legislation above. In 2016, the EEOC settled 97,443 complaints. These complaint numbers do not include the statistics for federal government employee cases, only cases against private employers. In as much as 152,000,000 people were in the labor force in December 2016 this means that that the share of employees filing complaints is very small. (RI.gov, 2017). Perhaps it is between one-half and one percent. The EEOC claims settlement statistics include both current year and prior year charges. The commission determines most new cases, 84 % are without merit or it dismisses them for other reasons.

Conciliation services are voluntary. Investigators offer them when there is a finding of discrimination. Settlement offers and counter offers occur. There is no cost to use the process and it saves the time, expense, and aggravation associated with litigation. Employers lose 1.8% more cases then they win in conciliation.

In addition, EEOC provides a free voluntary mediation service prior to the investigation of a complaint to reach a settlement or resolution. Both processes are confidential and if successful result in ending consideration of the complaint.

There were several paths to positive outcomes for complainants. First, during 2016, Employers paid $438,000,000 to settle complaints in which the employee is successful, or an average of $21,242 to each of the 16,382 people receiving a settlement. Negotiations were successful for some employees. Employers and employees reached settlement in 7.4% of the complaints managed in 2016, and Complainants withdrew complaints with benefits in 5.4% of the complaints. Monies paid to complainants also include cases litigated by EEOC. Table 5-2 indicates the types of charges by percent. Not included is the fact that 42% of all complaints are for retaliation. The person making the complaint contends that because they discussed employer discrimination against them, or their intent to file an EEOC complaint that the employer subsequently discriminated against them. This statistic means that at least one other person in the company, a coworker, manager, or the accused knew about an employee complaint or dissatisfaction. This statistic is a powerful recommendation for establishing a well-publicized, effective employee complaint process. The total number of complaints exceeds 100% because many complaints fall into more than one category.

(U.S. Equal Opportunity Commission, 2016) *Family and Medical Leave Act*. The Family and Medical Leave Act of 1993 (FMLA) is a federal law that requires employers to provide employees leave time for medical and family events. These include employee illness, or pregnancy. The use of leave time to care for a newborn, for an adoptedchild, a child in foster care, or an ill relative is permissible. Companies having 50 or fewer employees within a 75-mile radius are exempt from complying with the law.

A detailed discussion of the act is in the employee benefit section of chapter four

Table 5-2 Percent of EEOC Complaints by Category	
Category	Percent of Complaints
Race	35.3
Disability	30.7
Sex	29.4
Age	22.8
National Origin	10.8
Religion	4.2
Color	3.4
Equal Pay Act	1.2

Setting Precedents, Equal Treatment and Discrimination Claims

Agency precedent is very important in examining equal opportunity and discrimination claims at PCWAs. In the absence of written policies and procedures, management actions concerning any employee sets the precedent. For example, the agency grants an additional 12-week leave to an employee to care for a newborn, in addition to the 12-week FMLA leave. If there is no agency policy in this area than the granting of the additional time off creates a precedent, and the agency should grant similar requests from other employees. Sometimes management will not wish to follow a precedent due to special job related circumstances. The denial of the second request further defines the circumstances for additional leave. It applies to future requests. The difference in the work circumstances between the first and second person making the request should be clear. For instance, the agency grants the first request to a receptionist due to the ease of bringing in temporary help through an employment agency. In the second situation, a therapist counseling sexually reactive boys makes the same request for 12 weeks of leave to care for a new born in addition to the FMLA leave. The basis for denying the request is that granting the leave time will not allow for continuity of the boys' treatment plan, as getting a replacement staff member for close to half a year, that has specialized training in working with sexual offenders is unlikely. If the agency gets a third request, consider creating a practice statement

Upper management needs to assure that there is consistency in handling things such as raises and promotions. If a manager promotes a candidate of one race rather than a candidate of another race, it should be clear to an outsider reviewing the facts and circumstances of the promotion that the person elevated was the superior candidate. An outsider might look at the criteria used in making other promotions within the last five years to see if they are the same in making this hiring decision. In reviewing a complaint, a person might ask about the employment tenure of each candidate. They would review both candidates' performance evaluations, and history of discipline. The review may examine the candidate's educational background, job history, and salary history. The use of an employee complaint officer to avoid the filing of EEOC complaints in these kinds of situations can be invaluable.

Disability Processes and Issues.

There is no legally binding list of what constitutes a disability. A problem is a disability if it seriously limits the person's ability to function. These include an inability to move, see, or think. An employer does not have to change the essential elements of a job description because of a disability. Employers grant reasonable accommodations to enable the employee to perform the job. However, an accommodation does not place unreasonable burdens upon the employer. Like most other EEOC matters, these are matters of facts and circumstances, traditions, and case law.

Building Accessibility

PCWA property handicap accessible status can involve several physical features most notably, handicapped parking, a ramp or lift for building entrance accessibility, handicapped bathrooms, and elevators. What the PCWA does depends on several factors. The first is the type of use. For example, if the agency plans to open a group home, the building will need to conform to three separate sets of rules all of which may state the applicable accessibility requirements. These are the zoning code for the home's location, the building occupancy permit for the physical structure. and state program licensing regulations covering both the building and the program, I use the word applicable because if the building has only one floor and the building entrance is level with the street there is no need for a ramp or elevator.

Two other factors, age of the building, and any renovation work done can make a difference. For example, a PCWA buys a building that is 40 years old to use as a group home for ten children. There have been no major renovations to the building. There is a good chance that a PCWA will not have to make accessibility modifications except as needed by handicapped consumers they decide to serve or as required by zoning or licensing authorities. However, in certain, but not all circumstances when there are major renovations the building code regulations require the owner to make accessibility modifications to the building. The key determinant is the building age and use at the time of the renovation. If the owner selling the building to the PCWA made major renovations to the property twenty years ago but occupied the building as a homeowner then there is no accessibility modifications codicil. This is because home-owners and not regulators decide on accessibility modifications to single-family homes they occupy. However, if the seller used the building as a group home and undertook a major renovation project 20 years ago, then the installation of a handicapped accessible bathroom and building entrance ramp is part of the renovation project. If the seller did not do this, the office issuing the occupancy permits in the state may require a new occupant to do it. If after the PCWA purchases the building it makes major renovations to the building than the applicable accessibility modifications will be in force. Finally, if the agency uses federal funds to purchase a building, it must conform to all applicable accessibility requirements.

If the agency buys a building to use as a drop-in center in which many different youths go in and out, then the building is a public use facility that needs to conform to all applicable accessibility requirements. Requirements for a building for three youth participating in a residential independent living program are likely not subject to these regulations unless a client has an applicable handicap. In part this is because the low number of residents falls within the definition of a family in many jurisdictions.

Reasonable Accommodation Requests

Reasonable accommodation requests always involve management decision making. Consumers, potential consumers, or an employee or potential employee may initiate these requests and the employer's obligation to comply with these requests depends on the facts and circumstances of each situation. This includes, considering the appropriateness of the accommodation considering the disability, the cost, and the practicality of the accommodation.

For example, an agency office building entrance and parking lot is already accessible. A car hits a current employee while they are taking a walk in their neighborhood. The employee permanently loses their mobility and uses a wheel chair. The employee requests, as a reasonable accommodation, that a handicapped accessible bathroom be available. On the first floor, there is an existing bathroom of sufficient size to accommodate a person in a wheel chair. However, the toilet height and the door width do not meet standards for a handicapped accessible bathroom. In addition, the present pedestal sink is too high. The staff member and any wheel chair bound visitors require a lower sink than exists. There is also some question about whether the sink is too close to the present toilet to allow the wheel chair to maneuver. Would this be a legitimate reasonable accommodation request? The answer is" it all depends". The nature of the disability and need is clear. Can the renovation of the bathroom on the first floor make it ADA compliant, or is there some odd location issue that prevents it? If the agency installs plumbing for the sink is this a minor renovation or a high cost item? What is the total cost of the accommodation project? What is the financial size and circumstances of the agency in terms of the affordability of the expense? For instance, if the agency has a $100,000 operating budget and three employees, and there is a projected loss for the coming year, and a very low cash fund balance, the answer could be no. If it is an organization with a significant budget and a high fund balance the answer might be yes.

Regarding employment procedures, it is a violation of the ADA to ask an applicant if they have a disability during an employment interview. If the employer brings up the subject during the interview and the candidate is not a hire, the employer's question is the evidentiary basis for an EEOC disability complaint. It is advisable to describe the job during interviews with all candidates, and to specify the essential functions a person will need to do to perform the job. Make sure to include mental and physical aspects, such as the ability to analyze consumer data, walking up two flights of stairs to visit consumers in their own home, the ability to drive a car, lift a box of files, write case notes, etc. Be clear about the hours of employment and give a summary of the paperwork requirements. After responding to any questions about the job description ask the candidate: Do you believe you can do all the components of the job? If there are some things you are unable to do please tell me which ones and why. For some applicants with a disability their disability may be evident to the interviewer, such as arriving for the interview in a wheel chair. If the observation leaves the hiring manager concerned about the individual's ability to do the job the hiring manager may ask if the applicant feels that will be able to perform specific aspects of the job i.e. walk upstairs.

Depending on the physical appearance of an applicant or employee and their presentation, the hiring manager may not know whether they have a disability. In addition, there is no obligation on their part to inform the agency about a disability. The disability only becomes relevant if it affects work performance.

The expectation is that the agency grants a low or no cost reasonable accommodation to an applicant with a disability. This includes unpaid time off to keep doctor's appointments. A first-floor office location if one is available, for a person who has limited walking ability, as well as a parking spot close to the building are reasonable accommodations. The PCWA grants a late start schedule to an employee receiving treatment for depression if it will not interfere with the functioning of the agency. If there is no indication of a disability during the pre-employment medical exam, if the employee claims a disability, sometime after they begin employment the PCWA has a record on the timing of the claim. In this situation, the employee should present evidence of the disability and the PCWA has the right to have the employee examined by a qualified physician of its choosing.

Once a manager knows about an employee's disability, they initiate a conversation with the employee about their ability to perform their job and any reasonable accommodations they need. The management of an employee disability situation is a mutual responsibility between the employer and employee. For example, a supervisor is in the PCWA lunch room and one of their supervisees comes into the room and lets out a loud yawn and then says to the manager, "excuse me I started on a new anti-depressant medication three days ago and I have been feeling drowsy ever since". The manager knows that the employee is getting medical care for depression. At their next meeting, the supervisor should ask the employee if they judge that the depression is disabling. If the employee responds in the affirmative then the supervisor asks, if and how, it is affecting their job performance. If the employee states that they do not think their depression is disabling or that it does not affect their performance then the supervisor ends the conversation. The supervisor in their notebook notes the date, time, and content of this discussion. The manager does not offer a specific accommodation. It is the employee's responsibility to make the request. In addition, a disability does not necessarily result from the depression. It is a disability only if it affects a major area of life functioning related to work.

Conversely, if the employee responds that they find it hard to get to work on time because of the "hangover effect" of the medicine, the manager asks the employee to obtain a letter from a physician stating the type of disability, and type of accommodation needed. If it is reasonable within the job requirements, the supervisor approves a late start schedule. If for some reason related to the job description this is not reasonable, then there is no scheduling accommodation. For example, it would be reasonable to delay the time an in-home counselor starts work by an hour or two. However, if the employee is a childcare worker, working first shift in a group home a late start time is not a reasonable accommodation because it would entail changing the schedules of all the other staff. A reasonable accommodation for the childcare worker is to switch to a middle shift position once one becomes available.

Asking the manager to accept poor quality work is not a legitimate reasonable accommodation request. Extended deadlines for the submission of written reports that do not adversely affect the business constitutes a reasonable accommodation, if learning disabilities are involved. Extra time to complete work is not a reasonable accommodation if the GCWA caseworker requires a report by a certain date for a court appearance. Granting a reasonable accommodation request could help the employee maintain good performance if the accommodation mitigates the effects of the disability. Taking the initiative demonstrates that the agency culture is sensitive to individuals with disabilities and is proactive in working with the employee to reach a solution. It also protects the agency against potential litigation in a case of a firing related to poor performance in which the employee says employment ended because of their disability, and that management knew about their disability but did nothing to help

Avoiding Employee Litigation

Employee litigation or threats of litigation occur most often when there is a firing or a staff member wants to leave the job with tail end compensation. These situations are time killers for upper management. They involve responses to federal, state, and municipal agencies that investigate these complaints. They involve multiple hours spent by and with a lawyer preparing documents, and preparing for testimony. In most situations, the insurance company decides to settle these actions for small amounts due to the risks and expense involved in litigation. These are sometimes nuisance lawsuits. The value of staff time and the cost of attorney's fees far outweigh the settlement amounts. The goal of the employee is to get termination compensation. They often hire attorneys who take many cases and generate their income through quick modest settlements.

Avoiding and faring well in these kinds of lawsuits involves having strong written policies prohibiting discrimination associated with race, sex, sexual orientation, sexual harassment, or age. Training for managers and employees regarding these behaviors is essential and occurs every year or two. In addition, the existence of an employee complaint officer is extremely helpful. One approach is to permit all to register a complaint with the officer for any reason. The broadly written anti-discrimination legislative language entails a greater use of judgment than with other laws where the codicils are less open to interpretation. At a minimum, the officer reviews the written complaint and interviews the complainant, the subject of the complaint, and other people as well. This system has the advantage of giving the employee a fair hearing, and of dealing quickly with managers who need to make changes in their behavior. Sometimes complaints are from employees who do not have EEOC coverage, and about matters that are management prerogatives such as complaints about performance evaluations. This kind of complaint has two advantages for the organization. First, if there are several complaints in this area and they are all against a single manager or all about a single area of the evaluation instrument, the complaints allow management to take corrective action. Second, it is the chance to get a good idea of the employee's "case" prior to a complaint or litigation. Once administration knows the facts and circumstances of a situation there is a good basis to act and get things settled in an informal way, and minimize the time and financial costs

Government agencies are likely to view organizations that have an internal complaint process, a good set of policies, and a training program as making a good effort to conform to EEOC legislation. This kind of program also allows the organization to distance itself from managers and employees engaged in illegal behaviors because it is clear in policy statements, and training curriculums that discriminatory behavior is against agency policy.

Because of the power of executive staff if a complaint involves some one at a high level, perhaps program director and above organizations ought to consider a BOD committee acting in the complaint officer role. As an alternative to an internal complaint officer, some organizations contract with an outside company to handle all complaints to avoid the integrity question that occurs about internal complaint programs under management control.

Another piece of an effective employee litigation prevention program is having a good labor attorney who acts as a consultant. Often the "ready, fire, aim" approach does not work well. In talking with an attorney before the agency acts, the manager has a good idea of the possible consequences, and good instruction on the way to implement a decision to minimize damage.

Chapter 6 Succession Planning

Succession plans exist to prepare current staff to fill management positions. The first step is to develop a written succession plan. An important consideration is the scope of the plan in terms of positions covered. One could do a plan that starts with first line manager positions and covers every position up to and including the position of president. This kind of organization wide planning has the advantage of giving every staff person the opportunity to engage in management development. Inclusive succession planning is worthwhile; however, it is time-consuming. A more limited and focused effort is to plan for only the top organizational positions. In doing this the plan will result in one of three choices for filling management positions: 1) eliminate the position when the present program manager retires and combine the program with a similar agency program, 2) hire from the outside because there does not appear to be any qualified internal candidates and 3) hire an internal candidate who is participating in management development training, unless there is a better candidate for promotion who is not in the training program. The BOD adopts a written succession plan and the personnel committee of the BOD oversees plan implementation. From the beginning, everyone understands that the BOD hires the president, and sometimes participates in the process of hiring the senior vice president.

The incumbents in the top management positions review and update their job descriptions. They bring forward people who would benefit by participating in succession planning activities. Unless the organization is very large, this would be between two and four people. The incumbents also specify recommendations for training, experiences, activities, and personal development tasks that prepare the person to perform the duties of the position they could assume. This might include proposal writing, public speaking engagements, and developing a business plan for a new service. The training components will vary by the experiential and academic background of the participant. If someone is a social worker, or family counselor some business courses or entry into an MBA program might be a plan. Course work in finance, strategic planning, and human resources will often be of use.

For top spots within the organization, this will include participation on BOD committees. Select the three most important BOD committees and have the succession planning participants attend each of the committee meetings for one year and then rotate on to another committee. This gives the participants a chance to get to know, about some of the BOD committee work. Of more importance, it gives BOD members a chance to get to know them.

Leadership during a Planned or Emergency Absence
When the president leaves, the BOD puts together their emergency plan prior to the discharge or resignation. This plan includes an email to the staff and major customers. It states, "Ms. X is no longer affiliated with the organization. Ms. Y (telephone # and email address) the executive vice president will act as president until the BOD concludes its search for a new president. If you are aware of a good candidate to become the next president of the organization, please contact (insert name of search committee chair). We appreciate your patience and understanding "The email is signed by the board president. The BOD decides one month prior to the discharge meeting with the outgoing president on whether to use a professional search firm. If the BOD engages a firm conduct interviews and select the firm prior to the discharge of the president. If the board is conducting the search, prepare to send out the requests for input on the job description.

A planned absence is a period of more than 25 working days when executive staff are away due to medical, vacation, or personal reasons. An unplanned absence is due to death, serious disability, or desertion of employment by the president. During an absence of the president, the executive vice president is the acting president. The president, if available, executive vice president, and other vice presidents will decide how to divide the president's work. The president's administrative assistant will initially screen incoming communications and distribute these communications as appropriate. The officers and committee chair people of the BOD will be responsible for providing consultation and advice as requested by the acting president. As the situation dictates, the chair of the BOD will initiate activities to fill the position of president.

Promoting a Staff Member to the Position of President
When there is a decision by the BOD to promote an internal candidate then there is no search process. In this situation the current leader, the BOD chair, and committee chair people train the incoming president. The training period can vary, lasting up to a year to cover all the situations that will arise. Doing this assumes that the president that is taking another job or retiring is willing to train the new leader. When this is not the case, the path of the new leader is like that of an external hire except the promoted leader has knowledge of the organizational culture, programs, and many of the

protocols. The training and activities focus on those areas in which are new leader is inexperienced and or ignorant. Usually the promoted leader has a good clinical background but has not been extensively involved in finance, private and perhaps government fundraising. Depending on their duties, they may also need to learn more about the human resource function and planning. Contracting with a PCWA president at another organization to train and mentor the new leader in selected areas is a method for the new leader to become knowledgeable. Alternatively, board members and staff can help with some of the needed skills and knowledge. Coursework or independent reading is also useful. This is a good method for the learner who is motivated, but perhaps more importantly knows the right questions to ask.

There are advantages and disadvantages to being an internal candidate as compared with being an external candidate. One of the disadvantages is that the blemishes are better known, and naturally seen as a disadvantage to the candidacy. Whether through counseling, personal coaching, or, a personal development course, internal candidates need to implement a strategy that will change other's perception of their perceived weaknesses. For the internal candidate review the training material in chapter four. Also, review the post hiring material below.

Recruitment

Recruitment begins with the appointment of members to an ad hoc presidential search committee. The committee's life span begins when there is a need to recruit a new president and ends when the committee agrees that the new president's onboarding process is complete. The outgoing leader does not sit on the hiring committee. A committee of between six and nine members is adequate. The committee includes the chair of the BOD. It is useful to have a committee member that has significant experience in the executive search process. This could be a BOD member, or an employee or retiree from a local college or hospital that has experience in conducting searches for executives or high-level professionals such as physicians, or college presidents. Have a person that has experience with the hiring function carried out by the human resources department of a corporation or sizable charity. This person will be of help in reviewing resumes, composing questions to ask candidates, and assuring the process is compliant with EEOC laws. Have one or two youth members, between the ages 17 – 21. Due to their age, they will have different questions and observations than other committee members. The best choice is someone who is or was a service recipient. If this is not possible, a local high school assistant principal or college professor can suggest a student. The committee has a member that has experience as a PCWA president. To recruit this member a committee member contacts a foundation, the local United Way affiliate, and / r the PCWA's largest customer and asks them for the names and contact information for leaders that head an organization like your PCWA. The committee reviews the list and asks one president to serve on the committee. Having a PCWA president as a committee member is important because their depth of knowledge about the position and the field results in questions for, and observations about applicants that may not occur to BOD members.

Other committee members should have expertise in the areas of responsibility of the new leader. Members of the BOD finance, fundraising and planning committee are good choices. The board chair selects an internal PCWA administrative assistant to act as the committee secretary. This person places employment ads, maintains the committee minutes, and agendas, and notifies members of meeting times.

The Leader's Position Description

The committee's first job is to construct a position profile that lists the duties as well as the desirable characteristics, and background of an applicant. Have the BOD committee chairs, three key employees, three large customers, and the three large donors complete the following tasks:

> Review the existing job description
> Propose additions and subtractions to the current duties and background criteria
> Name challenges the agency could face during the next five years
> Cite five important characteristics for a leader to have
> State the assets and deficits of the departing leader

The search committee reviews stake holder inputs and adds and subtracts duties, knowledge, experiences, and skills judged to be important to the position description. This includes the types and years of experience that the ideal candidate will have. What level of experience will suffice? Does the hiring team want only candidates who are or have been president of another PCWA or does the team also wants to consider second in command candidates that are seeking to advance to the president level? Does the group want to set both a total of years in the field and / or number of years in senior management? The group specifies the desired type of academic degree. Must a candidate have a human service degree or does the agency seek a business leader with a master's degree in business administration? Is either kind of degree acceptable? Does the most desirable candidate have a background in both business and youth services? Some people believe that to assure quality, develop new programs, and be acceptable to the professional staff many of whom have human service degrees that a human service professional is the preferred leadership type. Other people believe that most social service people do not have a good enough grasp of budgeting, cost control, and marketing to make good leaders and a person with business experience is a better choice. When the hire is a business leader it is essential that the senior vice -president or director of operations is very knowledgeable about the assumptions that underlie the program of services as well as knowledge about the wider field of youth social services. The business president spends significant amount of time learning about the clinical operations and the details on the financing of each program.

Use the updated job description to screen applicants. Consider both technical and human relations skills. A technical skill is the ability to analyze a financial statement. A human relations skill is to be a community leader. If a good candidate does not live in the service community and will not relocate to the community than it may be difficult for them to become part of the community. Although a candidate knows the ins and outs of fundraising ask yourself if they can engage the BOD and staff in implementing the mission. If a candidate is clinically proficient, ask yourself if they can acquire the fundraising, financial, and business skills needed for the organization to flourish.

In addition to a list of duties and personal characteristics recruitment materials describes the agency and community. The material summarizes the compensation package and highlights any special inducements. Also, indicate the efforts the agency is willing to make to assist in spousal employment, the location of good quality childcare, and the search for a home. State if there is a sign on bonus or relocation assistance. Some believe that it is better to restrict the search to local candidates because they are already committed to the community. The next question for the committee to ask is: Do they want to hire an interim president or a "permanent" president.

Interim Leaders

Three special circumstances call for engaging an interim leader for two years.

> ➤ There is a major crisis in the organization. This could be a major funding loss, or scandal. There may be a question about the agency's ability to continue to fulfill the mission. Perhaps there will be a merger.
> ➤ A house cleaning is in the organization's future. There are several people in conflict and a leader must resolve the situation. Once people refocus on the mission and away from interpersonal conflict, those staff that cannot support change may have to go elsewhere.

> A long time or founding president has retired. Along with the leader's longevity comes the development of a culture and committed working relationships. A new leader who has different ideas and wants to move them along quickly can end up in difficult conflicts.

> Be clear in advertisements and other recruitment materials that this is an interim appointment. Also, tell leadership staff about the decision and the rationale for it. Before interviews begin it is important to know the tasks that the agency wants accomplished during the interim period. Recently retired PCWA presidents and candidates that have previous experience as an interim president are good candidates.

Using a Search Firm

Discuss and decide upon a search strategy. One choice is for the committee to conduct the search and the other is to use a search firm. One dimension in making this decision is the agency's tradition with executive replacement. Some PCWAs have repeatedly used the same search firm because of satisfaction with their work. Several firms specialize in executive searches for human service agencies. The advantage of using one of these firms is that they will outreach to specific candidates they are aware of who could be a good match for the organization. They will take the time to interview key people in the PCWA. In addition, they will prescreen the candidates and check the references of each finalist. They will prepare career and psychological evaluations. They will negotiate compensation packages with the candidate selected by the BOD. The PCWA hiring group does the interviews and decides on whom to hire. Many search firms will repeat the search process, both if the initial effort does not result in selecting a new leader or if the new leader leaves before a time period specified in the contract with the search firm. Be aware that if the agency hires a person who is a current staff person, or who was known to the PCWA prior to contracting with the search firm after the effective date of the search firm contract the search firm often reserves the right to bill in full for their services. The fee will probably range from the upper five-figure range to the mid six-figure range.

There are two big advantages of using a search firm. While most PCWA's hire a new leader infrequently, the search firm locates candidates often. Second, the workload of the search committee is much lower when using a search firm compared to the job duties of the BOD search committee conducting the search. Search company salespeople will say that they have access to a bigger, better pool of candidates than the agency will. BOD thinking about the quality of candidates often depends on the quality of the most recent leader. This is a mistake. The committee focus is on the available candidates that can fulfill the position description. The location of the community will influence the interests of many potential candidates not already living in the community. The east and west coasts seem to be the most desirable locations. Candidates favor major cities over rural areas and small cities. As with other vendors, check the search firms' references before engaging them. Also, interview the staff people that will work on the search. Be cautious about new search firm employees unless their last employer specialized in human services executive searches and will provide a good reference for the person.

BOD Led Searches

For the PCWA unable or unwilling to pay the search company fee the BOD search committee bears the lion share of the search responsibility. One choice is to conduct a BOD led search for three months before engaging a professional search firm. There is a lot a PCWA can do to assure a successful search. Aside from advertising in a national online job-listing site such as Indeed, Monster, or Craigslist some actions hiring committees can take to successfully procure a new leader are the following:

1. Interview <u>all</u> interested internal candidates. Skipping this step will cause morale problems among these staff and cause them to resent the new leader

2. If the PCWA is within an hour and a half drive from a major city advertise in the newspaper or any other media source that city-based candidates pay attention to. With big city newspapers explore with the advertising department if there is a specific section of the paper where advertisements for hospital executives and school superintendents appear. This is the section to use for the ad. Also, place the advertisement where possible candidates will learn about it. Some ideas are the Child Welfare League of America, the National Association of Social Worker news, National Network of Youth Services. The Chronicle of Philanthropy and state membership organizations. A Google search using the term "nonprofit jobs" will yield many job sites.

3. Publicize the current leader's retirement or resignation with key constituencies. This creates publicity about the position opening and is good customer relations. The constituencies include government customers, foundations, major individual donors, BOD and staff members. Indicate the PCWA will hire a replacement ASAP, and ask these stakeholders to nominate replacements.

4. Have the president from another PCWA that serves on the search committee contact the other PCWA presidents named in the survey outlined under committee membership. Ask them to serve on a professional advisory committee to the BOD search committee. Also, ask other people who have contact with PCWA's. These include United Way and foundation staff and PCWA leaders that have retired in the last two years. During the first meeting, the chairperson explains the committee purpose and shares the job description. The advisory committee members brainstorm the names of possible qualified candidates that they know. During the second advisory board meeting review, the membership lists of the local united way, any other local lists such as the chamber of commerce membership list. Also review, state and national child welfare, and behavioral health provider's organizations. At the conclusion of the brainstorming and list reviews, each member agrees to contact five of the organizational presidents listed as a possibility. For those that are interested share the job description. Ask them to submit a resume to a designated email address.

5. Set a salary offer range, and decide on the benefit package. If your top three candidates find turn you down find out why. Negotiate within reason, and budget constraints with the candidates you make an offer to. Do not make an offer to a relatively undesirable candidate. Consider instead if you should hire an interim president. If that person is a senior vice president, be sure to assess their strengths and weaknesses. Plan to add staff or consultant services to deal with weaknesses. For instance, if the interim is an experienced clinical leader see if a BOD member will volunteer some additional time to coach the interim leader and closely monitor organizational financial performance. If this is not possible contract with an accountancy firm to do this. If the interim is an applicant for the position of president consider a promotion after a year if their performance is very good. If not plan a new search for the next president within twelve months.

Interviewing Applicants

The next decision is the interviewing regimen. An ad hoc subcommittee reviews the applicants resumes using the agreed upon job description and selects the seven most qualified applicants. The subcommittee circulates these vitas to the whole committee and each committee member ranks each resume 1-7. The committee decides on paying the out of town applicants travel expenses. If the organization does not or cannot pay travel expenses than conducting the first interview using Skype is a good alternative. The chair of the subcommittee than calls each candidate to invite them for an interview. Discuss characteristics of the area with out of town candidates. Discuss the average cost of a home in an area that has excellent schools. An interview appointment is set. For candidates that are going to interview the caller asks each candidate to thoroughly review the PCWA website. In addition, email the position description and parts of a grant application that describe elements of the PCWA that are not on the website. The subcommittee decides on a list of interview questions. Any committee member may ask a question that is not on the list. The entire committee interviews the candidates. Separately a staff group consisting of all vice presidents, a line supervisor, a member of the finance department staff and two direct service staff, interview each candidate.

Following each interview, all interviewers rate each applicant using an anonymous written ballot as excellent very good, good, fair, or poor. Alternatively, interviewers can complete a rating form comprised of the key job description items. The ballot also leaves space for comments. The committee administrative assistant tabulates the search committee and staff ballots separately and emails the information to the search committee members. The summary indicates a candidate number, the number of interviewers and the mean (average score) and mode (most frequent score) for each candidate indicated separately for the staff and search committee groups. These vote tallies are advisory and not prescriptive. At the same time if there are wide differences between the two groups, with the staff group having a relatively low opinion of the candidate the BOD members favor carefully consider this. Proceed with a job offer to the highest rated candidate.

Some possible interview questions for the search committee group to use are:

1. Will the present board chair give you a positive reference? What comments will they make about your performance – the strengths and growth areas?
2. What part of your current job do you enjoy most? Least?
3. What are the key things you look for when you examine the PCWA balance sheet?
4. As you, consider future funding for our PCWA what will be the role of child welfare funding, behavioral health funding, and donations?
5. What are the characteristics of BODs that are performing well? Performing poorly?
6. After reviewing the information on our PCWA website, do you have any questions about the organization?

7. How do you use your relationship with the staff to achieve excellent results?
8. When you consider the service array at your present PCWA are there things that would strengthen our service offerings?
9. What are the personal characteristics and leadership style of a BOD chair that are helpful? Not helpful?

Some questions to consider for the staff interview are:

1. If you are the next leader of our PCWA, what will be the major goals and how quickly will you implement them?
2. What will you do to assure the agency maintains its reputation for excellent services?
3. Do you keep an open-door policy for all staff?
4. In an environment of no or limited rate hikes what strategies have you used to maintain excellent health care coverage for the staff?
5. Do you believe in merit based or across the board increases when awarding annual salary increases?
6. Talk about your view of a leader's chief duties and how you divide the work time between them.
7. How do you approach professional training for the direct service staff?
8. In working with your direct reports do you keep authority centralized or do the reports have substantial authority.
9. How do you involve direct service staff in the strategic planning process?
10. Describe the circumstances involved for each of the last three staff you fired?
11. Do you believe in bonuses that primarily benefit executive staff?

How Will Each Candidate Get Along With the Existing Senior Managers?

An important part of a PCWA success is the long service of the lead program managers. Several factors are relevant They are 1) the ability for managers to have reasonable authority in their area of leadership, 2) the organization's growth and success, and 3) a high degree of their commitment to the core organizational values - helping children and families succeed, high quality services, and hard work. The level of support from the BOD also made a difference. How will each candidate mesh with the current managers? Should the new president seek to retain the current team or replace them?

Onboarding a New Leader

Exhausted by the many hours spent interviewing candidates the BOD is often glad when they select a candidate and board members are ready to take a break. Despite this, the successful onboarding of a new leader requires their attention and effort.

It is very important that the board chair for the first year or two of the new leader's tenure has a substantial history with the organization and held the position of board chair in the past. It is also essential the staff and other board members respect the chairperson. More over the chairperson has good community relationships. They can get the new president oriented and acclimated to the community. An inexperienced board chair who professionally and in terms of board participation is on their own personal growth track limits the type and quality of the assistance that the new staff chief will be able to get.

The BOD chair, members, and leadership staff need to introduce the new leader to key customers and donors. The new leader participates in organizations that provide the opportunity to meet peers. This could include joining a committee at United Way or a local government task force. Becoming active with a Chamber of Commerce, Rotary, or Kiwanis to meet business leaders is also worthwhile.

Getting to know key employees is important. Some of these staff will be direct reports and others will report to a Vice President. The new leader gets to know the key activities of these leaders, their goals, and the major projects they will be involved with during the coming year. They ask about the method of supervision provided by the last leader for their direct reports, and what the reports found helpful and unhelpful in the supervisory relationship. The new president takes the time to attend staff meetings to understand the agency programs and belief system. On these occasions, the new leader makes a brief statement about their professional history. They solicit questions from the direct service staff. From day one, they perform the duties listed in the job description. There is very little emphasis on change during the first year except as required due to a crisis or circumstances. This allows the new president a time to become oriented, learn about the past, and present before leading the organization into the future. The goal for the BOD chair is to assure the onboarding process is successful and they do not pressure the leader to start major projects except when circumstances require it.

Evaluating the New President

Evaluate the new president after three, six and twelve months of employment and annually thereafter. Because of the importance of the position, timely feedback to the new leader is important. Executive evaluation is the responsibility of the BOD chairperson. An internet search results in several examples of evaluation formats. Key evaluation instrument tool attributes are that it covers job description duties as well as important parts of the strategic plan. The BOD chairperson rates the president in each category using a Likert scale, (including a not applicable category) and the evaluation has a comments section and a suggested goal section. The BOD chair asks each of the following stakeholder's groups to provide feedback to the BOD chairperson 1) the chair people of each BOD committee that the president staffs, 2) the president's direct reports, 3) the president's peers at three large government customers, and 4) three large private donors. In considering the input from stakeholders the chairperson looks for patterns. The evaluation document prepared by the Chair provides for an overall rating and goals for the next period. If there is a variable compensation component of the president's salary include every specific measurable objective in the six months and one-year evaluations

Executive Compensation

Salary The first important principle is that the salary paid to the executive encompasses all the work listed in the job description and there is no additional compensation for completing usual and customary duties. Annual executive compensation, other than annual cost of living adjustments increases or decreases, when there are substantial changes in the job description. Some organizations like the idea of paying a base salary and then additional salary for specific accomplishments or goals (variable pay opportunities). A third approach to executive compensation is the use of bonuses. I do not favor bonuses for key employees (those paid more than $150,000 per annum) because the IRS can interpret these payments as distributions to officers of the corporation that violates private non-profit status legislation.

When hiring a new president beware of offering too little compensation. For some there is the temptation to offer a salary that is 75% to 85% of the salary of the exiting leader. The thinking is that the salary ought to be lower than that of the preceding leader because of the new leader's lack of seniority in the organization. They reason the new leader's salary will rise over time. Also, if the organization has sustained budget cuts, those hiring, reason that hiring a new leader at a relatively low salary will help reduce costs. These kinds of strategies limit the applicant pool and the organization may miss the opportunity to hire a talented leader that can be successful.

Whatever the method of compensation executive salaries at private nonprofit organizations conform to Internal Revenue Service guidelines. The duty of the executive compensation committee of the BOD is to assure that total executive compensation (salary, benefits, deferred compensation, housing allowance etc.) is in line with the usual compensation for comparable positions at like organizations. The key dimensions of similarity are geographic proximity, and budget size. Some organizations prefer to use an outside consultant to conduct the salary study rather than doing it themselves, avoiding the fox in the hen house problem. A second advantage of an outside firm is that they will investigate the types and value of noncash benefits that is not discernable in the Guidestar study cited below. However, studies done by outside consultant firms may cost more than is acceptable for small and midsized PCWAs. A good study available for the positions of president, lead financial officer, and other key executives is the annual Guide Star Nonprofit Compensation Report, (Guidestar, 2014). It is a good resource because it contains information on a very large number of charities, and it is possible to analyze the data by charity types, region, as well as budget size. The last Guidestar study that I reviewed did not control simultaneously for specific IRS code organizational type (children and youth, foster care) and for geographic location. To control for these factors, one might inquire with Guidestar about a custom report. To do your own executive compensation study get the names of twenty PCWAs within 200 miles of the corporate home city. Get the compensation information for each Chief Executive Officer the organizational net cash assets, annual revenue, and expenses by reviewing each of the organization's 990 filings on Guidestar. In as much as the data is digital gathering the comparable organizational information is not onerous. Choose the ten organizations closest in size to yours. In comparing information, remember that the Guidestar compensation information is inclusive of the cash value of all benefits. At this writing, there is no charge for reviewing organizational 990's on a one at a time basis so this is a low-cost way of getting information on comparative executive compensation.

Executive Benefits These can include leasing a car for exclusive use of the executive. The incumbent keeps mileage records on the business use of the vehicle. Non-business use lease costs including normal travel to and from the incumbent's residence to the work place is ordinary taxable income. An alternative is to allow a fixed amount as a monthly car allowance that pays for leasing plus operating, and car insurance costs. Other benefits include reimbursement for business travel and for business entertainment expenses, including expenses for a spouse or partner. In addition, the PCWA pays for costs for memberships in community organizations i.e. Kiwanis or Rotary type groups. Some BOD leaders also want the president to belong to a country club for donor access. This is often a productive use or organizational funds but some people regard it as a frivolous use of charitable donations. In addition, sometimes executives have higher amounts of life insurance than other staff. Where health insurance, dental insurance, vision insurance and a pension or 401(k) plan exist for the staff the executive staff also participates in the existing plans. The same goes for the long-term disability insurance policy.

Employment Contracts The president as protection against a sudden or whimsical discharge often initiates these agreements. They also protect the BOD against the sudden departure of organizational leaders. These contracts exist for a fixed term often three to five years, record salary and benefits and provide for compensation for different circumstances when the president resigns or the BOD fires them. Of course, each contract is individual and contains any terms agreeable to both the BOD and the president. They cover the following type of items:

1. *Salary both base and variable*
2. *Executive benefits including:* Supplemental retirement plan contribution, automobile allowance, housing allowance, club membership fees, sabbatical leave,
3. Requires the president to have an annual physical examination that certifies continued ability to perform their duties
4. Requires BOD approval of outside BOD memberships.
5. Requires the president to keep all non-publicly published material confidential
6. For the time limit specified the President may not work at a similar PCWA in a specified geographical region
7. Requires that the president does not recruit staff to work at another organization for a fixed period
8. President agrees to cooperate in any litigation brought by or against the PCWA
9. Separation Provisions:
a. due to disability occurs when the length of disability is longer than six months
b. due to death require health insurance in force for
     children, spouse, or partner to continue for 12
          months
10. resignation requires six months' notice
11. Termination without cause require salary, health benefits, and life insurance to continue for twelve months
12. Termination with cause – salary and benefits cease at termination
13. Agreement to end or continue employment 90 days prior to the contract termination date.

Deferred Compensation Plan

Part of the way to encourage longevity in management is through a deferred compensation program offered as a 457(f) plan or other type of plan. An important decision is the positions that participate in the plan. In a small to midsize PCWA, usually only the president and perhaps executive vice president participate due to financial constraints. In midsize and large PCWAs, it may be possible for all vice presidents and program directors to also participate. The wider the participation the greater the incentive for managers to remain PCWA employees.

The 457(f) is a "non-qualified Plan" under federal ERISA guidelines. As such, the organization has a great deal of freedom in plan design, and government paperwork is minimal. However, this is a "deferred compensation plan" meaning the participants are responsible for all payroll taxes upon receipt of the funds. In some plan designs, the participant meets the vesting requirement prior to retirement, but receives the deferred compensation upon retirement. In this situation, the payroll tax payment precedes retirement and comes from the participant's account balance. This occurs due to a triggering event. The event most often is the employee reaches the age of eligibility to retire but continues working. The participant gets the account value upon reaching retirement age or after a fixed number of years. In the latter arrangement, the PCWA pays a participant when their age and their years of service reach a specified number, perhaps 65, or 70. The terms of the plan are in a deferred compensation plan document. If the employee resigns or the program director fires them prior to vesting there is no payment. The PCWA invests plan account payments. They may be subject to the organizational investment policy.

The 1) financial retirement goal for the executive staff members, 2) fixed percentage payment or the 3) the financial condition of the PCWA approach are examples of methods than can all be of used to make contributions to a deferred compensation plan. However, the criteria and annual amount of payments into participant accounts is at the discretion of the BOD. State the method for contributions and distributions in the plan document. Adopt any parameters that are legal and do not violate regulations, particularly IRS compensation guidelines.

The financial retirement goal approach considers a percentage of salary the BOD executive compensation committee judges as appropriate for a retired executive to live comfortably. A brief scan of internet sites suggests 80% of salary as an appropriate retirement income goal. An actuary calculates annual plan contributions. The factors considered in setting a contribution amount are the years of employment, the age at retirement, life expectancy, social security income, and the value of the retirement plan offered to all employees.

With the fixed contribution approach deposit a percentage of the fixed portion of compensation annually into each participant's plan account. The financial condition approach considers performance and the change in cash net assets between the current year and the immediately preceding year and the total organizational cash net assets. The 457(f) plan managers are usually members of the executive compensation committee of the BOD and the BOD chairperson appoints the members annually. It is a good idea even if there is a deficit in a year to make a modest contribution to each participant account to demonstrate the organization's commitment to the plan. Participants in the plan receive an annual statement of account value. The PCWA often contracts with a private firm for the bookkeeping and to send participants an annual statement. The plan is set up as a trust (aka a rabbi trust) so the employee accounts amounts are not subject to the terms of a merger or bankruptcy. It is common for the PCWA to use the same firm(s) to manage plan funds
that manages other organizational investments.

Chapter 7 Prevention of A Pain in the Neck – The Effective and Successful Board of Directors

The Nonprofit Organizational Form

The private non-profit charity is an important and unique American organizational form. It is the "third sector" – business and government being the two large sectors. As of 2013, there were nearly a million charities having combined revenues of $1.73 trillion and assets of more than $3 trillion. Only 13.3% of their revenue was from private giving. (Mckeever, 2015) The private nonprofit form is a way for a group of likeminded people who share a common mission to act in concert to benefit others. Private charities exist primarily to provide services to help people. Charities exist to achieve a particular purpose such as providing healthcare or education, protecting animals, helping a disadvantaged group, advancing a political agenda, or conducting research. There are also private-nonprofit organizations such as foundations that provide money rather than services, and membership organizations that exist to help only their members. It is an organizational form regulated by law that is tax advantaged. Charities that help people are exempt from paying state sales taxes, and do not pay income taxes on activities related to their mission. Although many large charities receive government, support there is no obligation of government or private individuals to support any charity. Like any other business, a private nonprofit must maintain a positive bottom line, but it is unique in that there is no individual profit taking by the employees or BOD members.

Board of Directors Recruitment

There is a process to elect leaders of units of government, corporations, and private not for profits organizations. In government registered voters elect their county commissioners etc. The election of corporate boards is the job of the shareholders Most commonly in PCWA, current directors nominate people they know personally or people they seek out because they have a specific skill or help the BOD meet a social goal, such as racial diversity. In many organizations, a larger group of organizational members elects the BOD. These "member" elections are meaningful in organizations like labor unions. In PCWA elections, the members vote on a list of nominated officers and directors by a voice vote at the annual meeting. If there is a serious organizational rift, (which is rare) in which people take different sides, elections are more formal. Use a written ballot when there is more than one candidate for one or more offices. A BOD nominating committee is responsible for cultivating BOD member prospects, nominating prospective members and monitoring BOD member attendance. A second choice is to have the nomination functions carried out by the BOD development committee. There is more detail about this function in the committee description section of the appendix.

There is a great deal of diversity in the size of PCWA BOD. Depending on state rules, there can be as few as two members. Many BODs have between seven and fifteen members, and many have larger boards. There are characteristics of the type of people, and the BOD roles that tend to vary by organizational size. People elected as directors of large PCWAs organizations are philanthropists, wealthy, affiliated with corporations, professionals, or successful small business people. They possess a skill that is useful in the work of the BOD of directors. They can contribute $1,000+ gifts, and often have social relationships that are useful to the organization. They are involved primarily with stewardship, policymaking, and fundraising.

For smaller organizations, people who are highly attached to the mission, and people who are willing to contribute time and services that the organization needs are likely to be BOD members. They are likely to communicate the vision, provide free legal, accounting, IT, property management, and other services. They help with modest fund-raising events. In organizations with no or few staff, the BOD members may play a dual role involving both traditional BOD responsibilities as well as service responsibilities. If an organization evolves in terms of budget size, the type of BOD members often also changes. However, if the charity does not have a significant private funding component the type of BOD may not involve those capable of giving and getting charitable gifts. This happens when PCWA operate only or mostly on a fee for service basis. Usually in organizations of all sizes, there is a mix of BOD members. So even in the smallest organization, there can be a member or two who gives significant gifts. Sometimes in the large PCWAs, a BOD member wants to help families or children directly.

Skill grids match the skill set of the current members against organizational needs. At many PCWAs, the priority is the ability of the potential member of the BOD to give and get significant gifts. While this is good as a rule, it is better to recruit large donors who also meet one or more of the priorities identified by using the grid method.

The grid lists each of the current members and their geographic location, skill sets, race, and sex. The aim is to have the BOD represent the community diversity along these dimensions. The first goal is that the number of female and male members is about the same. A second goal is that the racial composition of the BOD and the community are similar. The grid also reflects strategic plans. The PCWA seeks nominees with either special expertise or who have affiliations with potentially important partner organizations. For instance, if the agency will put on a major push to have youth attend college than someone from the local community college on the BOD could help with planning and implementing the project. A few times each year the nominating committee chair will report to the BOD on the number of members sought, state the committee recruitment priorities, and ask the directors to suggest possible nominees.

When diversifying the racial and gender makeup of the BOD the main trick is to recruit people who are equal or close in status to the current members. When the new member has a lower job and social status than the present members there can be a lack of attachment to the BOD on the part of the new member. Although the present members are very welcoming, the new member can feel out of place. They feel that there are few people like them in the group. When this happens, the new member has a poor attendance record and may resign after a short time.

The BOD elects available and interested people who have superior ability to support the organization financially or are distinctive in other ways even if their profile does not fit well with the recruitment priorities. The reason for this is that there are relatively few people in the community who possess distinctive characteristics such as significant wealth, or real political influence.

Potential BOD members usually get interested because of their relationship with the person who approaches them and their attraction to the mission. There is often a relationship between a BOD member's perception of their usefulness to the organization and their attachment to the organization. Usefulness is a strong American value. A wonderful example of the ethic of people being of use, as the most important value in life that is relevant to private child welfare is John Irving's book Cider House Rules (Irving, 1985). The story is about the children and the staff of an orphanage. If you have an interest in child welfare history, it is worthwhile to read. In the book, the director of the orphanage continually tells the children and everyone else "to be of use". He abhorred a life of idleness and thought there is always much to do.

One way to ensure BOD member commitment is to find a niche in organizational life where the member judges they are accomplishing something. The "something" needs to be meaningful to the organization and utilize knowledge and skills the new member possesses. This niche could be serving on a BOD committee such as finance or program, through direct work with a family, or creation of a fundraising event. They may want to help in an administrative task such as quality assurance, efficiency, or program evaluation. The president who wants to get and keep a good BOD will get to know each of the members and try to involve them in committee work or a specific project the member will find meaningful and satisfying. The president takes the time to talk with members annually about their satisfaction with being a BOD member. Usually all is well, but sometimes-midcourse corrections occur as the BOD members' interest change.

There are opposing thoughts about the desirability of the reelection of former BOD members. Many people believe in continually bringing in "fresh blood". They believe that members have already contributed their ideas and expertise during their term of service and new people will bring new energy and new thoughts to the process. Also new members bring new donors, and former members will continue to help and donate to the organization whether or not they are members of the BOD. To get the best of both worlds some boards invite selected former members to serve on an emeritus basis. Emeritus members attend BOD meeting as they like, but do not vote. The second school of thought favors reelecting long-term BOD members because of the issue of continuity of ownership. That is, when a business sells it is often on the condition that the present owner will stay involved for several years because of the knowledge and relationships they have. Another advantage to long-term BOD members is their loyalty to the organization. They are especially important in times when there is a new president or organizational crisis.

Although it not always possible, it is preferable, if someone on the BOD knows a possible nominee and thinks, they will be a good BOD member. In addition, use readily available internet search tools to learn things about a potential member. If the organization does not elect a member after a recruitment meeting, the situation is awkward. For this reason, it is important for the discussion about the proposed BOD member to be frank, and include any possible conflicts of interest that will be difficult to manage. After the committee discusses a potential candidate, a member calls the person of interest to arrange a meeting.

The higher the work/community status of the nominee the lower their participation will be. However, their donation will be generous and they will be helpful in gaining access to other potential donors and access to elected officials and community leaders.

Meet the candidate at one of the service sites at a time youth are present, because the potential member can get a good sense of the work by taking, a youth led tour. A member of the nominating committee and the president conducts the interview. Begin with the BOD member giving a history of their involvement followed by the agency president giving a brief overview of the organization. Talk about the time commitment involved, and that the expectation is that members donate generously within the context of their ability. In some organizations, the custom is to ask for a fixed amount, and if so, talk about this. Give the person a BOD s' member job description with the fiduciary, mission, policy, philanthropic, nominating and mission roles. Also, give them the list of current members, and the last annual report. Discuss any real or potential conflicts of interest and develop a plan for managing them.

Tell the potential member why you are interested in having them join the BOD and talk about potential committee assignments. Ask them about why they are interested in becoming a director. Ask them about what kind of tasks are most appealing to them. Ask about their family life and relationships with children and concern about children's issues. Be prepared to respond to the following questions from potential directors. Where, when, and how often are meetings held? Is there any pending litigation? What have been the organizational financial results for the last several years? Is the organization a member of the United Way? Attending a BOD meeting as a guest is sometimes helpful. If the meeting is at a service site and the potential nominee is rude to the youth doing the tour or the meeting takes place at a restaurant and the person is rude to the server, cross them off the list due to the arrogance factor. Do not take a "beggars cannot be chooser's" attitude toward recruitment. It is better to have a small BOD with members who are committed and purposeful rather than a large group marked by poor attendance, and inattentiveness to agency business. The nominee election process ends following election, with a letter of congratulations that includes the committee assignment, and board and committee meeting calendar. The letter also references the BOD manual. An online search using the words "Nonprofit board of director manual" will yield many examples of manuals. I found those that I viewed to be tomes. As a rule of thumb keep the manual brief. Make the manual and the documents referenced part of a cloud-based board of director website

The job the nominating committee finds difficult is dealing with members with poor attendance. If the poor attender is a major donor people usually look the other way; however, for others one method is as follows. First, specify in the by-laws, that the BOD expel members who miss a fixed number of meetings. The chair or a member of the nominating committee calls the lax attender and informs them of their attendance slipup. The caller states that the BOD needs their regular attendance to conduct business, and the caller ends the conversation by saying to the member that they hope to see them at the next BOD meeting. If attendance does not improve, wait until their term expires, and then do not nominate them for another term. For this reason, one or two-year terms are a good idea. Be sensitive to the fact that people do not like to toss others off the BOD.

<h3 align="center">Board Building</h3>

There are two circumstances when board building is important. The first situation is the president does not put in the effort to have an effective board. This happens for any of several reasons. Sometimes the president is unable to devote the time and energy to have an excellent BOD. In other situations, the president does not have enough personal contacts to recruit the type of board member that they want.

The second situation is when the president, board member or other stakeholder wants to have a development program that raises significant amounts of money from private sources. In this situation, there is a good working board but the private fundraising function is weak. The board is functional, and engaged. Attendance is good. Members are also good stewards, and relationships are collegial. However, they are unable to make substantial gifts, and do not have the contacts to secure sizable gifts. Their political and community influence is not strong. The PCWA hold one or two events a year that have modest success, and procure a few foundations grants a year.

Building a board that is primarily working on stewardship, fundraising, policy, and ambassadorship takes about five years. It occurs due to a few members who are financially able, socially prominent and have had trouble as a child, or with their own child. They are action orientated and steadfast. They will be good BOD members in many ways but the most important thing they do is network with their friends and recruit them for the board. Do not ask them to help with recruitment until they engage with the organization. Locate these people through finding one or two families a year that have used the services that are financially capable. Due to the nature of PCWA work, the agency will have five or fewer of these consumers a year. When the direct service staff spots these families, the president invites the mother, father, or both to lunch and asks one if they would be interested in being a board member. If things go well follow the usual nominating process, but do not violate the family's confidentiality. Whether or not they discuss their personal situation is their decision. Over 30 years about 20 of these parents have been VYH board members. Most did not share their personal situations with the other directors.

Board of Director Operations

In private charities, the BOD represents the taxpayers, donors, consumers, and community interest in the organization. Although they cannot use organizational assets for personal purposes, they as a group are the owners of all organizational property. They assure assets go to implement programs or for future purposes. In general, they rarely have personal responsibility to pay organizational liabilities if things go wrong This presumes, they have acted with due diligence and honest intention. The corporate structure, various organizational insurance policies, and volunteer and Good Samaritan legislation usually protect directors against individual liability. However, there is no protection against gross negligence or criminal behavior. This includes self-dealing, violation of organizational by-laws, and not using the prudent person standard of judgment. Not attending BOD meetings for a long period can sometimes constitute negligence.

BOD members act as a group in conducting business. The group has two key responsibilities; the first is the fiduciary role to assure that the conduct of financial affairs is reasonable, ethical, and lawful. They listen to the finance committee and treasurer 's reports. They pay attention to information about income and expenses, and assets and liabilities. Members assure that financial procedures and practices meet regulatory body standards, grant conditions, and American Accounting Board standards. While the president and finance director assure these on an operational level, these are good areas for BOD members to ask the auditor about when an audit firm partner presents the audit to the board.

The BOD enacts the annual budget. They ask questions about budget line items or individual expenditures that seem unusual or unnecessary to the work of the organization. They understand the key budget assumptions and ask about areas of risk in the budget. They ask how much the PCWA will spend on direct service and how much on fundraising costs, and administration.

There is attention to special transactions. These include building purchases or sales. The BOD also approves mortgages and other borrowing. The BOD review budgets for programs that begin after they approve the annual budget. Ongoing concerns are excess executive compensation or payments to BOD members, or loans or gifts to these people. As part of the audit report review, inquire into the auditor's findings in these areas.

The second key responsibility of the directors is to warrant that the organization is implementing its mission. This includes assuring there is a good match between the mission and the programs offered. A review of service statistics indicating the number of consumers served, number and types of services provided and the outcome of service provision are tools to support adequate implementation of the mission.

The finance committee chair presents the financial statements at BOD meetings. They summarize income, expenses, and assets and liabilities. There is an annual independent external audit report. The committee also reviews the annual 990-tax filing with the BOD. Program directors summarize annual services levels, consumer characteristics, and outcomes.

Some agencies elect the president as a BOD member - some do not. The advantages of the president serving are that they are likely to attend most meetings, helping to fulfill quorum requirements, and satisfy the contribution expectations of membership. It is also a way of the BOD communicating to the president that they regard them as a peer. Some people feel election is not a good idea because it blurs the lines of authority in the organization. In addition, things can get uncomfortable if the BOD members have performance concerns about the president.

Board of Director Officers

Many charities use a model with four officers' chairperson, vice chairperson, treasurer, and secretary. Smaller organizations may combine the secretary and treasurer role or do not have a vice chairperson. The chairperson leads the BOD meetings. They supervise the president acting as their consultant and evaluate the president's performance. The chairperson, appoints members to committees, initiates new committees as necessary, and represents the agency at public events; they attend each committee meeting once a year unless there is a specific need for them to attend more often. If the chairperson decides to attend most committee meetings, which is their prerogative, the committee will look to the chairperson for solutions rather than function independently. The president provides orientation to the chairperson at the beginning of their term, and a calendar of BOD meetings, and community events they should attend.

Most chairpersons want to leave a positive legacy. My advice to them at the beginning of their term(s) is to choose one or at most two things they want to accomplish. Their choice involves something for which they have experience and knowledge, and will benefit the organization. For example, a chairperson who is an internet pro eliminates 90% of the paper communication with members, by creating an intranet site. A president with expertise in human resources guides the agency through the succession planning policy process. An unpleasant task that falls to the president or chairperson is dealing with bad BOD member behavior. For instance, if the male chair of the program committee gets frisky with the female head of a program, but the behavior does not constitute sexual harassment than the chairperson calls the person and says the finance chair has too much to do and reassigns the man to be a finance committee co-chair. However, if the behavior rises to the level of sexual harassment the chairperson follows agency policy. The chairperson of the audit committee of the BOD assumes the role of the complaint officer. As appropriate, the chairperson also recommends sanctions to the BOD.

The vice chairperson functions as the chairperson when the chair is absent. The tradition at many organizations is to have the vice chairperson succeed the chairperson when their term ends. In addition, there can be special circumstances when the vice chairperson plays a prominent role during the term of the current chairperson. For example, the chairperson who due to a conflict in meeting schedules is often twenty minutes late for the BOD meeting. In these situations, the vice chairperson calls the meeting to order and leads the meeting until the chairperson arrives.

The treasurer supervises organization funds, and regularly reports to the BOD on the amounts and locations of funds. They have the authority to make decisions about account types and banking relationship but usually work with the staff finance director when substantial deposits move from one institution to the other, or there is a decision to change banking relationships. They usually are members of the finance committee. The treasurer often approves expenditures exceeding the amount that the president is authorized to approve, but is lower than the amount the BOD approves. The treasurer signs checks above a certain amount in small organizations and stands in for regular staff signers when they are unavailable to sign checks above a certain amount. Refer to the "credit card" section of the chapter titled "Treasury, Investment, and Related Financial Policies" to learn more about expenditure and check signing authority. The treasurer is often the chairperson of the finance committee and is a member of the audit committee

The actual work of the secretary varies usually according to the organization's size. Their traditional duties are to take and prepare the minutes of the BOD of directors, and to sign as a witness on contracts and other agreements. In smaller organizations, they will perform these duties directly. In larger organizations, the BOD designates these duties, by resolution to a staff member, usually an administrative assistant.

Meetings involving Board of Director Members

When planning any one to one, committee or BOD meeting, always ask yourself – What do I want from the BOD member(s)? What do I want to accomplish because of the meeting? The answers to these questions are the basis for the meeting agenda. It could be to review and discuss program performance and make recommendations for improvements, deciding upon hardware purchases to enhance the information and technology functions, or to meet with the company that manages the investments and decide the satisfaction with the company's performance. Meetings that have little discussion and member involvement, and with members' listening to staff reports are sometimes boring and often do not use the participants skills. Before you present any report tell the group what feedback or guidance you want from them. If there is nothing, summarize the report very briefly and have a few copies for people who want to read it. Meetings that engage directors have important discussion items. The agenda contains policy questions. If there are, any items currently in the news that relate to the agency bring them up. If time allows ask people at committee meetings if there are strategies or policies that their companies have that could be of interest to the agency. Leave time at the beginning of the meeting for people to say their hellos and engage in a few minutes of informal conversation before calling the meeting to order.

Whether at the BOD or committee level one of the president's important jobs is to finalize an agenda with the director, who will chair the meeting and keep the chair informed and as prepared as possible to lead the meeting. This includes letting them know about outcome(s) you would like, and the materials you plan to distribute.

The BOD members will become more deeply engaged if the atmosphere at the meeting is informal, friendly and has humor. Convivial relationships make these meetings events to which they look forward to. Some BOD members became my friends. We would never fail to give each other a bit of a "hard time" much to the enjoyment of the other attendees. In other words, **work hard but have fun.**

BOD Meetings - The number of times a year the BOD meets as a group is discretionary, and the range is usually monthly, quarterly and sometimes semiannually or annually. The frequency that business matters need attention, and the distances the members are from the meeting site often determine the number of meetings. It is more likely that boards whose members live all over the United States meet less often.

If BOD members come to meetings from a short distance away it is preferential for the BOD to meet monthly, except for the summer and to hold meetings at multiple service sites so that the members see the different programs in action. If a meeting is at a site the members do not visit often, offer a tour of the site, led by a youth. Holding the meetings at service sites allows youth to have casual interactions with the BOD members, and to talk about their lives and experiences with the programs. The youth involved know the BOD members are important adults and the interaction is a self-esteem booster for the young person. The BOD members put a face on the organizational purpose through seeing and talking with youth and having youth talk to them.

The meetings run formally in terms of following an agenda and handling motions. Some general familiarity with Roberts Rules of Order is necessary. In preparation for the meeting, the president and BOD chairperson spend some time on the phone two weeks before the meeting to review the agenda. Then three or four days before the meeting they talk again briefly regarding any important updates, or things that a member could raise at the meeting, such as a news article about a community event or situation.

If meetings occur at mealtimes provide something to eat. Consequently, the beginning of the meeting allows for a brief period of social interaction among the members while they get their food and find seats at the table. During this time, the president circulates around the room to greet the attendees and make them feel welcomed; moreover, they express appreciation to them for taking the time to attend the meeting.

Assign an administrative assistant (AA) to handle all BOD related tasks. At the meeting, the AA takes the minutes, and uses a tape recorder as a backup. They also ensure the telephone system, video teleconference, or Go to Meeting or other technology works, so those at the meeting location and those at remote locations can hear what people say at the meeting and vice versa. If the agency has a small BOD group, the speakerphone function on a regular telephone may be fine. For larger groups a telephone with two remote speaker-microphones is o.k., but video conferencing or other more advanced technology has additional advantages. The AA also does the meeting set up (food, agendas for each director, last minute meeting materials) and after meeting cleanup.

The AA emails most meeting materials to the members three or four days before the meeting. These include an agenda, the annual program report of the program that staff will present at the meeting, a list of motions, and copies of background material regarding the motions and sometimes copies of business plans. In addition, all meeting materials are on a website for BOD members. The AA also emails the minutes from the last meeting, and a two-page summary of the income and expense statements. The president provides a one-page synopsis of all the materials that serves as a cover sheet. The cover sheet summarizes: 1) monthly and year to date income and expenses, and changes in assets 2) a summary of the program presentation 3) motions 4) key discussion items and BOD education items.

A monthly BOD meeting ideally lasts between 50 minutes and an hour and 15 minutes. Members are busy and it is important that they know they can reliably move on to other commitments and not be stuck in long discussions. This meeting length presumes the existence of an operating committee system, and a BOD that meets frequently rather than quarterly or annually. BOD meetings that are quarterly or semiannually may be a half day in length. If there are no or few committees monthly BOD meeting will be longer, perhaps an hour and 30 minutes.

Following the call to order the meeting always begins with a program presentation. The program presentation by a different manager each month includes an oral summary of the written annual program report (which has a pre-established outline and that has been prepared and submitted in advance of the meeting). If the agency has, only one program includes a discussion about it at each meeting. Do this by discussing one consumer story each month. When possible have the consumer alone, or better still with their parents tell their own story. It is less formidable for the youth if the program director involved talks about the program piece and the consumer talks about themselves. The BOD members are usually very interested in these presentations and ask many questions. The stories of the consumers put the human touch on the presentation. They serve to remind the BOD members of the mission. In making presentations to the board, at fundraising events, and legislative meetings youth participation is essential. People may disregard statistical evidence when there is a call to action to donate money or support legislation; however, the issue is more difficult to ignore when they are face to face with a few articulate youths and hear about their life circumstances.

Following the presentation, the secretary presents the meeting minutes from the last meeting for approval. The Treasurer indicates the institutions holding organizational assets, and account balances. The adoption of a motion to approve the treasurer's report confirms the directors' acceptance of cash assets as stated. Next committees presenting motions make their reports with the committee chair or their designee making the motion and discussing the rationale for it. Sometimes committee chairs distribute brief written materials stating the motion and key facts. Usually without or after brief discussion the BOD approves each motion, but sometimes there is controversy or the matter is complicated and the discussion is more extensive. Sometimes there is a request for committee reconsideration of the matter. Sometimes the no votes exceed the yes votes. If the motion under consideration is important to the president, they make notes during the discussion of the reason for the negative evaluation of the proposal. Subsequently they revise the proposal to satisfy these objections, or modify their presentation, or both and present the motion again at the committee level. Also, if only a slim majority pass a motion than it is better not to proceed with the action. Although votes are on a majority wins basis, there is wisdom in the Quaker tradition of trying to reach consensus. When the president implements an action based on a small majority vote, if things go wrong, they will be continually hear "I told you so" from the dissenting BOD members and the directors as a group will be more reluctant totake remedial deal with the problems. When there is a consensus or near consensus the directors are much more likely to feel that "we are all in it together" for better or worse.

The remainder of BOD committees then report out. If there are no or only a few brief motions the meeting includes a presentation by the president or vice president on a special area of focus. This will be either an education and / or input piece. The topics vary and could include progress reports on programs in development, information about important changes in funding or regulations and issues facing the agency.

The President limits the other staff attending BOD meetings to the vice president, director of development, and the AA taking the minutes. Others believe that multiple vice presidents and others should attend BOD meetings. This is a good idea if the president in not knowledgeable about key parts of the organizational operations. Otherwise, the fewer staff who attends the better. The danger of having too many staff at the meeting is that staff can dominate the discussion and take responsibility for areas where the directors should be making decisions. In addition, the BOD members always should feel like the meetings are meetings of the BOD and not staff meetings. The BOD members always lead the discussions, and staff participation consist of giving information on request, responding to questions and making brief recommendations.

Leadership Staff and the Board of Directors

The way the BOD and staff interact is functional for each organization. The most common model is that the president reports to the chairperson of the BOD. In this relationship, the chairperson represents the attitudes, values, and goals of the BOD, and the president does the same for the staff. The BOD chairperson leads in policymaking and stewardship, and the president in policy implementation and operations. They are mutually responsible for matters related to the organizational mission, and assuring financial and programmatic integrity. If the president is unavailable, the executive vice president fulfills this role. The understudy for the chairperson is the vice chairperson. BOD members will also have task-oriented relationships with staff who sits on BOD committees as resource people such as the finance director, the information technology officer, and the director of development. Staff members who participate in the succession program for the positions of president and executive vice president attends BOD committee meetings as part of the process. The person BOD members are in most frequent contact with aside from the president is the AA. This relationship is around the many details associated with organizational life, such as meeting times, and paperwork. Beyond this BOD-staff relationship is occasional and functional. Prior to nomination it is best to think through potential BOD member conflicts of interest regarding staff, primarily when one person in a family is a BOD member and another is a staff member.

Most BOD members will understand that in all matters they act as a member of the BOD or a BOD committee, and not individually. This should be committed to writing in the section of the BOD manual dealing with BOD staff relationships. Individual BOD members never become involved with an individual staff member's problem, compensation, work assignments etc. If BOD members cross this line, it is the job of the board's chairperson and not the president to address it with them. The only exception to this if is they are a member of a committee investigating a complaint against an executive, or evaluating executive performance.

To facilitate excellent BOD functioning and relationships the president identifies and cultivates the third of the BOD members who are formal or informal BOD leaders. This includes most officers of the BOD as well as long time members. The most important parts of this cultivation process are getting to know the BOD member's values, interests, family life, political philosophy, goals, and work. Some of this will come through individual meetings with these leaders. Other information is in the public domain.

A great deal is apparent by the president paying attention to what people say during BOD meetings and committee meetings and what questions they ask. This enables the president to encourage action on the part of these leaders in a way that they will find appealing and adopt. For example, if the chairperson of the program committee is politically conservative than stress the goal of a new program in promoting self-sufficiency. If they are liberal, stress the new assistance that will become available through the effort. If they have an interest in Latino children stress the number of these children that the program will serve. Perhaps more importantly by meeting individually with leaders with some frequency you confirm their importance to organizational life. As time goes on some BOD members will come to you as the need arises for help with a difficult situation regarding one of their own children or a child of a friend or coworker. If the president or a member of the direct service staff helps in this situation, the BOD member is usually appreciative, and gets a better idea of how the work of the agency is useful and important.

The relationship between the president and the BOD is one of collaboration, and joint organizational ownership. The BOD members are not an audience for the president's pronouncements.

The president needs to carefully listen to BOD member ideas and try to figure out ways in which to integrate them into the organizational context, unless they are counterproductive. A good example of a counterproductive idea that works for corporations is to lay off employees to reduce cost, and ultimately to improve the bottom line. While layoffs are necessary when there is a major and sustained reduction in a charity's income in other circumstances layoffs is a bad idea for PCWAs.

Layoffs to reduce costs work in corporations for many reasons. Cost savings and increased profits are likely to please shareholders and Wall Street analysts. Layoffs, along with stock buybacks can help companies meet projections when business revenue is weak. They help companies remain competitive in the international marketplace where other countries have lower labor costs. For most corporations the bottom line is high earnings. There are also some exceptions to this in which the goal is organizational growth and business building. For instance, in its 2014 Annual Report Amazon states "Amazon.com opened its virtual doors on the World Wide Web in July 1995. We seek to be Earth's most customer-centric company. We are guided by four principles: customer obsession rather than competitor focus, passion for invention, commitment to operational excellence, and long-term thinking". (Amazon, 2015). This sounds suspiciously close to the thinking that guides PCWAs committed to excellence.

For the PCWA improved lives and children protected is the bottom line. Because salaries are much higher in the private for-profit sector when a layoff occurs, the remaining labor force is willing to assume the work of the people who leave by working longer hours. Teacher salaries are higher than social worker salaries. For most positions, a bachelors or master's degree in human service is necessary to qualify for jobs. This is because of state licensing requirements, managed care credentialing requirements, and the knowledge necessary to achieve positive outcomes. The PCWA has the unusual situation of many well-educated workers who earn low salaries. This situation exists for several reasons. The biblical teaching that we are our brother's keeper has become a value attached to charity work. Staff do not expect to earn salaries that are comparable to people with a similar education. The willingness of the staff to accept low compensation is a litmus test of their sincerity of heart.

Automation is prevalent in many businesses. Often the pubic embraces technological change. For example, customers accept the idea of going to a company website to complete a transaction rather than working with a customer service representative. In child welfare work there are two primary jobs, counseling youth and parents, and supervising youth in out of home care. Much of the direct service work is labor intensive so that although technology is useful in many ways it does not the reduce the consumer contact required.

The revenue model for PCWAs is very different from that of the for-profit sector. During the decade in Pennsylvania, following the last recession, service payment rates to PCWA have remained flat for the most part. This is not surprising considering the deep recession. There was a 31.7% loss in the amount of revenue that states generated for two years following the 2006-2007 fiscal year (Thomso, 2013) , Fifty seven percent of those participating in a Harris poll stated that taxes were too high (Robin,2016). A few customers at the federal, state, and sometimes local level decide agency income potential. The reverse situation prevails in terms of the customer base in the business sector. There are likely to be many potential customers for most businesses. In the retail sector, there are many thousands of customers.

The large majority of the PCWA workforce is women, many of whom have children. Layoffs are not a good strategy because this is a highly mobile workforce, and even when funding is easy to procure, the turnover rate is usually in excess of 10% annually (Children's Bureau, 2016). Unless there is an industry wide malaise workers will obtain other employment rather than work substantially longer hours.

All this is to say that sometimes circumstances in the private for profit and private child welfare sector are different so that solutions are not always transferable. However, often they are.

PCWA can often benefit from business practice adoption. For instance, a BOD member is doing quality assurance in their corporation through a detailed process review and wants the PCWA to adopt this quality assurance program. The BOD member raises this at a BOD meeting. The president may feel that this is great in theory, but has no idea how to free up staff time, or get the money to hire a consultant to implement this at the agency. The president also feels positively about the agency current work processes and is unsure if there will be any real gains made by implementing the BOD member's recommendation.

One response the president could give to the suggestion is to state that they think this is an interesting idea, and wants to discuss it further with the BOD member. At the end of the BOD meeting, the president makes an appointment with the BOD member to discuss the quality assurance idea. At the meeting, the president listens to the BOD member's idea. The president says "This sound really interesting. My management approach is to start small so that there is an opportunity to get the kinks out of the process and see early results. We have twenty cottages on the campus. I have thought for a while that cottage 12 where we help adjudicated female delinquents could use some special attention. Our work with this population is relatively new and we have been using our usual process with them. I think it is worthwhile to examine if we are on track in doing this. Will you volunteer to lead a quality review process for this program?" This kind of response accomplishes a few things. It lets the BOD member know you think this is a worthwhile idea to explore. It limits the size of the project to something that is manageable. Because the project relates to work that is new to the agency there is a potential quality gain. Starting with one cottage will provide an initial sense if the quality assurance program is worth expanding. The BOD member's commitment to the process is likely if they do part of the work.

Another important task of the president is to provide issue analysis, choices, and recommendations on individual matters coming before the BOD. The president's first job is to know enough about issues that will have a direct impact on the agency. These include likely increases or decreases in income and expenses. For example, the president or other staff are interested in starting a youth business, both to provide work experience for the consumers and provide new revenues for the PCWA Also leaders are aware of changes in program licensing regulations, referral patterns as well as facility licensing. They identify issues that the BOD may want to weigh in on. For example, the administrative offices are located in a lovely and large historic building. The president thinks that an income generating idea is to rent out certain rooms in the facility for evening and weekend wedding receptions. This will entail bringing liquor on premises which the agency has not done this in the past.

Also, leaders know the local news, and if they have a business BOD, it is beneficial to scan the Wall Street Journal or read two or three of the columnists in Barron's. They pay attention to other media sources about child abuse and neglect through child welfare membership organizations, child welfare journals and websites. For example, child sexual abuse by priests and the cover up by church leaders is in the news. In addition, multiple news stories about sexual violence perpetrated by powerful men against women is a result of the Me-Too movement.

The president knows about any major staff issues. They are familiar with pending child welfare legislation and customer news and issues. If the president is uncertain about whether the BOD will want to discuss a matter then they talk with the Chair and one or two informal BOD leaders and act accordingly.

It is disconcerting when a BOD member bushwhacks the president. This happens when a BOD member raises an unexpected issue at a BOD meeting. This could be the result of a media report, or something that is happening in the members business or family life. For instance, there is a story in the local paper about disorder at a local high school where there are regular fights and gang activity. The BOD member asks at a meeting if the agency ought to contact the school and offer to help. The president is not a mind reader and is unable to anticipate every issue. However, if the president is up on current events, they are better able to comment on a situation and give a meaningful response.

The president knows the values of the members and the history of important actions. For example, the president knows the BOD is committed to having a balanced budget. The budget adoption process is going to begin and early estimates project a deficit for the coming year. The president needs to anticipate that this could be an issue for them. If maintaining a balanced budget is a strong BOD value, then the BOD needs to decide whether to cut costs to achieve this. The president analyzes the budget to learn the cause of the projected deficit, and knows the choices available to bring the budget into balance. Furthermore, the president needs to recommend a course of action to the BOD. This is because the BOD members view the president as the expert and want their opinion on what to do. If a BOD member asks the president what to do the president does not with any regularity say, "I do not know". If they do not know, say, I want to look into this and I will include on the agenda for the next board meeting.

For instance, the PCWA has provided state funded services for ten years. The state reduces the budget for child welfare services by 5% due to a loss in tax revenues associated with poor economic performance during a recession. Because maintaining their workforce is a high value to due to the existence of bargaining units covering the state caseworkers, as well as the existence of the civil service rules, the state agency informs the PCWA that the contract will be 10% lower next year. The agency's main choices are to cut program expenses by 10%, try to get other income to support the program, or use agency funds to make up all or some of the lost funding. Since the program reduction occurs in a poor economic environment, the demand for this service will rise. The president's colleagues at other area agencies indicate that they will reduce services in proportion to the budget cut. It appears that the economic downturn is in the beginning phase and reduced funding amounts will be a reality for the next several years. Using fund balance earnings and perhaps a small part of the principal to fund part of the cost reduction could distinguish your agency from competitors. Also, your agency could direct some of the fundraising results to subsidize all or part of the deficit. Doing this though, may reduce other program offerings that a fundraising event supports. The customer might appreciate this and keep this in mind in awarding other funds. The community may appreciate the commitment to the mission. However maybe nobody will notice the benevolence.

Agency priorities come into play. People who value a balanced budget will favor reducing costs. Others will want a balanced approach-involving making both cost reductions and devoting fund-raising results to the deficit reduction effort. In the end, which choice or combination of choices is best is a judgement call. The important thing is for the president to know and understand the issue, present the choices, and a recommendation for action.

This is an example of leadership. BOD members sometimes advance other ideas or make a choice that is different from the one the president recommends. The main point is unless the BOD regards the president's recommendation as demonstrating awful judgement, they will respect that the president knows the issues presents them intelligently and gives some decision choices.

The president considers shared values and value differences between the staff and BOD in BOD policy making and staff practice adoption. The president communicates these differences to each group as needed. The common values shared by the staff and BOD are 1) commitment to the mission 2) the value of children 3) the service(s) provided 4) the belief that child abuse and neglect are wrong 5) the belief that children are vulnerable and need support, guidance, and protection 6) the belief that positive parenting is important 7) the belief that advocacy on behalf of abused and neglected children is worthwhile and 8) other mom and apple pie values such as predatory behavior toward children is wrong. Consider these beliefs held by both groups as well as the value differences highlighted below when the BOD and staff interact BOD members like the idea of agency services because although, it is government funded it is a private organization. They judge that a PCWA will be more efficient and effective than if the government runs the program directly. Staff come to the work because they see it as an opportunity to make the world a better place for the disadvantaged and are not so concerned about the private auspices.

BOD members usually prefer a merit-based salary increase plan whereas, the staff likes the idea of everyone getting the same percentage increase. BOD commitment to private fundraising is in part a result of the belief that government funding is not dependable. When the BOD members are mainly business people the value differences with staff may play out as listed in Table 7-1

Board of Directors Committees

The most common way most charities accomplish the work of the BOD is through committees. At most agencies, the chairperson establishes the different committees and appoints committee members. The PCWA bylaws provide for the establishment of certain committees.

Fewer committees with broader purposes, rather than more committees with a narrower focus have some advantages. Most people are busy. They have limited time for committee work and most members want to serve on only one committee, although there are frequent exceptions. The BOD chairperson and president review committee assignments annually. The ideal goal is to have five or more members on each committee not counting staff. The purpose is to assure enough members on each committee.

Unexpected member resignations reduce the number of committee numbers each year. Poor attendance at a committee meeting by one or more members affects the functional size of the group. A special committee assignment sometimes leads to an expansion of the size of the committee. For example, when the program and planning committee are preparing a new strategic plan it is a good idea to have enough committee members to make the workload manageable. Tie the number of members of a committee to its task list. I think that the finance and development committees need the most members due to the workload. Discuss initial committee assignments with new members at the recruitment meeting. Confirm the assignment in writing after the person's election as a BOD member. During an annual review, assignments sometimes change. A BOD of directors' committee structure that works is:

> Audit Committee – Meets 3 times a year
> Development and Nominating - Meets Monthly
> Executive Committee – Meets irregularly only as needed
> Executive Compensation Committee- meets twice a year
> Finance and Property - Meets Monthly
> Information Technology - Meets quarterly
> Program and Strategic Planning - Meets quarterly
> Personnel - Meets three times a year
> 401(k) Plan committee - Meets twice a year

Adjust the number of meetings listed above to the organization's needs and capabilities. The agenda drives meeting frequency. Adjust the number of members and committee duties specified in the or pay professionals to perform BOD duties that are outside of the expertise of the BOD members or involve spending a greater amount of time to complete than BOD members have available. For example, a small PCWA receives a state grant to purchase two vans to transport consumers. The state requires reports detailing the bidding, purchasing process, deployment and maintenance of the vehicles. The BOD decides to develop a contract with an accounting firm to submit the reports. The number of committees listed above and their duties change according to the circumstances of each PCWA. Three of the committees listed above have two different and related functions. The main reason to combine committee purposes is to limit the number of meetings. The finance and property oversight functions are the responsibility of a single committee because the financial elements of property purchases and building maintenance are the main areas of interest of the BOD. A BOD member employed in construction management or as a builder makes a good addition to the committee. The audit committee can be a subset of finance committee members. Combine the program and strategic planning committees because changes to the services are the most important part of the strategic planning process. Having the development committee manage the BOD member nomination process makes sense as the committee is always on the lookout for

<u>**Table 7-1**</u>

<u>**Board of Director and Staff Value Differences**</u>

<u>**Board of Director Values**</u>	<u>**Staff Values**</u>
A successful economy is the best way to ensure success for all	Even in a good economy there are winners and losers
The social value of individuals and their rewards are merit based	Everyone is valuable and equal
The financial bottom line is most important	Client improvement is the PCWA bottom line
Job one is to achieve results potential	Job one is to develop human
Technology can solve many problems	Social equality can solve many problems
Individual achievement is key to a Nation's success	Achieving justice for all is very important
Government regulations detract from Economic efficiency	Government regulations assure social assistance
Big government stifles economic growth	Transfers to the needy provide a minimal income for poor people
The PCWA assures abused children are responsible adults	The PCWA assures abused children become better functioning adults

people to donate to the PCWA. At a minimum, an executive, finance, and development committee exist, as does an executive compensation committee if there are highly paid executives. If not, there is no need for one.

I do not believe in the strong executive committee structure. A strong executive committee creates an in-group/out group situation. The executive committee consists of the officers and two at large members, who are BOD members. The President is a non-voting member. A majority of the committee members constitute a quorum. The committee convenes at the request of the BOD chairperson. The committee meets irregularly under three circumstances (often on their cellphones). 1) in a major emergency 2) when a motion requires action but there is not a quorum at the BOD meeting 3) when a decision is essential and there is a very short timeframe to make it. In some organizations, it is essential to have a strong executive committee. For example, one of the acts of genius of the Boy Scouts is that they have a very large the number of BOD members. There are many reasons for this including the number of volunteers compared with staff, and the large number of scouts and troops. It is a wonderful fundraising strategy but governance would be unwieldy if the total BOD had to be involved in the business of governance; therefore, a strong executive committee is essential.

My observation is that most PCWAs have a BOD size between ten and twenty members. Larger boards result in an easier workload for all, and will increase the results of the annual board appeal.

Both the 401(k) and executive compensation committee have BOD approved charters. These committee charters exist because of the regulatory environment. ERISA legislation, regarding the 401(K) and the IRS safe harbor provision regarding executive compensation, suggests the adoption of a committee charter, which makes it clear that the group operates in conformance with the applicable regulations.

A committee statement of purpose or charter for each committee outlines the responsibilities. Committee descriptions indicate the committee purposes, duties, number of members, and the committee's relationship to the BOD of directors. As mentioned above a committee may also adopt policies and hire advisors in the course of conducting committee business. It is common for BOD finance committees to have investment policies that guide them as well as investment professionals who manage the organization's cash assets, endowments, etc. When there is a new task item, the chairperson decides which committee will address it.

The Committee Meeting

The manager responsible for staffing the committee and the committee chairperson draw up the agenda. The manager writes a first draft and the chairperson approves it, or amends it. Establishing a committee calendar is useful. Mark the calendar with the meeting dates for the year. The members then decide which items they will review at each meeting.

At the beginning of a committee meeting, ask the members if they have anything to add to the agenda. For example, a program committee member reads an article about an opioid drug prevention effort that has model program status and wants to discuss if it is suitable for the PCWA. One role of the committee chairperson is to possess general knowledge in the field that is under the auspices of the committee, and bring items up items for discussion. For instance, the chairperson of the personnel committee works in the human resource department of a large corporation shares that they have achieved efficiencies through computerizing many of the personnel tasks using a software program and wonders if this is a good software program for the PCWA. In addition, the chair responds to questions or remarks raised at BOD meetings.

The agenda includes any committee action items, motions to make at the board meeting, and any educational or information items. For example, several years ago the Internal Revenue Service increased the amount of information they gathered about fund raising processes and results, executive compensation, and BOD operations. This resulted in the IRS significantly expanding the charitable organization tax filing – the 990 form. One of the new mandates is that charitable boards review and approve these filings. In this situation, the chair of the finance committee is responsible for informing the BOD of the change. They tell BOD members about the rationale for the change, and its implications for the organization. The BOD needs to know about their duty to review the tax return, and approve the 990-tax filing submission. Another example is the duty of the strategic planning committee chairperson to obtain input from the BOD members as part of completing the plan. This could include a plan review at a regular BOD meeting, written questionnaires or a special meeting to provide input to the plan. Determining the method to get member opinions is a BOD agenda item. Test line staff problems with a specific first line supervisor or policy by periodically tabulating exit interview questionnaires. Compiling the reports every two years and discussing them with the personnel committee of the BOD is one tool to keep policies and practices current.

Chapter 8 Four Powerful Ideas to Use in Child Welfare Policy Making

Each of the chapters that follow covers subjects that have a policy-making component. The type of policies the PCWA adopts is wide ranging including personnel policies, gift acceptance policies, and strategic plans. Adhering to four concepts in formulating and implementing policy will achieve success. The concepts are child safety, professional practice, good business practices, and the prudent person standard.

Child Safety

The first and most important concept is assuring child safety. Policies and practices in this realm include safety plans for children living with parents or caretakers that have abused or neglected them. It means that if children, especially infants and young children live in potentially unsafe homes that staff make frequent home visits during which they observe the physical condition of the child. It means that children who are older than 10 who are participating in agency programs receive verbal and written information on what to do if someone is hurting them. For children in residential care, a vice president meets with the children without any of the other staff present to get the children's impression of how they are doing and if anything is going wrong for them. PCWAs consider the adequacy of staff - child ratios for all program activities where there is a safety risk, such as swimming. Adequate supervision of the children always occurs. Staff always has sight supervision of the children during the day. In residential programs children are in common areas during the day and cannot be in their bedrooms except if they are sick. When children are asleep staff tours the bedroom areas hourly. The installation of a small window in the bedroom doors makes these bed checks less intrusive for the children. If there is a pattern of children getting hurt, it damages the PCWA credibility as a safe place.

Professional Practice

Professional practice means that organizations engaging in child welfare work, represent that their staff, programs, and businesses practices meet professional standards. Laws, codes of ethics, purchase of service contracts, government grant stipulations, program and staff licensing standards embody many of the standards of professional practice. Agency policy informs staff of the need for their professional actions and behaviors to conform to the requirements contained in these documents. PCWAs develop specific policies as the conditions of child welfare work necessitate them. For example, a personnel policy provision prohibits staff from sharing information with other people about consumers without the consumer's written permission. Laws and professional codes of ethics embody this principle in child welfare. Although plumbers are licensed, they are not required to keep their relationships with their customers confidential. Grant agreements list professional standards. For example, it is a violation of federal grant provisions to supply needles to addicted youth in a group home. Sometimes customers incorporate laws by explicit reference in contracts. As an example, most purchase of service agreements has language that there are not any delinquent taxes owed to the contracting government.

Professional practice standards also shape administrative practice. State licenses are a prerequisite to the operation of residential child welfare programs as well as selected out client programs. Licensing standards are likely to specify the staff-child ratio, the academic and experiential qualifications for different types of staff, and staff training requirements. Licensing requirements for residential programs will include facility requirements such as having more than one way of leaving the building, and minimum bedroom room sizes. Additional local fire safety and food safety licenses are likely to exist. Administrators assure that business operates within the context of IRS requirements. For example, leasing is preferable to purchasing.

State licensing boards establish standards for social workers, family therapists, psychologists and other human service professionals. The licenses and licensing standards for each profession vary by state. The American Association of Social Work Licensing BOD website (aswb.org) has a wealth of information about state licensing boards, and licensing standards. This includes information defining practice. The licensing BOD in many states license social workers for different levels of practice - bachelors, masters and clinical. Individuals who have completed social work degrees, psychologists, as well marriage and family therapists who pass an examination, and obtain state licensing board approval of their license applications, may engage in practice. The clinical license level also has practice hours and supervision requirements. State licensing boards accept complaints against practitioners. If they believe the complaint is valid, they take a variety of action including license revocation.

Each state defines practice. The definitions vary by state. By way of example, the definition of social work practice in California is:

"service in which a special knowledge of social resources, human capabilities, and the part that unconscious motivation plays in determining behavior, is directed at helping people to achieve more adequate, satisfying, and productive social adjustments. The application of social work principles and methods includes, but is not restricted to, counseling and using applied psychotherapy of a nonmedical nature with individuals, families, or groups; providing information and referral services; providing or arranging for the provision of social services; explaining or interpreting the psychosocial aspects in the situations of individuals, families, or groups; helping communities to organize, to provide, or to improve social or health services; or doing research related to social work.

Psychotherapy the use of psychosocial methods within a professional relationship, to assist the person or persons to achieve a better psychosocial adaptation, to acquire greater human realization of psychosocial potential and adaptation, to modify internal and external conditions which affect individuals, groups, or communities in respect to behavior, emotions, and thinking, in respect to their intrapersonal and interpersonal processes."

(Association of Social Work Boards, 2013)

Readers interested in social work licensing law issues and recommendations can review the Association's model licensing laws. (https://www.aswb.org/wp-content/uploads/2013/10/Model_law.pdf)

Both social workers and psychologists have codes of ethics that govern values and behaviors of practitioners. The National Association of Social Workers has an extensive code of ethics, which govern ethical behavior in practice, regarding consumers, peers, and
employers. The code URL is
http://socialworkers.org/pubs/code/default.asp. Similarly, readers can
review the Ethical Principles of Psychologists and Code of Conduct at the
following URL: https://www.apa.org/ethics/code

Professional association codes of ethics do not have the force of laws. However, officials and attorneys consult these codes when there is an allegation of wrongful behavior on the part of individual practitioners and there is civil litigation. Codes of Ethics are resources used to answer questions about appropriate practice and behavior. In addition, alleged victims can file complaints against members. If the association rules in the victim's favor the victim can use the ruling to bolster civil rights and litigation claims, and the perpetrator suffers the consequences, which could be a rebuke, a report to the state licensing body, public embarrassment, and termination of association membership.

Good Business Practices

The third important concept is good business practices. This covers a wide range of subjects applicable to PCWAs. The conduct of all business matters meets applicable standards, conform to laws, meet organizational ethical standards, and result in customer satisfaction. Concepts such as efficiency, effectiveness, and honesty characterize business operations. PCWAs have an adequate governance structure. It includes the existence of basic organizational documents, such as by-laws, a mission statement, policies, and practices that provide a lawful and rational basis for operation of the agency. These include conflict of interest, whistle blower, and business ethics policies. Accurate business records including financial reports and supporting back up documents exist. PCWA's complete required documents including government grant program and financial reports, quarterly employee earning reports, and federal census reports in a timely and accurate manner. Potential BOD members, significant donors, and government agencies do not want to be associated with poorly organized agencies. They will expect business practices on par with the peer agencies. If the invoicing system is weak, and government customers cannot submit reimbursement claims to higher levels of government, they will not continue doing business with you. If the president has a very high salary, it will raise questions for GCWA and other government agency staff. They may be too embarrassed to discuss this with you, but they will be thinking about it when it comes time to consider rate increases.

Prudent Person Rule

The last important concept is the prudent person rule. This applies to actions taken by BOD members and staff. It states that a person acquires the same knowledge, does the same research, and considers the same factors that any prudent person in the same situation would. This means that the action is reasonable and that the person taking it uses the same due diligence that the average person dealing with the same situation performs People can rely on information given to them by legitimate sources. Careful consideration marks professional action. If you are a childcare worker in a group home and a child does not feel well and goes to their room to rest, it is prudent to check on them hourly. It is imprudent to let five hours pass before you check on them.

In thinking about what can happen when PCWAs do not use the prudent person rule think of the line appearing in several of the Laurel and Hardy comedy movies made in the 1930's "Well, here's another nice mess you've gotten me into". A fictional example of a "nice mess" that occurs when the BOD and president ignore the prudent person principle.

Case Example: Prudent Person Rule

Little Lambs Children's Services is a small but growing PCWA primarily providing foster care services. Their annual budget is $2,500,000. Ninety percent of the income is from GCWA per diem foster care payments and ten percent is from private donors. Little Lambs has a $400,000 cash fund balance. The agency rents offices. Dr. Oops, the head of clinical services, successfully sought the position of president, when the founding president retired. Prior to the appointment, the BOD conducted a search for a new president. Several applicants including Dr. Oops interviewed for the position. The BOD concluded that none of the other applicants compared favorably to Dr. Oops.

A year after Dr. Oops begins as president, the chair of the finance committee introduces a motion at the BOD meeting to purchase a property in the city of Nuplotz to use as a boys group home. The purchase price is $250,000. Dr. Oops distributes a business plan after another board member seconds the motion. The business plan includes a capital and operating budget, letters of endorsement from potential customers, and a letter from the Business is Business Foundation pledging a gift of $150,000 that will fund most of the house purchase costs. The document also includes a floor plan showing the utilization of each room, a list of furnishings, the supplies needed the results of the property inspection, and a timeline. Dr. Oops is very enthusiastic about moving ahead with the purchase and the new program because it meets a community and customer need, and it will expand the agency. The business plan does not indicate anything about the program or the zoning of the property, property insurance costs or the prices of other neighborhood homes that have recently sold. None of the BOD members thinks to ask about the items not discussed in the plan. A BOD member for a year, Mr. Charlie Sleepwalking, is an attorney specializing in property transactions. The BOD chair asks Charlie what he thinks. Charlie says that he does not know much about the proposal other than what Dr. Oops and the others have said, but if everyone thinks it is okay, then it probably is. Another BOD member, Ms. Nevergettomeetings, a commercial realtor as usual is not present at the meeting. On the finance chair and Dr. Oops's recommendation, the BOD votes to purchase the property. The meeting minutes record the discussion and motion. The agency purchases the property after receiving a check from the foundation, and takes out a mortgage loan for $100,000. A month after the home opens a neighbor complains that he cannot get a parking space near his house anymore and that the boys are noisy, though they are not any noisier than a family with several children. The program director rents parking spaces for the staff at a nearby commercial lot, and instructs the childcare staff to minimize noise. The neighbor is satisfied until someone vandalizes his car *and he suspects one of the boys did it. He reports this to the police, but the results of the investigation are inconclusive. When the investigation comes up during roll call at the station, the police captain is surprised that the group home is in this neighborhood. The city uses sector policing so the captain is familiar with property uses in the sector. He thinks this is a residential neighborhood. The captain happens to see the city-zoning officer at the water cooler and asks if a group home is an allowed use on the block where it is located. The zoning officer says he is not sure, but he will check into it. He learns that the block is in a district zoned only for residential use and group homes are not an allowed use. The zoning officer visits the group home and tells the program director that the group home property is in a residential zoning district that does not allow group homes. Considering the home is already in operation, the zoning officer gives the program director 30 days to apply for a zoning variance. Dr. Oops asks the head of the law firm that represents Little Lambs to assign an attorney to prepare the variance request, and represent the agency at the zoning hearing. The group home is in a middle-class neighborhood with single-family homes many of them occupied by long-term residents. As per requirements, the zoning hearing board clerk notifies the neighbors whose properties are located close to the home about the hearing. The written notice includes the time, date, and location of the meeting. The notice states that the purpose of the hearing is to consider an application for a zoning variance to operate a group home in a residential district. The notice also appears in the local newspaper. The home's nearest neighbors fear their property values will decrease and that the neighborhood will not be safe. They notify other neighbors and thirty people attend the hearing to oppose the request. The neighbor who had their car vandalized testifies about this and the noise from the home. Another neighbor testifies about a recent home break- in attempt. She reports the person she suspects looks like a teenage boy. Several other neighbors testify about their safety and home value concerns. There is loud applause after each neighbor testifies. The attorney for Little Lambs does a good job of presenting how the group home operations would conform to the requirements for a zoning variance. The attorney states the boys are child abuse victims, and are not delinquents, and do not have behavioral health problems. The zoning code specifies that the zoning board can grant or deny the variance request at their sole discretion. Three weeks later Dr. Oops gets a letter from the Nuplotz Zoning Hearing Board denying the variance request and directing the home to cease operations within 30 days. The city hall beat reporter is there when the zoning hearing board announces the decision. The story appears that night on the six o-clock news along with the fact that the group home is a major project of the Business is Business Foundation. The* day after the newscast the foundation chair calls the foundation president, Mr. Moneybags to tell him to convene an emergency meeting of the foundation BOD to discuss the bad publicity and decide what to do. At the meeting, the members express anger and embarrassment about the foundation's name being associated with the Little Lambs debacle. They wonder why Little Lambs brought the home without first obtaining a zoning variance. They conclude that they should get the foundation's money back ASAP and invest it in something worthwhile for which the foundation will get credit. The next week Mr. Moneybags calls Dr. Oops and says that the foundation BOD members expect that Little Lambs will return the grant money to the foundation within 30 days, as Little Lambs cannot continue to operate the group home. Mr. Moneybags says the foundation members are mystified that the Little Lambs organization did not know that the zoning code did not allow for a group home use before they purchased the property and thought this would certainly be part of their due diligence process. Dr. Oops apologizes for the situation and the bad publicity and tells his peer he understands the Foundation's position. He says that Little Lamb's does not have enough cash on hand to return the money immediately. When the property sells, they will return the funds. Mr. Moneybags says he will talk with his chair, but he is sure that the foundation BOD was clear in their instruction to him and a delay in returning the grant funds will add to the board's negative impression of Little Lambs. Dr. Oops calls the agency attorney Mr. Sleepwalking about the ruling. The attorney says that in as much as the zoning code allows the zoning board to rule on these requests, and since abused children are not a protected class that there is little basis for a court appeal. Little Lamb's cash, balance is insufficient to instantly repay the foundation, and maintain the cash flow to pay for operational costs and the total principal of the new mortgage. Dr. Oops and Ms. Nevergettomeetings talk. Based on the prices of recently sold properties in the neighborhood, she suspects that Little Lambs will get less money than they paid for the property, and that properties in the area are taking about two months from the listing date to sell. Little Lambs owns no other property so there is a limit to the amount they can borrow.

There are issues concerning the lack of good business practices and the failure to use the prudent person rule that contribute to this situation. Dr. Oops is an experienced clinician and knows about foster care services. The good doctor has no business experience prior to becoming president and is learning on the job. Dr. Oops fell short on the prudent person front by not consulting Ms. Nevergettomeetings and Mr. Sleepwalking as he developed the business plan. As a professional realtor, Ms. Nevergettomeetings would have been of assistance in supplying information on comparable property *sale prices so that Little Lambs would have paid an appropriate price for the property. Mr. Sleepwalking as an attorney who handles real estate transactions would have noted the need to check the zoning codes to see if a group home is an allowable use in the zoning district in which the property is located. Dr. Oops's failure here is not the absence of knowledge about real estate purchases, but not meeting the expectation that a prudent person would seek out, readily available, relevant expertise, as part of the decision-making process. This amounts to not knowing what you do not know and not thinking to ask someone who does. These are due diligence issues.*

The behavior of the BOD members also did not meet prudent person standard. Dr. Oops's and the board finance chair's excitement about the project, propelled the BOD to quickly decide to purchase the home. The group's enthusiasm fueled their action. In the process, the BOD members lost sight of the prudent person rule. A $250,000 purchase is a relatively large expense for an organization the size of Little Lambs. The BOD needs to conclude the purchase is judicious and the purchasing process is adequate. The BOD members did not see the business plan prior to the BOD meeting. A prudent BOD requests to have time to review a business plan and then vote on the resolution later. As some of the BOD, members are homeowners they ought to have raised questions about price negotiations. Mr. Sleepwalking said nothing wrong. On the other hand, the BOD chair did not have the insight to notice the fact that Mr. Sleepwalking as a relatively new BOD member did not want to upset the apple cart. In addition, the chair knew but did not utilize Mr. Sleepwalking's professional expertise, by asking him to review the business plan and report to the BOD regarding his impressions at the next meeting. The chair also could have contacted Ms. Nevergotomeetings before taking a vote on the motion. All this amounts to "I just didn't know". This is fine, but the prudent person makes a reasonable attempt to find out before they act. State legislation protects BOD members from individual liability in this situation unless gross negligence is involved. Ordinary sloppiness is different from gross negligence. Paying back the foundation, selling the property, financing operations are all challenges faced because enthusiasm rather than thoughtful consideration prevailed.

Chapter 9 Program Development

Six Paradigms that Direct Action
1. Use of the Case Based Method in Program Development

One of the most important elements to success is listening to the stories of the children and thinking about the implications for practice methods, and program services. This is an outgrowth of the casework method. The work involves understanding the presenting problem, social situation, and history of the child. This information results in a social diagnosis, and the development, and implementation an intervention plan. For individual children, this process guides what needs to occur, to enable the child' life to improve. On the organizational level, listening to many of these stories guides the next steps in program development.

2. Mixed Environmental Scanning A second perspective that is of use in program development is the mixed environmental scanning approach (Etzioni, 1967). The idea is to be aware in a general way of everything that is happening in the environment. From this, you eliminate what is clearly not relevant. You pay attention to fringe as well as main line ideas, as fringe ideas can change into mainline ideas. For example, what started as a small federal program, a component of the Runaway Youth Act, (Transitional Living Programs) serving a few hundred youth nationally became a major federal effort when the IVE foster care program was expanded to help older foster care youth transition to adulthood, Environmental scanning is important because it gives the organizational planning process an external component beyond the external stakeholders the staff knows (customers, foundations, donors). In addition, a lack of awareness of what is going on in the world of child welfare can lead you to overlook important trends that the organization should address or important strategies that can be of help in constructing a program to meet a certain need. For example, although one of the programs that many PCWA's offer is group home care several environmental factors caused this to change. The Casey Foundation, one of the oldest, largest, and most influential private foundations focused on child welfare, led a national campaign to reduce residential care, and make more efforts to increase family involvement. In addition, there was a desire to decrease child welfare expenditures. Moreover, there were questions about the effectiveness of group home and institutional programs in helping children. These trends combined to decrease residential care and increase extended family care.

Some scanning tactics are to sign up for Google Alerts for the words child welfare, foster care, etc. Ask a staff person at the congressional district office to forward copies of any child welfare legislation, when an elected official first introduces it. Become a member of the Child Welfare League of America. Check the child welfare pages of the National Council of State Legislatures. Listen or read the news daily.

3. Values Translate into Decision Making Criteria A third element in service development is thinking about logical next steps considering agency values, which translate into decision-making criteria. Some agencies use similarity criteria. A foster care agency then might be likely to add a therapeutic foster care program, or an emergency foster care model to their basic program. Other agencies use a diversification approach and will balance their service portfolio by having residential, in-home, and educational programs. At some organizations, there is a focus on innovation rather than duplication. The decision is to use a service innovation model and not offer some traditional services.

4. Service Selection Style

The agency adopts one or a combination of service styles. A competitive and duplicative style involves opening the same type of program that already exists in different service areas. The goal of this style is to substantially grow the size of the agency. This style is beneficial when there is an additional need for an existing service, or when the existing services are of poor quality, or too expensive. The advantage of this strategy is that the service need is clear. If there are already PCWAs the agency will be competing for market share, which will likely keep per diem rates low.

A second style seeks to develop a continuum of care for consumers. Here the focus is on program expansion based on consumer need. PCWA establish new programs related to the first program. For organizations that operate a runaway and homeless youth shelter, developing longer-term aftercare counseling services for youth makes sense from a continuum of care perspective. The shelter is a crisis based short-term intervention. Out client counseling services, provide an opportunity for families to work on solutions to chronic problems over time. For a foster care program, a continuum of care expansion could be to offer home studies for potential adoptive parents.

A third service selection style model is innovation. This involves providing a service that does not exist in the community. In addition, the service may be an original intervention. An innovative program in behavioral health could be a specialized eating disorder program where none presently exists. The advantage of offering innovative programming is that it distinguishes the agency from other youth service PCWAs. The challenge is to assure effective program design and implementation

5. Matching Available Money to Program Ideas

There are two principal methods to align program development with financing. The first is the search process. For this, the agency needs good donor records, access to foundation directories, a comfort level in using grant.gov and a good knowledge of the types of programs of interest to GCWAs. After the search, it is clear if a funding source exists, that is interested in the program. If no one at the agency has the time or ability to do a search, develop a contract with a professional fund-raising firm. The advantage is their staff is already familiar with these resources and the search process will be quicker and more efficient. If there is no money to pay for a contract, recruit a grant writer as a volunteer or BOD member.

If there is not a good match between your idea and your search results try a donor and customer cultivation process. Begin by writing a brief standard proposal narrative and budget. The purpose of the proposal is to assist in the preparation of your elevator speech. Then make telephone calls to the best customer and a few of the regular large donors.

The important things to do when the agency is trying to get financing for an innovative program is to convince prospects of the inherent value of the idea. This could be better outcomes, major improvement in efficiency, or a needed service. Put forth the idea in a way that compels the donor or customer to act. When something is new and the results are unknown, the donor or customer is taking a leap of faith based on their respect of the president's competence and ability to produce results. The president's ability to convey confidence, and enthusiasm, about the idea is important in convincing supporters to invest. When you lose all hope, shelve the proposal for future submission. Often as time passes, there are new opportunities to develop old ideas. Sometimes the idea is just ahead of its time.

The second important financial consideration is the match between cost and revenue. If a funding source pays $30 a day, for a program that costs $40, it may be best, not to start at all. The more of the service supplied the more money lost. Most of the time public customers have a range of customary rates they will pay for a service and they are reluctant to pay more. An alternative in this situation is to do a small startup project letting the customer know that the agency is doing it at a loss. If the results are excellent, go back to them in a year and see if they will purchase the service at full cost. If not be prepared to use agency or private funds to support the loss if there is a very strong commitment to continue. Keep the amount of services matched to the donations or agency money you are willing to commit to it.

6. Accreditation Accreditation is a worthwhile credential to have. It indicates a commitment to quality of care. Accreditation demonstrates that a program component meets "best standards of practice". It provides the accountability sought by public customers and private donors alike. Often one or more customer requires accreditation. One caution with accreditation is that the accompanying administrative and direct service staff hours required to meet the standards is considerable.

Criteria for Starting a New Program

The Project is Consistent with the Agency Mission Do not pursue a proposed venture that is inconsistent with the agency mission. Although it is not usual sometimes, a project suggests a logical expansion of the agency mission, and if so, the next step is to review the mission. For example, the mission is to assist youth, but much of the work involves families. A logical expansion of the mission is to focus on the service needs of the parents of consumers. This suggests the development of new services perhaps an employment program for the parents of these consumers. However, if a community needs a geriatric service a PCWA is not a resource.

A Valid Child Welfare or Behavioral Health Need Exists

We sometimes know about a need through our own experiences with children and families. In addition, other local PCWAs might cease operations or stop offering a program. Occasionally GCWA need additional programs to comply with new legislation. In other situations, the service array in a community needs a new component due to changes in community population trends.

The Service is Aligned With the Agency Service Selection Criteria

One service selection style is competition through geographic expansion. A competitive model entails gaining a larger market share. It is quite successful when implemented by regional and national PCWA and behavioral health organizations. This strategy has the advantage of developing an in-depth knowledge of an existing program that should facilitate high quality and lower costs. It also results in higher service levels. Public agencies are often glad to have more PCWAs to contain cost and prevent any one agency from being dominant in any geographic area.

The Organization Possesses the Required Expertise Possessing the competency to offer high quality services that improve the lives of children and families is a key to program expansion. However, when the agency focuses on innovation, chances are staff will not know it all when you begin. Bringing new competencies into the organization through hiring, or staff training, modeling the program after what others has done, and focusing on best practices all enable the development of expertise. Evaluate if existing agency experience and ability suggests that the agency has some of the competencies required. If a primary service is counseling it is reasonable for staff to learn a new counseling model.

The Project is Financially Viable

This is an area in which the president and the BOD members need to be vigilant. Financial viability means that a customer or donor is committed to pay for the service at a rate and volume that allows for an annual operational surplus of between 2 and 5 percent. The customer or donor has the financial ability and willingness to fund the project. The customer has a legitimate method for determining the actual level of need.

An issue to consider is that the customer really may not know the level of need. If it turns out the number of consumers referred is low, the PCWA may not realize enough income to pay for project costs. The risk for the PCWA is that the government customer is not usually willing to enter into anything other than a per diem or per hour reimbursement contract. A startup necessitates a tremendous amount of time and effort to rent space, hire staff etc. If the referrals are slow to come the costs exceed income, sometimes for a year or more and a large deficit is possible. Some alternatives to managing this risk with a GCWA is to ascertain if they will purchase slots, at an established per diem rate if usage is below an agreed upon number, after six months of operations. Another method is to scale programs up slowly so that any deficits will be small. If the GCWA is not willing to cover some of the agency losses then consider closing the program after a year or two if it is not operating on a close to breakeven basis.

Additionally, the GCWAs that are the customers of PCWAs periodically deal with funding reductions from federal and state government. They often will make across the board reductions to PCWA allocations in response to a reduction in their own funding. Also, managed care organizations will sometimes offer rate reimbursements that are lower than costs to limit service volume when a service is responsible for a disproportionally high share of expenditures. For example, total outpatient behavioral health service expenditures are high and service reimbursement rates are low. If things go well for PCWA, they can come close to breaking even in this service and perhaps achieve a surplus. However due to problems in hiring psychiatrists (because the demand far exceeds the supply) and high consumer appointment cancellation it is equally possible that a deficit will result.

Organizational Management Capacity Exists This has a few dimensions. The first is, can upper management supervise additional projects? Is there funding to add the management staff necessary to manage the new project? Agencies have often stretched the envelope on this dimension. The first reason this has happened is that as growth occurs the agency hires the necessary staff at the program director and supervisor level. However, at the vice president level little changes. This results in a situation in which upper management capacity is minimal and additional growth occurs due to the good will of your top people to take on an ever-growing workload. The downside (or perhaps not) is that there are limits on the ability to grow at any given time. The reason I say perhaps not, is that I think gradual rather than explosive growth is better.

Is the Location of the Project Favorable? Is the new service opportunity in a community that fits with the agency growth strategy? This depends on the growth strategy stated in the strategic plan, and if the agency culture incorporates opportunity theory into its geographic growth plans. That is, if the strategic plan provides that the agency will consider expanding into counties that are adjacent to the current service area and a great opportunity comes along that is located outside this area does the agency undertake the project because the opportunity is attractive? Is the new community saturated with services there being little opportunity to develop services beyond one specific program? Does the new community have the financial resources to support their present and intended program of services? This has to do with the sufficiency of the local tax base to support services, unless the community has a record of attracting a lot of money from out of the area.

A second belief about geographic proximity is historical. The BOD is likely to live proximate to the service community. They serve on the PCWA board in part as a community activity. They believe that the PCWA ought to limit geographic reach. This kind of "home boy" thinking is more common when many of the directors are either born in the community or has lived there a very long time. Due to the mobility of American's, there are fewer "native" community members and the board may become more expansive on the geography of the service area as time passes.

Strategic Risk Factors

Eight important strategic elements present significant risk for agencies. 1) A failure to use readily available information about service trends to remain relevant in a changing service environment can cause financial difficulties for an organization. This relates to changes in what customers want, funding trends and reductions, emerging trends and missed opportunities related to new funding or programs, or new funding for present programs. 2) Failing to develop key services or a reputation that differentiate the organization from others providing private child welfare services. This is likely to be a threat when funding is insufficient and government customers choose between excellent and good PCWAs. The extent to which PCWAs have a positive reputation with customers and offer unique services can sway a customer to use one organization over another. 3) There is a lack of diversification in services. When an agency offers only one or two services, they face diversification risk. If services, due to customer, regulatory or internal operational issues cannot continue, there is not much of a fallback position. 4) There is a lack of enough customers. Even though funding for PCWAs is primarily government funding, there are many potential government customers. These include child welfare, juvenile justice, behavioral health, and substance abuse service customers. In addition, these public funding sources exist on the federal, state, and local level. This risk is highest for a PCWA that has only one customer, usually a large city. In this situation, there is also risk of rates not increasing for a few years. If due to a consumer related problem, or government jurisdiction issue there is a loss of business from one customer than the organization can withstand it, if the customer is one among many rather that one among a few. 5) The inability of the PCWA to retain staff that customers like. Purchase of service decisions occur at the caseworker level in the field of child welfare. When GCWA caseworkers like a particular PCWA staff member they will repeatedly refer cases to them and tell their peers about the staff member. Again, in private child welfare services quality staff are assets in addition to being expenses because their work generates revenue and their reputation with customers can result in higher or lower revenue 6) Direct staff members fail to provide services that satisfy customers. If the PCWA staff does not protect children, provide levels of supervision to families desired by customer staff, or fails to meet customer expectations in another way, referrals from that GCWA can dry up. From a marketing perspective in child welfare services the most important people to high customer satisfaction are the direct service staff members.7) Direct service staff hurt or kills a child in residential settings or allows other residents to hurt or sexually abuse a child. This is usually present when there is a, misuse of physical restraint or lack of sight supervision of children. In addition, when childcare worker salaries are very low and the staff hired is not well suited to the work problems can develop. GCWA workers investigating alleged abuse perpetrated by residential staff is quick to let those who make placement decisions know about these events. GCWAs suspend referrals to the PCWA. In residential programs with prescribed staffing patterns and other fixed costs, the resulting low occupancy will put a strain on agency finances. Quick corrective measures and effective customer communication is important. The actions must convince customers that the necessary changes have occurred to keep children safe. Beyond terminating the employment of staff make changes to your system of care that will help keep children safe. 8) Leadership does not act on the business basic of having a balanced budget over an extended period. When this happens, the agency shrinks and then usually merges, with a financially stronger agency, and the agency loses its identity.

Program Closing Criteria

Use a well -reasoned process to decide on program closings. A pro forma policy follows:

The BOD approves program closings upon the recommendation of the program committee of the BOD. The president recommends closing a program to the committee. The president makes both a verbal and written presentation to the committee about the facts and circumstances pertaining to the closing recommendation.

These reports address the applicable points below:

- ➤ The reason(s) there is a recommendation to close the program.
- ➤ The reason the program cannot become a part of another existing program
- ➤ The plan to link current program consumers with a resource that can address their needs.
- ➤ The tail end cost of closing the program.
- ➤ The implications of the program closing for current program and administrative staffing
- ➤ If the program housed at an agency owned site, is there a plan to repurpose the program space
- ➤ A program closes if any of the circumstances listed below exist:
  - Expenses have exceeded program income by more than 10% for twelve months or 15% for 24 months. Efforts to mitigate financial losses have not been successful and are unlikely to be successful.
  - There has been a significant reduction in financial support from the program's primary customer(s) that will continue. It is not practical to continue program operations on a smaller scale and have expenses and income match
  - There are an insufficient number of referrals to the program to justify its continued operation
  - The outcomes of the program are unsatisfactory for 24 months. Efforts to improve outcomes are not favorable.
  - The risks of operating the program have become unacceptable
  - Due to a change in circumstance, the program purpose is not consistent with the agency mission or values.

Program closings are sad events, entailing a loss of service for children and a reduction in agency capabilities. Financial failure precipitates most program closings in one way or another. A strategy to avoid these kinds of closing is to use surpluses from other programs to support the program that is losing money. In as much as money is fungible the issue to decide is, among the entire agency priorities, is it the best use of a surplus to subsidize a money-losing program. The President and BOD consider both values and facts when they make these kinds of decisions. When thinking about choices in using organizational surpluses choose the option that is most consistent with the mission statement.

Closings due to program ineffectiveness demonstrate organizational integrity. Spending money on ineffective efforts is wasteful. Sometimes operating costs are prohibitive. For instance, with equestrian programs, expenses include feeding and providing labor intensive services for the animals as well as high insurance premiums due to the risk of injury to the children. If there are a few claims there may not be a carrier willing to insure the program. The agency could self-insure, but in the end, the BOD members think the risk to children and the insurance costs are excessive.

Another reason for closing which is even rarer is a change in program circumstances. For example, an agency provides a counseling program for youth living in the county juvenile detention facility. To save money the county decides to bring in a vendor to operate the program. As time goes on it is clear that the vendor staff is engaging in disciplinary practices with the youth that agency staff regard as excessive and destructive. The BOD decides to discontinue the service because respect for youth is an important agency value.

Business Plans

Business plans are of use in two circumstances, when considering a large capital expenditure and when considering a large new program. Good business plans outline the necessary steps to complete the project and demonstrate how you accomplish them. Plans provide the case statement for fund raising campaigns and support financing applications for the project. Business plans are not necessary for incremental expansions of existing programs.

Writing a Business Plan

Begin with the purpose of the project. This section provides an overview and serves to introduce the reader to the contents of the plan. First, discuss the gains made by the consumers due to the project. Emphasize behavioral changes that are important for consumer's success in life. Next, discuss the gains made by the agency. Emphasize what the new services are and how the service meshes with the mission and current programs. For property purchases is there anything specific to the property that permits different kinds of service provision? Will the purchase achieve certain efficiencies? Will the property purchase distinguish the agency from other PCWAs? For example, if the agency purchases a camp to offer adventure programming and create a healing environment for youth, the organization creates a resource that most agencies do not have. Next, define the property or program. Last, communicate the capital and/or program budget and make a brief statement about the financing of the program. (one page)

The second section is the program development history. It illustrates why the organization developed the program and discusses key people who are interested in the project.

Mention any relevant BOD motions, and significant work or false starts. For instance, if the purchase of an apartment building for independent living youth is on the table and a building donation fell through mention this. For property, acquisitions discuss the program usage for the property and for a new program discuss the capital requirements. Note comparable pricing materials that a real estate agent has provided on similar property sales. For programs, mention program reimbursement amounts for similar programs offered by other PCWAs. (1-2 pages)

Third, tell about the purpose of the present plan. If for instance a property needs extensive renovation this might be a focus. A major expansion to another state of an existing program might be the purpose. Include property maps, news articles and other relevant content. (1-2 pages)

Fourth, supply a time line indicating the important tasks, both those that you completed and those you will complete. List the task, the proposed completion date and the person or group responsible for completion. For building or property purchases, this includes due diligence items, zoning hearings, development of the sales agreement, major repairs (i.e. a new roof) a required environmental remediation (asbestos removal) and essential improvements. For programs, it includes contract development dates, hiring, training, and the program start date; outcome measurement dates (1-2 pages)

Fifth, provide a more detailed program description. This is an expanded version of the topics discussed in the one-page program description without the finance section. Depict the needs assessment. Cite relevant community statistics and testimony from potential customers. Describe the size of the service population and their characteristics. Write project goals and measurable project objectives. Describe the present and anticipated competition. Explain the rationale for selecting a program compared to alternatives. Mention site visits made to other organizations offering the program. Discuss any research that indicates this is a best practices program. If this is a building or property purchase, give a detailed description of the property and building. Provide drawings of the property and label the use for each room or space. Describe the purpose of repairs or alterations. For instance, if the agency is purchasing a building to operate a Child Advocacy Center describe interview and observation rooms, medical examination facilities, and videotaping equipment needed Discuss any important assumptions about the future nature of the agency that are important to the project. (2-3) pages

The sixth section discusses on an item-by-item basis all the items listed in the time line. For example, it discusses the property inspection process, and the phase one environmental study. It discusses the property zoning and if you require a special exception. Provide a discussion of the zoning code and the probability of success, and who is providing legal representation. For programs, discuss who will do the hiring, the number, types, and qualifications of staff, and brief job descriptions Discuss training plans, workload expectations etc. Describe the program staffing and staff management plan. This includes new hires, transfers, and whom the program manager reports to and why the reporting relationship makes sense. (2 pages)

The last section of the plan is capital and or operating income and expense budget summaries as well as a budget narrative that explains the numbers. Emphasize financing arrangements such as mortgages or a planned capital campaign or special operating campaign. It is important for the BOD to know that if they approve the plan that they are signing on to conduct a capital campaign. Expect that readers will pay special attention to this section and present a clear plan to finance both the capital and operating portion of the project. (2 pages)

Chapter 10 Child Welfare Specific Policies

Document Policies

Record retention policies discuss the different kinds of documents that are common in the organization and their protection, retention, and destruction.

Electronic record protection includes computer passwords and additional passwords to enter certain software programs. A finance department staff member makes backup of electronic records and stores them off the premises. Cloud storage of records is now common. Paper records are in locked filing cabinets. Lock all agency buildings after business hours. Most policies provide for shredding paper files that are past their retention date. The backup of electronic files is a departmental responsibility. Good clinical record keeping software will facilitate record retention and destruction. If there is no clinical software, before destroying electronic files wait until the end of the year and search the files for the information needed to assemble the annual report. Then move the record to a new folder renaming each file with the family name and the date each case closed. Then delete the file when they reach the destruction date. The creation of offsite records storage facilities, for paper records that are inactive, is sometimes necessary. As needed decide upon a central location or scattered site storage options approach. Consider renting a storage facility. A better choice if it is affordable is to pay a document management organization to store the paper files and to destroy them when the record retention date passes. In decision-making, consider how often there is a need to supply copes of paper file information. For electronic files keep offsite copies of the records. External hard drives are one possibility to accomplish this.

When the organization considers adoption of a records retention policy it is time to involve people from each functional department (finance, fundraising, information technology, and each major clinical program) to provide input into the draft policy and get information and different ideas about existing procedures that work. Get input regarding record retention requirements, needs for record accessibility, and present storage practices. After the president approves a final version, it becomes the agency practice.

The following are selected passages from the Internal Revenue Service (2018) Compliance Guide for 501©3 Charitable Organizations. Both the president and chief financial officer should read this publication. The IRS has a very large amount of information applicable to PCWA. However, it is often difficult to get the information you want. This publication does the best job of anything that the IRS has in summarizing the important portions of the tax code that are applicable to PCWA.

> "...In general, a public charity must maintain books and records to show The charity must be able to document the sources of receipts and expenditures reported on Form 990... ...If an organization does not keep required records, it may not be able to show that it qualifies for tax-exempt status or should be classified as a public charity... Records must support income, expenses and credits reported on Form 990 series and other tax returns. ... Books and records of public charities must be available for inspection by the IRS. If the IRS examines a public charity's returns, the organization must have records to explain items reported..."

> "...An organization should maintain a list of its donors and grantors and the amount of cash contributions or grants (or a description of the noncash contributions) received from each..."

> "...Substantiate Revenues, Expenses and Deductions for Unrelated Business Income Tax (UBIT) Purposes An organization needs to keep records of revenues derived from, and expenses attributable to, an unrelated trade or business... "

> "...A public charity that makes grants to individuals must keep adequate records and case histories to demonstrate that the grants serve its charitable purposes.... Case histories on grants to individuals should show names, addresses, purposes of grants, manner of selection and relationship (if any) that the recipient has with any members, officers, trustees or donors of the organization... "

> "...A public charity can choose any recordkeeping system, suited to its activities, that clearly shows the organization's income and expenses. The types of activities a public charity conducts determines the type of records that should be kept for federal tax purposes. A public charity should set up a recordkeeping system using an accounting method that is appropriate for proper monitoring and reporting of its financial activities for the tax year..."

> "...If a public charity has more than one program, it should ensure that the records appropriately identify the income and expense items that are attributable to each program..."

> "...A recordkeeping system should generally include a summary of transactions. This summary is ordinarily written in the public charity's... accounting journals and ledgers. The books must show gross receipts,

purchases... expenses (other than purchases), employment taxes and assets. For most small organizations, the checkbook might be the main source for entries in the books while larger organizations would need more sophisticated ledgers and records...Documents for expenses include: canceled checks, cash register tapes, contracts, account statements, credit card sales slips, invoices and petty-cash slips for small cash payments..."

➢ ".... Organizations that have employees must keep records of compensation and specific employment tax records..."

➢ "...Assets are the property, such as investments, buildings and furniture that an organization owns and uses in its activities. Liabilities reflect the financial obligations of the organization. A public charity must keep records to verify certain information about its assets and liabilities. Records should show: ▪ when and how the asset was acquired, ▪ whether any debt was used to acquire the asset, , ▪ documents that support mortgages, notes, loans or other forms of debt, ▪ purchase price, , ▪ cost of any improvements,, ▪ deductions taken for depreciation..."

➢ "The organization must keep records that support an item of income or deduction on a return until the statute of limitations for that return runs. The statute of limitations has run when the organization can no longer amend its return and the IRS can no longer assess additional tax. Generally, the statute 19 of limitations runs three years after the date the return is due or filed, whichever is later. An organization may be required to retain records longer ...Record retention periods vary depending on the types of records and returns. "

➢ "...*Permanent Records* – Some records should be kept permanently. These include the application for recognition of tax-exempt status, the determination letter recognizing tax-exempt status and organizing documents, such as articles of incorporation and bylaws, with amendments, as well as board minutes. ..."

➢ "...*Employment Tax Records* – If an organization has employees, it must keep employment tax records for at least four years after filing the fourth quarter for the year. Records for Non-Tax Purposes – When records are no longer needed for tax purposes, an organization should keep them until they are no longer needed for non-tax purposes..."
(IRS 2018)

When there is a complaint under investigation, litigation, customer audit or other special circumstances, the agency retains records until three years after they resolve the matter. Due to variations in funding source requirements record retention policies should always allow that the PCWA keep financial records for as long as a government grant or contract or grant supplied by a foundation or individual requires. Also, State record retention requirements sometimes exceed Federal requirements.

Except for the above, the IRS is silent on the retention of records. Keep all committee minutes, 990 filings and the substantiating back up materials for three years as well as executive compensation salary studies, and materials related to conflict of interest situations

In addition to documenting 990 responses, the information might be necessary to make voluntary responses to any number of people reviewing the 990. For example, if a donor comes to a charity and says, "Your organization's mission is close to my heart because of my personal family history. I am considering making a \$100,000 gift. I do not know the BOD members and want to make sure this is a well-run organization. I naturally have reviewed the 990 forms. I do not want my money going to excessive salaries for key employees. I want to make sure the agency has a functioning BOD and an executive compensation process in place. Send me a redacted copy of the compensation committee minutes for the last two years

Service records contain information regarding each consumer assisted, and typically will include identifying information, assessments, releases of information, individual case notes for each client contact and, case summaries. Client record retention practices are consistent with the requirement of the contracting governmental agency or foundation. When there is no retention requirement stated, retain records in accord with federal grant regulations; that is retain clinical record three year past the submission of the last fiscal report. (U.S. Government, 2013)

For readers that want to look at a comprehensive list of documents and suggested retention periods the guide issued by The Massachusetts Society of Certified Public Accountants, Inc. Federal Taxation Committee is worthwhile. Access it at: https://www.cpa.net/resources/retengde.pdf

Electioneering Policy

Agencies that promote the participation of employees in political campaigns risk losing their 501©3 status. Agencies adopt an electioneering policy so that employees know that they may not engage in activities promoting a political candidate on work time or use agency resources to promote a political candidate at any time. The policy provisos are that agency employees may not do any of the following during working hours:

> Conduct political campaign activities. An example is going door to door to ask people to vote for a candidate. Another is assembling signs asking people to vote for a candidate.
> May not attend a political rally for a candidate
> May not at any time use agency equipment, resources or facilities to prepare political materials advocating the election of a candidate. For example, they may not use the agency copier and copy paper to make a copy of a political speech for a candidate.
> May not use agency funds to pay for campaign supplies or materials
> May not associate the PCWA name with any candidate.
> May not in any one to one conversation, group conversation, or staff event, email or use any other agency written communication to provide information advocating for the election of a candidate, or distribute campaign information such as notice of a political rally. Staff does not post on agency media sources favorable information about a candidate.

Voter registration drives, which are not associated with a particular candidate, are not political advocacy activities.

(IRS 2018)

Child Death Practice Policy

Because the organizational mission of PCWAs is to better the lives of abused and neglected children, a child death is an especially traumatic event. Practice statements focus on four areas 1) communicating with the aggrieved family 2) providing support and trauma assistance to the family's direct service provider(s) 3) participating in likely police and child welfare investigations of the death 4) cognizance of the possibility of civil litigation against the agency on the part of the family.

The practice statement should include the responsibilities of the various people involved. The child's direct service worker should immediately notify the supervisor of the child death, including the circumstances, and needs of the family for support. The worker reports the death to the police and the appropriate GCWA. The worker documents what they know about the circumstances of the child's death in the child's record. They assure the record is up to date, and are familiar with the contents of the record to prepare for participation in investigations by public agencies. These include GCWA, the police, and the coroner. Staff maintains consumer confidentiality except as necessary to further the investigations of involved authorities. Staff communicates with their supervisor, but not any other staff about significant issues. They do notspeak to the media.

Staff preserves all clothing and personal items of a residential consumer. Handle items the police deem relevant according to instructions. This is likely to be a time of grief for the worker, and they may have feelings about the consumer's death that they have difficulty managing. The supervisor should approach the direct service worker(s) about the agency providing grief-counseling services for them. The direct service worker supports the family by attending the funeral service, and arranging for the agency to send flowers, make donations etc. In their communication with families and others it is appropriate to say "I am sorry for your loss" or "I will miss ______"

Staff is not to make any comments except to their supervisor about their performance regarding the case. Specifically, they should not say things like "If I had it to do over again, I would do things differently", or "I feel badly I did or did not do this or that". In answering the investigator's questions, they are to make only factual comments.

The supervisor is responsible for notifying the program director or vice president about the child's death. They are responsible for supporting the worker and indicating that the agency provides malpractice insurance coverage and other supports for them and presumes unless there is substantial evidence to the contrary that the worker discharged their responsibilities to the child and family in a professional manner. They arrange for grief counseling for the worker as needed. They review the consumer file within 48 hours of the death to assure it is complete and accurate. The president reviews the entire situation with the program director, communicates with the media, and informs the BOD of the child's death. The BOD has enough information about the nature of the situation to be able to respond to comments of people they know in the event a media piece appears. The president reports any claim to the insurance carrier and works with counsel.

Emergency Preparedness Policy

PCWAs act "in loco parentis" the Latin for in place of the parent in many different situations. These situations all involve the child participating in a staffed agency program when the parent is not present. The worker(s) exercises the judgments and performs the duties normally performed by the parent. However, this status does not allow for the violation of any of the child's rights. The staff acts as the child's caretaker when a child is participating in any agency program at any agency site such as a camp, an office, or even their own home if the parent for some reason is not present.

One of the core roles of staff acting as the temporary parent is to assure the best interest of the child. In emergencies the staff does, within the law, what is necessary to keep the child safe. Many government organizations purchasing child welfare services and federal grantors require PCWAs to have emergency preparedness plans. In considering the scope of the plan, an emergency is a serious, unexpected, event that has the potential to harm children and requires immediate action on the part of the staff.

Emergencies include suicide attempts, serious acts of homicide, serious property destruction, bomb threats, malfunctions at facilities such as loss of heat or water, release of toxic substances in a specific geographic area such as a railroad or truck spill of harmful material, and major and minor terrorism attacks.

Suicide attempts involving ingestion of enough drugs to result in an overdose, very large amounts of alcohol, loss of more than a quarter cup of blood, attempted suffocation, gunshot or knife wounds should result in a call for an ambulance and medical evaluation and treatment. Threats and attempts using non-lethal methods result in a mental health evaluation to determine the need for services such as acute psychiatric hospitalization, medication, and counseling.

When there is a homicidal situation that staff is unable to control, the first thing to do is to call 911. Calling the police is always the first thing to do when a weapon is involved or the staff judges that the person acting out is in a state of psychosis, or is on a rampage.

However, staff successfully manages situations when there is no weapon involved and there is not much physical aggression, using two techniques. The first is separating the rest of the residents / youth from the individual acting out to ensure their safety. One staff member stays with the group. The other staff member listens to the expressions of anger, of the acting out individual and allows them to talk themselves out to a point where they are calm and have regained self-control.

Organizations should always have an on-call protocol that starts with the direct service worker, followed by the supervisor, and goes up the chain of command to the program director, vice president and president so that consultation is available to people handling an emergency. Other communication protocols include contact with child welfare caseworkers, juvenile probation officers, or parents. **Advance training and preparation will be useful for facility and environmental emergencies**

Equipment and supplies at each agency facility include

> ➤ A fire extinguisher
> ➤ Several days' supply of water and nonperishable food
> ➤ A non-electric can opener
> ➤ Paper plates, cups and utensils
> ➤ A battery-operated radio
> ➤ A first aid kit
> ➤ Flashlights and extra batteries, candles and matches

> Road maps for the state that the facility is in as well as all adjoining states
> $200 in cash
> A list of the office and home telephone numbers of all the people in the chain of command

Check every six months to make sure these supplies are present and not past their expiration date.

For each facility, the staff on each shift knows:
> The location of all utility shutoffs and how to activate them
> The location of the emergency supplies
> The administration of first aid

Emergency preparedness includes the following practices:
> Each staff member keeps a change of clothing, sleeping bag and a 3-day supply of personal medications and personal items in their car or office.
> At each facility, limit the flammable materials stored inside the site to a minimum.
> post a facility floor plan, including the evacuation route, on each floor of the facility
> Conduct fire drills quarterly and keep a log.
> Have a facility evacuation plan in case of fire as well as a predetermined meeting place.
> After the evacuation, confirm everyone has left the building. If possible, take child medication and health records.
> If someone has contact with hazardous materials get medical attention as soon as possible.
> Evacuate the facility in the case of a bomb threat and notify the police.
> For each residential facility, the counselor informs the residents and other staff of an alternate meeting place within walking distance of the facility, in cases where people cannot re-enter the building.

In the event of a power outage, heat loss, or water loss determine if it is wide spread. Report outages to the maintenance staff and utility suppliers
> Check the fuse box, oil burner button, water source valve as necessary
> Be sensitive to the needs of residents who use signaling devices in the event of a power outage
> Procure battery operated lanterns, portable toilets, electric radiators etc.
> Obtain cooked food from outside sources

Depending on the length of the outage, discuss with the supervisor relocating residents to another agency site or a motel For evacuation situations caused by area wide emergencies, such as a release from a local nuclear facility, staff follows instructions on media sources or the Emergency Alert system from area emergency management personnel.

Staff uses agency and personal vehicles to evacuate youth to predetermined, out of area sites that provide shelter. This might be a motel/hotel or a residential service PCWA with which the agency has a reciprocity agreement. Staff uses evacuation routes recommended by emergency management personnel.

> Staff carry credit card with a $2,500 minimum available credit limits
> Staff assure residents pack a three-day supply of clothing,

Staff takes all resident medications, the first aid kit and consumer records.
Staff secures the building before they leave.

> Staff use the specified agency number as a communication point,
> Staff carries a personal or agency cellphone. They use the cellphone for alerts and situation updates.
> Staff notifies agency personnel of overnight stops as possible or to get needed assistance.

Hazardous materials accidents may result in a shelter in place situation. All staff and residents stay at the facility. Lock all windows and doors. Turn off fans, close fireplace dampers, turn off air conditioning, and other systems that draw air from outside the building. Stay in rooms with the fewest windows at a place above basement level. Remain aware of updates from emergency management officials.

Diversity Policy

Customers and donors who consider embracing diversity as a best practice now frequently require diversity policies. Large corporations and nonprofits adopt them. The items covered by diversity policies are typically the same as covered by law - race, color, religion, gender, national origin, age, disability, and, sexual orientation. The main points of the policies are valuing and respecting diverse populations. Diversity is a social good. The organization states its active interest in having the participation of diverse communities and in understanding the nature of each of these communities. Policies include a commitment to equal opportunity in employment and inclusion. I looked at many diversity statements. The following U.S. Coast Guard diversity statement does a good job of capturing the concept of diversity

Training Monies Repayment Practice Statement

Increasingly, agencies pay substantial training fees for staff to gain the needed credentials to provide services. The most common of these are clinical licensure supervision requirements where the agency hires a supervisor with a certain credential to supervise staff wishing to attain the credential. In addition, extensive training fees are involved in having staff certified to provide model programs such as Functional Family Therapy. The repayment policy seeks to specify the employee obligation to the agency should they end employment during the training period or for a certain period following the completion of the training. The economic reason for this repayment practice is that the agency will have spent money, but not have received the value of the expenditure during a period of continued employment, and the need for the organization to make this expenditure again in order to have other staff that is certified provide the service.

The core of the practice is for the worker and the agency to sign a written agreement regarding the amount paid by the worker to the agency, and the conditions that trigger repayment. The agreement indicates that the worker accepts the agency is investing significant staff time and effort and / or money in providing supervision or training for the purpose of the worker achieving a specific credential. The agreement lists the specific resource and its cost i.e. number of

DIVERSITY
POLICY STATEMENT

Diversity, though not easily captured in a single definition, allows the Coast Guard to benefit from the talents, abilities, ideas and viewpoints of a workforce drawn from the richness of American society, including men, women, minority groups, people with disabilities and veterans. It is achieved by using two key enablers: providing unfettered enlistment, appointment or employment opportunities to all qualified citizens equally, and creating and sustaining an organizational climate in which people of diverse backgrounds, cultures, races, religions, ethnicities and experience are fully included, valued and respected.

Diversity is vital to mission readiness and excellence. Diversity sparks innovation by incorporating new approaches and fresh perspectives to problem solving. Attracting and employing a diverse and talented team of active duty, reserve, civilian and Auxiliary members ultimately enables us to better perform our challenging maritime missions.

We must strive to create a climate of equity that fosters an environment where all individuals have the opportunity to prosper, advance in their careers and contribute their utmost to Coast Guard missions. We must strive to ensure that our Coast Guard recruits, retains and sustains a diverse, talented and highly skilled workforce. Our Diversity Strategic Action Plan will guide our efforts to achieve these goals. I encourage all members of our workforce to become familiar with the plan located on our diversity website http://www.uscg.mil/diversity/.

I am personally committed to making the Coast Guard the Service of choice for all Americans who seek to serve our Nation and its people. Achievement of this goal is an all-hands evolution.

R. J. PAPP, JR.
Admiral, U. S. Coast Guard

hours of clinical supervision over a two-year period valued at a specific dollar amount. The employee acknowledges that if they leave employment that the organization will have lost it investment but the worker will have benefitted from the training/supervision received. The agreement lists a period, (I suggest two years) during which the employee will continue employment following the completion of the training. The agreement indicates that the employee will repay the organization a fixed sum of money encompassing all or part of the agency expense if they leave prior to the end of the agreed upon period. Additionally, the agreement has a repayment schedule if the employee ends employment during the training or post training period. The agreement states that payment is due in full on the last day of employment. There is also additional language in the agreement that is particular to contract law so Have your business attorney write it.

The difficulty with this practice is collecting the repayment. Some people are very good about repayment, and others are not. Contact the person if they do not make a payment within thirty days to see if the agency can work out a payment schedule. Failing this, some organizations use a collection agency. Another choice is litigation. If the amount falls within the small claims court guidelines this can be a good choice because staff can represent the organization. If the amount is large, the agency may want to institute a lawsuit. As with all litigation, the PCWA needs to consider the costs of lawyers' fees with the amount due, and the person's financial ability to make the repayment. In non-payment, situations report the nonpayment to the three main credit bureaus. The early resignation and payment failure are part of a reference statement for the employee.

Excess Compensation Policy

"...A charity may not pay more than reasonable compensation for services rendered. .... the compensation of officers, directors, trustees, key employees, and others in a position to exercise substantial influence over the affairs of the charity should be determined by persons who are knowledgeable....Under (the rebuttable presumption) test, compensation payments are presumed to be reasonable if the compensation arrangement is approved in advance by an authorized body composed entirely of individuals who do not have a conflict of interest with respect to the arrangement, the authorized body obtained and relied upon appropriate data as to comparability prior to making its determination, and the authorized body adequately documented the basis for its determination

concurrently with making the determination. Comparability data generally involves looking to compensation levels paid by similarly situated organizations for functionally comparable positions. One method is to obtain compensation surveys or studies from outside compensation consultants for this purpose. The compensation consultant must be independent from all members of the BOD as well as all staff members whose compensation is determined by the BOD. The consultant must undertake a study or analyze existing data to establish executive compensation recommendations... "Once that test is met, the Internal Revenue Service may rebut the presumption that an amount of compensation is reasonable only if it develops sufficient contrary evidence to rebut the probative value of the comparability data relied upon by the authorized governing body."
Internal Revenue Service (2008)

Information Technology Policy

Social service information technology policies contain a general statement that equipment, software, and Internet access are tools for staff to fulfill their job description. Specify in the policy that all files, pictures, and any other material on agency computers are agency property. Include a statement forbidding the use of technology resources by friends and family members of the employee. The policy should outline any behavior that the agency does not want employees to engage in. This will include things like not sharing passwords. Although the agency will probably want to allow personal use of workstations during break times, managers may want to prohibit certain activities such as mass emails, chain letters, or accessing pornographic materials.

The policy should address each employee's responsibility for protecting proprietary agency information, and for protecting consumer information. Outline the reasonable efforts employees make to prevent the theft or destruction of hardware and software, including "IT hygiene" expectations. A policy specifically addresses the confidentiality of information that is in electronic consumer files, as well as consumer billing information. Often policies prohibit tampering with files, and remind employees about agency ownership of materials, including electronic media developed during work time. Prohibit the use of software not licensed to the organization. If the agency does home or school-based work, decide whether to provide laptops to the staff. Laptop theft prevention protocols exist for staff who takes laptops on appointments in consumer homes. The password system uses a double password, one for the laptop or workstation and a different password for the consumer record system. The agency may affix tracking devices to laptops.

The manual has a section on new employees getting a password from IT staff, as well as having the password deactivated when employment ends. In addition, the policy has the method for setting up and closing email accounts. Indicate that users cannot use software that disables the virus protection software.

There is a section on personal use of the internet. For instance, you may want to prohibit employees from making negative comments about their supervisor, the agency consumers etc. on social media sites. The policy specifies that staff do not download software; games, screensavers etc.

The policy may specify that email exists to conduct agency business, and employees have no rights of personal privacy when they use the agency email system. All emails of any type and email related software belong to the agency. Due to the sensitive and confidential nature of consumer information, the policy should emphasize that employees are not to leave their computer screens open while they are away from their desks.

The policy needs to charge the IT committee of the BOD with having periodic external audits of the vulnerability of the IT assets to criminal action. The audit report makes specific recommendations of actions needed to reduce IT system vulnerability. There is an emphasis on protecting consumer files, personnel files and financial records from hijackers, and destruction of data and computer systems.

Public Communications Practice Statement

Indicate by position titles who may communicate with the media. The policy states that except for the positions authorized, or people given specific authorization to talk to the press, staff does not communicate with media sources.

Contagious Disease Practice statement

These types of policies direct staff behavior when there is a widespread outbreak in the community of a highly contagious disease. The goal is to prevent the spread of the disease, and recognize that alternative staffing patterns may be necessary in programs if there is an occurrence.

In the event of infection for those working in office-based or in-home programs, the infected staff person communicates with their supervisor who, in turn, will arrange for the cancellation of any appointments, until the infected individual is in good health and returns to work. Additionally, the supervisor is responsible for establishing a rotating on call schedule of uninfected staff to provide telephone counseling to families whose worker is infected and who experience a crisis while their worker is out on sick leave.

For those residents who have or may have a reportable communicable disease, medical precautions apply which include segregation. Infected youth may not have visitors. Achieve adequate staffing that meets state regulatory requirements by the following strategies:

Programs pool residential staff resources to cover residential sites. The goal is to maintain staffing patterns that meet but do not exceed requirements. Supervisors activate on call and part time staff to cover shifts in addition to the regularly scheduled staff as needed. Supervisors work as direct service staff as needed. In the case of low to moderate census, consolidate two or more programs at a single site. Utilize non- residential staff to work alongside trained residential staff if necessary. The policy also emphasizes the use of universal precautions in hand washing and facility cleanliness, and the protocol used in handling mucous and blood.

Limited English Proficiency Policy

In accordance with federal law, establish a policy of providing language access services to consumers who have limited English proficiency. Such services provide the ability of consumers to participate in programs. To accomplish this, family members when appropriate, provide interpreter services. Signage for key locations in agency buildings is bilingual. In addition, PCWAs use translator services.

Public Inspection of Documents Policy

Section 501(c)(3) organizations are required to disclose information about their organization to the public. You are required to share the following documents with the public when requested:

• Annual returns for three years after the due date. This includes returns like your Form 990, 990-EZ, 990-PF, and any Forms 990-T filed after August 17, 2006, including your extensions.

• All Form 990 schedules (except portions of Schedule B), attachments and supporting documents.

• Your application for exemption and all supporting documents, like Form 1023, if you filed it on or after July 15, 1987. • And the determination letter from the IRS that shows your organization has tax-exempt e: No, you're NOT required to share all business documents. For instance, you don't have to disclose some information found on Schedule B of Form 990 or Form 990-EZ, documentation for unfavorable rulings or certain types of information that the IRS approved

• Portions of Schedule B of Form 990/990-EZ – You don't have to identify your contributors by name, only the amounts and natures of the contributions.

• Unfavorable rulings – An earlier denial of tax-exempt status is an example of an unfavorable ruling.

• Certain types of information that the IRS said could be withheld – This could include trade secrets, patents, processes, styles of work and national defense material.

Remember that there are consequences to not complying with these. You or employees of your organization can be fined $20 for each day of noncompliance, up to a maximum of $10,000. If the failure to comply was deemed willful, the employee could face a penalty of $5,000 per return or application! "

(IRS 2019)

Gift Acceptance Policy

The gift acceptance policy often originates in the development office and is important for the organization in handling donated items. Having a gift acceptance policy can protect the organization from risks, including public relations risks. For example, a charity with a capital campaign in full swing would want the ability to refuse a gift that necessitated naming its new building after a notorious figure. The Al Capone wing of a new building might not present the desired public image. The policy should allow for the refusal of gifts when costs associated with the gift make it undesirable. This sometimes happens with gifts of real estate, when the repairs needed to a building are extensive.

Workplace Safety Practices

The federal government Occupational Safety and Health Administration (OSHA) exists to ensure safe workplaces. View a list
of employer responsibilities at:
https://www.osha.gov/as/opa/worker/employer-responsibility.html_Policy elements include posting, in each agency site, a placard indicating OSHA employment contact information.

Generally, the employer is responsible for maintaining a safe work place for staff by keeping the work place free from known sources of harm. For PCWAs, this includes emergency procedures when a staff member feels physically threatened by a violent child. PCWAs provides safety training for staff. Staff have access to masks and other supplies that protect them from an outbreak of infectious disease, or from complications of dealing with a consumer blood loss situation. The policy has provisions for the medical examination of staff for injury detection and treatment. Color code hazardous items. Employers keep records of injuries. OSHA receives report of serious injuries and fatalities.

Chapter 11 Policy Making, Bylaws and Conflict of Interest Policies

General Policy Making Considerations

This chapter discusses non- financial policies and practices. First, identify an area where the PCWA should consider policy or practice adoption. My general attitude is the less policy the better to facilitate organizational agility and flexibility. The identification process can have many origins. A new law sometimes leads to a new policy. For instance, most businesses needed to amend their personnel policies after the enactment of Family and Medical Leave Act legislation. Another situation is that a PCWA adopts a policy that demonstrates alignment with a funder policy. For example, some time ago United Way became interested in fund recipients adopting a diversity policy. Other times external events like the Penn State sex abuse scandal, cause a BOD to enact special reporting procedures when wrongdoing involves top management staff. Sometimes tragedies like the death of a child, in care, precipitate the adoption of a child death protocol.

Whenever considering a new policy the first thing to do is to study the issue to educate policy makers. The questions to ask are what policies exist? What makes for an effective policy? What is the nature of the debate about the available policy choices? What are the main things the policy should include? From this, an issue paper is prepared. Boilerplate polices in many cases, are readily available through Internet searches. Reviewing three or four of these is useful in learning how others manage the policy construction process. However, state and local laws, the preferences of stakeholders, the services you offer, and the organizational culture, will determine the applicability of other policies to individual organizational situations. For example, a children's hospital child death policy is likely to focus on a review of the medical care given. In a PCWA group home the focus is on dealing with the trauma that the child's family and other residents of the home experience. Staff responsibilities in cooperating with child abuse and criminal investigations are also components of the policy.

After the key constituencies on the BOD and staff review and comment on the issue paper one of the leadership staff members, as a professional development activity, prepares a first draft of the practice statement. The vice presidents and program directors then review the first draft and provide feedback. As necessary, discuss the main differences in their input at a leadership meeting. As the group discusses the possibilities, the key considerations usually become known. Either the president or chief clinician finalizes the practice statement. It usually takes two or three drafts and reviews to nail things down. People think differently and give different kinds of feedback. If this is a policy adoption situation rather than a practice implementation situation, the president refers it to the appropriate committee of the BOD. The BOD approves organizational policy but not practice statements. If there is a question of whether to involve the BOD, the president, and chairperson address it. The president implements the policy once the BOD has approved it, and the BOD is the only ones who can modify it. The president and whoever else have the authority can grant exceptions or modify practice statements. In the rare case that a situation arises in which the president grants an exception to a BOD policy the president writes a memo to the BOD chair describing the situation and the exception.

The IRS and Organizational Governance

"The IRS encourages every charity to adopt, establish and regularly review a mission statement to explain the organization's purposes and guide its work. Significant changes in your organizational documents should be reported to the IRS... An active and engaged board is important to the success of a public charity and compliance with the tax law. A governing board should be composed of persons who are informed and active in overseeing a charity's operations and finances. To guard against insider transactions that could result in misuse of charitable assets, the governing board should include independent members and should not be dominated by employees or others who are not independent because of business or family relationships... Although the IRC does not require charities to have governance and management policies, the IRS does encourage boards of charities to consider whether the implementation of policies relating to executive compensation, conflicts of interest, investments, fundraising, documentation of governance decisions, document retention and whistleblower claims may be necessary and appropriate... Board members are encouraged to regularly review the organization's financial statements and information returns, and consider whether an independent auditor is appropriate."

(IRS 2008)

Key Policies

The key organizational policies are the articles of incorporation, by-laws, and mission statement. In addition, vision statements and value statements guide actions. Agency leaders read these documents often. This will protect them from self-recrimination when a BOD member asks at a meeting about the procedure for amending the by-laws, and the president does not know the answer. More important they will prevent the organization from acting in violation of existing rules. For example, if the agency articles of incorporation that is sixty years old, state that the business office is   in Muncie do not write in the annual report that it is in Gary (even though it is). Be silent on the issue, and decide to amend the articles of incorporation or relocate the office back to Muncie. If the by-laws state most of the BOD has to approve the sale of real estate, do not sell the house received from a donor without a BOD vote. Keep a copy of these documents in your office.

Articles of Incorporation

The articles of incorporation are the document used to legally create the organization and register it with state government. State government prescribes the content of the articles, associated fees paid, and other necessary organizational start up paperwork. It includes the name of the charity and the address used to register the PCWA. Indicate the purpose of the agency within the IRS definition of purposes for exempt organizations. The document contains wording about the earnings benefiting only the corporation. Officers, BOD members, and employees do not receive distributions of earnings. However, they get reasonable pay for work. The organization does not participate in activities aimed at electing candidates to public office. Lobbying activities conform to IRS regulations. The company will not conduct any activities that are not allowable under law or regulation. The articles state the organization is to exist in perpetuity or a specific number of years. The dissolution process provides for the payment of final bills and distribution of the assets to advance a charitable purpose. A minimum of two incorporators sign the articles.

Know where staff keeps the articles. Sometimes you need an original for an audit, or business transaction. This document is not something that people look at on a routine basis, yet it is advisable that several people have a copy of the articles. Amendments are infrequent. The most common reasons to amend the articles of incorporation are if the organization's name has changed, or the organizational purpose has changed. The filing and amendment of articles of incorporation is in the states' jurisdiction. It is necessary to notify the IRS of any changes to the articles of incorporation in the 990 filing. Be careful not to change the organizational purpose in a way that might cause the IRS to question the organizational charitable status.

The IRS has a lot of information available for tax-exempt organization on their website http://www.irs.gov/Charities-&-Non-Profits/Charitable-Organizations

By-Laws

It is a good idea to review by-laws every five years. The Internet has model by-laws that are of be use as a starting point if they are better than your current by-laws. Make sure that the substantive topics covered in the present by-laws are present in the new draft. The subjects the bylaws address, and the content about each is spare. This maximizes the authority of the present BOD who will face situations, not anticipated, when you write the by-laws. In addition, the more mandates contained in the by-laws, the more chance there is that current staff and BOD members inadvertently break a rule. Less is more. For example, rather than specifying the BOD committees, authorize the BOD or the BOD chairperson to create and eliminate committees. On the cover page write the adoption date Attach any amendment adopted to the last page of the bylaws. List the date of the amendment. The bylaws usually include a general statement of purpose that mirrors the statement in the IRS tax-exempt status application as well as a more detailed statement of PCWA activities. Each state determines the required structure and content of organizational by-laws. In many states, the language is general and there are few requirements. The IRS does not have specific language or content rules for by-laws. The IRS does mandate that each organization select a fiscal year.

Membership - Set a minimum age for voting rights that is specific to state law usually age 18. The number of board members required is low and there is variation by state. From a community perception, and workload capability perspective, a good minimum is ten members. Anecdotally many PCWAs BOD size is between ten and twenty members. An idea is to set a minimum number of directors and empower the board of directors to determine the maximum number. In addition, if you have someone you really want on the BOD when there are no openings put a provision in the by-laws that the BOD, by vote, may raise the maximum number of members. Set the circumstances when the directors declare that the position of a member is vacant. These can include a failure to accept office, because the member does not attend meetings after election; the conviction of a member of a felony, a judge declares the member to be of unsound mind by a court, or the member dies.

By-laws identify membership criteria such as age. Also, include election, and removal conditions. Election and removal usually occur by majority vote of the BOD. There is a vote to fill vacancies if the size of the BOD shrinks or expands. Indicate that missing four (or use a different number), meetings a year or failure to perform duties is grounds for dismissal from the BOD. It would not be advisable to kick the best donor off the BOD if they are unable to attend many meetings, so there is discretion in enforcing this provision. In this section indicate the length of a term (usually between one and four years) and the maximum number of terms (if any) a member can serve. One method is to have two to three-year terms, and allow for a maximum of three or four terms.

Set the quorum requirement at between 60% and 80% attendance. If the PCWA is just born, it is likely that enthusiasm is high, so the number of attendees will be high. As organizations mature, the agency has higher status members attendance will drop and so should the quorum requirement. This is a bit tricky in that the president does not want poor attendance to prevent the BOD from conducting business but they do not want to make major decisions without the input of a good number of BOD members. An alternative is to accept low attendance for general matters but set higher requirements for selected decisions. For instance, the bylaws can specify attendance by 51% of the BOD constitute a quorum in order to conduct organizational business, but 75% of the Directors must approve the purchase or selling of property, and incurring debt, such as mortgages. Charities having difficulty with attendance are in good company, as the large majority of registered voters do not show up at the polls for local elections.

Officers - **N**ame the officers, their duties and the length of their term, usually one or two years. The most common officer positions are president, vice president, secretary, and treasurer. Some organizations have more than one vice president position. Other's with smaller boards combine the treasurer and secretary positions, or eliminate the vice president position or do both things. The important position most often is the chair. Along with the president, they are the public face of the agency, and the president's boss and confidant. The second most important officer is the treasurer who is the steward for organizational funds.

Meetings - The by-laws address regular, annual, and special meetings, and the meeting notices required. For example, the by-laws can specify that regular meetings occur at least four times a year, and any director may convene additional special meetings. There is five days' notice of any meeting. Indicate acceptable methods, such as email for providing meeting notices. Do not forget to convey in writing information required by the bylaws at the annual meeting. This information can include a summary of the income and expense, assets and liabilities, and service accomplishment for the prior year. Check your state statute for annual meeting requirements.

Contributions - This section is optional. Some by-laws specify fixed annual financial contributions by the members of the BOD. This reflects the concept of organizational dues. The idea is that there will be higher contributions if the gift request is specific. In addition, having giving amounts stated in the by-laws depersonalizes the process. Since many people do not like to ask for money this is another advantage. I do not believe in prescriptive giving. I prefer asking BOD members to contribute a generous gift annually within the context of their ability to give.

Voting Alternatives Some by-laws allow the adoption of motions by a majority of all members of the BOD in writing, with all directors voting in writing in lieu of a duly called meeting. There is no harm in this provision except when you try to use it. The time and effort involved in hunting down the two members who do not submit their written ballots after numerous requests is extensive. It is a much easier to empower the executive committee to act on behalf of the board, wait until the next scheduled meeting, or even to call a special meeting.

Confidentiality - Some by-laws have confidentiality provisions for the BOD that prohibit the discussion of organizational business outside of the BOD meeting. This is a heavy-handed tactic in the age of the Freedom of Information Act and an emphasis on transparency. An alternative would be to ask the BOD of directors not to discuss any confidential matters on the agenda, outside of the meeting

Duty of Loyalty and Due Diligence - BOD member service to the organization includes care in the discharge of their duties including prudence, skill, and diligence. They are loyal to the PCWA. The member does not put their personal interest or the interest of another organization above what is best for the PCWA.

Indemnification - This section absolves BOD members from personal liability, except in cases of gross negligence or a violation of law. Generally, state volunteer and Good Samaritan legislation prevents litigants from holding BOD members liable if they have acted in good faith. In practical terms, this means the organization will pay for the defense and settlement costs in cases of litigation that name the members of the BOD. For more information on this, see directors and officer's policy in the chapter on insurance.

Amendments - Do not make the process to change the by-laws onerous. Ten days written notice to the BOD of a meeting in which there will be a proposal to amend the by-laws, is sufficient.

Conflict of Interest - Some by-laws incorporate word for word from the IRS conflict of interest language. The disadvantage of doing this is that some of the IRS language reflects legislation, but some of it are IRS recommendations but are not requirements or law. Once it is in the by-laws, it codifies the IRS best practice recommendations and creates a higher standard for BOD conduct than existing laws require. In addition, adversaries will use publicly available information and self-imposed standards of practice against the BOD in contentious situations. Contentious situations though are not common Also be on the alert for changes in IRS charitable regulation and best practice mandates if congress introduces legislation to reduce business regulation during President Trump's administration.

Conflict of Interest Policy

The IRS states that a conflict of interest policy:
> Delineates what determines a conflict of interest
> States the organizational classes of individuals included in the policy
> Describes the process used to disclose potential conflicts of interest
> Describes how conflicts of interest are handled
> Describes how the organization monitors transactions to determine if there Is a conflict of interest
> Describes any limitation faced by a person having a conflict of interest
> Describes the financial level of the transaction at which a conflict of interest exists and what level the conflict is investigated

The IRS defines a conflict of interest as follows
"A *conflict of interest* arises when a person in a position of authority over an organization, such as an officer, director, manager, or key employee can benefit financially from a decision he or she could make in such capacity, including indirect benefits such as to family members or businesses with which the person is closely" related.
"A conflict of interest exists when a BOD member or key employee or their family members have an ownership interest in a business and are involved in a transaction with the agency... A principal concern is that a transaction results in excess financial gain for the individual business, or that the business receives preferential treatment in the bidding process or obtaining a contract involving a business transaction. A person with a conflict of interest does not participate in the decision regarding the transaction and declares annually in writing, as well as on an ongoing basis where potential conflicts exist. Between the annual declaration date individuals covered by the policy are obligated to declare to the group designated by the agency of a conflict of interest that has developed due to a change in the circumstances of the person, or due to the agency proposing to enter into a new business transaction.

The IRS proclamations about conflicts of interest include the following, which highlights this standard:

"The directors of a charity owe it a duty of loyalty. The duty of loyalty requires a director to act in the interest of the charity rather than in the personal interest of the director or some other person or organization. In particular, the duty of loyalty requires a director to avoid conflicts of interest that are detrimental to the charity.'"

(IRS – Life Cycle of Charity2004)

What follows is conflict of interest policy I wrote. A sample IRS conflict of interest policy is available at: https://www.nigp.org/docs/default-source/docs/chapter/resourceguide /ConflictofInterest.pdf

An important advantage of using the IRS sample cited above is that if there is ever a situation where an outside agency examines an organization's conflict of interest policy, following an IRS template will be a best practice. In addition, several organizations that supply conflict of interest templates use the IRS sample word for word.

I take the approach of requiring competitive bidding to deal with conflicts of interest as opposed to allowing the person with the conflict to make a presentation to the BOD, and subsequently having the board make the decision as to whether or not a conflict exists. In my sample policy, those bidding who have a conflict cannot communicate with the BOD and staff during the bidding process regarding the bid item.

I do not like the IRS approach for several reasons. The first is that BOD members as part of the same body usually have cordial relationships. I think telling one of their peers that they have a conflict of interest is a difficult thing to do, and members will not want to do it. Second, I think giving the director with the conflict the opportunity to address the BOD, about the issue, gives them special access over others who might be interested in doing business with the agency.

I like using competitive bidding for a number of reasons. Federal regulations recognize competitive bidding as a best practice. It does not punish a person with a financial interest, who also gives time and money to the charity, by prohibiting them from submitting a bid. Not allowing the BOD member with a business interest, to communicate about their bid to any director or key employee or to attend meetings where there is a discussion about the transaction allows for an arm - length transaction. Not having anyone with a financial interest participate on the decision-making committee is a safeguard against self-dealing. I think the best interest of the charity is when it receives the best value for its money. My experience is that BOD members with a business interest will often submit a lower bid or offer better services than the competitors offer as a demonstration of their loyalty to a cause that they care about. The safeguard offered by competitive bidding is that if a bidder submits the bid offering the greatest value to the charity than they and not the BOD member will be the winning bidder.

Author Sample Conflict of Interest Policy
Article I
Purpose

The purpose of the conflict of interest policy is to protect Caring Children's Services here in after referred to as "the organization" interests when it is contemplating entering into a transaction with a disqualified person as defined in Article II. This policy supplements but not replaces any applicable state and federal laws governing conflict of interest applicable to PCWA.

Article II
Definitions

1. *Financial Interest*

A disregarded person has a financial interest if the person has, directly or indirectly, through business, investment, or blood relations, has an actual or potential ownership or investment interest in any entity contemplating having a transaction with the organization.

2. *Disregarded Person*

A disregarded person is any BOD member, principal officer, highly paid employee, or key employee of the organization or member of a committee with governing BOD delegated powers, or any donor making a \$5,000 or greater donation during the preceding 12 months who has a financial interest in an entity that is contemplating entering into a financial transaction with the organization whose annual value exceeds \$10,000. There is a five year look back to determine who is a disregarded person

2. *Conflict of Interest*

A conflict of interest exists when a disregarded person, contemplates a financial transaction with the organization that puts their interests above the interests of the organization and / or violates the principle of free market competition. Conflict of interest transactions include excess profits, use of insider information, and the failure to use competitive bidding.

Article III
Procedures

1. *Duty to Disclose*

In connection with any actual or possible conflict of interest, a disregarded person must disclose the existence of the financial interest in writing upon election to the Board of Directors or employment by the organization, or within 30 days of donating more than \$5,000. Each director, principal officer, highly paid employee, or key employee thereafter makes a disclosure on an annual basis

2. Annual Statements

Each disregarded person shall annually sign a statement that affirms such person:

a. Has received a copy of the conflict of interest policy,

b. Has read and understands the policy,

c. Has agreed to comply with the policy,

d. Records the name and address of any person or business that could be involved in a transaction with the organization, with which they have an affiliation, and specifies the nature of the affiliation.

If a disregarded person begins an affiliation with an organization that could enter into a financial transaction with the organization between the filing of annual statements, they will make a supplemental declaration in accordance with III,2, d above.

3. Monitoring of Transactions

The administrative assistant to the president monitors the completion of written conflict of interest disclosures. The name of each person making a disclosure along with the company or person that can possibly be involved in a business transaction with the organization appears on a list. Every four months, the administrative assistant who maintains the list sends an updated copy of the list to the president, vice president, the chairperson of the Board of Directors and the chairperson, of the audit committee. The president and vice president are responsible for notifying the BOD chairperson and the audit committee chairperson of the BOD any time the organization proposes a business transaction covered under this policy. The audit committee chairperson indicates to the disregarded person their awareness of the proposed transaction and the applicability of the conflict of interest policy to the transaction.

4. Competitive Bidding

For any transactions contemplated between a disregarded person with a financial interest as defined in Article II and the organization, the BOD engages in a competitive bidding process. The organization issues a request for bids using the organizational purchasing policy. A disregarded person with a financial interest will not discuss their bid, or the goods or services bid out with any member of the committee selecting the successful bidder unless the selection committee decides to meet with all qualified bidders. In addition, a disregarded person with a financial interest will not discuss their bid, or the goods or services bid out with any other disregarded person, or any other member of the BOD, key employee or principal officer. As per the purchasing policy, the decision makers select among qualified bidders based on a best value received basis.

5. Violations of the Conflict of Interest Policy

a. If a person has reasonable cause to believe, a disregarded person has failed to disclose an actual or possible conflict of interest, or has violated this policy in any other manner; they will report the situation and the circumstances involved to the chairperson of the audit committee. In the case of a good cause report, the audit committee members will meet with the person accused, inform them of the basis of the accusation, and afford the disregarded person the opportunity to explain the alleged violation. The name of the person making the report is confidential.

b. If, after hearing the disregarded person's response, and after making further investigation as warranted by the circumstances, the audit committee shall take appropriate disciplinary and corrective action commensurate with the violation. There actions can include introducing a motion at a BOD meeting, or executive committee meeting to censure, suspend or expel a member and/ or censure, suspend without pay or terminate employment, as well as eliminating the bid from consideration in the current transaction, cancelling a transaction as far as possible, and forbidding the business involved in a conflict of interest from submitting bids for consideration of future transactions.

Article IV

Records of Proceedings

The minutes of the governing BOD and all committees with BOD delegated powers shall contain:

a. The names of the persons, found or who disclosed a financial interest in connection with an actual transaction,

b. The names of the persons who were present for discussions and vote relating to the transaction, the content of the discussion, including any alternatives to the proposed transaction and a roll call by name of each yea and nay vote.

Article VI

Periodic Reviews

To ensure the organization operates in a manner consistent with charitable purposes and does not engage in activities that could jeopardize its tax-exempt status, the audit committee shall conduct periodic reviews. The periodic reviews shall, at a minimum, include whether executive compensation arrangements and benefits are reasonable, based on competent survey information, and the result of arm's length bargaining. In addition, there is a review of excess benefit transactions. In the case of excess compensation or an excess benefit transaction the audit committee chairperson assures the beneficiary repays the principal involved along with a penalty of 1% for each month between the date the beneficiary receives the excess compensation and the date they repay the amount involved to the organization. These rules also apply to the monetary value of any excess benefit other than money. The committee chairperson reports the name(s) and the nature of the transactions to the Chairperson of the BOD who in consultation with the executive committee decides upon non-monetary consequences for the person(s) involved in the transaction. In a situation where any BOD members hold any of the offices cited above are involved in an excess benefit transaction, or of receiving excess compensation do not include that person in the consultation process. The consequences for people involved in excess compensation or an excess benefit transaction will be the same as in article III4B. Also, as appropriate the BOD may bring criminal charges or file civil litigation against the person.

Article VII

Use of Outside Experts

When conducting the periodic reviews, the organization may use outside advisors. If the organization uses outside experts, their use shall not relieve the governing BOD of its responsibility for conducting periodic reviews.

receiving the complaint at the next committee meeting. Members share their thoughts. They have the following questions. 1) Did the process to award the cleaning service contract conform to the agency purchasing Policy? 2) Was there competitive bidding? 3) Was Jake's Cleaning Service the bidder offering the lowest price? 4) Prior to Jake joining the BOD was he a donor? 5) If so, what is the amount of his gifts and dates given in the last two years? 6) Did Jake discuss the fact that he was a donor with the members of the committee charged with selecting a cleaning service? 7) What is the date of Jake's election to the BOD? 8) Did Jake reveal his ownership interest in Jakes Cleaning Service when he completed his conflict of interest form? 9) What are the Cleaning Service payment arrangements? 10) What is the content of the termination clause of the agreement? 11) Is the performance of the office cleaning work satisfactory? The audit committee chair asks the president to prepare a report that gives the background of the complaint and is responsive to the questions raised.

The president's report states:

John Tattletale, a member of the BOD reported to Valarie Vigilant, audit committee chair that he was making a complaint about a conflict of interest on the part of fellow BOD member Jake Sparkling who has a contract to clean the agency offices. Ms. Vigalent receives the report on July 1, 2016. There is a cleaning contract between the agency and Jake's Cleaning Service, of which Jake Sparkling is the owner. An annual contract, which began on September 1, 2015, is for $45,000 annually, paid monthly. Either party can cancel the agreement without cause by giving 30 days written notice to the other party. Prior to entering into the agreement, the organization sought competitive bids and there were four bids. Jake's Cleaning was the low bidder. The BOD elected Jake Sparkling to membership on February 1, 2016. He stated his ownership interest in Jake's Cleaning Service on his conflict of interest disclosure statement. The staff report the company has done a good job cleaning the offices and Little Lambs counselors and administrative staff is happy with the work compared to the former cleaning company. Jake has been a long-time donor to Little Lamb Children's Services. He started his support after his nephew Aaron was abused by his father who is Jake's brother. Aaron received counseling, and foster care services at Little Lamb. Jake's gifts during 2015 and 2016 are $7,500 each year. Jake and three other potential cleaning service vendors made verbal presentations to the contract selection committee as part of the bidding process. During his presentation, Jake emphasized his strong connection with the agency due to the help his nephew received and the many donations he has made. He assured the committee that if his business won the cleaning contract that his donations will continue.

After reviewing the president's report at the next meeting, the audit committee minutes, recorded the following: 1) the committee received a conflict of interest report and investigated it within 60 days. 2) The particulars of the complaint are in the investigation report, which is in the committee records file.

xxxxxxxxxxxxxxxxxxxxxxxxxxxxxxxxxxxxxxxxxxxxxxxxxxxxxxxxxxxxxxxxxxxxx

The committee finds that the BOD member is not involved in an excess benefit transaction and did not violate organizational conflict of interest policy provision related to a business interest based on the following: The BOD elected the member several months after the contract start date, and therefore the member conflict of interest policy is not applicable. The work was subject to competitive bidding and the member's firm was the low-price bidder. The contract performance indicates the payments made are not more than the value received. Upon election, the member did disclose his ownership of the business on the agency disclosure form.

This is a conflict of interest situation because the BOD member, a long-time donor, made cash gifts to the agency exceeding the $5,000 amount specified in the agency conflict of interest policy within 5 years of the contract. The member discussed these gifts with the contract selection committee. The BOD chairperson signed the cleaning contract on behalf of the agency. The Chairperson did not recall that the person was a significant donor when he signed the contract. The agency does not inform any of its large donors of its conflict of interest policy.

The agreement has a 30-day cancellation clause. The committee directs the president to notify the member that the agency is exercising its 30-day cancellation right and will rebid the contract. The BOD member can bid again, but cannot discuss the contract, the bid, or the donation history with any BOD member or key employee. In addition, he cannot attend any committee or BOD meeting during which the contract is under discussion. The president also informs him that his behavior and contract performance is without fault. The president contacts Mr. Tattletale and informs him that this is a conflict of interest situation, but there was no wrong doing on the part of the person reported. Valarie, the audit committee chairperson makes a verbal report to the BOD highlighting the committee process, finding of facts, and decision. Valarie does not use Jake's name. The audit committee sends its minutes to the directors. The investigation report is confidential and to protect Jake Sparkling's good name considering the circumstances of the situation the other BOD members do not get a copy. Note the president's error in violating the confidentiality of Mr. Sparkling and his nephew in his report to the audit committee. Jake also does this in his presentation to the selection committee.

Mission Statement

The mission statement informs every important action the organization takes and everyone affiliated with the organization agrees with it. It describes what you want to accomplish, the population you will serve, and briefly describes the types of services the agency provides. Review it carefully every two years to assure it remains relevant and current. Think about the appropriateness of every organizational action taken using the mission statement "lens". Child and Family Services in Buffalo N.Y. have a good mission, vision and values statements. Access them at http://www.cfsbny.org/cfs/mission.aspx. For instruction on writing a mission statement, see: https://www.thebalancesmb.com/how-to-write-the-ultimate-nonprofit-mission-statement-2502262

Whistle-Blower Policy

The IRS inquires in the 990 filing if the charity has a whistle- blower policy. It is not mandatory to have a policy, but the IRS considers a comprehensive policy to provide evidence of good governance. People possessing credible evidence concerning criminal and unethical acts perpetrated by organization leaders make whistle-blower reports. Whistleblowers can be agency employees, consumers, or other stakeholders. Whistleblower laws and policies provide protection from retaliation by employers against employees making whistle blower complaints. Examples of retaliation include blacklisting, firing, demotion, denial of benefits, denying a promotion, and harassment.

The scope of the applicable sections of the Sarbanes – Oxley legislation of 2002 to nonprofit agencies is related to the investigation by law enforcement officials of Federal Crimes. The areas of interest are IRS investigations into tax evasion and criminal violations involving federal funds. The IRS recommendations, are much broader stating that whistleblower policy cover employees that report violations of any organizational policy.

Accounting fraud in connection with federal and state grants and purchase of service contracts are other risk areas One example is a manager who steals grant funds through manipulation of the agency accounting system. Purchase of service fraud occurs when agencies bill governmental bodies for services not provided or bill for services in excess of what the agency provided. This includes billing for excess days of care, or billing for individuals who never received any care. The whistle blower is the person who reports the theft to the federal agency involved.

A non-financial violation that affords whistle-blower protection, to reporters, is the failure of the agency to provide a safe workplace. These are violations of the federal Occupational Health and Safety Administration regulations. For PCWAs, this would most often involve environmental hazards in the work place that causes worker illnesses or injury. The federal government Equal Opportunity Employment Commission prohibits retaliation against employees filing discrimination complaints. If the BOD adopts a broad policy it will likely conform to most federal whistleblower protection programs

However, if a PCWA employee who is angry about a negative performance evaluation and slashes the tires of their supervisor's car it is not a Sarbanes matter. The employee is guilty of violating agency anti-violence policy as well as committing a criminal act. However, because criminal statutes are under state auspices no federal crime is involved.

A trained employee complaint officer or human resource staff can handle all whistle blower complaints except those where a program director, vice president or the president is the subject of the complaint. In managing complaints, the officer maintains their normal review process when the subject of the complaint is a direct service worker, administrative staff member or a supervisor. The employee complaint officer's manager is a vice president or the president. The process involves the employee complaint officer informing their manager when they receive the complaint, the investigation plan proposed, the result of the investigation, and the proposed corrective action plan. If the complaint involves a program manager, vice president or the president the employee complaint officer is the chairperson of the BOD audit committee. For a more in-depth discussion, a model policy, and recommendations for policy dissemination see the DC Bar Pro Bono Center alert at https://www.lawhelp.org/files/7C92C43F-9283-A7E0-5931-E57134E903FB/attachments/B2D746C6-B926-A6C3-DC91-9D2D7233A7AA/whistleblower-policy-alert-2017-update-final.pdf.

The filing of the complaint with a government agency often sets up an adversarial relationship between the whistleblower and the charity because of the possible consequences for the agency. In addition, there Is a bad feeling on the part of managers if the employee did not air the complaint internally, before turning to a government agency. Managers sometimes feel that it demonstrates a lack of loyalty and fairness to the charity. At the same time because these complaints involve executive staff the employee may feel it is unsafe to use internal mechanisms. Setting up opportunities for whistleblowers to handle concerns internally lets the whistle- blower know the organization has a commitment to good practice.

Fictional Whistleblower Complaint Story
Darling County Children's Services (DCCS) is a program that assists abused and delinquent youth. The agency offers a community rehabilitation program for juvenile delinquents that provides individual and family counseling, a wilderness program, and a community service component. The program uses Community Development Program funds granted by the city of Stumpenfest to fund program costs. DCCS's President Stan Stupawitz owns Always Transport a bus company. A bus transports consumers to the wilderness program and to a recycling center where the youths render community service because DCCS's program is based on a Balanced and Restorative Justice (BARJ) model. DCCS's finance director Sidney Suds is in a rage because Stan issued two written reprimands to him in the last three months for coming to work drunk. Sidney wants to get revenge and makes a complaint to the Department of Housing and Urban Development (HUD) which administers the Community Development grants program claiming that that Stan is defrauding the federal government through excessive billing for transportation services. Sidney gets a quote from two other busing companies operating in Stumpenfest and finds both quotes are about 75% less than Always Transport's fee. Sidney also states in his complaint that Stan has never sought competitive bids for the bus services and DCCS is Always Transport's only customer. Sidney files his complaint. Unfortunately, Sidney's drinking continues, and the next time Sidney comes to work drunk Stan requires him to undergo an alcohol screening test which comes back positive. Stan writes Sidney another reprimand and requires him to participate in DCCS's employee assistance program. Sidney does not do this but his drinking continues, and Stan fires Sidney. Mean time HUD has their Office of the Inspector General (OIG) investigate Sidney's complaint. Stan is informed that OIG is coming to audit DCCS' books. OIG also determines that Sidney's information from the other busing companies is accurate. Also, the other contentions in the complaint are correct. At the end of the investigation Stan is indicted on a Federal charge of fraud. Sidney files a whistleblower complaint to get his job back claiming that Stan fired him in reprisal for filing the HUD complaint. HUD has a whistleblower protection program for employees who file complaints, prohibiting employers from taking adverse actions, such as firing the employee. The Department also states that the employer bears the burden of proof to establish that it would have taken the same adverse action regarding an employee, if they did not file the complaint. Because Sidney received multiple disciplinary memos regarding his drinking, failed a drug test and refused to get help with his drinking by participating in DCCS's employee assistance program HUD

judged that DCCS did meet the employer's burden requirement and did not require DCCS to reinstate him to his former job.

Chapter 12 The Rightfully Feared and Deservedly Avoided Strategic Planning Process

Organizational Planning

Confidence in the value of organizational planning is widespread. After World War II there was a belief that comprehensive centralized planning was superior to other methods. Robert Moses work in New York City embodied this philosophy. Although he is responsible in developing important infrastructure projects, he was not without his critics (Caro 1975) Comprehensive planning manifested in social services in the trend of long-range planning. These plans covered a decade, contained detailed program expansion efforts, and had extensive budget projections and the plan's scope was comprehensive.

During the last 20 years, a new trend perhaps best labeled as strategic planning has come to dominate charitable planning. The plans cover 3-5 years, are more concerned with specific tactical decisions, than a high-level view, and use specific techniques. The most popular is SWOT (Strengths, Weaknesses, Opportunities, and Threats).

Part of the value of planning is in the process. The plan involves the participation of the primary constituencies of the PCWA so there is an opportunity to learn from others committed to the agency. It provides a structured opportunity to think about practice rather than engaging in practice. The latter happens daily, but because of daily demands, the former does not occur often. Beyond the formal use of the information gained in constructing the plan it serves to sensitize key leaders to be attentive to the information they learn. For example, if a GCWA representative informs you that their highest priority for new projects is to double the number of day care slots they purchase consider opening a center. If this is a one-program agency helping teen mothers and the agency decides not to offer day care services, figure out what synergies exist between more day care availability and the program. The availability of more day care allows more teen mothers to engage in educational, training, or work activities.

The value of the plan is not only that stakeholders act but also in achieving a consensus about organizational efforts. For both those committed to the PCWA, as well as other readers, it is a handbook of action for the future. It gives anyone reading the plan knowledge about the mission, values, and direction of the agency. In considering, a planning process for the agency think about both the key issues, and who will use the plan. Is it primarily for internal use? Will the agency submit it to potential and current funders, or others disregarded in the organization?

The Planning Process

A review of the material in the remainder of this section provides information about possible planning components. Plans can be simple and useful or on the other end of the continuum they can be sophisticated, and the basis for important gains in organizational performance. The quality of the plan, like most other things in life, is a result of the time and effort expended. The material here provides a variety of possible planning inputs and activities. PCWA leaders determine which of these, if any, will increase the efficacy of the agency. At one end of the spectrum, the planning process can be brief and the resulting basic plan is simple but meets the organization's needs. The basic plan is appropriate for agencies, with budgets of $5,000,000 or less, that are stable. When these organizations face important challenges, the goal can be to develop a basic plan but do a deeper analysis into one or two areas that are crucial. As previously noted, the planning process can be extensive, result in important business intelligence, and a plan that has the potential to provide superior organization performance. Organizations with budgets greater than $9,000,000, organizations that are service oriented with inadequate infrastructure, and organizations that are complex engage in a more extensive planning process. The last part of the chapter provides a table of contents for a comprehensive strategic plan,

A good first step is having a brainstorming session with four or five BOD members, the president, the director of each major service, and any other staff who are usually important to decision-making. Also, include two people from outside the organization who have a macro level knowledge base about the target population and service, and one or two youth consumers. The first discussion question for the meeting is Are there any major internal issues that can really hurt or help the agency? One example is that there is an exception on the annual independent audit and the auditor tells you that the fiscal staff is not current on non-profit accounting practices. Is there a staff training need and a training plan? Should the agency be making staff changes? Should part of the work be done by an outside accounting firm? A second example is that the agency has just hired a first-rate director of development but there is no fundraising program or history. The agency will need a plan and personal contacts to maximize the fundraiser's results.

The second discussion question is: Are there any major external issues that will significantly affect the agency? One example is that the property owner of a site where the agency staff sees 300 consumers a day is selling the building. Decide whether to move or buy the building. Another example is that a class action suit brought by parents of autistic children has been successful and the state will have to fund services, some of which the agency offers, to all autistic children who wish to participate in them. This is a real growth opportunity for the agency. Devote 10-20 minutes to a discussion of the two questions. Next using white boards, or an easel with paper, ask each attendee to list up to three things that they would like to see accomplished during the next few years. The things can include programs to add or eliminate, populations to serve, attention to important community changes, and attention to infrastructure issues such as fundraising and physical facilities. Emphasize that there are no wrong answers and that the group will prioritize but not critique ideas. Write each item down. Instruct the participants not to repeat items that you have written down. There is no discussion of any item, except if there is a need to clarify the meaning of a suggestion. This may take 15-30 minutes. Last, prioritize suggestions through voting. Each participant has five votes and cannot use more than one vote for any suggestion. After everyone has voted, tally the number of votes for each suggestion, to establish the key issues at hand and the planning priorities.

Other questions that shape the planning work are:

1. Is there a reasonable consensus about the mission?
2. In most organizational matters do people agree or is there a lot of conflict in decision- making?
3. Do external regulatory agencies, or funders request to see the plan?
4. Will the president retire or move to another job during the next two years? Except for items requiring immediate attention, delay the planning process until a year after you hire a new president.
5. Is there a lot of uncertainty about future funding? or the future of the agency?

Plan development and the BOD

The BOD adopts the strategic plan. It is then organizational policy. To start, get input from the BOD about the decision to engage in the planning process. If the president cannot make the case to engage in strategic planning with the BOD either abandon the project or present it again in a way that responds to BOD objections. Outline the planning process the agency will use, and share a first draft of a plan table of contents. Discuss the BOD's thinking about plan input. Do they want a retreat? Do they want to devote a BOD meeting to providing input? A retreat is time consuming but is appropriate if there are many BOD level issues to discuss, one or two very complicated issues, or some issues where members have strong feelings though they do not agree with each other. If members feel things are going well one special two-hour meeting or use of a BOD meeting to provide plan input will do. During the BOD planning meeting first review the mission statement and see if the members think it still accurately describes what you do. Get an idea of some changes they might want, but do not use the meeting to rewrite the mission statement. Ask the questions that are worthwhile from the following list. Once members make the key points, promptly move on to the next question. Ten minutes before the meeting will end if you get the sense that there is still a lot of ground to cover schedule another meeting of the BOD to complete the work.

1. What are the main reasons members agreed to serve on the BOD?
2. What are the most important things the members would like the agency to accomplish   during the next three years?
3. Are there changes in BOD operations that would make the experience as a member more satisfying?
4. Is there anything that will improve BOD or BOD committee meetings?
5. Considering the administrative functions fundraising, finance, information technology, and building maintenance are improvements needed.?
6. Do members get enough and the right kinds of information to fulfill the responsibilities of financial and program stewardship?

Update the BOD at each meeting on the progress of the planning process. Use BOD meeting time if a major unexpected item comes up as the process proceeds. Major items are building purchases or extensive renovation projects, new programs that are significant in size, changes to the mission statement, or controversial items. Once the plan document is ready, distribute the plan at one meeting and ask the members to review it and come prepared to discuss it and perhaps vote on it at the next meeting.

The committees of the BOD are the venue to discuss the BOD member's specific thoughts on functional segments of the plan. (finance, fundraising, marketing, personnel, program, information technology, and a capital improvement project). The areas of consideration are desired changes in committee charters and functions, and a review of existing committee plans and goals for the period covered by the plan. There is an emphasis on new projects as well as reductions. Some examples are: the IT committee members recommend a new HR software package, and institution of a three-year useful life criterion for the purchase of workstations. Finance committee members think another accounting position ought to exist in light of past and likely future growth in programs, and accountability requirements. Program committee members are not convinced program results are equal to program costs and efforts and want to see a program quality improvement effort. The people who are the regular staff members of each committee are responsible for communicating BOD committee input to the planning committee members.

Minimum Plan Scope
If the decision is to limit the time and effort expended on the plan, review existing agency statistics, and financial information. Cover the following topics in the written plan:
1. The current local environment including consumer statistics and readily available community demographics and trends
2. An affirmation or change to the mission statement.
3. Discuss whether the PCWA will continue current programs, or eliminate them. Will programs grow, or shrink? Discuss new program development or program phase outs.
4. State the strategies to maximize organizational agility
5. State plans to maintain or improve support services - finance, fundraising information   technology, and building maintenance
6. Review the current budget and expected increases or decreases During the plan term
7. State the significant challenges facing the organization and how the PCWA will respond to them.
8. Discuss the fundraising efforts

If the agency is going to do a more extensive planning process do, all or some of the studies and focus groups listed below.

Nine Step Full Strategic Planning Process

A. Staffing the Extensive Planning Effort
A committee chair and the committee members are the core-planning group. The committee has four or five members from the BOD. If the BOD is small, fewer members participate and recruit more outside committee members. Preparing a strategic plan requires substantial time and talent. To

keep workloads manageable, have a core committee of 5-7 BOD members and executive staff. One option is to create the planning committee when the planning process begins and dissolve the committee after the BOD approves the plan. Another approach is to use an existing committee, perhaps the BOD program committee, or executive committee and assign the planning responsibility to this group.

The main purpose of the group is to receive, review, and distill the plan inputs into a strategic plan. These will be the ideas for the plan from various stakeholder group meetings. These groups are BOD members, consumers, customers, donors, and the staff. Other inputs are statistics that describe the staff, clients, and community. The committee recruits the category of members as follows.

> Recruit two or more outsiders who have special expertise on the client population and services. People from the staff of the two largest customers are good choices. A youth consumer or their parent is another good idea.
> Recruit an outside facilitator who helps other groups prepare plans to keep the committee on track. As an alternate the BOD chairperson or president can perform this role
> Recruit a staff member at the local city, county or regional planning agency, who has access to social statistics. A high value member is the person who compiles the social statistics for the local GCWA, or regional office of the state agency
> Recruit a college professor who teaches statistics in a social science department seeking a personal research project, to analyze the planning data. Another idea is to use agency graduate interns who need to do a research project. If a volunteer cannot do this, consider a modest contract to get the data analysis work done.
> Ask the program directors of two of the largest agency programs to join the committee. They represent direct service staff, and the clinical concerns of customers
> Appoint a person as the committee administrator. They keep minutes, gather, organize, and distribute information that comes to the committee. The administrator and committee chairperson develop the committee meeting agendas, and remind members about meeting dates.

B. Planning Committee Task Description

> The committee meets monthly,
> At the first or second committee meeting the members: compose a preliminary plan table of contents. This changes as time goes on. Its

main function is to organize by subject area the information the committee receives

- ➤ The committee decides about the number and types of inputs, (from staff, clients and BOD committees, social statistics etc.) and a preliminary schedule of due dates for submission
- ➤ The committee establishes a preliminary date for submitting the plan to the BOD for review
- ➤ One member works as a liaison to the people doing the environmental scan. The member meets with the people gathering and analyzing the data as appropriate
- ➤ Two more committee members are the liaison to each of the following groups. They attend meetings of these groups, and assure the group meets deadlines for submission of input. They present data from each of the groups at planning committee meetings. The groups are: the BOD, the finance, fundraising, program, and information technology committees. Other groups are the staff and the consumers.

The committee reviews these inputs jointly and makes group decisions on what is in the final plan document. Do not make inclusion decisions until the committee has most of the inputs. Look at the commonalities among the groups. Ask the "so what?" question. Will inclusion of an item in the plan make an important difference for the agency? If it involves a program, will it further the mission? If it is an infrastructure or capital improvement suggestion, will it support the accomplishment of the mission? If three or more groups bring up the same issues include it in the plan. Also, look for synergies in the suggestions. If the committee will not include a popular topic or action in the plan, indicate the reason as part of the BOD planning progress reports.

After the committee receives most of the planning inputs, staff member(s) or committee member(s) write the plan. Within each subject area, prioritize items when possible. For example, if the agency has a presence in ten counties, divide them into high, medium, and low priority groups for agency growth purposes. Doing this focuses marketing efforts and provides guidance in case there are multiple requests, and the PCWA cannot accommodate all of them. Do the same for existing and new services. Rank them into groups according to their priority. If there is a very controversial idea, discuss it with the BOD as part of the update reports. For each new initiative, assign an accomplishment date and indicate BOD committee and staff responsibility. In the budget section of the plan, add the necessary cost, if any.

One method for plan presentation is a written narrative. Make the narrative as short as possible, twelve pages or less. Another option is to write the whole plan in the form of Power Point slides. This makes presentations to the planning committee, BOD, and other groups easier, and the plan will be more concise. The administrative staff person distributes plan drafts to discuss at future meetings.

The committee chair submits an initial draft to the BOD. The BOD usually will adopt the plan, unless there is a controversial item. If more than 20% of the BOD is unwilling to adopt the plan because of a specific item, omit it from the plan. Consider the BOD comments and if you like present the controversial item again at a future date.

Following plan adoption, the committee meets semi-annually to do a progress check and reports on plan accomplishments and changes to the BOD. When there is not progress on an item, the committee also reports this to the BOD. Put the plan on the website and email the staff, donors, and customers to thank them again for their participation, and so they know that a new strategic plan is in place. Either send the plan to all major stakeholders or let them know they can view the plan on the website.

C. Planning within the Context of Organizational History
How the Past Influences the Present

All agency leaders should know and think about their agency history, relevant environmental factors, and the cultural context of their own agency to understand the basis for organizational operations culture and program development. One committee member is the committee historian. They research the organizational history and present their findings to the committee Include a very brief history in the plan emphasizing key values, and agency identity to date.

Thinking about the historical context provides an understanding of the organization's identity, values, and culture. History and organizational culture interact. The nature of the initial agency program(s) effect agency organizational development and culture.

Some of the readers will be part of an organization that is old by American standards, some dating back to the late 1800's. Internal agency records along with a good book on social work history will serve to give an idea about values that people may not talk about anymore, but which still play an important role in organizational life. Organizational leaders should take the time to speak with those who were important in organizational development and review important historical documents. A good resource regarding the influences affecting older child welfare organizations is William Trattner's, *From Poor Law to Welfare state* (Trattner, 1998). For an example of a first-rate account of agency development within its historical context, review the history and archive pages of the Children's Aid Society website. (Children's Aid Society, 2019)

For agencies that started as a result of the great society effort, use the issues of the late 1960's through the mid 1970's as a context for their history. The runaway and homeless youth shelters opened in the 1970's amidst a decade long backdrop of youth distrust and alienation. Disaffection and feelings about the Viet Nam War characterized the youth malaise. Young people believed political leaders lied to the public. Large anti-war protests precipitated a feeling of empowerment among young people. Youth belief in individual choice was widespread and involved the rejection of the value of social solidarity that emerged in connection with World War II. The values of personal sacrifice for the national good were a bequest of World War II veteran to their children, but the generation broke with this creed.

The East Village in New York and Haight Ashbury in California had a large inflow of runaway youth. The Beatles song "She's Leaving Home" released in 1967 on their Sgt. Pepper's Lonely Hearts Club Band album captured many of the elements of the feelings associated with the runaway youth phenomena. The child leaving the home without telling the parents, and the child's sadness about the lack of emotional attachment to the parents. The teenager's quest for freedom is their central desire. The song emphasizes the values of the parents - personal sacrifice for the good of the family and children, and the struggle to be successful. Their commitment to care for their children, and provide for them is strong

The conflict between the youth values of love and freedom of choice versus the parents' values of obligation and material success were the back-story to the phenomena of runaway youth starting in 1968 and lasting a decade.

The establishment of the runaway youth shelter programs followed the assassination of President Kennedy in 1963 and the initiation of the great society programs by President Johnson the following year. This was an environment where there was great hope for conquering social problems. Simultaneously the community - based services movement took root, and the former methods of providing services in centrally located large facilities lost popularity.

This shift had important implications for the development of organizations beginning runaway youth programs.

These included:

> Breaking with the past of centralized institutional service provision and offering services at many smaller geographically dispersed sites.
> Developing a service provision culture where the overarching goal was making "connections" with alienated youth. These

programs broke with the authoritarian "doctor" / "patient" framework that characterized services.

> Having the staff express their ideas on how to do things recognized the important value Americans put on freedom of expression, and a participatory democracy characterized in the "anti-war" movement.
> Believing that change is possible and rejecting the idea of the status quo.
> Recognizing the importance of federal government leadership in funding services to troubled youth

D. Self-Assessment

The BOD chair and president rate the agency using a self-assessment instrument. The tool provides a list of areas that the organization may need to work on. There is a chance that a major item needs attention. As part of the input review process, the full committee reviews the chairperson's and the president's findings. The planning group decides which items if any, to address in the plan. An internet search will locate many self-assessment instruments. The Nonprofit Association of Oregon issues one that assesses agency BOD and administrative functioning. The
instrument is located at: https://independentsector.org/resource/self-assessment-tool-for-nonprofit-organizations/

E. Planning Environmental Scan

The committee arranges for an environmental scan. The data is as local as possible to the main geographic areas served. Some Census data is available by city and county as well as census tract. The Kids Count Data Center is the primary source for most of the data items listed below(https://datacenter.kidscount.org/) The Data Center has information available by state, city, county, territory and nationally. If there is not data for your area, choose an area in the state that is similar. Also, for items 1-7 check with the state or local public child welfare agency for data. For state data check the national reports on the incidence of child abuse and neglect.

State government may issue a data book. If it is feasible, review the following data. Do not despair if the agency cannot get all or most of the data. If time and resources limit you, select the items from the list that are most relevant for your situation. Something is better than nothing. In addition, for demographics the U.S. Census Data, state Vital Statistic Reports, and State reports on participation rates in the Medical Assistance, SNAP and AFDC program yields interesting information.

1. # of child abuse reports

2. # of child abuse reports investigated
3. # of child abuse reports substantiated
4. Per capita child welfare expenditure (calculated by dividing
    Total GCWA Expenditure by total child population)
5. Per client child welfare expenditure (calculated by dividing
    total GCWA expenditure by GCWA caseload)
6. % of GCWA cases receiving in-home services
7. % of GCWA cases receiving out of home services
8. Infant mortality rate
9. Child mental illness rate
10. Adult mental illness rate
11. Race of child population and race of GCWA population
    expressed as percentages
12. Children under 18 by age group
13. % of teens not working and not in school
14. % of children repeating a grade
15. % of children missing 11 days of school
16. % mother only families
17. % of single parent families
18. % of persons 25-64 without a high. school diploma
19. % of children in poverty
20. % of children living in high poverty communities
21. Child supplemental security recipient rates
22. Median family income
23. State gross domestic product
24. percent democratic and republican registration
25. Percent of voter turn out

Perform a correlation analysis between the child welfare variables (1-7) and the other variables (8- 25) if possible. If not simply review the results. Consider what the data suggests about the following questions:

1. Does a substantial gap between the reporting rate and the substantiation rate of child abuse suggests the need for community services for children funded by other sources?
2. If teachers, social workers, medical personnel etc. make child abuse reports but the percentage of these reports substantiated by child abuse investigators is very low, it may mean that another service that will help children could be of use. I.e. afterschool programs, family counseling etc.
3. How does expenditure per client data, which covers GCWA as well as service costs, square with the services the agency
4. offers and their costs?

5. Will the service utilization be low because the fees are high?
6. Looking at the GCWA expenditure data by age; Are there implications for program development for the organization?
7. Are there some problem rates in the service area that are disturbingly high such as high rates of children repeating a grade, or adults without a H.S. diploma? What is the implication of this for the current services, service partners, and referral networks?
8. How does the community's income and gross domestic product compare to similarly sized communities in the state? What are the implications for fundraising and financial goal setting?
9. What is the political party registration in the service area? Tailor the core marketing and fundraising messages to the predominant group.
10. How do poverty averages compare with state data? High poverty rates indicate program needs, and program partners. Also, it suggests that plans consider developing Medical Assistance, funded services.

F. Human Resources Review

The information in this section comes from the organization's human resource officer. If the organization does not have a computerized system or a human resources officer this could be an assignment for a student. If it is too burdensome to gather the numbers than perhaps the staff members on the committee should respond to the questions using estimates based on their experience.

How many staff work at the agency? How many work part time, how many full times? Do the number of part time staff impact service quality?

1. What percentage of services do contractors provide?
2. What share of budget goes to pay for the staff?
3. What percent of the staff are high school graduates, hold bachelors, masters, and doctoral degrees? How many have no degree? How does this match with programming envisioned during the years covered by the plan period? Is there a need to concentrate on recruiting staff with specific academic preparation?
4. What is the staff turnover rate? How long does it take to fill vacancies? Should new staff retention initiatives be part of the plan?
5. What is the implication of all of this for new hire salaries, and salaries for current staff?
6. What is the age range of staff? What is the expectation around retirement during the plan period of key employees?

G. Consumer Focus Group(s)

One way to do this is with the youth in residence. One person from the planning committee attends, and the residential supervisor, leads the group. The committee attendee creates a record of the key ideas. If several people attending the input session agree with an idea, or it appears to be of special merit, include it on the list of key ideas. Input meeting notes do not need to be comprehensive. It is enough to record two or three responses to each question. The group is no longer than ninety minutes and the maximum number of participants is fifteen. If there is a youth advisory BOD or other ongoing youth club or effort at the agency use them if they are representative of the consumers served. It is also worthwhile to do youth focus groups for out-client and in-home programs consumers as well as parent groups. However, getting sufficient attendance is often a challenge. Below are some possible questions to ask youth in residence.

1.Does the staff spend the time with you that you need?
2. What is your favorite thing to do here?
3. When you leave here, where would you like to go to live?
4. What happens here that is the most helpful?
5. What are the things that are least helpful?
6. Do you feel safe here? If not why not
7. What service is absent that you need?

H. Direct Service Staff Focus Groups

The direct service staff groups discuss a list of specific questions. The program director is the facilitator and a committee member records the key points. Allow all staff a chance to participate. Although this is time consuming, when the plan is complete, they will most likely support it and "own it" because they have participated in its formulation. Try to keep each group to fifteen or fewer people. Allow 2 hours or less for the meeting. Select from the questions below as applicable to your organization. Have the planning committee review a relevant question list to see if they have additional questions. Staff meetings or a staff retreat are good venues to get staff input.

1. After reviewing our mission and values statements, do you believe we need new ones?
2. When you think about our organization compared with other area child welfare / mental health organizations what things make us unique?

3. Of the key things, we do with consumers, should we do any of them in different ways?
4. Should we be providing other services to consumers that we do not provide now?
5. Of the services, we provide are there any we should eliminate?
6. When consumers leave our program what are, the types of services if any they are likely to need as they move on with their lives?
7. What are our consumers' most important unmet needs?
8. If you have been in the field for at least five years what are your observations about the most important changes in the characteristics of people we help?
9. When youth and families we serve talk about their service experiences with us are there particular things they liked or did not like about the services?
10. What have been the strengths and weaknesses in service provision of other places you have worked?
11. Based on your experiences in working with them which agencies do you regard as doing the best job in providing a.) mental health services to adults b.) substance abuse services to adults?
12. During the work with children and families, what private organizations do you work with most often?
13. What do you think is most important to county child welfare workers about our services?
14. Overall, what is the biggest complaint GCWA caseworkers have about our services?
15. From the conversations with GCWA caseworkers, what do you sense are their most important frustrations and unmet needs?

H. Customer Interviews

Meet with the 3-5 of the largest public customers. Use what is worthwhile from the list below and use the list to stimulate your own thinking on what you would like to know. For the meeting with the director, ask them to bring a supervisor, and two direct service staff members with them who are familiar with the services. In addition, or as an alternative email them the question list a week or so before the meeting. Begin each interview by saying thank you for choosing the agency as one of their vendors.

1. Do you expect caseloads to increase, decrease, or stay the same?
2. Over the next few years, what do you anticipate in terms of the mix of services the agency will purchase as compared to today?

3. What changes do you anticipate in the mix of consumers in terms of the ages of the children, and the types of abuse and neglect involved?

4. Do you think the federal and state funding for GCWA services will increase, decrease, or stay about the same?

5. Will the regulatory environment for the agency change?

6. What are the top service priorities for the coming year?

7. Based on the results our state achieved on the last federal review, are there things that you do differently?

8. When you compare the capabilities of the private PCWAs with the anticipated service needs are there gaps?

9. Are there areas where there has been or will be reduction in purchase of service contracts?

10. In terms of the political climate, do you think there will be pressure to reduce the public child welfare workforce and contract out additional services? If so what services?

11. Are there any areas you think we should expand or contract?

12. What things do we do well and what things could we do better?

13. Regarding our record keeping administrative process etc. are there things that would be helpful for us to do differently in response to feedback the office gets from federal or state agencies?

I. Large Donor Meetings

Meet with a few large donors. Within the limits of time the more donor meetings the better. The BOD of directors' chair, development chair, development director, and president can do the interviews. Try to cover at a minimum, United Way if the agency is a member. Get two large donors from the following three groups: individuals, foundations, and corporations. In addition to the following questions, if the agency is considering a capital campaign ask for some feedback on any preliminary campaign ideas. Begin each interview by saying thank you for past support.

1. What motivates you to support our agency?

1. Do you hear from us often enough? Too often?

2. In terms of your personal or the group's priorities, are there other things we do, or could do in the scope of our mission that are of interest to you?

3. In terms of our relationship and handling of the gifts, are there things we could do better?

4. Are there changes in our services and how we operate the agency that are important to you?

J. Potential Strategic Plan Table of Contents

- ➤ . Environment
  - o From the data analysis and stakeholder feedback lists Strengths and weaknesses
  - o List strategies to eliminate or reduce areas of weaknesses and maximize strengths
- ➤ Opportunities and Threats
  - o From the data analysis and stakeholder feedback list the principal opportunities and threats the PCWA will face
  - o List specific actions that the PCWA will take to deal with the to reduce vulnerabilities and explore opportunities
- ➤ Mission
  - o A statement of the agency history, mission, organizational vision and values.
  - o Discuss significant revisions.
- ➤ Unique Characteristics of the Organization
  - o What separates it from other organizations? i.e. emphasis on a certain age group or geographic area,
  - o special expertise and competence, unique programs offered, special outcome evaluation efforts etc.
- ➤ Services
- ➤ List and prioritize areas of potential growth.
  state which major child welfare services the agency will not provide
- ➤ For each program offered state:

- o the Strategic partners highlighting those providing
- o funding and referrals and any additional partners needed for plan implementation
- o Prioritize geographic areas for expansion by county
- o Finances - Present a summary income and expense budget for each year covered by the plan
  - o Provide a brief narrative describing key income and expense line items
  - o Explain any year to year difference greater than cost living
  - o Provide a summary capital expenditure budget listing the project and amount for each year
  - o Discuss any capital campaign plans
  - o Briefly outline the organizational fundraising program plan including events, annual campaign, and planned
  - o giving program. List fundraising goals for each

significant component of the fundraising program
o   Discuss planned fund-raising expenses and staff
o   Briefly outline the marketing program plan
    including key messages, media outlets, activities,
    annual budget and staffing.

Chapter 13 The Big Money - Public Child Welfare Contracts

Introduction to Government Purchase of Service Organizations

While PCWAs often have substantial programs aimed at private donors, their main work consists of helping children referred to them by government agencies or served in government-sponsored programs. It is worthwhile for government fundraisers in child welfare to understand how their customers function, their priorities, and their challenges. In the GCWA job one is assuring the child's safety. The second mandate of the GCWA is to strengthen family functioning. The major areas of involvement for the GCWA are intake, assessment, information and referral, child abuse and neglect investigation and child protection. GCWAs frequently collaborate with the police and courts. They contract for residential services, primarily foster care, group home care, and congregate care and family preservation services. Family preservation services consist of a very broad range of services; those that seek to involve extended family known as "family finding". and those that seek to empower and involve families through a family group decision making process as well as, in-home counseling services. Extended family foster care and guardianship arrangements are now very common and reduce professionally provided out of home care. Total child welfare expenditures are significant:

"Child welfare agencies use a mix of federal, state, and local funds to support the children and families they serve.... in SFY 2016, more than half (56 percent) of all dollars child welfare agencies spent came from state and local sources... Over the past decade, the proportions of total child welfare agency expenditures from federal and state/local sources held steady. Child welfare agencies reported spending \$29.9 billion in federal, state, and local funds on child welfare services in SFY 2016... There was a 5 percent increase in total child welfare spending between SFY 2014 and SFY 2016."

(Rosinsky and Williams 2018)

Child Welfare Legislative Background

Federal legislation prescribes federal and state responsibilities for public child welfare system operations. Each piece of federal child welfare legislation indicates the federal government's purpose, client eligibility conditions, the services funded, the funding mechanisms, and requirement that each state submit a detailed implementation plan to the federal government. In 2014, the federal government covered less than half of the total child welfare expenses. This continues a decade long decline in support of child welfare service. States and localities together pay most of the costs. Not counted is PCWA expenditures on public child welfare programs from private donations and drawdown from cash assets.

Although some of the federal child welfare money is for program evaluation and, program demonstration grants most of it goes to the states. Most federal funds provide foster care payments, adoption subsidies, and guardianship payments for children from poor families. The term foster care covers foster care programs operated by both GCWAs and PCWAs, family foster care, and the portion of group home and congregate care costs attributed to room and board. However, most of the funds for all children in out of home are state and local tax dollars. The children paid for by state and local dollars comes for families that are not poor enough to meet the IVE means test, which remains fixed at the 1996 level.

In addition, significant amounts of federal financial support are for preserving families; Table xx provides information on the purpose and funding amounts of the significant federal laws. The information in this overview and table XX are based on: "Child Welfare: An Overview of Federal Programs and Their Current Funding", (Stotzfus, 2017) Reading this report is a good way for PCWA leaders to achieve familiarity with the important federal child welfare legislation. Aligning services with these federal programs offers PCWA an opportunity to receive financial support from State and local GCWAs. The discussion here does not include other important legislation covering substance abuse, mental health, and runaway and homeless youth funding managed by other federal agencies

Most child welfare programs are state administered. The state systems use a variety of service delivery models. In some of these, a state regional office covers several counties. Other states use a colocation model, having service centers in a greater number of counties compared with the regional model. These "one stop shops" serve food stamp, disability and child welfare service consumers in a single location. Nine states have a local provision model in which the state licenses and funds local GCWAs. The local offices investigate child abuse reports, provide child protective services, case management services and awards service contracts. Court adjudication of children as dependent and other custody matters are determined by the orphan's court in these counties and cities. The states having a county-based system are California, Colorado, Minnesota, New York, North Carolina, North Dakota, Ohio, Pennsylvania, and Virginia. Hybrid child welfare models operate in Maryland, Nevada, and Wisconsin. In these states' services are partially the responsibility of the State and partially the responsibility of the counties. (Child Welfare Information Gateway, 2012)

Federal Monitoring of State Child Welfare Programs

The federal government assesses the extent to which the state child welfare agencies operate in conformance with federal laws and regulations uses five methods. These are 1) the Adoption and Foster Care Analysis Report system (AFCARS) 2) Periodic Children and Family Service Review (CFSR), 3) National Youth in Transition Data Base, 4) Statewide Automated Child Welfare Information System (SACWIS) in addition to 5) case management system and IVE claim reviews (Children's Bureau, 2017)

The AFCARS review process is an evaluation of state information systems utilizing case level information of children in foster care or adopted. The review team identifies problems, investigate the causes, and suggest solutions during the review.

The periodic CFSR reviews of state child welfare systems a) Ensure conformity with federal child welfare requirements, b) determine what is happening to children and families as they are engaged in child welfare services, and c) assist states in enhancing their capacity to help children and families achieve positive outcomes. After a review, each state develops a Program Improvement Plan. The instrument uses several different measures including the reoccurrence of child abuse, child abuse report investigation speed and length of foster care stays. Of all of the federal monitoring tools the CFSR results report for your state is the most useful in understanding the GCWA plans for improving performance. The 2018 aggregate report is located at the following URL: https://www.acf.hhs.gov/cb/resource/cfsr-aggregate-report

The National Youth in Transition Database (NYTD) is a federal reporting system designed to collect information on youth transitioning out of foster care. The John H. Chafee Foster Care Independence Program (CFCIP) funds services for older youths.

SACWIS contains a complete case management history. After a state's automated child welfare system is operational for approximately 1 year, the Division of State Systems (DSS) conducts a review to assess the system's functionality.

The regulatory reviews of the title IV-E Foster Care program determine whether children in foster care meet the federal eligibility requirements for foster care maintenance payments. Visit, for more information on these monitoring efforts. Visit https://www.acf.hhs.gov/cb/research-data-technology/reporting-systems for more information on these efforts. Also use the search function at the Child Welfare Information Gateway for other efforts.

Table. 13-1 Fiscal Year 2016 Child Welfare Funding by Major Fiscal Year Programs (nominal dollars in millions; parts may not sum to total due to rounding)	
Program	**Amount (in millions)**
Total	**$8,689**
Total Title IV-B of the Social Security Act	**$668**
Stephanie Tubbs Jones Child Welfare Services (CWS) investigation of child abuse and neglect, caseworker expenses, counseling, emergency assistance, and arranging alternative living arrangements; family support, family preservation, and family reunification services. support for adoption, guardianship; and foster care payment programs, training, and foster and adoptive parent recruitment	$269
Promoting Safe and Stable Families (PSSF)	
Promoting Safe and Stable Families Program: family support services, family preservation services, adoption promotion and support services	$381
Child Welfare Research, Training, and Demonstration Competitive Grants, contracts, and other arrangements to support child welfare workforce training and to advance practice of child welfare via research or demonstration	$18
Family Connection Grants - Kinship navigator programs, family finding, family group decision making, residential family treatment	$0
Total Title IV-E of the Social Security Act	$7,833
Title IV-E Foster Care, kinship and Guardianship for very poor children and adoption assistance for special need children	$7,609
Tribal IV-E Plan Development and Technical Assistance	$3
Chafee Foster Care Independence Program (CFCIP) Assists youth to make a successful transition from foster care to adulthood: financial, housing, counseling, education, employment, coaching, training and-cost payments to former foster youth ages 18-20 years of age	$183
OTHER PROGRAMS Adoption Opportunities Program - establish national adoption information exchange and resource centers, adoption training, recruitment of families to adopt older, special needs, and minority children in foster care	

Table. 13-1 Fiscal Year 2016 Child Welfare Funding by Major Fiscal Year Programs – page 2 (nominal dollars in millions; parts may not sum to total due to rounding)	
Program	**Amount (in millions)**
Children's Justice Act Grants improve the assessment, investigation, and/or prosecution of child abuse and neglect cases — particularly cases involving suspected sexual abuse and exploitation of children, child fatalities suspected to be caused by abuse or neglect, and those involving children who are disabled and children with serious health disorders	$20
Adoption and Legal Guardianship Incentive Payments eligible states earn an incentive for improving the rate (or percentage) of children who leave foster care for adoption or guardianship	$39
Abandoned Infants Assistance -Services for the infant and their families when infants remain hospitalized due to a lack of a non-hospital home	$0
Victims of Child Abuse Act Children's Advocacy Centers, Court Appointed Special Advocates, and Child Abuse Training for Judicial Personnel) Child Abuse Prevention and Treatment Act - grant funding to states to improve their child protective services, competitively awarded funds to support research, technical assistance, and demonstration projects related to prevention, assessment, and treatment of child abuse and neglect	$31
TOTAL appropriation	**$98.10**
CAPTA State Grants—Formula grants to states and territories	$25.30
CAPTA Discretionary Activities—Competitive grants, contracts or agreements to eligible entities	33.00

(Stotzfus 2017)

Customer Cultivation

Plan to meet, once or twice a year with the director (or their assigned representative) of the 5 largest GCWA customers. Also, meet with other government customer staff on a schedule that is commensurate with the current purchase of service volume as well as based on any planned program or geographic expansion. These customer relationship cultivation meetings can accomplish a few things. 1) They provide the opportunity to get feedback on agency services,.2) The president provides an update on new programs and other important agency changes and gets a sense of the customer's interest.3) If the GCWA agency has a bad service situation with the PCWA, do damage control, by indicating the changes that have been made or will be made to assure the situation does not reoccur. If the situation really upset GCWA leaders then a special meeting is immediately scheduled. 4) Get an update on important issues at the GCWA. Explore if you can help in addressing them. 5) Ask if the state has IV-E waiver projects, and if so, ask the funding amount and a project description. Ask If it involves a service you provide, or a new service you could provide. Many states have waiver projects designed to reduce out of home care.

To prepare for the meetings try to get answers to as many of the following questions as possible. Much of the information is on the Internet. The business intelligence the agency gathers will give insights into customer concerns and funding focus. This knowledge will shape the marketing efforts and program offerings with each customer.

As a starting point read the federal legislative summary that I cite above. Next get to know the contents of your state child welfare legislation. Third, find out how the State GCWA fared on their last Federal CFSR review. To do this click on the URL cited above. Review any existing state consent decrees. Consent decrees are settlements of class action lawsuits brought on behalf of a class of people that believe that failures of state child welfare systems have an adverse effect on them. Between 1995 and 2005, there were consent decrees in 32 states.

"Most decrees that have been active within the past ten years have addressed the state's failure to:

- ➤ properly license and train foster parents;
- ➤ place children in adequate and safe foster and group homes;
- ➤ properly report, investigate and address abuse and neglect incidents;

> ➤ provide needed medical, dental, and mental health services to foster children;
> ➤ ensure adequate parent-child or sibling visitation;
> ➤ ensure social workers have manageable caseloads, training and supervision;
> ➤ Provide children and families with adequate case planning and review".

(Koanavich, 2005)

What is the structure and organization of the GCWA internally as well as within the context of the larger governmental system? Who are the key decision makers? Moreover, who reports to whom? Some of this information will be available on websites and in annual reports; other information is from staff. How are the relationships with the courts and police structured? Does the court have a positive regard for the child welfare agency, and if not, what is the GCWA doing to improve things? The outcome of knowing the above information is the ability to think about new services, and present services in a way that helps a GCWA deal with their organizational challenges. For example, if a state has a new consent decree because stays in foster care are too long, can the services you provide be part of the solution. Can the agency rejigger the family support or family preservation work into a re-entry service that helps parents improve skills so that their child can return home from foster care?

What is internal work and what is contractual work? What are the pressures on the PCWA to contract out because of government wide decisions? For example, if there is a hiring freeze within a unit of government than there is likely to be more outside contracting. Can the agency help deal with this hiring freeze by managing the GCWA foster care service, so child welfare caseworkers can do other work?

For the PCWA, good networking with elected officials and child welfare leaders yields information and how this information influences the priorities and behaviors of managers and caseworkers. Quite often, the GCWA labor force is in a union and part of the state civil service system. In part, due to pension and health care costs for current staff and retiree legacy costs (pensions and health care premiums), elected officials prefer to contract out work to a PCWA rather than hire staff.

Purchase of Services

In the private for-profit sector, there is usually two buying methods 1) retail - when the consumer makes the decision and 2) the purchasing model in which a single or multiple people make purchasing decisions for an organization. For GCWAs there are also two levels but they are different from the commercial sector. Executive staff at the GCWA creates or assures the continuation of the range of contracted services the GCWA requires. Many of the leaders in GCWAs are long-term employees. They are seasoned and knowledgeable. When awarding contracts, they share with their casework staff a concern that the services be of high quality with the goals of improving the child's functioning and life chances. Reasonable costs are also important. The leaders determine the service choices of the casework staff by selecting to contract for some services with certain PCWAs, but not others. It is common for the GCWA to have purchase of service contracts for the same services with several PCWAs. When this is the situation there is market share to gain or lose and a downward pressure on per unit costs. In addition, individual and group practices also provide services. In these situations, the popularity of the individual or the distinctive services offered are the basis of the contract. Two examples of a distinct service are psychologists who evaluate sexual offenders and social workers who perform adoption home studies. In addition, those professionals who judges think highly of may hold individual service contracts. Also, homemaker health services, day care centers, and nurses who provide home visiting services have service contracts.

The experience, knowledge, and career differences between the GCWA leadership staff and casework staff are very wide. Leaders are typically career civil servants; caseworker turnover is very high. Caseworkers are often ages 22-30 and leaders are 45+.

The purchasing process is usually that the PCWA has a mission aligned with part of the GCWA mission. Knowing the services that the GCWA generally purchases the PCWA develops a service to meet their need and the GCWA decides on whether to purchase it or not, and how much it wishes to purchase. In some circumstances, the GCWA will issue a request for proposal for a new service to receive responses that vary in method and cost. The GCWA will usually try to have multiple PCWAs provide a service to avoid any PCWA from being too powerful. In the current financial environment, there is more concern about pricing. There is a trend of GCWAs to settle for lower levels of staff credentials to achieve cost savings. Formerly the expectation was that the PCWA direct service counseling staff holds s a master's degree in a human services discipline, now bachelor level staff sometimes provides the services.

The role of the GCWA casework staff in making purchasing decisions has implications for PCWAs. Through visiting the children, reviewing case reports, and discussions with their co-workers, caseworkers form positive or negative impressions about a PCWA's service that influence future purchasing decisions. The direct service staff is the face of the PCWA to GCWA caseworkers. In addition to their role in helping the children and families they act as the PCWA's liaison for each child receiving services. Their competence and relationship with the GCWA caseworker are the most important part of the agency marketing effort. The GCWA worker's satisfaction with the services for the first child they refer will be important in future buying decisions. Another essential element in buying decisions is service availability. Child welfare is often an "emergency service" If a PCWA cannot deliver services promptly, GCWA caseworkers seek another PCWA who can.

When a PCWA is trying to develop a new contract, their best strategy is to develop a service that the GCWA wants. With the trend of providing services locally PCWAs with centralized services, located significant distances from the location of the family home of the child may want to consider decentralizing to provide services closer to consumer home areas. Recently, national PCWAs have become more interested in-service areas traditionally served by local agencies. This has happened because of their interest in growth.

Depending on legal requirements and the political situation in the purchasing jurisdiction, officials will seek competitive bids. Administrative staff is not likely to seek competitive bids unless the PCWA will not negotiate a rate that the GCWA finds acceptable, there have been substantial problems with services, or there is designated funding for a major initiative. In addition, a very powerful control that GCWAs have is to "vote with their feet" and stop purchasing services from an agency. This is most likely to happen when there is a child death or a case of serious physical or sexual abuse to a child in residential care.

Elected officials are sometimes interested in competitive bidding to save money. They reason that many people get quotes on car insurance, home oil delivery purchases, and go to gas stations offering a lower price. They believe that when they get bids for services that new PCWAs will bid to supply services, and that bidders will offer prices lower than current rates to get and keep public contracts. Although this thinking makes sense, my experience in bidding out residential and community-based contracts for behavioral health consumers did not have the intended result. I invited over a hundred organizations to submit bids from a five-state area. The result was that 90% of the bids were from the current providers and that the pricing was the same as in the current contract. I did not follow up with qualified applicants who did not bid so I am not sure of their rationale.

As a cost control measure, many GCWAs have centralized the authorization for a purchase of service for a child, to one or two people in the office. When this happens maintaining a good knowledge and positive impression of the service by the decision maker(s) is important. Once the GCWA establishes the quality of the care, then cost is uppermost in their minds when they make purchasing decisions. The decision makers are aware of program outcomes, and cost competitiveness. Upon forming relationships with them the managers at the PCWA learn that these decision makers favor one type of service over another. Learning the way these decision makers evaluate service approval decisions and their service preferences may help get referrals.

As previously mentioned, due to working and environmental conditions, there is a high turnover rate among GCWA caseworkers. The jobs involve going into homes where there is a risk of harm to the caseworker because of the angry parents who are upset about the investigation. Moreover, many of the parents have substance abuse and/or mental health issues, which make their behavior unpredictable. In addition, many neighborhoods are high crime areas. The situation is worse when funding shortages lead to the GCWA having too few positions or the decision not to fill vacant positions results in higher caseloads.

For the PCWA, this means there is an ongoing need to orient new GCWA staff to agency services, and position the agency so the new staff will consider making appropriate referrals. Part of marketing to these staff is having an easily used set of materials on the website as well as, hard copies that list the services that the PCWA provides. The materials include the program name, a brief discussion of the program services, program contact information, and any other information required as part of the referral package. The likelihood of the referral is proportional to the number of barriers to program entry. The fewer barriers the more likely it is that the GCWA will refer the child. For the PCWA that already receives referrals from the GCWA staff, the task is easier because senior GCWA workers educate junior workers in an informal way. In marketing to new GCWA staff, an optimum method is to ask to be part of their staff orientation process. Another common practice is to ask to speak at a GCWA staff meeting. Some PCWAs have staff visit GCWAs unannounced, bearing a box of doughnuts, talking to whoever is in the office when they drop by. Those performing the marketing tasks need to be sensitive, to the fact that new GCWA caseworkers have extensive training requirements that they must complete within a certain period. Therefore, they may not have the ability to meet, or pay attention to information at the very beginning of their employment. PCWA staffs need to be attentive to "windows of opportunity" to reach these people.

The director of the GCWA or other appropriate liaison staff will usually be willing to meet periodically. Prepare very carefully for these meetings knowing as much as possible about the answers to the questions posed above. Also, be clear on what the meeting strategy is. Do you want the agency to use the service because the organization achieves better results than current PCWAs do? Will the agency provide a less expensive service than is currently in place? Will the agency provide a new service? If the administrative staff will not meet with you after the agency have done the cultivation work then the next step is to see if an elected official will.

Child Welfare Contracts

Government contracts codify the terms of the service relationship. Government contracts are the primary source of income for many PCWAs. The contracts describe the services provided, the payment terms, and the GCWA policies that are applicable. They describe the duties of the GCWA and the PCWA. In the majority of the state's GCWA services is a state responsibility so that child welfare contracts will be uniform according to the practices of the state involved. Prices and service description may vary by region, or be uniform for each type of service. In addition, service standards may be uniform. Some major cities may have additional performance standards that are different or exceed state requirements. Because the federal government provides some child welfare funding, adherence to federal laws and regulations will likely be part of service agreements. Additionally, because the federal government measures state child welfare performance using certain standards, some of these standards may be in the contract.

PCWA contract managers communicate these service standards with program staff who implement them. The standards are part of each program's operations manual. In a situation in which there is, dissatisfaction with the PCWA services these standards will come into play in making judgments about whether services complied with expectations.

Most child welfare contracts are annual so there are no long-term funding guarantees. However, to keep rates steady and avoid extensive contract preparation work GCWAs often specify an initial term of one year with a right to add additional one-year terms. Sometimes a contract will end up being a 5-year agreement. The rate for the initial contract period is important for the PCWA in that the rate could be the same for several years. Plan on this possibility when setting the initial rate. If the PCWA is in a situation where the GCWA offers a fixed rate multiyear contract, try to write the program description in such a way that if the PCWA gets into a difficult spot financially, some elements of the service are not obligatory so it can adjust service costs. Another strategy is to put aside surpluses from the first two or three years of the contract in a fund account and draw down on the account during the last two years of the contract to cover any losses.

If the state fixes all three – the per diem or hourly rate, the term of the contract, and the program description the PCWA may face financial deficits with a contract that has a three-year or longer term. If this is the case either limit the number of referrals you accept or know up front the commitment the agency is making to contribute charitable dollars, or organizational funds to underwrite public funding by calculating a cost of living increase amount for each year the rate is unchanged. It is important that at least one person at the PCWA organization does a line-by-line review of GCWA contracts and acts as an information disseminator. This means that one person understands all the contract terms and gets the necessary information out to the appropriate staff. For example, if there is a provision that the agency must get the government body's approval, prior to the purchase or rental of a service site building it is important that those staff and BOD members involved with property procurement are aware of the requirement.

Program Descriptions

There are three types of program descriptions: The first is proscriptive, in which the GCWA specifies what constitutes the service. The second is PCWA constructed using broad categories determined by the government agency, and the third is a very detailed description that responds to a long list of questions posed by the GCWA. In the latter two circumstances, specify any subcontracts proposed and assure that the subcontractors will abide by all applicable federal and state laws. Contracts may mandate certain services, for example life skills training, for teenagers in placement.

Specify in the program description that public dollars will not fund any software, technology, public reports, or copyrighted material. It is judicious to document the funds used to pay for intellectual property in case the GCWA asserts a claim of ownership rights. If the agency uses contract dollars to fund intellectual property the ownership of the software resides with the payer not the PCWA.

Laws and Regulations

Some contracts have requirements that PCWA report any legal violations, community incidents, and problems to the GCWA. If so, line staff should know the organizational policy on reporting infractions, especially minor ones, like speeding tickets, municipal fines for not mowing the grass etc. I suspect if the PCWA report anything related to a serious risk to child safety the agency will be in good shape. If you start reporting every little thing, it creates a cumbersome amount of paperwork. Be aware that if an adversarial neighbor finds out the agency has a GCWA contract they may contact the government unit to complain that the hedge is too high, the kids are too noisy, or the flowers in the planter are dead.

The contract will state that PCWA personnel are to obey all federal state and local civil rights and disability legislation. These acts together prohibit discrimination based on race, color, national origin, sex, handicap, age, and religion. Sexual harassment and discrimination against GLBTQ persons are forms of the sex discrimination. In addition:

- The PCWA must conform with state or local conflict of interest legislation
- The PCWA conforms with dual employment prohibitions or notification requirements for persons who are employed by both the PCWA and the contracting GCWA
- The PCWA must hold state licenses appropriate to the services provided (i.e. foster care, residential, behavioral health, etc.)
- A 501(c) organization maintains its status with the IRS
- There are no legal proceedings that will prevent performance of the contract. For example, there has not been a zoning hearing board finding that a PCWA group home is in violation of the zoning code.
- The PCWA is not delinquent in tax payments to the government body. For example, because things were tight financially the PCWA did not submit payroll taxes for the employees during the last two quarters.
- The PCWA or any of its employees are not debarred. The most common example would be debarment of a PCWA, or PCWA employee by Medical Assistance because of a fraud finding.
- The PCWA may not conduct worship services or provide religious instruction.
- PCWA report requests for donations by elected officials.
- The PCWA does not use contract funds to engage in lobbying activities.
- GCWA staff may not give or accept gifts
- The PCWA indemnifies the GCWA against any harm associated with PCWA or PCWA's employee acts.

Other Important Contract Provisions

Location of the Child - GCWA contracts require PCWAs to account, every day for the physical location of every child receiving residential services. GCWA caseworkers need to be able to locate children in an agency's care immediately for any number of reasons including a court date, illness or a death of a family member, a medical appointment, etc. The inability of a PCWA to locate a child in their care is a contract violation and a public relations embarrassment.

The PCWA staff maintains a residential roster of children. The roster includes all children receiving residential services, those recently discharged or who have run away. Each afternoon the administrative staff amends the roster to reflect children who are new admissions, moved from one physical location to a different physical location, on runaway, or discharged. Direct service staff email administrative staff daily about any child who moves and makes a note in the child's file. In the situation that a child moves from one agency foster home or group home to another agency location the staff at the receiving location sends the email and also notifies the child's GCWA caseworker. When a child runs away, the unit staff emails a notice to the administrative staff and notifies the GCWA caseworker for the child.

The roster entry for each child includes:

1. The child's name, date of birth, and the address of their current physical location,
2. The child's PCWA and GCWA caseworker's name and cell phone number. A central residential program includes the name, address, email, and telephone numbers for the foster home or group home
3. The names and cellphone numbers for all staff in the GCWA and PCWA emergency contact chain of command
4. Contact information for the child's parent(s).
5. For ninety days after the date a child leaves the PCWA, the name of the receiving person or agency including the name address, email and cellphone number.

The PCWA central office staff maintains the residential roster. The administrative staff member trains two other staff members, one of them working weekends, in the maintenance of the residential roster. The residential roster is on the agency intranet site, and is accessible to staff who oversee the agency during non-office hours. The central office record contains all of the information in 1-5 in the previous paragraph.

Critical Incidents These are serious events involving for the most part, harm, or potential harm to a resident. A list of incidents that are subject to a report to the GCWA is in the contract or licensing regulations. What is on the list differs by state. It is important that one internal person who reports to the president is aware of all reports and discusses reports involving serious harm to a child with the president. The president is interested in both the frequency of the reports and any patterns that exist by types of injury or program. As necessary, the leadership staff starts a discussion with staff providing services, on what changes will reduce reports. It is common for any instance of suspected child abuse, the arrest of a child, a fight between children that results in an injury, suicide attempts and any instance of physical restraint of a child to be reportableitems

Runaway Children - Clear internal policy on who gets reports when a child runs away from care exist. It is important to take a picture of each child upon admission, so staff can copy it for police and other potential searchers. A discussion of the notification process is in the last section. Be clear on bed hold requirements, in the contract and make sure the intake staff is aware of them. In the economics of residential care, occupancy is the main determinant of a surplus or deficit because the expenses are stable for the most part. The ability to reaccept a runaway child that returns is very important in terms of continuing the child's relationship with staff they trust, and other youth in the unit that they probably regard as quasi-family members. Internally or through a subcontract with an emergency shelter facility, arrange to reaccept these children, and then work them back into a regular program, as there is an opening. The fewer placements the child experiences the better. Their placement stability predicts their potential according to some experts in the field.

Rejection of Referrals and Unplanned Discharges

Some contracts require the PCWA to maintain a list of all referrals received, indicating the date of the referral, the GCWA caseworker who made the referral, demographic information about the child, the presenting problem, and the disposition of the referral. Staff also notes a decision not to accept a child and the reason. GCWA workers may give the PCWA notice when they disagree with the PCWA's decision not to accept a referral. Some contracts allow for contract termination if the number of referral rejections exceeds customer standards.

Similarly, unplanned discharges often become contentious events between GCWA staff that now have a new unplanned assignment to locate another placement for a child, whereas PCWA staff often feel defeated and exhausted in dealing with the child's bad behavior.

This kind of conflict happens because the GCWA is more concerned about using its power, which is considerable, rather than paying attention to how to meet the needs of difficult children. PCWAs who rigidly continue to provide services that do not meet the needs of substantial numbers in their service population are laying the groundwork for their own irrelevance.

When these premature discharges become frequent, the GCWA may penalize the PCWA by not making any further referrals. If the agency serves one major city as its primary customer than cutting off referrals threatens the existence of the agency. What is happening is that there is a gap involving hard to serve children and the program offered by the PCWA. The GCWA must serve these children. Most PCWAs do not like an unconditional care rule because one agency usually cannot offer the full range of services needed for all children, and so they want the right not to accept referrals. In addition, children with certain behaviors may have a history of not doing well in their program. When this gets into a conflictual situation between PCWAs and referring agencies it means good proactive planning is not occurring at the GCWA, and this might represent a service opportunity for an enterprising PCWA

When the GCWA does a good job of planning they profile these children and sort rejected youth into groups with homogeneous factors such as history of assaulting staff, children with other serious conduct disorders, and those who truant. Next, the GCWA completes a study of the programs that have the best chance of helping these youths. New programs start through a competitive request for proposal process. Due to the firefighting culture of some GCWA's this type of analysis and new program development may not occur. There is no reason that the PCWA cannot engage in this process. PCWAs who want to distinguish themselves in a competitive market will create new programs that help youth using new strategies, and research-based approaches. Many of these youth do better in settings where passive physical restraint in not used or only used in limited circumstances. Selected youth are more aggressive when they feel physically threatened. Hands off settings, which model respect and nonviolent conflict resolution, will make a difference for some violent youth, but not for others.

In addition, private and public agencies need to do a good job of reporting serious assault situations to the police. Although nobody likes to see a young person enter the juvenile justice system, the juvenile justice system operates closed residential settings, which some youth may need for a time. In addition, PCWA staff balances the intervention needs of violent children against the safety needs of the other residents. One job of the GCWA is to nurture the development of programs for hard to serve youth and understand that pounding a square peg into a round hole only causes frustration among all concerned. Sometimes public agencies become too concerned with holding PCWAs accountable to what they believe the PCWA has committed to in a program description. This kind of shoving match between public and private agencies takes the focus away from their service missions.

Child Safety

Part of the Adoptions and Safe Families Act (ASFA) provisions focus on assuring child safety. Both GCWA and PCWA staff must assure that the living arrangement for each child is safe. For each child, at risk, there is a written safety plan, and at each visit to a home staff asses the identified child's safety. Contracts state that PCWA staff must document the safety of each child during every face-to-face contact and notify the child's caseworker if there is a safety risk, specifying what steps the PCWA agency takes to assure the child's safety. Whatever the contract specifics are, child safety is very important. If a child dies or sustains a serious injury while in the care of a PCWA, the consequences: loss of life, tragedy for the family, possible suspension of referrals to the PCWA and the potential for civil litigation are risks so severe, a risk reduction program is worthwhile.

For a PCWA a risk management program includes knowledge regarding:

> A child's potential for self-harm
> A child's potential to harm other children and staff
> The risk of physical or sexual abuse of a child by a visiting parent or friend
> The risk of physical or sexual abuse of a child by a staff member
> The risk of physical or sexual abuse by another resident

PCWA Action Plans include:

> Staff reporting impaired colleagues to their manager.
> Staff maintain sight supervision of residents during their waking hours and frequent room checks occur during sleeping hours
> Staff follow internal and contractual incident reporting procedures
> Leadership staff meets with each resident group quarterly, without any other staff present to learn if residents feel safe, and if not why not.
> Separation of the group of children from a child having a violent episode.
> Having the police handle youth violence.
> Use of passive physical restraint as a last resort, only to prevent harm to residents and staff.

Child Death Reviews

Some contracts require PCWAs to conduct an internal child death review following the death of a child in care. Such a review should only start after police and GCWA officials complete their work. Police and child welfare investigators are professionals trained for this work. Premature agency investigations may negatively affect their efforts. In addition, unless the PCWA trains staff, personnel do not possess the training or credentials for this work. Another serious concern is the self-interest of PCWA staff to protect themselves, peers, and the agency. If the budget allows and the PCWA wants to or must do a review, bring in an outside investigator to assure independence. Due to the possibility of findings of agency negligence and civil litigation, involve the PCWA attorney from the beginning in mapping out the review plan

Insurance Requirements

Contracts specify types and amounts of insurance that the PCWA must maintain in connection with the agreement. These usually include general liability, professional liability, property, directors and officers, workers compensation, and auto insurance. When policy costs are prohibitive, sometimes contracting offices will allow a waiver on policy coverage amounts and allow lower amounts.

Violation of Terms, Default, Failure to Perform Duties

There are usually several sections related to remedies that the GCWA has if they judge the PCWA have violated the terms of the agreement. What constitutes a violation varies and can involve not accepting referrals, entering bankruptcy, closing a program under contract, employing a debarred person, etc. The remedies specified are usually wide- ranging including suspension of referrals, suspension, or termination of the agreement, litigation to recover funds, withholding payment related to work under investigation, and other actions. It is much more likely that financial consequences will result from an audit of agency financial records than from a contract violation. This occurs most often when fiscal staff bills for services that professional staff do not provide Sometimes staff provide a less expensive service than what is in the contract. For example, the contract is for group counseling but instead youth participate in a group recreation program. Government customers usually deal with dissatisfaction with services by suspending new referrals and depending on the specifics of the situation may remove children from care. The latter action occurs if the child is in an unsafe situation.

Paperwork

The paperwork required will vary by contract. The trend over the past decade is to make more of the paperwork the responsibility of the PCWA. Government cost reduction strategies can entail minimizing new hires in GCWA departments, and reducing positions, where they can, through not filling vacancies, or filling them through interdepartmental transfers. This has led to PCWA staff being responsible for more paperwork. It appears that this responsibility has largely gone unfunded in terms of PCWA rate increases. This leads to staff spending more time completing administrative requirements and spending less time with youth and families. This along with a lack of resources for annual contract cost of living increases lead to threeresults:

1) Degradation of services. This occurs when PCWAs lower experience and academic standards for staff to save money, or fail to attract and retain high quality staff. 2) PCWAs subsidize public dollars with charitable donations, and agency reserves. When doing this, use an "endowment" approach on spending reserves. The goal is to use the earning on reserves to subsidize services, but not the principal. Other strategies to supplement public dollars include additional fund-raising activities and pursuing unrelated business income opportunities such as renting out unused property, a youth oriented business, etc. 3) During any given year service

volume is limited to what can be supported through the public payments combined with the results of resources from item 2.

The agency's paperwork requirements are in the agreement. The list below indicates some items that are common in agreements. If the agency is new to government contracting review the effort required to prepare the rate determination paperwork. This varies from state to state. The amount of time will be greatest in the first year because in addition to recording the information, staff creates the templates. If this financial task is considerable, include the time spent as an administrative expense in determining the rate

I Clinical Paperwork
- PCWA service plan
- Quarterly reports
- Discharge from care plan
- Discharge plans for older youth transitioning into independent living

II Administrative Paperwork
- Incident reporting related forms
- Paperwork that supports state or local government receipt of federal TANF funds
- Documentation that criminal record check and fingerprinting is complete for all staff

III Financial
- Monthly invoices
- Independent audit or
- Program specific compliance audit
- Rate determination forms
- Reports of program Income

CHAPTER 14
THE YELLOW BRICK ROAD
TO GRANT WRITING PROFICIENCY

The share of agency budgets generated by foundation and government grants varies by organization, but is often substantial. There are many government grants that support PCWA programs. I discuss a few of them, as well as how to conduct a grant search. The first section of the chapter describes a way to approach initiating a grant program at a PCWA. Next, there is a detailed description of the grant writing process.

Things to Do to Start a Grant Writing Program at The Organization

Identify Program Prospects Identify three agency programs for which the agency could seek a grant. Describe each in writing in two pages. Evaluate the three descriptions by asking three staff and three board members to read them and tell you which idea appeals to them most. Do not tell them your opinion. If one idea gets at least four votes choose the program for the first grant search. If the agency chooses a current program that is losing money keep in mind that federal and state grant makers do not allow for sup plantation of funds. Sup plantation is substituting new Federal grant money for other monies the agency already uses to operate the program, and then using the "old funds" for another program. If the agency is seeking a state or federal grant to fund an existing program, in which the agency is losing or have lost monies emphasize the point very clearly in the application. Still most federal and foundation grants are interested in funding specific programs, rather than deficits. It is fine to ask for money to expand an existing effort.

Identify Grant Makers Learn about what federal grants are available to the organization and the grant makers that might consider funding your program(s). The best place to start is the youth.gov website. At the top, choose from the menu. The result will be a wealth of information about the federal activity. This will include funding, program information, statistics, and related federal resources. Also, you may get ideas about non-federal sources. Although staff will use grants.gov as described below youth.gov is a superior beginning website for PCWAs. If the agency participates in a membership organization or connects in another way with peer agencies, staff can find out what grants they get. In addition, there are fee- based grant newsletters.

Locate the library in the area that is an affiliate of the Foundation Center Funding Information Network. This is one of the best foundation resources. Visit the library to conduct the search. Use the tutorial to get familiar with the site features before beginning your search. Focus on foundations that have made grants in your geographic region. While you can apply to appropriate national foundations, the competition is very fierce. With national foundations review the list of charities that the foundation has funded during the last five years to discover nonprofits in your area that are grant recipients, and other aid organizations that have staff you know. If you do not have any personal contacts you know, check the grant recipient's 990 filing to see if you share any BOD members in common. If so, ask your BOD member to make the initial telephone call. Contact the recipient agency and ask them to call their grant officer to ask if you might call or visit to discuss a possible grant application. If you cannot use this method it is generally best to write a brief cover letter describing your project and requesting an in person or telephone interview.

The advantage of the Foundation Center materials that like other library reference materials it is free to use at the library. Many libraries are subscribers. However, like a reference book the center's materials and resources do not leave the building. Staff cannot do it online from an external location unless the agency subscribes through the center. If staff cannot access it through an area library, budget for a short-term subscription. Between the Foundation Center database and youth.gov, you will identify many of the grants available to fund your project. In addition, obtain the annual reports of local and national organizations similar to yours and review their donor listings, usually included in the back of the report.

Larger sister organizations are especially good resources and you may want to make a personal contribution, to one or two of the best, to get on their mailing list and receive their reports and solicitations. This will give an idea of how an organization with more resources than yours approaches solicitations, who gives to them, and the key points they make. Family foundations often do not appear in guides. Local news and donor listings from other area charities alert staff to them. Prepare yourself to deal with a very common situation in which there is somewhat of a match between the program and a funding source's area of interest, but the match is not exact. You need to decide if you can fashion a proposal that meets the funding source criteria and at the same time advances your mission. With available private foundation staff, request a meeting to see if they will consider supporting the program the agency offers.

Also, get the sources of state government grants. Contact a state senator or house member office and ask their constituency service staff to look into this for you. Also, OJJDP makes grants to states to fund youth programs as well as direct grants. The federal grants are listed at this URL: https://www.ojjdp.gov/funding/FundingList.asp.

Review Instructions from Two or Three Grant Makers and Write a Boilerplate Proposal Go to the foundation, state agency, or grants.gov, website, and select specific grant program(s). Download the grant application instructions, and read them. Note the general kinds of information they request. Use this information to write the first draft of a boilerplate application that the agency will use to develop a proposal when staff is ready to apply. Many funders want to know 1) what is the need? 2) What are the measurable objectives of the proposed project and the evaluation plan? 3) What is the organization's experience and credentials? 4) What is the nature of the proposed program including the service population, method of intervention, and expected service numbers? and 5) What is the project budget? Gather the necessary attachments. They could include documentation of 501© 3 status, an organization chart, a list of the BOD members, and the organization's annual budget. The grant maker may require the most recent audit, strategic plan, by - laws, and articles of incorporation.

Create a Social Indicator Data Book The data book includes any social indicator information that is available for the overall service area, as well as for the major subdivisions such as cities, counties and school districts. Check and see if a foundation or other organization in the area acts as a central data-gathering site. A good person to ask is a staff member at the local planning commission, or a staff member at the city, county or state human service office. Often, they will have access to municipal and state data that they use in doing their own human service plans. If a central community data book already exists, it will save a great deal of work. Look for state specific organizations. The Annie B. Casey Foundation's Kidscount data center is also a very useful resource. There is a wealth of census data available by census track, city, county, and state. https://www.census.gov/data.html) Other good sources will include school district data, state annual child abuse and neglect reports the best source of data may be the organization's own client records. This includes demographics, problem types, and outcomes.

Develop Relationships with Others in the Community Who Will Play a Role in the Grant Program and Developing the Application

Representatives of other community organizations may play one of several roles in the grant application process. First, ask them to write letters of support for federal and state grant applications. Presumably, the agency ordinarily works with these organizations. They include schools, medical personnel, police, GCWAs, juvenile probation agencies, and private organizations and practitioners who know the agency's work because staff refer either children to them for service, vice versa, or both. Second for certain grants (HUD as one example) if the organization and other organization(s) provide services to the same consumer, the value of the services another organization provides are of use as grant matching funds. Third, there maybe projects where the agency develops a subcontract with a community organization as part of the grant. Fourth, United Way and local and state government funds often match federal funds in applications. Other relationships develop due to special expertise. This may include a successful grant writer in another area who acts as an outside reader of the draft. A university-based research and methodology professor assists in developing program outcomes, an evaluation plan, and the logic model.

Developing the Knowledge Base To demonstrate the competency to deliver particular services you need to be knowledgeable about the field in general, as well as, current needs and trends. If you are a good writer, but not knowledgeable about the focus of the application, take the time to acquire the knowledge that validates the organization's competency to deliver the services. Review the last annual report that the unit of the federal government issuing the FOA submitted to congress, the relevant legislation, and any research relevant to the grant conducted by the Congressional Research Office. The child welfare information gateway website (https://www.childwelfare.gov/) is the central federal government information resource on child welfare issues. There is a great deal of information there, and it is a good starting place to learn and focus on specific areas in the field. As mentioned above youth.gov is another good resource. The Casey Foundation has expertise in child welfare research and state child welfare policy makers take their recommendations seriously. They issue many worthwhile reports in addition to the data that is on the KIDSCOUNT website. It is advisable to review the National Incidence Study on Child Abuse and Neglect. The National Juvenile Judges Court Commission and National Institute of Justice provide a focus on the role of the court and issues in juvenile delinquency. Identify and read the publications of experts.

Review one local newspaper a day for relevant stories, which will include useful anecdotes and local statistics. Another good information resource is Chapin Hall at the University of Chicago. Rand Corporation and Kaiser Permanente have current information on child health issues. Kids Count, the National Research Council, and the Lucille Packard Foundation are good sources for child data. The Heritage Foundation provides a conservative perspective, and very good analysis work on government spending in addition to analysis of Congressional Budget Office data. An online library literature search and college textbooks can also be of use. The electronic resources at a university and a big city library are very useful in conducting literature reviews.

Review federal grant instructions to become knowledgeable about approaches emphasized. These may include consumer issues such as trauma informed care; harm prevention, anti-discrimination, and harassment strategies. Ensuring youth safety is often of interest. If the agency will approach a foundation, review their website focusing on the purpose, areas of interest, and current grantees.

Identify the Grant Writer The ideal grant writer is a person who has an excellent knowledge of the field for which they write and is an excellent writer. Their writing style is responsive to the grantor instructions and is factual, but at the same time, it excites and engages the reader, and conveys the organization's knowledge and competence to take on the task. They have excellent fiscal skills, and collaborate with the organization's fiscal staff. They know the procedures of the funding sources. They have good attention to detail so as not to miss any important part of the process or instructions. Keep material that is usually part of grant applications in a file. The file includes job descriptions, resumes, salaries, program expenses, a BOD list, and a copy of the strategic plan. In terms of personality, they are someone who works well with others, but can stay on task and work alone a good deal of the time. They also possess good organizational skills.

However, consider contracting with a grant writer for the application if you think the agency will not apply for many federal grants. Alternatively, if the agency is planning a federal grant-writing program at the organization you may want to seek a person with grant writing expertise as a member of the BOD. Writing the application with only internal staff has the advantage of building organizational competencies. However, sweat equity is necessary.

Deciding on Whether or Not to Pursue a Particular Grant Applying for sizable federal grants ($200,000+) and national foundation grants are time consuming. Depending on what kind of cut and paste material the agency has, the knowledge base, and grant writing experience staff will spend between 40 and 80 hours on a project. Due to the amount of time involved in the grant writing process, consider if staff has the work hours available to commit to it. The theory of "opportunity costs" applies. Presuming there is limited time available for grant writing, consider, that for every grant you apply for, you may forgo the opportunity to write another. Consequently, carefully assess if the one(s) you select will be of benefit to the agency in a strategic way.

The way to make this decision is to read the request for proposal summary, and then if the grant is a good fit for the organization read the actual request for proposal. The things to consider are: 1) the number of grant awards in the jurisdiction. For instance, if there are less than 20 awards nationally a grant award will be difficult to obtain 2) How good is the fit between the program you propose and the program type that the grant maker wishes to support? Federal and state grants are usually quite competitive. In many situations, the federal government funds only 10% of the applications. If there is not a "goodness of fit" between the idea and the grant maker's priorities, it is better not to apply.

Does the time between the grant announcement date and the application due date allow the agency to prepare an excellent application considering other responsibilities? A key to successful grant writing is that the grant writer uses the application to demonstrate the organization's competencies. The grant reviewers are unlikely to form a positive impression of the organization's competency to complete the proposed project if the agency submits a poorly crafted application.

Is there an internal team available and ready to put in the time and effort? Do they want the grant enough to work for it? At a minimum, the team consists of one or more people who are very knowledgeable about the program that is the subject of the application. Chances are this will include a program director and supervisor of the program. Direct service staff who knows the program details, and administrative staff responsible for statistical reporting, can also be good team members.

In multi-service agencies where the grant writer submits proposals for many different programs, they usually do not possess the depth of expertise held by the program staff. In these situations, staff team members carry a high level of responsibility. They provide information on program content and processes. They often write either bullet points or full draft sections of the narrative, and locate evaluation tools and evidence-based program models. They proof read application sections written by the grant writer and provide feedback. The grant writer is the team leader in organizing and setting the agenda for team meetings, final writing of the narrative, writing or having the finance department write the grant budget, and conducting any necessary liaison work with the funding source. They also act as liaisons with partners and sub-grant agencies. They create a logic model that begins with needs, identifies goals, objectives, services population, service numbers, outputs and outcomes. They prepare grant time line charts that include key tasks and who is responsible for their completion. With some funding sources like United Way and local government departments, they attend meetings, along with management staff, related to upcoming competitive bidding opportunities. They keep the other members of the team on task; establishing time lines for task completion. In addition, there is an outside reader that does not work with the rest of the team, but has a good knowledge of the field but not necessarily the specific program. The outside reader reviews the grant instructions, and criteria for awarding points, reads, and gives feedback to the grant writer on the "final version" of the application.

Does the grant writer have the time to collaborate on the application with any required partner organizations? Collaborations require additional meeting times and incentives to involve the needed organization. It entails working with the other organization's internal timeline and decision-making process Start the inter-agency work early in the application process to assure there will be enough time to get information and signed cooperation agreements from partners.

Are many potential competitors likely to be successful because of their experience with the service population, or area served? In government grant making, federal staff is likely to make grants in a way that many geographic areas receive awards. The same is true for state grants. If the agency and a like organization in the same or adjoining geographic area will both be applicants, it is better to collaborate on the application than submit competitive applications unless you are sure that your application will be much better than the one submitted by the other organization. From a cultural perspective, the expectation of state and federal agencies is that organizations in the same community will cooperate with each other. A failure to collaborate with another applicant may result in either a perception that you are uninformed or an isolationist. For other grant-makers it is customary to receive several applications from the same community. Talk with grant-maker staff to determine their expectations for collaboration.

Research is necessary to figure out which organizations are likely competitors. Long-term staff will know many of the organizations in the community that deliver services similar to those provided by your agency, giving some ideas of possible collaborators or competitors. Federal grants are for specific programs so it is best to know who the current grantees are for the program. This gives some idea of the competition as well as programs that are worthwhile. Each federal entity will have a website that provide detailed information on the programs that grants fund and reviewing the sites is part of the background research. The distribution method for federal grant programs is an allotment of the total funds available to each state. Also, for several federal programs there are regional offices that cover several states. Sometimes both the federal and regional staff participate in the grant making process, and sometimes only the federal staff in Washington D. C. make the decision.

The grant writer reads the prior year FOA for the grant they are considering seven months in advance of the current year anticipated application due date. Presume the application due date will be close to the prior year's due date. However, there is not a predetermined announcement or due date for any grant. If the anticipated FOA date passes without an announcement, check grants.gov every few days for the FOA. There is likely to be a delay in the FOA issue date when the legislation authorizing the grant is up for renewal, when there is a new president, (due to the need to appoint office heads) and when there are significant changes in the available funding. Then review the grant applications of three or more of the current grant holders in the state. These are available from the federal agency. Submit a Freedom of Information Act request if the federal officer does not share the grant applications on a voluntary basis.

The FOA will often include a list of current grantees. The federal agency that awards the grant has a list of the grantees on their website. Grantees usually compete for a grant once every three to five years, but there is some single year or two-year grants as well. They receive noncompeting continuation grants during the other two years in the three-year (five year) funding cycle. For instance, a list of current basic center (runaway and homeless youth) grantees, organized by year of the award, is available at the Family and Youth Service Bureau website: https://www.acf.hhs.gov/fysb/news/rhy-program-announces-fy2018-grant-awards A strategic approach is stronger when you know the grantees, and the number of grant awards in the state. This can change annually. A new applicant applies in the year when there are a relatively high number of grant awards to increase their mathematical odds of success. A second choice is to apply in a year when another organization received a grant, but had a relatively low score, to increase the chance of getting a grant due to weaker competition. For grants made as one-time awards, a strategic approach based on the extent of competition is not possible.

Does the agency have the organizational infrastructure to meet the grantor's record keeping and reporting requirements? For federal grants, you complete periodic program and fiscal reports. The program reports entail demographic and service statistics. Grantees summarize program accomplishments and failures. Federal grant conditions sometimes require the use of grantor software to record consumer information. State licensing standards and the local zoning code determine maximum occupancy for residential programs. Local government determines food safety procedures, and fire safety requirements for residential programs.

Federal grants

The runaway and homeless youth Act (RHYA) program makes grants to provide shelter and other services to homeless and runaway youth. In addition, RHYA funds transitional living programs that assist older homeless youth, including mother child pairs to transition into adulthood. Last, the program makes grants to establish street outreach programs to reach street youth and link them with shelters and other services. The URL for these grants as well as other grants offered by the Federal Youth Service Bureau is: https://www.acf.hhs.gov/fysb/grants The Housing and Urban Development department (HUD) provides grants to house and provide services to homeless populations, including young mothers, older adolescents, and young adults. Each state has its own method of making HUD grants. These grants provide support for program operating costs for efforts that provide services to assist older homeless youth, or to purchase and renovate a property towards this purpose. Get a general idea of the types of HUD grant at the

following URL: https://www.hud.gov/ program_offices/spm/ gmomgmt/grantsinfo There are various grants available through titles IVB and IVE titles of the social security act and other child welfare grants discussed by Stotzfus. (Stotzfus, 2017). Visit the Substance Abuse and Mental Health Service Administration website for other grant programs that fund programs that assist consumers with mental health and/or Substance abuse issues. The website address is https://www.samhsa.gov/grants Federal grant programs also support pregnancy prevention programs. The URL is: https://www.hhs.gov/ash/oah/grant-programs/teen-pregnancy-prevention-program-tpp/index.html   Again consider applying for an juvenile delinquency prevention or treatment grant. The URL is: https://www.ojjdp.gov/funding/FundingList.asp

A full list of federal programs with brief descriptions is on the youth.gov website.

Application submission for grants listed on the grants.gov website is electronic using website protocols. The federal grant process is uniform in that there is enabling legislation, regulations, grant submission instructions, and post award obligations.

Assign an administrative assistant to manage the data downloading and application uploading process. The grants.gov website site uses Adobe Reader. If the agency has the Adobe PDF free version, make sure it is compatible with the grants.gov version. If the organization has the Adobe PDF free version, and the team working on the grant is using Microsoft Word get an annual subscription to an online service that converts Word files to PDF files as well as PDF files to word files. This is not a submission requirement. Staff can upload the application in Word as well as other software programs but the instructions strongly advise to use the Adobe file format.

Plan to submit the application electronically a day or two before the due date. Federal grant managers do not review applications that arrive in their offices after the due date. An exception is possible if the applicant can demonstrate that a problem with the grant.gov system within 24 hours of the due date prevented uploading the application exists. If there is a problem with your agency computer system or the dog eats the application, or the PCWA does not upload, the application for any other reason on or before the deadline date, as they say in Brooklyn, fuggetaboutit.

Start by completing the steps in the prior section on starting a grant program before staff begins the application. In addition to a narrative, there are standard forms: identifying information forms, budget forms detailing federal and other support for the project, and certification forms to complete regarding lobbying, human subject protection, etc.

Download from the grants.gov website several types of materials: 1) instructions for electronic application submission. The first step is to register on the grants.gov website, which entails indicating the Employer Identification Number and DUNS number, and having several people identified as contacts, through the business office. See the website: grants.nih.gov/grants/duns_qa.doc for information on how to get a DUNS number, which is a unique nine-digit organizational identifier. In addition, staff downloads the forms for the application in which you populate preformed boxes, the general application instructions, and then the most important item the specific instructions for the program of interest. The amount of information is tremendous. Do a few things to prepare to write the application.

First, download and print out the instruction information. Share all or parts of downloaded files with people who will be working on the project as needed. Use the printed version for reading and making notes, if it is undesirable to read a significant amount of material on the computer screen. This is just a personal preference. It is more efficient to do it all on the computer rather than keeping track of, and carrying around a pound or two of paper. Read the instructions twice. Underline (highlight) what is important and make notes in the margins (add comments) of issues or questions that specific passages raise. Read carefully to find the answers in another part of the instructions. Use this information to form the agenda for the first group meeting with the team. At the meeting, the grant writer will share thoughts, with the others, and solicit their input regarding questions where there is not much of an idea of what to write.

When the grant writer gets to a point where they have a reasonably good grasp of the instructions they start writing. Prepare what the PCWA is going to be submit using an iterative process, which while time consuming, is a method that produces good quality applications. This method works for me because if I have too many things to think about, at once, I feel overwhelmed and I am unproductive. Then the writer goes back to the instructions to see if what they have written is responsive to each item of instruction. More often than is desirable one finds they have communicated unclearly on some points, and is wrong on others, and then the rewrites "begin". By the time the application deadline is approaching, usually four written four drafts have been prepared. The most important outcome is that the writing is clear, communicates the agency's knowledge and competence, and is responsive to the application criteria and questions.

The Federal Grant Application Package Parameters

There will be a page limitation to the application, which is specific to the office issuing FOA. In addition, there is a page-formatting scheme. The use of 81/2 by 11 paper, Times New Roman 12- point font, and one-inch margins is common. In addition, there will be instructions on the organization of the application contents. A common format is 1) table of contents 2) abstract 3). objectives, outcomes, and need for assistance 4). Approach 5) organizational profile 6) budget and budget justification.

There is also a limit to the amount of material that applicants can submit as appendices. The grant maker may require the following type of material: organizational charts, statement of organizational experience, job descriptions and staff resume, copies of agreements with participating organizations, and copies of existing indirect cost agreements. Half the states require Single Point of Contact reviews (SPOC). This process, created through an executive order from President Reagan allows the state as well as local jurisdiction input into the federal grant making process. If the organization is in a state with a SPOC requirement, the agency participates as part of the application process.

The nature of the participation varies by state and sometimes a state requires registration, and a state identification number that applicants enter on the federal forms. Subsequently, depending on the state, the applicant may need to submit the narrative and other forms to the state for review as well. The state than submits their input, if any, to the federal grant making agency, and federal staff review the input as part of the grant making process. Depending on the state, the comments are advisory or binding in nature. In reviewing SPOC, requirements note how the SPOC deadlines interface with the grant submission deadline and plan accordingly.

Grant Specific Instructions In addition to reading the extensive grant instructions, read the original enabling legislation. A legislative citation is usually in the executive summary of the funding announcement.

Knowledge of the legislation keeps the applicant on track with the history and spirit of the program. Bearing these in mind results in an application that is on target. Pay special attention to contents of the annual reports mandated in the legislation. Federal office heads make the reports to Congress, and are a way that elected officials know about program accomplishments. If you reference the above items, whether or not they are part of the instructions you will impress federal staff with your depth of the knowledge about the grant program. Work these items into the objectives section of the application

The definition section is also worthy of the attention because it provides parameters that are important in creating the project, such as age limits of the consumerpopulation.

The application instructions often specify a program model or criteria. These provide the "lines you draw within" and provide another checkpoint to determine if the program serves the purpose of advancing the agency mission.

The "lines you draw within" usually have four dimensions in the instructions. First, are the general purposes of the program. Second, are the program services provided and specific instructions on their nature. This includes the program population demographics and problem types, facilities, staff types, and specific methods. Third is the philosophy that underpins the service design. Ensure the narrative addresses the theoretical orientation of the grant maker such as *harm prevention, trauma responsive interventions, or anti-discrimination and harassment strategies.* Ensuring youth safety is often of interest. In addition, *positive youth development and a risk-protective factor rubric* are common paradigms mentioned. Take the time to learn the terms in italics so that the grant writer can integrate them in a meaningful way into the program design. The youth.gov website may have information about "special terms" listed in the application instructions. Last, get some ideas of appropriate qualitative and quantitative outcomes. Some of these might be the prevention of out of home placement, homeless youth reunited with their families, older youth establishing independent households, with the outcomes varying by the program area.

In thinking about service numbers, tie them to the grant amounts plus any required matching funds and any other financial or in kind, resources the agency will donate to the project. It is a mistake to make wild promises about service numbers for two reasons. First, grant reviewers will look to match the specific services you propose, their cost, and the numbers served and they will probably spot if the writer is over reaching. Second, if the government awards a grant the application is part of the agreement with the federal government stating what the organization will do and how many youths it will serve. If the number of youths served is substantially below plan this will be a problem when it comes time to submit program reports. Service projection numbers should be aggressive but realistic. Last, if the application proposes to serve too few youths the application will come off as inefficient. One approach is to decide on a cost per child served and then project service numbers based on this. Third are the general goals and purposes of the program. These provide some beginning orientation, but by this point, you and the reviewers probably know this information.

Chapter 15 -
The Other Big Money Winning Large Federal Grants

Criteria

The instructions for the content of the narrative appear in two different sections of the FOA. The first of these outlines the type of material to include in each of the sections. This description is somewhat generic and intended for many different types of federal grants. The second place the narrative instructions appear is in the criteria section of the FOA that lists the basis used to assign the points for each section of the applications. The criteria section of the FOA lists the maximum points earned for each section uses the same subheadings as the generic instructions, but lists the specific topics relevant for the grant that is the subject of the application. It is essential to organize the proposal according to the points awarded criteria. The content in each section of the narrative starts by referencing the criterion addressed. As needed the grant writer divides the criterion into subsections. Number each criterion according to its label in the FOA and number the subsections. Place a few lines of each FOA subsection text immediately before the response. For example, Criterion 1: Needs and Objectives. On the next line, write 1A. Need for the project. Then write the specific kinds of information requested in the criterion that addresses the need for the project. Start a new paragraph, label it 1B Project Objectives, and list the project objectives. Be mindful of completeness and responsiveness to the criteria as you review and edit the application. The narrative is the primary basis for evaluating the proposal, presuming it meets the minimum administrative requirements previously discussed.

The narrative begins with a table of contents that list the different sections of the application and corresponding page numbers. Next is an abstract that very briefly discusses the proposed project and the needs it addresses. It also lists the services proposed and the service population. List the organizational contact information on the top of the abstract page. The contact person is whom federal staff will call if there are questions about the application or if certain changes in the application are necessary prior to awarding a grant to the organization.

This section of the application describes the social problem the agency wants to address and the extent, nature, and dimensions of the problem.

First, write a qualitative description of the problem. For runaway and homeless youth, indicate the dimensions of the crisis they are experiencing - their need for shelter, and services needed to keep them off the streets. Indicate their risk of sexual exploitation while on the streets. Discuss their needs for medical care. For a community group home for adolescent sex offenders write about their own history of victimization, the diminishing probability of non-offending behavior as they grow older. Talk about the high number of potential future victims. Talk about the cost to the community of imprisoning them.

The data book referred to in chapter 14 prepares the writer with most of the statistical information required for this section. However, some of the data needed is grant specific and requires additional work. An effective response to this section requires a list of any aggregate data, about the population experiencing the problems, or having the characteristics the proposal will address. If the agency is already serving the population and have automated consumer records, provide a description of the consumers. Use census data for the geographic area involved, uniform crime code statistics, and service use information available from local governments and state reports and local school district data. For example, the state child welfare agency will usually have data on number of youths they are serving. However, this is not universally true. Create a state level child abuse report on the Kidscount software. If the state is not on the results page, the state is not reporting child abuse information to the Federal Government. This may mean that the data does not exist, or exists in a form that is difficult to use. Planning commission and other communityservice data is often useful.

An effective presentation of the data uses comparison data that illustrates that the data for the population that is the subject of the grant application indicates higher problem rates than for comparative populations. What constitutes the comparative population depends on the geographic area the agency will serve and the data that is available. If the agency is proposing a county or multi-county effort, use state level data for the comparison. If the agency proposes a statewide program, use national data for a comparison. As an example, the agency is proposing a program to increase the graduation rate at Any High School in Any City, in Any state For census type data (race, household type, [two parent, single parent, etc.,] child poverty rates, unemployment rates, median family income, home ownership rates, family size,) compare the census tract data from the tract in which the school is located, with city, county and/or statewide census data to document that

Any High School is located in a very low income area. Chances are the Any High School drop-out rates will be higher than county and state rates. One can make the same case for other schools in impoverished communities. However, it will not serve your purpose to make this last point in your application.

Sometimes comparing data from earlier and later years documents you case for support. That is to say that you make the case that the problem rate has increased sharply over time. At the end of 2013, in the aftermath of the Penn-State sexual abuse scandal, Pennsylvania enacted several new child abuse reporting laws. A result of this legislation was to sharply increase the number of child abuse reports made. A grant application to provide a program for abused youth in any of the jurisdictions in the Commonwealth could bolster their application by citing the sharp rise in child abuse reports. For example, in 2017 there were 47,485 child abuse report in Pennsylvania, compared to 27,182 reports in 2012, more than 20,000 more reports. Keep in mind the quote attributed to mark Twain, but not original to him "There are three types of lies, lies, damn lies and statistics. Taken a different way by 2018 the number of Pennsylvania child abuse reports was 44,063, 3,000+ fewer reports than in 2017. (Pennsylvania Department of Human Services 2019, 2016)

Discuss community services used by the target population and needed services that do not exist. Indicate that the proposed service will fill a service gap, should this be the case. If school district students have recently participated in drug use surveys or a problem survey, this information is generally helpful. Include relevant news stories. Letters from others in the community such as school counselors, police, etc. that can speak to the problem the agency is addressing, and/or the efficacy of the project.

Letters from politicians and others who give a general endorsement to the agency proposal, but do not have any substantial information to share are not productive to include for most reviewers. Experienced reviewers understand the letters are a constituent service. In this section, the grant writer also provides the needs assessment. It is quite common that the exact data is not available, and the organization provides derived estimates. For example, if the national runaway youth rate is a rate per 1,000 youth ages 12-18, multiply the national rate by the number of youth 12-18 in the project area. The application will score well, here, if the number of youths needing the service is high, and the write up can make the case that community problem indicator rates are substantially higher than state or county averages. If problem rates and the consumer population are low, the application has less of a chance of success as the same federal expenditure would likely assist many more youths in a needy high population density community. However, if the problem rate is low but the numbers are high due to the density of the living area, then focus on the numbers rather than the percentage of youth involved. If the need is low, but there are no services within 100 miles than make this point. Keep the grant request amount in line with the need. If the agency wants money to shelter runaways, and the maximum grant is $200,000, and the review of the report to congress, indicates that overall, grantees reached x number of runaways through y grants of z amount calculate the average number of youths served per grant dollar. If your proposed service number is within 25% of this average then request the maximum amount. However, if the number of runaways the application proposes to serve is half the average than request only half of the maximum. Sometimes the aim of the FOA is to assist rural youth, or indicates a certain proportion of the grant will go to rural areas. If so, smaller service numbers are fine.

Outcomes

Next in the application, state the program outcomes. These outcomes express what the agency hope the participants achieve. The outcomes are also part of the logic model that is in a later section of the application. In addition, the outcomes form the basis of the program evaluation.

Outcome evaluations are one of two types of program evaluation. Process evaluations seek to define the program offered in detail. This includes the theoretical underpinnings and the different components of the program, staff qualifications, the service setting, etc. If at some future time an agency wishes to establish that the program is an evidence-based model program, a careful process evaluation is necessary to document the program characteristics. For purposes of the grant application, a limited process evaluation takes the form of the program description.

In this section of the grant application however, the interest is in outcome evaluation. The goal of an outcome evaluation is to learn if the program works. What results do the youth achieve?

Outcomes are the changes in the behavior, status, knowledge, or circumstances of the population participating in the program. The outcomes are hopefully the result of the services provided. Although the outcome section is only the second major part of the grant request narrative, its basis is information that the applicant supplies later in the submission - the logic model. Outcomes are usually the last section of a logic model. A logic model is part of the federal grant applications for youth services. It depicts and summarizes the application. The logic model usually requires the applicant to specify the problem of interest, the objectives of the program, the services provided, (type and how much [a.k.a. the dosage]) the outputs (what the program accomplishes) and outcomes (what changes because of the outputs). Different federal departments and even programs in the same department use different forms of the logic model and applicants use the logic model listed in the FOA instructions. Think through what to write in the outcomes section of the application only after the grant writer has constructed the logic model. Consider the situation of a fictional John Urban High School.

Only 25% of 634 John Urban High School 11th grade students in 2014 achieved proficient or better scores on the Pennsylvania System of Student Assessment (PSSA). The school faces multiple challenges including insufficient funding due to the relatively low city real estate property values and the state funding formula, a high turnover of students in the school, and many students who come from poor families. Many things need to change to achieve the academic success of these students. The fictional grant program described is only one of many efforts needed.

Although each outcome is only a brief statement, the process of composing them is somewhat complex and an annotated example of fashioning an outcome follows. Well-written outcomes indicate: -

1) *A description of the population that is going to take part in the intervention.* This could be foster care youth, students, victims of sexual abuse etc.

2) *The number of participants that is going to be involved in the intervention.* This could be any number, the higher the number the better. To be of use in an outcome evaluation a minimum of 100 participants who take the pretest and posttest and participate in the prescribed dosage is preferable. Lower numbers suggest sampling bias to some scholars.

3) *The intervention is the program that the participants complete.* This could be a best practice such as FTT or a homegrown program, such as the athletic component of a residential program.

4) *The dosage is how much of the intervention is necessary to achieve the outcome.* This might be 60 days in foster care, 20 in home counseling sessions, or monthly medication monitoring visits with a psychiatrist.

5) *The measurement tool determines the change in the behavior, attitude etc. that is the object of the intervention.* This could be days of truancy, number of fistfights, or psychological test score results.

6) *The output is the score on the measurement tool.* This is the change achieved by the intervention. This could be fewer days of truancy fewer fist fights etc.

7) The outcome is the change in behavior, knowledge etc. This could be positive school attachment, or the development of social problem-solving skills.

The outcome example that follows is for a remedial math program aimed at improving student scores on the PSSA.

Outcome: Seventy percent of two hundred John Urban High School students completing at least 37 of the 41 instruction sessions of the University of Chicago School Mathematic Program in both the 9th and 10th grade will achieve or exceed grade level proficiency on the 11the grade administration of the PSSA and graduate to the 12th grade.

The outcome has the following parts: 70% proficient rate on PSSA (output part 1) of 200 (number of participants) John Urban students (description of population) completing at least 37 of the 41 instruction sessions in both the 9th and 10th grade (dosage) of the Chicago School, Mathematic Program (intervention) will achieve or exceed grade level proficiency (output part 2) on the 11th grade PSSA (measurement tool), and graduate to the 12th grade (outcome).

For the purpose of the logic model example, I assumed that the fictional federal grant program the school district applies for, is under the auspices of the federal department of education, and exists to fund curricula improvement in order to increase academic performance. John Urban High School in its application proposes collaborating with The What Works Clearinghouse (WWC) and using the Clearinghouse evaluated math curriculum (University of Chicago Mathematics Project Multiple Grades developed by I. Wirszup and K. Mchenry). It is not unusual for an applicant to work with a partner that has a special expertise to achieve the purpose of the grant.

A logic model for the grant application follows. Take note of the model's parts, and how they include the most important elements of the application. It lists the problem, the grant objective, the service site, service population, service numbers, services provided, dosage, output, and outcomes.

Problem: In 2014 75% of 635 11th grade John Urban High School students are not proficient in mathematics as measured by the PSSA.

Objective: John Urban High School students will become proficient in mathematics

Service: In 2015 and 2016 all students in 9th and 10th grade (service population) at the John Urban High School (service site) are taught using the University of Chicago School Mathematics Project Multiple Courses Curriculum instead of the current state and school district approved mathematics curricula (service provided) and attend 37 of 41 sessions provided each year (service dosage)

Output: 80% of those students who receive the full-service dosage in both grades will demonstrate proficient or greater in the PSSA in Mathematics in 2017

Outcome: The school promotes 70% of the students achieving proficiency or better scores on the 11th grade PSSA to 12th grade with a grade of at least C in mathematics

Note that in the output section above only students who complete both the 9th and 10th grade at the high school and then test in the 11th grade is in the output and outcome groups. In the John Urban High School between grades 9 and 11 there are 10% fewer students due to students dropping out of school each year. Also, the regular attender percent will drop because of the students who move in and out of the district and so only participate in the University of Chicago program for a limited time. So, the problem and service portions include the total number of students, but the output and outcome sections only include the percent of students who receive the full program dosage of two academic years. Also note that the outcome percent is 10% less than the output percentage. This difference allows for the students who drop out or leave the district between the time the school administers the PSSA and the end of the school year.

The outcome posits that the percent of proficient test results will improve after the students learn using a new math curriculum. This is a pre-post approach also called, a before and after approach.

This is a good evaluation plan. However, an evaluation design, which researchers reviewing an application would view more positively, is the comparison group approach to outcomes. This approach involves comparing the John Urban High School students that learn using the new University of Chicago curriculum, and a second group of high school students, at another high school that continued with the existing state curriculum. The challenge to using this kind of evaluation is finding a close enough comparison group where the characteristics of the students (race, English as a second language, poverty rate, similar scores during the 2012 test period, etc.) match. A second challenge is a finding a school district staff that is willing to track PSSA scores, drop-out rates, and student entrances and exits from the school over a three-year period. It is unlikely that a matched group would agree to serve as a comparison group, except if the second-high school and the John Urban High School are in the same school district, and the Superintendent supports the evaluation design.

The last approach, which is the research gold standard, is to divide the John Urban 9th and 10th grade students into two groups, one that participates in the new math curricula (the experimental group) and a group of students who are instructed using the state approved curricula for math (the control group) using random assignment to the experimental and control groups.

Although the outcome evaluation movement in federal grant making has picked up a lot of steam during the past two decades, grant makers often do not require academic rigor in evaluations for many grants involving youth service provision. The result is that the social service research effort is unsatisfactory when compared to medical and physical science study procedures. However, using a logic model which requires, a before and after, a comparison group design, or a control group design is an improvement over past evaluation practice.

A note of on program completion rates. Many of those participating in social service programs are poor. Income insecurity is often associated with housing loss because the parents cannot pay the rent. Program completion rates suffer because families move. Program completion for any program that does not provide for family housing stability in areas with a high poverty rate can be low. The easiest way to provide for housing stability is to link families with the community program(s) that provides rental assistance. This may require a case management service to link parents with rental assistance programs.

Approach

This is the single most important part of the narrative carrying the highest point value. The successful application presents a plan of services that meet grant maker requirements and reflects the applicant's knowledge about service delivery. It describes the characteristics of each program service, and the quantity provided. The applicant rather than the grant maker usually selects the service type, but this is not always the case. Sometimes the grantor will specify the intervention used. In addition, it is now more popular for grant makers to have applicants select an intervention from a list of evidence-based programs that the office issuing the FOA approves. If the applicant chooses an intervention not on the list then they bear the burden of presenting research evidence that substantiates the program is a best practice.

The federal g overnment provides support for child welfare organizations to operate shelter programs for runaway and homeless youth. The funding maximum of $200,000 per year, while generous, make this program difficult to operate financially unless the grantee uses a host home model, or a group home model includes the provision of emergency shelter for abused and neglected children in addition to services for the runaway and homeless youth. Another option is some other complimentary function that is a good match for the federal runaway program and at the same time supplies additional income.

The Administration for Children and Families of the Department of Health and Human Services administers the Runaway Youth Act Basic

Center Program. The FOA provides a very detailed description of the program components and the theoretical underpinnings used in the application in its 2015 FOA. A portion of the FOA follows: (Administration for Children, Youth and Families, 2015)

"In reviewing the approach, reviewers will provide appropriate scores to the extent applicants have successfully considered the Comprehensive Youth Centered Service Model in their project plan:

I: Access to shelter, gateway services, and assessment (0-20 pts.)

Established a logical outreach strategy that will attract and engage runaway, homeless, and street youth to the Basic Center Program services.

Discussed the proposed screening and assessing tools used to effectively gather information during the intake process to assess each youth's situation and determine service prioritization.

Explained a reasonable strategy to provide gateway services to run away, homeless, and street youth.

II. Coordinated case management, follow-up/aftercare services, and continuum service linkages (0-20 pts.)

Outlined a clear and acceptable project plan that includes the successful coordination of intensive case management for youth and a clear strategy for helping youth establish permanency.

The approach to coordinate services, and how the working relationships will enhance the services the homeless youth population will receive to support the BCP project.

Detailed procedures to effectively provide follow up/aftercare services to youth who receive shelter services or are provided alternative living arrangements.

Considered the statutory authority, § 311(a) (1) of the Runaway and Homeless Youth Act, 42 U.S.C.§ 5711(a) (1), throughout the proposed operational plans of the BCP project.

Includes a sound positive youth development approach, trauma informed care intervention, and an evidence-informed approach in the proposed BCP project that promotes social and emotional well-being of service delivery.

Demonstrated an understanding of the need to provide inclusive culturally competent services to run away, homeless, and street youth, and explained procedures to prevent harassment of any kind.

Illustrated a plan for continuous quality improvement that reflects a clear understanding of the required performance evaluation plan".

(Administration for Children, Youth and Families, 2015)

The services addressed in this FOA are highly specified, as are the important philosophical underpinnings of program service provision. This is not always the case in the approach section of an FOA, and sometimes it is incumbent on the applicant to select the specific service provided. As previously stated sometimes the applicant selects from among a list of evidence- based services maintained by a federal agency. This is often the case with Substance Abuse and Mental Health Service Administration Grants (SAMSHA) grants for drug prevention efforts among teenagers.

The tact of the Administration of Children and Families (ACF) in this section is to say that they have a uniform tried and true model that the applicant is required to use, because two of ACF's goals are to maintain model fidelity among the approximately 300-400 runaway programs that are funded nationally, and to implement a best practices model. The applicant has or gains expertiseabout key concepts listed by the grant maker. For this FOA, applicants know what positive youth development, trauma informed care interventions, and cultural competency mean, and how to implement them within a shelter or host home.

Each applicant decides about the service site type. Will it be a host home model, a shelter, or through arrangements with an existing agency? A host home design uses several families that provide shelter in their homes.

The grant writer describes each part of the service approach in enough detail so that the reader can envision program start-up and operations. For example, if the plan is to provide a group home shelter the applicant needs to discuss the number and types of rooms: bedrooms, counseling offices, eating areas etc. The applicant needs to demonstrate that youth can get to the shelter by public transportation, if possible. If there is no public transportation, describe how they will get to the shelter. The applicant needs to depict the methods to supply personal care items and bed linens to the residents. The grant writer describes the youth orientation and discipline procedures, the shelter staffing pattern, services offerings and state licenses the agency has or will acquire.

In writing this section emphasize the organization's experience in working with the population that is the subject of the application. Emphasize years of experience, types of service provided, and number of youths served. If the agency is a previous grantee, state this. Highlight the program's ability to assist consumers in achieving outcomes, and state actual outcomes currently achieved. The evaluation of experience differs by FOA. In some FOA's the federal agency issuing the FOA awards points for experience. If the agency is in a geographic area, where another PCWA has received the grant applied for, the experienced PCWA will probably receive these points, and the new applicant may be at a disadvantage.

One of the tactics an applicant can use if the agency is a new comer is to demonstrate the need exceeds the current grantee's capacity, or the application proposes to serve a different part of the city. If this is not the case, propose to serve a specialized population that is a priority of the grantor such as GLBTQ youth. Before applying read the grant application of the current grantee. If the program of the present grantee is terrible, demonstrate this by references to media accounts, state inspection reports, Federal Program Performance reviews, letters from community agencies and former clients. If the federal regional office is unhappy with the current grantee performance, they may be interested in making a switch. Do not engage in slanderous behavior.

If the agency is proposing a new program give a clear start-up plan indicating how close to the grant start-date services will begin. Also, in the budget section, do not charge for youth service costs during the start-up period. In the start-up plan, include a timeline chart for obtaining the necessary program and health and safety licenses, and hiring the staff.

Discuss the organization's financial management capability. Include a discussion of key written policies, especially those aimed at fiscal control. Briefly discuss the accounting system, how often the agency will issue financial statements. Indicate if the agency has an annual external audit; discuss the financial and consumer data backup system, and the emergency plan for continuing financial operation in the event of a disaster. Similarly, outline a crisis operational plan if the agency loses use of facilities after a predicament. Indicate the use of passwords, locked consumer file cabinets, and information releases, to manage consumer confidentiality.

Discuss other integral community PCWAs the agency works with and any formal arrangements with them regarding the youth served through the grant. Indicate their role in implementing the grant and discuss their skills, experience, and competencies to fulfill these roles. If the agency is entering into a third-party agreement to provide a service, include a signed copy as part of the application. In a RYA grant application this could involve the grantee providing all of the services and a foster care agency providing the housing.

Discuss the staffing plan including the types, numbers, and function of each staff. If the agency is proposing a residential program, include a staff schedule. Include provision for an on-call service so youth can access a staff member 24 hours if the agency is proposing a host home program. Develop mini job descriptions for the program director, supervisor, and direct service PCWA positions. Also, include the resumes of representative present staff for these positions. Assure all staff will be participating in fingerprinting, criminal, child abuse record verification, and a drug screening. A favorable reaction results if experienced incumbents fill the director and supervisor positions.

Grant makers realize that some of the staff will be new hires but if the agency can utilize an experienced direct service person or two all the better. Discuss staff supervision in terms of frequency and the standard meeting agenda. Develop or document the existing staff-training plan. The training plan needs to focus mainly on the intervention modalities, theories, and standards that are important parts of the grant program. However, it is also important to emphasize staff safety training. Discuss the topics and the background of the trainers. Make at least brief mention of the personnel policies. If they already cover some of the federal polices the organization will need to conform with, indicate this as space allows (EEOC, ADA, sexual harassment, drug free workplace, and smoke free workplace).

Put together a plan to continue services in the event that the agency does not receive a second grant and cannot procure continuation funding. One way to handle this is talk about an orderly program shutdown assuring that staff gets consumers into other programs.

Budget

The basic center grant budgets are for operating purposes. Include only the first-year budget. In addition to the competitive year budget materials in each of the two non-competitive years of the three-year cycle, grantees submit a budget and a brief narrative. In other types of federal grants, the agency submits budgets for each grant year at the time they submit the applications.

One of the strategic issues in completing the application is to decide what to do because the maximum federal funds fall substantially short of the project costs. The maximum income from the Runaway and Homeless Youth Basic Center Grant has been $222,000 ($200,000 federal dollars and $22,000 matching) for many years. If the PCWA has a foster care program, the host home model is the simplest to provide. The easiest implementation strategy is for a number of foster families to commit to house an additional child or two on a short-term basis. The expense structure will be close to the foster care program, plus expenditures for services not normally rendered with foster children. Depending on the current service design, this includes youth and family counseling, operating a 24-hour phone service, and establishing an outreach program component. The agency will provide service as needed, serving more than the average calculated on some nights and less on other nights. For example, the agency applies for a grant of $200,000 and supply $22,000 in matching funds. The costs for foster care payments, counseling, a 24- hour hotline, and an outreach counselor are $85 a day. $222,000 divided by $85 equals 2612 days of care. 2612 days of care divided by 365, (the number of days in the year) equals service to approximately seven runaway and homeless youth a night. These calculations do not include a vacancy rate.

In a group home model, the challenge is to pay for the costs not covered by the basic center grant. One possible scenario is that several counties are interested in purchasing emergency shelter services. Three counties establish purchase of service contracts with the agency. These agency contracts cover expenses for the adolescents receiving emergency shelter services rather than runaway and homeless youth services. The plan is for the shelter to have a 12-bed capacity. Write the budget narrative and the budget detail to indicate that on average, the number of these 12 beds devoted to the youth who is a runaway or homeless child is in the same proportion as the federal grant, including the match funds to the overall budgeted expenses for the program. This is equal to an average of "x" beds, a night, of the total twelve-bed shelter capacity. The exact number housed on any given night depends on the number of runaways coming into the shelter. The math is similar to the above example. Supposing the total operating expenses for a 12-bed group home is $650,000. Dividing the total by 12 beds equals $54,167 per bed per year. $54,167 divided by 365 days a year equals a per diem cost of $148.00 a day. Allowing for a 15% vacancy rate the per diem rate is $170.00. This is the rate charged to the three counties for emergency services. For the grant divide $222,000 by $170 to calculate the number of bed nights per year which is 1,305. Divide by 365 days. The result is that the agency plans to shelter between three and four runaway youth per night.

The percent of full-time staff applied to the grant application budget, along with the other operating expenses, decreases each year, because staff salaries and supply cost increase annually but the $200,000 upper grant limit does not increase. A fiscal disadvantage to providing a basic center program, in a group home setting, is that in residential setting costs do not fluctuate substantially with occupancy rates. A second concern is that government grants and GCWA contract amounts do not always increase over time, and the gap between public income and program expenses can grow and you need to garner charitable contributions or use organizational reserve funds to make up the difference.

The budget detail lists the costs within predetermined categories listed in the grant application instructions. A general point that is applicable to all budget line items is to complete the budget narrative for all expenses listed in the budget detail. If it becomes necessary to move more than ten percent of funds from one budget category to another category, during any annual budget period, the usual procedure is to make a written request to the grantor federal fiscal officer (whose name will be in the grant award materials). However, check the terms of your grant award notice to see if this is applicable.

The budget package for the application has three components :1) the SF424 A-B that summarizes the budget information, 2) a line by line columnar spreadsheet style budget for the first year of operation, and 3) a budget narrative offering further comments on cost and cost determination. Applicants cannot use grant funds for building purchases or construction projects. Prior to making, an award ACF staff reviews budgets. They may contact applicants and make the award contingent on the applicant submitting a new budget detail and narrative, either to modify an expense amount or supply additional information.

The applicant decides on the format for items 2 and 3 above. For the budget detail pages, the eight-column set up for the personnel category listed below can be useful:

The details of a fictitious example follow. Taylor Doe is a shelter counselor who earns $31,132 per annum and spends 1/3 of the workweek helping runaway and homeless youth and 2/3 of the workweek helping emergency shelter youth. Write Taylor's name in column 1 and list the job title; counselor, in column 2. The counselor job title matches the written abbreviated job description title in the narrative. List the total annual salary in column 3. The salary amount is within the salary range for the counselor position listed in the abbreviated job description in the narrative as well as the PCWA personnel policies. The amount includes the cost of any cost of living or merit salary increase.

Taylor's salary cost calculation is the proportional cost for each of the years involved if the PCWA fiscal year differs from the federal fiscal year. In this example, presume the PCWA is on a calendar fiscal year. The federal fiscal year is October 1 – September 30. The grant application due date is May 30' 2018 and the grant project start date is October 1, 2018. The PCWA salary increase effective date is July 1, of every year. On June 30, 2018, Taylor's annual salary is $30,000 per year. On July 1, 2018, a 3% cost of living increase takes effect for all employees. Taylor's salary increases to $30,900 for the July 1, 2018 – June 30, 2019 period. Taylor's FTE per annum rate of pay is $30,900 between October 1, 2018 and June 30, 2019. On July 1, 2019, another 3% cost of living increase takes effect for all employees. Taylor's new salary is $31,827. The FTE grant cost (column 3 above) is 75% of $30,900 (for the nine months October 1, 2018 - June 30, 2019 period) plus 25% of $31,827 (for the July 1, 2019 - September 30, 2019 period) or $31,132.

In column 4 indicate that Taylor spends a third of the time working in the runaway and homeless shelter. Column 5 indicates his salary dollars allocated to the grant work ($31,132 x 33.3%= $10,367). Split the $10,367 between column 5 (90% of the total) and column 6 (10% of the total). This allocation is discretionary but the total of all expenses for the entire grant listed under the federal column (column 5) cannot exceed the total federal maximum. Again, the Federal agency lists the total federal funding maximum in the FOA. Likewise, the total of all grant expenses in column 6 must equal to or be greater than the grant match requirement. This is not to say that applicants cannot supply a higher match than the FOA require. To the contrary, this is a positive aspect to the application. The amount in column 7 is $0 (the field should not be blank) and column 8 is the total of columns 5, 6, and 7 $10,367. Also, the federal matching percentage varies according to the issuing agency.

Table 15-1 Example of a Personnel Category Budget Presentation Format For a Runaway and Homeless Youth Basic Center Grant							
1	2	3	4	5	6	7	8
Emp-loyee Name	Posit-ion Title	FTE Cost	% of FTE Charg-ed	Feder-al Grant Funds	Match-Ing Funds	Non-Grant Funds	Total Funds
Taylor Doe	Coun-selor	$31,132	33%	$9,338	$1,038	$0	$10,376

Time sheets on which staff records the portion of the time spent in each agency program every workday serve as backup for personnel cost allocations. Assure time sheets are consistent, accurate, and will be easy to locate in order to accommodate the auditor's sampling parameters. Add columns 5, 6 and 7, to calculate column 8. The allocation of column 8 between columns 5 and 6 is at the applicant's discretion but ifa large amount of federal or match funds supports a certain expense providean explanation in the budget justification. For example, if a foundation is interested in feeding children but does not fund staff. The designated use of matching funds results in one or more of the other budget categories to be different than the 90%, 10% division discussed above. To stick with the 90%, 10% plan for the most part, make the federal expenditure larger in a single budget category. The application lists their matching fund gift in the supply category under food.

The amount in column 7 is always zero. Include the column to make very clear that the only funds applied to the grant program are the amount listed in the grant budget (columns 5+6). In case of a federal audit of the grant the PCWA will want to limit the scope of the audit to the funds provided in the grant program and not have the auditor claim that the shelter income and expense related to the emergency shelter portion, is also subject to audit. Of course, in the case of a state child welfare audit of the shelter all the nonfederal monies are subject to the audit.

Another issue is the management of administrative costs with two methods available. The first is to establish an indirect cost rate agreement with the federal government. In this arrangement, the administrative percentage charged to the project is a fixed percent representing the overall level of administrative staff effort and other non-program expenses. Once established the indirect cost rate applies to all federal grants. Establishing a fixed cost agreement allows for simpler budgeting and less work in preparing the grant. On the other hand, if the expenses associated with operating grant programs are higher than the agency non-grant programs, due to reporting requirements etc. not having the fixed cost agreement allows for charging the true cost of administration. Another disadvantage to establishing an indirect cost rate is it is very time consuming.

When there is no fixed administrative rate, unless the administrative staff spends more or less time on the grant project as compared with the time, they spend on any other agency program; a proportional allocation method determines the amount of the salary and benefits of these staff to charge to the grant project. The allocation of salary and benefits for the administrative staff differs from the allocation for direct service staff in that the direct service staff customarily works is one or two programs. For direct service staff work who work in more than one program divide their compensation costs between the programs in proportion to the amount of time they work in each program. Assure their time sheets document the proportions. In comparison, the administrative staff works in all the agency programs. Administrative staff includes upper management, accounting staff, information technology, human resources and maintenance staff. Calculate the amount of administrative staff compensation listed in the grant by dividing the federal program cost by the total agency expenses, and then multiplying each administrative staff member's compensation by the resulting percentage. For example, a junior accountant earns $35,000 a year. The grant amount is $250,000. The total agency operating expenses for a year are $5,000,000. The grant expenses are 5% of the total agency expenses. Allocate Five percent of the junior accountant's earnings, ($1,750) to the grant budget. If the agency has, a well-paid executive staff be aware that there are limits to federal participation in executive compensation costs. In 2015, this was $188,000. If the PCWA president earns $225,000, a year the compensation cost basis chargeable to the grant is only $188,000, $37,000 less than the actual salary. As with the junior accountant position discussed above the presumption is that the total grant expenses are 5% of the overall agency expenses. Thirty-seven thousand dollars multiplied by 5% equals $1,850 less than the actual compensation cost that the PCWA cannot charge as a grant expense. Again, accurate time sheets showing the daily hours worked in each of the programs for administrative staff are the backup for the salary expense.

A columnar presentation format for the benefit category of the budget details is:

Table 15-2 Example of a Benefit Category Budget Presentation for a Runaway and Homeless Youth Basic Center Program						
Columns						
1	2	3	4	5	6	7
Benefit Name	Cost Calculation	% Basic Center Costs	Federal Funds	Matching Funds	Non-grant Funds	Total Funds
Employer Share Social Security	6.2% x $400,000 Payroll = $24,800	33%	$7,432	$826	$0	$8,258

In column 1 list the benefit items including medical, dental, and vision insurance, payroll taxes, EAP, life and disability insurance each on a separate line item and briefly show the math for the entire line item (in this case FICA) in column 2. Unlike the personnel costs, the calculation for benefits is for the entire staff that works in the program and receives the benefit. In column three indicate the percentage of the total benefit attributable to the grant program. In column four show the result of multiplying column 2 by column 3 and then allocate 90% of this sum to column 4 and 10 % to column 5. Again, column 6 is always zero Column 7 is the total of columns 4, 5, and 6. Space constraints will limit the ability to show all the information for many expenses. In the FICA example use for the shelter the assumption is that the total compensation for the direct service staff is $400,000 and that none of these employees earn more than the maximum taxable amount (the first $127,000 of salary in 2017).

Equipment For items that cost $5,000 or more (the federal depreciation threshold as of 2015) list only the annual amount depreciable during the budget year.

To purchase a van to transport youth that costs $30,000 and has a five-year depreciation period than list $6,000 minus the salvage value apportionment for the budget year. If the grant ends before the depreciation period than the PCWA finances the remaining cost not covered by the grant. In addition, in these situations the federal fiscal staff and the PCWA decide for the disposition of the item. These can include transferring the item to another grantee, or having the item transferred to the PCWA for program use. To avoid uncertainty with expensive equipment, consider a lease.

Travel The PCWA list the costs for grant required travel expenses, to meetings convened by the granting agency here. Also, list out of state meeting and conference attendance here. Do not list though any travel within the state. List travel expenses for trips within the state in the "other" budget section. List costs for mileage, food, and lodging. Be prepared for questions from federal staff when the per diem conference expenses exceed federal limits. Be prepared to reduce expenses here to get final grant approval. Use the following URL for the federal lodging and meal allowances. https://www.gsa.gov/travel/plan-book/per-diem-rates

Supplies List supplies needed for the program. List any piece of furniture that costs less than the depreciation limit in the equipment category. Keep the needs and behaviors of the consumer population in mind in setting budget numbers. In a short-term shelter for teenager's budget generously due to having many youths in residence over a year's time and because many teenagers are a bit rough on things. Breakage will be on the high side. Also, include here cleaning supplies, other building, and ground supplies. List the over the counter and prescription medications for residents here as well. Costs could be high if a portion of the consumer population has behavioral health issues, requiring psychopharmacology interventions. List the recreational supplies such as board games, weight sets, a ping-pong table, etc. Budget for clothing and personal needs. Again, budget liberally with the runaway and homeless population as they sometimes do not bring much clothing or their clothing is not seasonally appropriate (no winter coat, etc.). In situation in which the parents will quickly bring clothing to the shelter, costs will naturally be lower.

The biggest expense in this category for private child welfare residential programs will be food, although substantial savings occur if the local food bank will help. Often food banks will charge the agency a low per pound fee. The agency staff picks up the food. The major disadvantage is the limited selection that the foodbank has available. In addition, if staff makes civic and business organizations aware that the agency is interested in getting food that is uneaten at an event, the agency can get other food donations. However, because the receipt of this food will be irregular, and the staff need to plan for extra food storage space and devote time to receiving the donation, and working with the consumers to get the food stored the residential staff workload increases.

Contractual List any service provided for which a contract exists in this section. Do not list any items where the purchase is on, an irregular item-by-item basis. Some items to include here are payroll services, a share of the annual organizational audit, or the total cost of a program audit, if there is not an organization wide audit. See the FOA instructions regarding what the audit requirement is. It varies by the amount of federal funds the organization receives. If the agency has service contracts for office equipment repair and maintenance, extermination service, medical or psychiatric evaluation of consumers, legal fees, and Information technology consulting services list them here. In addition, for these services as well as for significant equipment purchases, bid them out. Discuss what the agency does in this area in the budget narrative. For example, some organizations bid out their audit services once every five years. On a different unrelated subject, if the agency does not bid out capital purchases or contracted services and you make the purchase from a BOD member or other disqualified person than the agency is at risk of sanctions if the IRS conducts an audit or someone reports the transaction to the IRS.

Construction The allow ability of construction varies by federal grant. Do not spend federal grant funds for construction costs in the runaway and homeless youth program. It is an allowable expenditure of federal Funds in some Housing and Urban Development programs, and certain other grant programs. Costs can include architectural fees, site acquisition, renovation, and construction. Carefully check grant requirements associated with federal construction funds. Typically, they involve following Bacon-Davis wage payment guidelines, which require paying union scale to workers, environmental impact studies, historical site clearance, and lead-free paint certification as well as certification that the grantee will use the property for its intended purpose over a fixed number of years. Consulting with a construction management company is useful to assure the agency does not exclude important costs. Unless a person on the staff or BOD has construction, expertise includes under personnel the cost of a construction manager who assures renovations meets the building code specifications, and conforms to the contract with the construction company.

Other List utility costs here as well as advertising related to staff recruitment. List the communication costs including postage and shipping, telephone, and monthly internet service fees. In addition, include staff training registration fees, but not costs for out of state grantor meetings. Include recreational activity fees for youth activities – movies, cultural events. Etc.,

Matching Funds

List the federal amount requested, and the matching funds required. List the source(s) and amount of matching funds. If you use private sources, include a signed letter from the source(s) on the donor's stationary which has a statement of commitment of the funds. If the agency is using state or local government funds likewise include a commitment letter. The Federal government does not permit other federal funds as federal grant matching funds. If the GCWA providing the match uses state or local government funds, the portion of these funds that originate from the federal government are not eligible for use. For example, a state GCWA agrees to provide the PCWA with $50,000 to establish a family intervention program aimed at preventing out of home placements. You are submitting a grant application to the federal Government for the rest of the funds needed for the program. The $50,000 of the state funds is from the state's allocation of federal IVE dollars that funds room and board costs for children in foster care. Your state has a federal waiver to use a portion of their IVE monies to establish the kind of program you propose. The $50,000 is not eligible to use as matching funds because IVE is a federal entitlement program with no required state match. If the state provides IVB funds 25% of the $50,000 is eligible to use as matching funds, because the states provide a 25% match to receive federal IVB funds and the purpose of the project aligns with one of the purposes of the IVB program. That is, the agency can use either IVE or IVB monies to fund the project but the agency can only use $12,500 of the IVB monies for federal grant matching purposes.

Budget Justification Statement

What follows are detailed instructions on the preparation of a budget justification statement that is responsive to the general requirements for a federal grant.

Personnel Discuss how salary ranges are set such as an organizational salary study, use of a Society of Human Resources study, or reviewing on line job sites. Discuss the process for deciding on the total amount authorized for annual salary increases such as BOD approval, approval as part of the annual budgeting process, etc. What factors determine the distribution of raise money? Is a merit or across the board method used to determine? For salaries paid for from federal grant funds, do not use a bonus system.

List each position using the same job titles used in the budget detail. For each position, write a few words about the duties. Counselor – counsel's youth and families. For accounting staff – participates in the preparation of accounting statements.

Fringe Benefits These could include health, dental, vision, life, and long-term disability insurance, retirement, worker's compensation insurance, and unemployment insurance. Use the same titling as in the budget detail. State the classification of employee that is eligible for the benefit (full-time, part-time or all). Describe what the benefit supplies. Indicate any employee copay (which the grant budget does not cover) and how you estimate the agency costs. For example, write "the applicant provides health benefits to all full-time staff upon hire (no waiting period). The health benefit is a choice between an HMO and PPO plan. The plan covers hospital and outpatient costs as well as testing. The health care company determines rates based on the employee's age, the plan classification (individual, married or domestic partner, and family) and the plan chosen. There is an employee premium copay and employee plan deductibles. The employer share of premium ranges for each employee ranges from $12,000 to $20,000 annually". Post costs for program staff in proportion to the percent of time worked in the program. Use this apportionment, as well for the other fringe benefits.

Travel Enumerate the costs associated with conferences and meetings required by the grantor. A few meeting details are in the FOA. List the number of attendees and position of each. List each item and indicate the math. For example, lodging for two staff for three nights at $200.00 per night. Do the same for food, registration fees, and mileage. Indicate if the agency is using General Service Administration rates, or actual rate quotes. Discuss any special circumstances that are relevant to high costs.

Equipment Discuss tangible items that cost more than the depreciation schedule floor. Again, the federal depreciation limit is items costing $5,000 or more, and state depreciation levels vary by state. Use the individual cost of each item. If the agency plans to pay $6,000 for six computers list them under supplies because they cost $1,000 each. If the state depreciation schedule is $1,000, discuss the purchase here. If the agency buys a $10,000 copier that has a five-year useful life list a $2,000 expense for each grant year. If the agency gets a three-year grant, but no continuation money than 2 years of the cost of the copier are unfunded. In these kinds of situations, consider a lease. Briefly summarize the competitive bidding process stating the group requesting and reviewing bids, number of bids received, and the decision-making criteria such as low-price bid, best value, bid etc.

Supplies Tabulate the expenses for the many different types of supplies. It makes for a more organized presentation if the application divides the supply items into categories for the budget justification explanation.

Office supplies - pens, paper, staplers, printer ink

> - Small furniture and equipment - Linens, dishes, and small kitchen appliances
> - Building and grounds supplies - cleaning supplies and minor facility repair supplies.
> - Medical supplies - first aid kits, prescriptions and over the counter medication
> - Recreation Supplies - supplies for crafts, computer games, and sporting equipment.

Food - Show the math multiplying the average number of consumers per night, in residence, multiplied by the cost of three meals a day and snacks, multiplied by 365.

Costs for an educational day program and school supplies (i.e., notebooks, pens, folders) Also, include meal and snack cost for day or out-client programs. Subscriptions and publications expenses pay for subscriptions to professional journals and subscriptions for magazines for consumers.

Contractual Include payroll services, the proportional costs of an agency wide audit, or the total cost of a program audit. The information consulting line item includes the cost of a computer-consulting firm that helps the IT staff maintain the agency's computer equipment. Enumerate other incidental contracts such as a contract for cleaning services.

Construction If the agency is writing for a federal grant for capital acquisition chances are you will have supplied a lot of the relevant information in the grant narrative. Discuss the due diligence. In addition, with a large building project, a BOD approved business plan is a good idea. Focus on the financial aspects of the project. Discuss both the initial construction costs and the plan for income to operate the building after it opens. Discuss handicapped accessible features of the building. Indicate Leadership in Energy and Environmental Design (LEED) rating category. If the agency will not seek LEED certification, discuss any environment friendly features of the building such as solar heating. Talk about the planned maintenance as this informs the reader of the intent to protect the initial investment. Highlight special safety features. This might include the installation or a sprinkler system, and hard-wired smoke detector. When considering a purchase discuss comparable recent sale prices. Discuss the basis of renovation costs. Discuss financing such as bank mortgage loans.

Other Include rent for a PCWA owned building at fair market value, for the class of real estate involved (A, B, or C). The amount to budget is the number of square feet in the office multiplied by the square foot cost. Keeps a current letter from a realtor estimating the fair market square foot rental cost on file. Again, in the calculations indicate the share of rental costs charged to the grant. This may be 100% if the space you use it only for grant related purposes. Also, discuss the utility costs: electricity, gas, cable, water, and heat. Record vehicle costs; including, gas, insurance, and repairs. Base repair expenses on experience, required maintenance (from the owner's manual) as well as a repair estimate.

Discuss the professional, liability and property insurance coverage. List the policy coverage limits. Telephone costs include operating costs; any lease payments as well as, the monthly bill. Costs for data communications include a monthly expense for Internet service. Postage includes the mailing of correspondence and reports. Recreational activities include the cost of admission for youth to attend movies, bowling, cultural events, and other recreational outings. Other expenses are for the cost of clothing, personal items, specialized items required for school or athletics, etc.

The Application Review Process

The application review process has four parts: validation, administrative review, competitive peer review, and staff review. Validation confirms that the uploading of the application to grants.gov is successful. Reasons for rejection include viruses in files and improperly prepared files. The administrative review involves confirming that the application is prepared in conformance with the instructions in terms of its length, format, order, funding request limit, required attachments, and other administrative requirements. If the grantor agency rejects an application at this level, they notify the applicant of the reason. Federal staff does not pass along disqualified applications for further review.

The federal government sometimes subcontracts out the peer review process. The company recruits' people familiar with the field, to read and score the application, in accord with the criteria listed in the application, using the point award system in the criterion section of the FOA. Reviewers who have a general knowledge of the youth service system participate, and there is some variation in their knowledge and familiarity with program operations. The panels consist of a minimum of three readers and a chair. The chair is sometimes a federal staff member and sometimes a panel member. Reviewers meet as a group at the beginning of the review process, and receive their instructions. Sometimes this meeting emphasizes certain points to consider in the review and reveals any anticipated problems. Each reviewer then reads and scores each application alone. The number of applications reviewed varies a bit depending on the number of applications and the number of reviewers recruited. It is common for each panel to review between five and eight applications. Some of the reviewers work at applicant agencies. These people do not review applications from the state in which they work.

The federal government uses two basic grant money allocation strategies. The first is the state allocation method where the GCWA divides the total money available nationally for a grant program among the states using specified criteria. The criteria often are the share of the nation's children in the state, and the state poverty rate or median income compared to the other states. In this case, each state has a specific allocation and separate panels for each state to review the grant applications. When there are many applications, there could be multiple panels for a state. The second method is the national allocation situation. Here all applications compete against all of the others and there is one national pool of grant funds. The degree to which a reviewer on a panel is a tough or easy grader is the luck of the draw, and may or may not affect the outcome. A person who is tough on all the applications does not affect the state allocation process unless there are several panels for each state. Sometimes a reviewer evaluates an application harshly giving it an unreasonably low score. It has occurred that a grantee that has a very positive reputation receives a low score and loses their grant. The fourth, and determining part of the process, is the federal staff review. It takes the peer review ratings into account, but uses other criteria as well to make awards. These criteria include geographic redistribution of the awards that can occur if there are not enough meritorious applications for a state and there is a desire to move that money to another state. In addition, staff may give preference to high poverty areas where few or no programs exists. Federal staff also consider past grantee performance when there is a new round of competition. Occasionally highly scored applications do not receive an award due to a political decision to fund a poorly rated application.

Post Award Information

Applications with proprietary information redacted are available to those requesting them under the Freedom of Information act. Grantees must not discriminate against anyone because of race, color, national origin, disability, age, sex, or religion. Grantees must take reasonable steps to provide meaningful services to people with limited English proficiency. Use no grant funds for any program of distribution of sterile needles or syringes for the hypodermic injection of any illegal drug. All Administration of Children and Families grantees submit an emergency preparedness plan (see policy chapter). Grantees agree to standards of confidentially regarding consumer information. Grantees make periodic program and financial reports in a format prescribed by the grantor agency. Staff compensation may not exceed federal guidelines for grantees or employees of subcontractors. An inventory records all equipment and residual supplies valued at more than $5,000.

Real property acquired with any federal Grant Funds is also reportable. Staff, youth, and visitors may not smoke cigarettes on the grounds of a grantee. Staff may not use drugs or appear at work
under the influence of drugs.

Chapter 16 Private Fundraising

Fundraising Averages

Human Services organizations (HSOs)—food banks, homeless shelters, youth services, sports organizations, family and legal services—are the organizations that many people think of when they think about the nonprofit sector. In 2014, HSOs constituted the largest percentage of all public charities (35.5 percent), but they received 11.7 percent of all charitable contributions "
(Giving USA, 2016)

The methodology of a comparison of 341 IRS classified children and youth agencies (p30) with income between \$10 and \$50 million involved entering each agency's audit data into the Profit Cents software program to identify financial ratios commonly used to evaluate business success. The appraisal found that the agencies were largely government supported through purchase of service contracts, (38.67%) and federal, state, and local grants, (47.61%). Philanthropy accounted for 8.54% of the total income. (Sage Works, 2015)

The Nonprofit Research Collaborative has been involved in fundraising research for many years. The respondents to their survey include organizations from all parts of the not for profit sector. A review of their body of work suggests that a good fundraising plan, sufficient staff, BOD participation, and the use of a variety of techniques are associated with meeting fundraising goals. There were 1200 responses to their winter 2015 poll. The participants are self-selected. Their study indicates that having recovered from the great recession (2008), 63% of the respondents raised more money than in 2013. Seventy-six percent met their fundraising goals, with the number of respondents who reach their goal increasing each year beginning in 2010. The larger the agency budget, the higher the rate of these organizations meeting their goals. Over 80% of the respondents used the following techniques to raise funds which are listed in order of their use, highest to lowest - major gifts, BOD giving, foundation grants, corporate giving, direct mail, online giving, special events, and email requests (Nonprofit Research Alliance, 2015) .

The Urban Institute income data on 4496 private child welfare organizations classified by the Internal Revenue Service as Children and Youth, Foster Care, Homes for Children and Adolescents, and Adoption agencies indicates that event income is 2% or less of total income among all agency income types (Urban Institute, 2015) .

The Role of Private Development

Each president and BOD assess, his or her organization's private fundraising potential. BOD members often feel strongly about private fundraising efforts, as they believe that decreases in government support is always a risk, and private fundraising is a primary duty of a director. Although the yield is relatively small, the 10% raised privately is often necessary to provide the difference between total service costs and what the government will pay. There are exceptions, and some PCWAs, Covenant House being one, have done very well in private philanthropy. It is too soon to judge the impact of The Tax Cuts and Jobs Act of 2017 on charitable giving. High income individuals still itemize deductions, however Fidelity estimates that the number of households that itemized their deductions in 2018 was less than half the number that did so in 2017. This involves 21 million tax returns. (Fidelity Charitable, 2019). The implications of this are that middle-class taxpayers whose charitable giving is predicated on the federal tax deduction will perhaps be less motivated to make charitable contributions, but higher earners will not. My own experience is that high worth individuals contribute many more dollars than middle income people, although there are exceptions to this. Perhaps Covenant House could be an exception.

The Development Effort

If the agency were raising less than 10% of its budget privately consider how impactful it would be if the agency were able to raise significant private dollars. In deciding on initiating a program to raise more dollars think about the following questions. What important things would the agency do if the agency receives more gifts that are private? Does the president, large donors, and selected BOD members have the will and time to upgrade the board to do private solicitation? Do the funds exist to invest in a development program? Are the BOD and staff leadership committed to improving the agency fundraising program? Does the agency have a plan that will result in increased private revenue?

Board of Director Activities BOD activities include making a generous annual gift to the agency, identifying and soliciting prospective donors, and working with the president and the development director on fundraising activities. For example, if the president is soliciting a major corporate leader for a gift, the BOD member supports the president by attending the solicitation meeting. It is beneficial for BOD members to talk about the agency's work at their places of employment and in work related social situations to raise the agency's profile with their company, coworkers, and employees. This can also make a difference in direct gifts and United Way designations. The BOD members periodically review lists prepared by the staff and development committee of potential donors and are the lead volunteer in cultivating each person they know. The agency president assists them in the cultivation process.

The Development Staff

If the plan is to have the ability to engage in a range of annual campaign activities, the development department at a PCWA includes the director, a second staff member who helps with events and major gift solicitation, along with a grant writer and an administrative assistant. If the PCWA helps children in several distinct geographical regions than there is also development staff in each region, where there is the potential to raise significant dollars. If the PCWA has low visibility in a region plan to also conduct marketing activities.

If the agency is making a start with only one position, hire a grant writer. The position will raise more money than the other positions listed. This is because generally most of the grant money available to PCWA's comes from government, foundation, and corporate sources. There are downsides to doing this. A grant writer will not give the organization much of a start in private fundraising with individuals and family foundations. For many PCWAs gifts from individual large donors account for the greatest portion of private giving.

If you have or plan a full-blown private development effort, the number of positions, and the activities depend on the PCWA ability and willingness to invest in fundraising. The number of staff positions vary by the current campaigns and activities plus new initiatives planned. Also, consider opportunities missed because there is not enough staff to perform the work. The development director in consultation with the BOD development committee, the president and significant donors, creates an annual development plan (the president ultimately approves the plan and supervises the development director's ongoing work). The plan indicates the elements of the current development program and new initiatives with agreed upon fundraising goals. Additionally, the plan identifies those responsible for implementation and due dates for each part of the plan

The president also handles the cultivation and solicitation work with between five and ten of the largest donors.

The development director attends, the BOD meetings and works with BOD members on projects as needed. Additional functions include cultivating and soliciting fifteen donors, supervising the major gifts officer, marketing staff, and the grant writer. The director ensures the success of departmental activities, such as, grant applications, cultivation and solicitation activities, and departmental publications

Major gifts officers cultivate and solicit donors who have significant giving ability that the president or development director does not cultivate. They also arrange for cultivation events and attend community events that give them the chance to interact with potential donors. These include chamber of commerce mixers, fundraising events of other charities, and United Way annual meetings.

The grant writer is responsible for writing and monitoring government, foundation, and corporate grant proposals and completing United Way applications. Many fishing expeditions for either foundation or government grants end up being a waste of time. Apply for only one major "stretch" grant a year. Foundations that have a record of accomplishment in supporting projects in the agency's geographic area are usually good prospects.

Sometimes the development director does not have the experience with government grant writing, a detailed knowledge of the youth services field or a detailed understanding of the agency programs. When this is the case, the manager who can be the most help in assuring the quality of the grant applications supplies the supervision. The supervisor is the development director when they can add value to the grant submissions. Another choice is a lead clinician. Sometimes the president has performed the grant writer responsibilities prior to the creation of a grant writer position and is the best choice to supervise the grant writer.

Marketing staff brand the agency within the community. They work with the development or marketing committee, internal staff, external media outlets, and assure that publications, websites and media messages are consistent and communicate key messages about the agency mission and activities. They focus on customer and donor messages and sometimes conduct Internet based campaigns. These can include email campaigns, linkage with existing web efforts, and Twitter campaigns. The first task is establishing recognition of the agency in the community. Working with print, television, and internet news sources to have the agency become the local experts on certain news topics can expand community awareness and respect for agency work.

Fundraising Events

Event staff, along with committees, implements annual events. A fact of organizational life is that there are some directors that enjoy specific events. Golf tournaments and Galas fall into this category. Sometimes if the BOD efforts coalesce around an event, it is a great morale builder. They often feel it is one way to fulfill their fundraising role. Be sensitive that although an activity may not be worth the time and effort, in terms of the funds raised, anything that ties the BOD members closer to the agency mission is worthwhile.

The key to successful events is to choose an event that attracts people to participate, to establish relationships with company leaders that result in high lead event sponsorships, pricing sponsorships at the level companies can afford and to ask for the sponsorship in an effective manner.

Sometimes events are better friend raisers than fundraisers. There is an added benefit to the event when the new friend will continue to support future activities. It is worthwhile to track the share of those attending an event that gets further involved in the agency. Communications to event participants demarcate the portion of their payments that pay for event costs and the portion that is tax deductible as a charitable gift.

Lotteries, Bingo, and Raffles

Raffles, small games of chance, and bingo are popular fundraisers for small and midsized PCWAs. They occur as independent activities or in concert with golf tournaments and other events to enhance the bottom line. In addition, small games of chance are popular and have the potential to gain modest donations from many givers. Highly priced raffles limiting the number of tickets sold and offering a highly desirable prize, (with the prize hopefully donated) are appealing. Small games of chance in which PCWA staff, volunteers, and Board members will sell tickets are both a fundraiser and marketing tool. Contact municipal authorities, to learn about buying a small games of chance license, to learn the types of games allowed, and prize money limits. Some states allow charities to partner with taverns. Local printers will likely supply tickets, and office supply stores sell generic tickets.

Donation of a Car or Boat

Sometimes members of the BOD offer to donate a car. Depending on programs and fundraising plans, PCWAs may want to solicit vehicle donations to raise money or to give or sell a car at a reduced price to parents of consumers. Having a car is important for employment in areas where there is no or limited public transportation. Vehicles needing repairs can be the basis of a youth training program.

Active solicitation to the public for vehicle gifts can utilize several media outlets. To minimize costs, use the agency website, newsletter, and email. Make announcements at staff and BOD meetings. See if media outlets will donate public service announcements, and if the local outdoor advertising companies have a charitable billboard program. Establish a relationship with an insurance agency that handles the vehicle transfer work and will arrange to insure the vehicle after you take possession. A relationship with a company that conducts car auctions is helpful.

If the car is near the end of its useful life, the donor can deduct up to $500 without anything except an acknowledgment from the organization, along with an appraisal and a price book value that is at or above $500. If the agency sells the car on the open market, the value of the deduction is the sale price, and the donor claims the deduction in the year the PCWA sells the vehicle. If the charity donates or significantly discounts the car for a consumer, uses it for its charitable purpose, or significantly upgrades the car, the donor gets the fair market value at the time of the donation. Depending on the scenario involved, the charity's communication to the donor has different components. Review the IRS's "A Donor's Guide to

Vehicle Donation". The URL is: https://www.irs.gov/pub/irs-pdf/p4303 .pdf .

Do a good job of monitoring costs for the private fundraising programs. Expect total costs (staff and materials) will run about 30% of the private dollars raised. Costs will be higher when initiating a fund-raising program where none exists and when there is a need for extensive marketing efforts to increase name recognition or more firmly establish knowledge about the agency's programs, and mission in the philanthropic community. Costs will be lower without events and limited individual solicitation work. However, a decrease in major gifts from individual solicitation is likely to occur.

Development Reporting

A monthly development report of private income by category is a basic management tool. Comparing the development and finance reports assure consistency. The development department report lists the annual goals for private fundraising results in each segment. The development goals are the budget income line items for the annual operating budgets. The report format should include categories such as BOD gifts, individual gifts, foundation giving, each event, and other categories if there is a major time investment in something else like direct mail. Depending on their number, church, civic, and corporate gifts go into one category. The categories chosen depend on the expected private income streams. For each category relevant to the agency, list the income for the current month, year to date, the annual fundraising goal, and the amount raised in the prior year. Staff prepares separate reports for capital or other special campaigns. These reports are for the campaign committee members.

Annual Campaign

The annual campaign often has several components. These include large donor solicitations, the BOD member campaign, direct mail, events, and foundation, church, and corporate solicitation. Capital campaigns occur every seven to ten years.

Private fundraising efforts include large donor identification, cultivation, and solicitation. Important reasons large donors give to private child welfare organizations vary. First, child abuse is a mom and apple pie issue. Most people believe that parents should love and value children and their hearts go out to children who parents brutalize them. They believe abused and neglected children deserve protection and assistance to lead happy and productive adult lives. Some religious people think the bible mandates people to protect child abuse victims. Others feel involvement with good works such as child protection is part of their religious obligation. Some donors contribute because they were a child abuse victim. Some are parents whose children exhibit troubling behavior (prostitution, assaultive behavior, etc.). These people had high, but unfulfilled hopes for their children. However, they believe supporting services to other troubled children would enable another child to do well. They believe in making lemonade out of lemons. Some of the most committed BOD members are those who have first- hand experiences with troubled children. Sometimes a donor has a relative who grew up in an orphanage, or they or a family member experiences a mental health problem. Many of these donor's support charities because they wish help was available when they or their family member needed it. Still others, communitarians at heart help so that their communities will be better places to live.

Corporate giving staff acts to fulfill corporate philanthropic giving goals that are often general in nature, such as seeking to improve community life. Sometimes, however, companies tie their corporate philanthropy to their business type. For example, a scientific instrument manufacturer may give only to nonprofits that advance science education among youth. Similarly, foundation giving reflect the organizations purpose and goals, which vary in accordance with the wishes of the person or organization that endows the foundation

BOD members' cultivation efforts work results in gifts. As previously stated, spotting potentially large donors involves asking the BOD members for names of prospects, as well as reviewing donor lists of charities like your own with them. The more difficult donor to identify is the wealthy individual who does not have a charitable giving history but is uncertain what to do with their considerable resources. These can be hardworking financially successful people who do not have children and do not have specific charitable interests. Often these givers help organizations who help them such as hospitals, or leave a large legacy gift to their church. Sometimes a friend who knows of their wealth and lack of a financial plan can interest them in making a gift to a particular charity. In addition, financial planners can be a source of gifts for these types of individuals.

If you are uncertain of a person's giving potential you can check the property records in the area to see the value of the donor's home. This is the easiest way fundraisers classify donors into or out of the large donor category. However, this like all methods is not fool proof. Sometimes a potential donor has an attachment to the house they own, although it is not a high value property.

The larger the potential gift the more time spent in cultivating a donor. Large donor cultivation often takes many years and is very time consuming. A hospital president I know visited a prospect every day for thirty-days while they were in the hospital. The effort resulted in the hospital receiving a multimillion-dollar gift. Also, be prepared that a large donor may see your organization as a likely vehicle for accomplishing a project in which they have an interest. This can be a dilemma for the staff in considering whether the project, which will come with major financing, is close enough to the organizational mission to implement. A second important consideration in these kinds of projects is the plan for ongoing support. If a service payer is not in evidence it is important to split the capital gift to provide for an endowment.

Capital Campaign

I think the main value of the annual individual giving efforts, and events, is to have a donor base to conduct a periodic capital or endowment campaign. These campaigns have substantial goals. At VYH a 2007 capital campaign that used half of the monies to buy a 32-acre camp and the half to endow a fund for operating costs, repairs and upgrades to the camp, attracted both capital and endowment gifts and exceeded its five-million-dollar goal

As a case statement, the camp was a much easier sell than a home for teen mothers and their children. Poor judgement by the girls for becoming teen mothers constituted an unfavorable perception for some donors, but not for most. The campaign also succeeded. Prior campaigns to pay down mortgages and expand the runaway shelter were also a success.

The common elements to making a capital campaign go well are:

1) Convening five top community wide leaders to attend two meetings to educate them about the need and get their thinking on implementing the campaign and project. The purpose is not solicitation, or cultivation, but rather to get the buy in and support of top-level community leaders.

2) Creating a solid business plan, which documents the need, talks about the project in some detail, indicates how the project generates ongoing income, and provides capital and operating budgets. These last two items receive a lot of attention in the plan review. The business plan is also a tool for a campaign group to use to develop a case statement and solicitation materials.

3) A chairperson who makes a generous lead gift (10-15% + of the total goal). The chair also needs to commit to solicit five donors for very large gifts. The president does the solicitation with the campaign chair, and accompanies the chair and any BOD member needing support on solicitation calls. The president needs to be cognizant that many large donors will want to have the confidence that the leader can execute on project implementation; therefore, they will expect a personal meeting to make that determination.

4) A feasibility study of 15-20 potential large donors who have made substantial gifts to the organization in the past. If you do not have many donors, who have made $1,000+ gifts to support operations in the last two years you may want to delay a capital campaign unless the campaign chair is so influential that many people will give because the chair asks them to.

The usual custom is to bring in an outside fundraising firm to do a feasibility study, interviews with prospective givers, on the theory that people will give responses that are more honest. If you think you will be unable to get into see the interviewees because they are not familiar with the organization, use of an outside firm is also useful. If you cannot afford to do this make sure you have a good fundraiser as a BOD member to help coach staff to do the feasibility study. The interviews are a ½ hour in length. The interviewer explains the project during the first five minutes of the meeting. During the interview, which uses a fixed list of questions, the interviewer carefully notes the questions, concerns, and objections of the prospective donor. Among the questions, the interviewer asks is the willingness of the person to support this kind of project and the range of a possible gift.

After the study, make a gift chart, which breaks down the amount and number of gifts needed to meet the campaign goal. The chart uses level system a) $1,000.000 gift b) $500,000 gifts, c) $250,000 gifts etc. The gifts are usually 3 to 5-year pledges. Organizational leaders will know after the feasibility study whether to proceed with the campaign. If there is a wide gap between the feasibility study results and the goal the organization can proceed with the campaign having a lower goal then that tested during the feasibility study and finance the remainder required. A badly failed campaign is terrible for everyone's morale.

In addition to the plaques, room and building naming set a donation amount perhaps a $5,000 donation or greater and call each of the donors to say thank you. Most people do not do this and a positive impression will result that the donor will remember.

Chapter 17 -Financial Statements, The Review Process, and Departmental Staff

The Organizational Role of Finance

While the children, the staff, and the programs bring the mission to life, and fundraising pays the way, the finance department is the organizational business manager. The finance function provides the controls to assure that the funds the PCWA receives go to their proper purpose, that the organization meets the financial reporting requirements of customers, and that ongoing business functions such as the submission of payroll taxes occur. The finance function also enables staff compensation including payroll and the management of the retirement plan. It serves as the organizational banker depositing checks, accepting electronic transfers, invoicing customers, making bank deposits and paying the bills. Additionally, it also monitors the organizational investments, and suggests cost saving measures to achieve efficiencies. The financial work products include key information about organizational functioning

Rules of the Road for Finance

1.) The operating account includes the PCWA cash that is not in a restricted account or endowment. Operate on a balanced budget basis. When expenses exceed income, year after year the PCWA will not be able to financially support its operations and will either merge or go out of business. If the expenses exceed the income in any year, the budget for the following year is a surplus budget returning the amount of the prior year deficit to the operating account.

2) Set goals and a plan with managers to achieve a surplus in any program that has a per diem or per hour fee. The surplus goal is between 2% and 6% of the projected gross program income.

Any grant funded programs are cost reimbursement programs. The two goals for these programs are a) to have expenses match, but not exceed the grant amount and 2) charge the maximum administrative expenses to the grant. Nevertheless, take care not to charge significantly more than the amount specified in the grant budget.

3) Add surplus, funds: add to: a) the agency "rainy day fund" b) the agency cash flow or c) restricted fund accounts established by the BOD for a specific purpose. These can include a building fund, a quasi-endowment fund, a new program startup fund, and an insurance deductible fund. Other than paying for the operations, the first goal is to build a contingency fund equal to three to six months of the annual budget. The money helps in managing cash flow when customers are slow to pay invoices or if there is a funding problem.

4) Limit significant deficit program funding when there is no solid plan to bring the program income and expenses into balance.

5) Issue financial statements that allow you to judge organizational performance on 1-4 above.

6) Conduct an independent audit of the financial transactions annually. This is the main tool to assure the internal financial statements are accurate.

7)Have good financial controls in place. Separate duties in a way that minimizes the possibility of theft and fraud. Document control procedures and other important parts of the finance function in a procedure's manual. Review and update all financial policies and procedures every other year.

8) Staff in upper management without formal training in finance becomes literate in the PCWA financial functions through study, mentoring, and coursework.

Financial Statement Characteristics, Components, Review Process, and Distribution

Transactions - Income and expense statements and other financial reports summarize the financial transactions of each program. There are many organizational transactions such as income received from GCWAs, payment of invoices, grant drawdowns, and donations. Expense transactions include staff salaries and benefits, food for youth in residential programs, and office supply purchases. Each income transaction conforms to invoicing and payment timeline provisions in contracts, grant drawdown provisions or donation documentation procedures. Create an authorization process for expense approval.

Record each operating transaction in an account. This is known as "posting to an account" The finance department staff members, decide on the account to which they post the transaction. Some budget line items summarize accounts. For instance, personnel expenses can include the professional, administrative, and supervisory salaries paid; benefit costs, and employer payroll taxes. All transactions taken together form the general ledger. The system to organize the transactions into different categories is known as the "chart of accounts" Due to the structure of most financial software, the account classifications are the same for each program, but specific accounts may not have entries in some programs because a particular income or expense type is not used in that program. The financial reports summarize the postings to the accounts in a way that is useful to staff and BOD members. In addition, independent auditors, outside funding sources and regulators review financial reports. The procedures used to account for the financial transactions conform to standards determined by the American Accounting Standards Board.

Financial Report Frequency and Speed

Accounting reports summarize financial aspects of the charity's operation on a historical basis. Deciding on the frequency of financial reports is somewhat subjective. In deciding, consider budget size, the agency financial condition, and the stability of agency income and expenses. The resources required to prepare the reports in light of the other finance department responsibilities are determined. If an organization is large, with much of the income based on per diem or per hour funding than monthly reports are customary. If the organization is small and more of the income is from grants or other steady sources of income than quarterly reports may be more efficient.

There are major corporations that issue financial reports within five to ten days of month end. Speed and accuracy work at odds. Quickly issued reports use more estimation. The size and complexity of the charity, the number and duties of the finance department staff, and invoicing and expense submission standards all influence reporting speed. The trend is for primarily GCWA funded PCWAs to generate statements more quickly than in the past. Public customers prefer prompt invoicing both because they want to close their own books promptly, and because of increasing accountability requirements of their funders. Moreover, because federal grant programs reimburse expenses electronically, the quicker federal grant expense information is available the quicker grant funds are available to the PCWA.

Method and Depreciation It is beneficial to use the accrual rather than the cash method of recording income and expenses. The cash method is to record income as it comes in and expenses as you pay them. The accrual method matches income to the related expenses and records them when the expense occurs and more accurately estimates income and expenses compared to the cash method. While some sizable organizations still operate on a cash basis, the risk of inaccurate financial records is greater than when using the accrual basis of accounting.

As a fictional illustration, Caring Children's Services (CCS) uses a cash system of accounting and operates on a July1, to June 30, fiscal year. CCS receives a letter from the Business is Business foundation in March of 2017 informing them that the foundation has approved their request for a $10,000 grant to make building repairs As the plan is to undertake the repairs over the summer, CCS submits a $10,000 check request to the foundation in May of 2017. The check from the foundation arrives on June 10th. The maintenance staff takes advantage of a sale at the Evergreen lumberyard and purchases $10,000 worth of lumber for the repairs on June 15th 2017. Evergreen delivers the lumber to CCS on June 20th. Evergreen invoices CCS for the lumber on June 25th. The terms are that CCS pays the invoice within 30 days. On July 20th CCS"s accounts payable clerk sends a $10,000 check to Evergreen. The income for the repairs comes in the 2017 fiscal year and the CCS pays the expense in the 2018 fiscal year. Using the cash basis of accounting the CCS overstates their financial condition for 2017 by $10,000 because there is an outstanding payable. Using the accrual method of accounting the foundation check is restricted income because it is for a specific purpose not yet fulfilled. The Evergreen invoice is a June expense and the financial staff releases the restricted funds to the unrestricted account in June to pay the invoice. Fiscal staff record both the income and expense for the repairs in the 2017 fiscal year.

Most PCWA have fixed assets. Fixed assets include buildings, vehicles capital improvements, and equipment costs that exceed the applicable threshold. The federal government considers any item valued at less than $5,000 an expense and any item costing more as an asset. Each state has financial regulations for state government-supported efforts. The thresholds are in the state fiscal regulations. Also, a certified public accountant will know the state threshold for PCWAs.

Account for expenses in the year they occur. Expense assets annually over the useful life of the asset. In determining depreciation schedule of an asset, consider the purchase price, useful life, and salvage value. The schedule determines how much of the value of the fixed asset depreciates each year, and is therefore expensed. For example, a PCWA buys a van to transport residential clients for $35,000. From experience with other vehicles used to transport residents, the finance director determines the useful life of the van to be five years. Using a used car guide the director estimates that at the end of five years the van's value is $5,000. Although there are several methods of depreciating an asset, PCWAs often use the straight-line method. The financial staff expenses the value of the asset over its useful life. $6,000 each year ($35,000 purchase price – $5,000 salvage value divided by the five-year useful life)

To make their financial situations look better some organizations do not record (expense) depreciation. The organization does not have a plan to replace assets, such as the van when its useful life is over, or the roof of the residence where the children live. The lack of a best practice in finance is apparent to sophisticated donors. Staff and the BOD rationalize the failure to record depreciation with plans to conduct a future capital campaign to raise money to pay for property replacement costs. The timing and success of a future campaign is not known.

Financial Data Aggregation – Who Gets What

For large organizations, monthly financial statements can exceed 100 pages. The level of detail and number of program reports is a discretionary decision and some individuals like the idea of consolidating several similar programs into one report. I take the path of aggregating data, more for the finance committee than for the staff, and still more for the BOD. The highest level of aggregation appears in the annual report, which uses about a dozen categories to summarize income and expenses. The lowest level of data aggregation is useful for the president, finance director, and the program directors. Maintaining detailed financial reports and limiting aggregation has two advantages. First, it may be the easiest way to meet funder accountability requirements. These requirements have grown and the trend seems to be for funders to require more financial detail each year. If there is enough detail in the financial reports, it is easier to rearrange them in a format, which a customer requires. If there is not enough detail, the number of "special spreadsheets" and the need to "double post" increases.

Second, the greater the detail, the greater the ability to spot budget variances. Detail provides information about customer purchasing trends, and allows for targeted cost control. The president saves time by having financial staff prepare, a program level summary report, listing income and expenses line items exceeding certain percentage or dollar value of the budget. Five percent of the year to date budget amount or $10,000 whichever is greater is a useful benchmark. This allows program leadership to work on budget issues as they arise. Prompt attention to deficit items avoids large unwanted expenditures that accumulate month after month.

The Most Current Report of Income – Census Reports

The best source of current financial data is census reports (the number of children in each program each day). It is important to know the breakeven census numbers for every program. This is the number of resident days in a month multiplied by the per diem, which equals the estimated monthly expenses. It is advantageous to have each program issue a weekly census report. These reports can aid management in determining the financial situation week by week. It is also good practice to send weekly vacancy reports to customers with the intent of letting them know how many openings there are. Use these census reports internally to help determine the financial situation week by week. Using census reports are the quickest way to get an idea of business income. Expenses for programs not in a startup or retrenchment mode are steady month to month except when there is a third payroll in the month, a managed care payment claw back or another onetime event (usually not a good one).

Financial Report Components and Review Process

Organizational leaders spend an hour or two each month reviewing the financial statement. The goal is to have general information about the bottom line, performance versus budget, customer buying trends, problem receivables, and changes in the balance sheet due to both operations and changes in the values of investments; debt instruments non-cash assets, etc. as well as changes in liabilities such as accrued vacation, retirement fund reserves, and bond or mortgage debt. The components of a financial statement package ideally include:

1. An agency wide summary of income and expenses statement
2. An agency wide program by program summary listing income, expenses, and results by program, actual versus budget for the current month and year to date
3. A program by program line item income and expense statement
4. Accounts receivable report-listing customers, their purchase amounts by the month for the first 150 days and then all 151 days and older receivables.
5. A cash flow statement that tracks the agency cash position and the factors related to increases and decreases in cash
6. A balance sheet that lists the cash and non-cash assets and liabilities.

First, review the agency wide income and expenses versus budget plan. Look for statement items where financial gains or losses exceed 5% of the budget. The main purpose of reviewing this statement is to spot the specific income and expense items that agency wide, have a significant variance and to focus the president, vice presidents and program directors on these items as they review the program summary report. Also, this report quickly shows the overall agency surplus or deficit for the month and year to date.

Next review the by program income and expense report. Be mindful that results reflect internal accounting decisions such as not charging off private fundraising expenses to programs funded entirely by a government grant. Also keep in mind an organizational decision that allocates administrative expenses in line with time use, rather than proportionately. These as well as other rules and practices affect performance. For each program of the agency, the report lists only total income and expenses and the net. The report contains the current month and year to date actual and budgeted income and expenses and the variance between the two. The reader easily learns which programs have gains and which have losses. For those programs that have losses for a month, a review of the year to date numbers reveals whether the loss is a onetime event or part of a pattern. Noting the magnitude of losses, above a certain threshold, will focus the reader on the importance of action where and when needed. Paying attention to the results of the programs with the largest dollar value assists in assessing the overall budget stability, in as much as these programs account for most of the income and expenses.

A fictional program summary report follows as table 14-1, PCWA Financial Summary Report April 2017. The format used shows the income, expenses, and net results for the month of April 2017 for the development office and 11 programs as well as the budget and actual year to date numbers.

For the month of April, the Total Program Operations section at the bottom of the report shows a surplus of $11,342 or less than 2% of total income ($741,585). This is a positive result as the overall monthly budget indicates a deficit because of the expected losses budgeted for the development department (-$19,169) and Camp Isaacson (-$20,140). The surplus for April is of a similar proportion to the year to date net, and this suggests that unless there is an unanticipated event that the PCWA will finish the year with a surplus. However, the percentage of the surplus compared to the total income is modest. Three programs, development, the drug prevention program, and the provider 50 program had the largest year to date surpluses. The most successful operating programs financially are Provider 50 and the Drug Prevention program. Not only did these programs achieve a large surplus but did so by controlling the increase in expenses while increasing revenue. The expenses only increased about half as much as the income when compared with the budget plan for the Drug Prevention Program and expenses were less than budgeted while income increased in the Provider 50 program. In April, significant losses occur in two programs Camp Isaacson and Independent Living.

Five of the programs operate at a loss for the month of April with the Camp and Independent living together losing $39,385. If these two programs operated on a balanced budget basis for the month the PCWA surplus would have been 6.8% of income instead of the 1.5% achieved. Five of the eleven programs (emergency shelter, Sudac boy's cottage, school drug prevention program, family based mental health and independent living accounted for 56% of the operations income in April. In total, these five programs have a surplus of $4,881, which bodes well for the annual results. This all suggests that due to serious deficits in two programs that PCWA will end the year with income and expenses being approximately equal, but a net loss for the year could also occur due to an unanticipated event because the surplus projected is modest.

The camp expenses are large compared to income. The camp budget anticipated a deficit, but not such a large one. In contrast, the Independent Living program staff has done a good job of controlling expenses, demonstrating agility in reacting to income reductions by making some expense reductions. The task here is to determine if the lower than budgeted income for the first third of the year in Independent Living will continue for the remainder of the year, and plan accordingly. That is, do not make staff reductions if the census will pick up during the next three months. However, if independent living referrals will be low because the state is shifting money away from services for older teenagers to purchase services for babies and toddlers in therapeutic nursery programs then the program should plan to adjust expenses to the "new normal" lower census numbers. If this happens, try to transfer the staff to another program rather than lay them off. The camp is more problematic. Due to the high value of the physical facility, depreciation accounts for a significant part of the deficit. The main use of the camp is for children who are agency clients. Also, there is a high staff expense due to life guard salaries. Perhaps swim hours could be more limited. There is a need to increase income through more usage by community groups, rental income from corporations using the camp as a team building site, and from families using the camp as a wedding venue.

Table 17-1 *PCWA Program Summary Report - April 2017*					
Program	Current Month	Year-to Date	Year-to Date		Annual
	Actual Budget	Actual	Budget Variance		Budget
Development					
Income	44203	6900	173277	27600	145677	82800
Expenses	30149	26069	118183	104275	13908	312826
Net	14054	-19169	55093	-76675	131768	-230026
Emergency Shelter					
Income	75970	66064	297801	264254	33546	792763
Expenses	74880	66283	293530	265133	28397	795398
Net	1090	-220	4271	-878	5150	-2635
Sudac Boy's Cottage					
Income	87344	79595	342390	318379	24011	955138
Expenses	90578	77610	355067	310440	44627	931320
Net	-3234	1985	-12677	7939	-20616	23818
Tremont Cottage					
Income	62398	65952	244599	263808	-19209	791424
Expenses	60880	60829	238648	243317	-4669	729950
Net	1518	5123	5951	20491	-14541	61474
Sudac Girl's Cottage					
Income	19073	22554	74765	90216	-15451	270648
Expenses	19242	22183	75429	88733	-13304	266198
Net	-169	371	-663	1483	-2146	4450
In-Home Counseling					
Income	65383	69218	256302	276874	-20571	830621
Expenses	69576	65263	272738	261053	11685	783158
Net	-4193	3955	-16436	15821	-32257	47462

Table 17-1 page 2

	Current Month Actual	Current Month Budget	Year-to Date Actual	Year-to Date Budget	Variance	Annual Budget
Drug Prevention Program						
Income	80038	51767	313747	207067	106680	621202
Expenses	65582	51098	257083	204394	52689	613181
Net	14455	668	56664	2674	53991	8021
Provider 50						
Income	53612	45500	210161	182002	28159	546005
Expenses	34122	43654	133758	174614	-40856	523843
Net	19490	1847	76402	7387	69015	22162
Fam. Based MH						
Income	72866	74065	285636	296261	-10625	888782
Expenses	68099	70422	266947	281688	-14741	845064
Net	4768	3643	18689	14573	4116	43718
Independent						
Income	98748	127600	387092	510398	-123306	1531195
Expenses	110946	120593	434908	482371	-47463	1447114
Net	-12198	7007	-47816	28027	-75843	84082
Mother-Child Supportive Housin						
Income	67512	54475	264647	217819	46828	653461
Expenses	64564	54557	253089	218227	34862	654682
Net	2948	-102	11558	-408	11966	-1224
Camp Isaacs						
Income	14438	16000	56599	63998	-7400	191995
Expenses	41626	36139	163172	144557	18616	433670
Net	-27187	-20140	-106574	-80558	-26015	-241675
Total - Program Operations						
Income	741585	679669	2907015	2718677	188339	8156031
Expenses	730243	694700	2862553	2778802	83752	8336405
Net	11342	-15031	44462	-60125	104587	-180374

An excerpt from the PCWA Sudac Boy's Cottage's May 2016 income and expense statement follows. The example uses only the personnel expenses and follows the format introduced above. The annual budget as well as the monthly and year to date budgets versus actual expenses form the core of the analysis. The annual budget forms the basis for each monthly budget line item amount. The BOD adopts the annual budget. Finance staff decides upon monthly allocations. In the example, the presumption is that the fiscal staff divides the annual budget into twelve equal parts. However, it is often the practice to allow for larger budget amounts during some months and lower amounts for other months with the total equal to the annual budget amount. The advantage of the second method is that it anticipates certain large expenses, such as months where the PCWA makes lump sum payments. The text refers to figure 17-2 below.

The year to date personnel expenses are $5,222 under budget. Total personnel expenses for the month of May exceed the budget by $4,178 or 8%, which at first glance is not of concern given the year to date results. However, if May actual expenses had followed the January to April pattern the year to date expenditures would be almost $12,000 under budget. If the May personnel spending pattern continues then the personnel expenses will exceed the budget at the close of the fiscal year by $24,021. If the January through April pattern had continued Personnel expenses would be $28,201 under budget at the close of the fiscal year. The gap between the two possible scenarios is $52,222. The comparison of possible scenarios points out the different results that are possible for an expense category depending on the patterns of actual expenditure. The important action for managers to take is to find out the reason for the relatively high expenses in May and determine if expenses will continue to exceed the budget then plan with the program director to reduce expenses, or increase income with the goal to bring the actual personnel expenditure in line with the budget plan. The third less desirable choice is to fund the deficit through surpluses in other program areas or through the agency contingency fund.

The accounts receivable report gives the amounts that customers, grantors, and individuals owe the PCWA. This includes GCWA

Table 17-2 PCWA Sudac Boys Cottage
May 2016 and YTD Personnel Detail

	Current Month Actual	Current Month Actual	Current Month Budget	Variance	Year to Date Actual	Year to Date Budget	Variance	Annual Budget
A Personnel								
Management Staff	3,592	3,592	3,326	266	16,298	16,631	-333	39,914
Supervisory Staff	10,249	10,249	9,490	759	46,499	47,448	-949	113,875
Direct Service Staff	27,955	27,955	25,884	2,071	126,831	129,419	-2,588	310,606
Maintainance Staff	820	821	760	61	3,722	3,798	-76	9,116
Total Personnel	42,616	42,617	39,459	3,157	193,350	197,296	-3,946	473,511
B. BENEFITS								
Health Insurance	5,989	5,989	5,545	444	27,172	27,727	-555	66,544
Dental Plan	508	508	471	38	2,307	2,354	-47	5,649
Life Insurance	86	86	80	6	390	398	-8	954
Disability Insurance	135	135	125	10	613	626	-13	1,502
Unemployment Insurance	224	224	208	17	1,018	1,038	-21	2,492
FICA	3,277	3,277	3,034	243	14,866	15,170	-303	36,408
Worker's Comp Insurance	378	378	350	28	1,715	1,750	-35	4,200
		0						
Retirement	3,187	3,187	2,951	236	14,458	14,753	-295	35,407
Total Benefits	13,784	13,784	12,763	1,021	62,539	63,815	-1,276	153,156
Total Personnel Expenses	56,400	56,400	52,222	4,178	255,889	261,112	-5,222	626,668

purchase of services invoices, managed care behavioral health billings, government grants, foundation grants, and unpaid pledges from individuals for capital and endowment campaigns. The accounts receivable report lists each customer's name, the name of the services purchased and the amount due. The fictitious PCWA accounts receivable statement below is for the month

of April 2017. The report includes the April 2017 billing and covers all unpaid invoices and pledges billed in April and prior to April. The first column has two labels, the month (April) and the words "current month". Each customer receives an invoice for the amounts listed in this column as soon as possible, usually within ten days of the end of the month the purchases occurred. The report also lists amounts of service purchases that are unpaid after 30 days, 60 days, 90 days, 120 days, and more than 120 days past the original billing date. For example, the accounts receivable staff bills the amounts under the 90-day column a few days after January of 2017 ends. The most important part of the report for most PCWAs is GCWA purchases. Most amounts are for per diem purchases, but any other types of purchases, such as program funding appear here as well. Commonly GCWA pay invoices sixty to ninety days after they receive an invoice. The finance director distributes this report along with the income and expense reports, usually fifteen to twenty days following the end of the month. They distribute the April report around the middle of May

The accounts receivable staff bills most child welfare customers on a monthly basis and most behavioral health customers on a service encounter basis, often daily. The PCWA bills for a consumer that participates in an emergency shelter services between April 2nd and April 5th on or before May 10th along with the billings for all consumers who reside at the shelter in April. In managed care, behavioral health claims are on a service encounter basis. The accounts receivable staff bills for a consumer who resides in an inpatient hospital program between April 2nd and April 5th on April 7th and the managed care company pays quickly, often within 15 days. Due to differences in invoicing and payment time frames the PCWA usually spends more resources on billing every service encounter but the MCO pays the claim more quickly than the GCWA.

The report identifies laggard payers. These are customers that have amounts listed in the 120 days and 120+days columns, meaning they have not paid for services rendered either four months ago, (120 days) or five or more months ago (120 days +).

Payment delays are often an issue for GCWA agencies, and makes keeping sufficient cash on hand an important practice. Sometimes, delayed payments are due to government holding cash received, as a cash management technique. In other situations, the government customer has little cash reserves, and is waiting for reimbursement from the state or federal government. GCWA delays in issuing contracts are often the reason receivables build up. Sometimes, government customers will not make payments until the authorized government official signs the PCWA contract. The contract review process includes a review of the PCWA program description, insurance policy endorsements and insurance waiver requests, rate calculations and rate schedule. Governments often divide the contract review process between several departments and this also adds time to the approval process. Last because the contracts are all for the same period and reviewed at about the same time there can be a bottleneck effect.

Concern about slow payers is proportional to the risks that customers will not eventually pay their bills. Some gentle prodding may be in order if the PCWA agency has serious cash flow issues. As long as there is no risk of default, or conflict about the billing do not get aggressive about collection efforts if you do not need to. Your efforts should be respectful. It is not a great idea for your customers to regard you as overzealous. Larger PCWAs with positive balance sheets are sometimes the last paid because of their financial strength compared to smaller PCWAs. However, if there is nonpayment due to a difference of opinion about an invoice item, then resolve the disagreement as soon as possible. In addition, even with government customers create an uncollectable allowance and use it in the receivable calculations. Naturally, one of the basic purposes of the receivable report is to communicate when it is time to contact customers to ask for payment on past due bills.

Act on any managed care behavioral health claim not paid within 20 days. This is necessary for two reasons. The first is that when a managed care behavioral health company does not pay a claim it is because they have a problem with it. The problem may be the accounts receivable staff makes mistakes in completing the encounter form, or because their records indicate, the consumer is not a medical assistance program member. The second reason the PCWA makes a prompt response to a claim rejection is that there are time limits for correcting billing errors, and appeals of non-payment of claims. If the accounts payable staff does not complete the necessary paperwork promptly, the company may not pay the claim.

The accounts receivable report is a good way of identifying month-to-month customer buying trends. It is easy to see which customers are buying more or less service by comparing the current, 30 day, and 60-day numbers. Most GCWA customers pay for invoices 60 to 90 days after receipt. However, it is common for longer periods to elapse before a customer pays a bill. When there is a 15% decrease or increase in customer purchase amounts for any program, when you compare the current, 60-day and 90-day amounts discuss this with the appropriate staff and ask that they follow up, with the reason for the change and the implications for future income and expenses in the program(s) involved. When the staff report back it will increase sensitivity about purchasing patterns due to changes in depreciation, uncollectable pledges, and other adjustments annually at the close of the fiscal year. The $2,845,368 is the value of the buildings.

customer budgets, and to problems that customers have with specific agency programs.

Another type of receivable is capital campaign pledges. For a capital campaign, list the total pledges that are outstanding by year. Most campaigns have three to five-year payment period. The first year listed is the first year the PCWA receives cash and pledge income for the campaign. Subsequent lines list the pledge income due in the current and subsequent years. In addition, record an allowance for uncollectable pledges. In stating the financial condition of a capital campaign, its customary to plan that

Table 17-3 PCWA April 2017 Accounts Receivable

NAMI PROGRAM	CURRENT April	1-30 March	31-60 Februay	61-90 January	91-120 December 2016	over 120 November 2016 & PRIOR	ENDING BALANCE
Bryant							
Shelter	53,366	42,915	37,432	45,362	50,786	115,621	345,483
Sudac-Boys						0	0
Sudac Girls			167		6,228	9,360	15,755
Indep.Living	28,885	26,324	30,245	29,622	31,432	43,321	189,829
Sex offender		27,550	23,246	25,742	19,742	63,875	160,155
Provier 50	18,222	22,102	20,987	19,817	21,497	17,643	120,268
Supp. Housing	5,886	5,051	4,951	5,206	5,972	5,400	32,466
Total Bryant	106,359	123,943	117,028	125,749	135,657	255,220	863,956
							0
Clayborne							
Shelter	6,433	7,508	0	0	0	0	13,941
Indep Living	4,940	4,940	0	0	0	0	9,880
Total Clayborne	11,373	12,448	0	0	0	0	23,821
							0
Deere							
Sudac - Boys	12,402	11,961	12,123	0	0	0	36,486
Supp. Housing	2,679	2,256	2,156				7,091
Sex Offender	17,781	20,987	14,074	0	0	3,085	55,928
Indep Living	18,245	22,790	20,819	800	320	5,771	68,745
Total Deere	51,107	57,994	49,172	800	320	8,856	168,250

NAME	PROGRAM	CURRENT	1-30	31-60	61-90	91-120	over 120	
Table 17-3 page 2		PCWA April 2017 Accounts Receivable						
						December 2016	November 2016 & PRIOR	ENDING BALANCE
		April	March	Februay	January			
Franklin								
	Shelter	30,659	23,030	0	0	0	0	53,689
	Sudac Girls	11,599	9,167	0	0	0	0	20,766
	Indep Living	1,747	0	0	0	0	0	1,747
Total Franklin		44,005	32,197	0	0	3	0	76,205
Graham								
	Indep Living	5,799	2,992	0	0	0	930	9,722
	Sex Off	47,207	39,183	0	0	1,206	1,806	89,401
	Sucac Boys	5,138	2,569	0	0	0	0	7,708
	Sudac Girls	8,260	10,675	0	0	0	1,906	20,841
	Drug Preventio	3,233	0	0	0	0	0	3,233
	Provider 50	4,869	9,985	0	0	90	157	15,101
Total Grahm		74,507	65,404	0	0	1,295	4,800	146,006
Hollaway								
	Sudac Boys	21,364	0	0	160	0	0	21,525
	Sudac Girls	19,826	22,440	0	0	0	0	42,266
	Proivider 50		3,418	0	0	0	0	3,418
	Indep Living	10,369	0	0	0	0	0	10,369
	Sex Off	24,321	22,984	0	0	0	0	47,305
	Drug Preventio	1,495	1,784	0	1,121		0	4,400
	FBMH			3,199	3,555	4,194	8,866	19,814
	SHELTER	11,363	8,484	0	0	0	0	19,847
	Camp Isaccson	27,921	27,921	0	0	0	0	55,842
Total Halloway		116,659	87,031	3,199	4,837	4,194	8,866	224,785
Subtotal Receivables		404,010	379,017	169,399	131,386	141,470	277,742	1,503,023

Table 17-	3 page 3	
DEVELOPMENT RECEIVABLES		
New Cottage Capital Campai		
2013 Pledges Receivable		24,000
2014Pledges Receivable		18,000
2015 Pledges Receivable		14,000
20165 Pledges Receivable		1,250
Reserve for uncollectible ple		-28,761
Total		28,489
Total receivables		1531512

between 5% and 10% of the pledges will go unpaid. Nonpayment is usually due to a downturn in the financial situation of the person making the pledge.

Less often, negative feelings that the donor develops towards the organization after the person made the pledge is the reason for nonpayment.

See page two of the fictional accounts receivable report. Assume a capital campaign in 2011 with a five-year pledge period. The campaign raised $300,000 in cash and pledges. Approximately 20% or $57,200 of the pledges is outstanding. Of these, $24,000 is for 2013 pledges. There is a significant chance that these pledges will go unpaid. When a pledge is unpaid, the campaign staff usually sends past due notices, and will make follow-up telephone calls. If these efforts do not yield any results, the organization uses their policy covering unpaid pledges, reducing the pledges receivable and listing a write off against the uncollected pledge allowance ($28,761).

The accounts receivable report is also a good planning and marketing resource. The report indicates which services of those offered are the most popular with government customers overall as well as on a customer by cutomer basis. Revenues for residential services in April are much larger than from in-home services. While this kind of macro analysis is helpful because purchasing decisions are made on a government unit basis the information on each GCWA purchasing practices are of more use.

An analysis of county-by-county purchasing patterns can help to formulating a sales approach for each county. For example, Graham County purchases signficant amounts of sex offender program services but the volume of their purchase of other services are more modest. Perhaps it is Graham County's preference to purchase services located in their county when possible and only use the PCWA sex offender program because it is a speciality program and it is not widely available. This raises the queston of whether the PCWA should think about opening a boy's group home or independent living program in Graham County to provide stepdown programs for the boys leaving the sexual offender program.

Next, briefly review the cash flow report to assure available cash is sufficient to pay agency bills. Spot the major items affecting cash on hand, and end the financial report review with a careful examination of the balance sheet.

The Balance Sheet

It is important for the finance committee, president, and lead finance staff to scrutinize the balance sheet because it provides information not covered in any of the other reports as well as being the most important indicator of organizational financial health. The balance sheet lists the assets (everything that the PCWA owns) and liabilities (everything that that the PCWA owes to others). There are three classifications of assets and liabilities, unrestricted, temporarily restricted, and permanently restricted. The first refers to assets that the organization is free to use for operating activities. The second are assets designated for a particular purpose and once the PCWA fulfils the purpose, the funds move to the cash account. For example, a foundation pays for a tutoring program in one payment. However, the recipient expends the grant over two years. This situation necessitates the creation of a temporarily restricted fund account. The recipient transfers the amount of the grant that remains at the end of the first program year to a restricted account. The recipient, during the second year of the program moves money from the restricted account to the unrestricted account for year two program expenses. The third column, permanently restricted assets is for donor designated gifts. An example of this is a cash donation in which the donor specifies the gift amount must remain constant and all income earned pays for building repairs to the shelter building

The first line of the balance sheet indicates there is $775,474 in unrestricted cash Remembering the PCWA income and expense summary (from Table 14-1) the PCWA annual expense budget is $8,336.405, or $22,839 a day. There is only enough unrestricted cash to cover 34 days of operations (unrestricted cash $775,474 divided by daily budget $22,839)

The next two lines list the PCWA investments. The types of investments for PWCAs usually include stocks, bonds, and mutual funds. However, the investments may include other types of instruments. The first line indicates that there are an additional $949,953 available as unrestricted funds. The PCWA has enough in unrestricted investments to support operations for an additional 42 days beyond the cash in the unrestricted account ($949,953/$22,656). A possible dilemma is whether to sell investments when customers are slow to pay and expenses exceed unrestricted funds. The PCWA will not want to liquidate investments if investment prices are low. The next chapter covers establishing lines of credit to handle the need for cash.

In addition, on the first investment line there is some money in the temporarily restricted account and a two-million-dollar endowment gift in the permanently restricted account. I discuss the purpose of these in the first paragraph of the balance sheet section. The second investment line, deferred compensation plan is separate from the other investments because the deferred compensation plan uses a specific policy, (a Rabbi Trust) that is different from the organizational financial policy to govern deposits and withdrawals.

Because the staff that participates in the plan receives payments upon retirement, the monies are in a temporarily restricted account. See the section on executive compensation in the succession planning chapter for more information on deferred compensation plans.

The next line, the accounts receivable is often a significant source of cash flow problems. The PCWA has $1,545,407 in accounts receivable. I discuss the issues that determine the amount of accounts receivable earlier in the chapter. A receivable is an asset but it is not cash in hand. Prepaid expenses are bills paid before they are due. Staff uses this to obtain prepayment discounts, or spend grant money that they cannot carry over between grant years to reduce expenses during the next year of the grant. The statement lists the present cash value of a life insurance policy, although the policy does not pay out until the donor dies. Note the next line the due/from account, which shows adjustments, indicates a decrease in the permanently restricted account, and increases in the unrestricted and temporarily restricted accounts. The increases in the first two columns are probably related to the decrease in the third, but the reader cannot know from the available information. More information about the activities in these columns is available from the PCWA chief financial officer. Above, is a discussion of depreciation the subject of the next category. Note that fiscal year end 2016 is the valuation date for the property and equipment. It is common for organization to make,

Table 17-4 PCWA Balance Sheet April 20			
ASSETS	Unrestricted	Temporarily Restricted	Permanently Restricted
Cash and cash equivalents	$775,474	$85,371	
Investments	$949,953	$108,673	$2,040,364
Investments, Deferred Compensation	$748,594	$0	$0
Contracts and grants receivable, less allowance for doubtful accounts of$ 60,000	$1,545,407	$0	$0
Other receivables	$1,220	$0	$0
Prepaid expenses	$309,482	$0	$0
Cash value of life insurance	$0	$0	$76,782
Due (to) from	$64,305	$97,600	-$161,905
Property and equipment, less accumulated depreciation 2016	$2,845,368	$0	$0
Total Assets	$7,239,803	$291,644	$1,955,241
LIABILITIES			
Accounts payable	$258,264	$0	$0
Accrued expenses	$562,650	$0	$0
Deferred compensation plan	$748,594	$0	$0
Deferred revenue	$4,773	$0	$0
TOTAL LIABILITIES	$1,574,281	$0	$0
NET ASSETS	$5,665,522		
COMMITMENTS AND CONTINGENCIES			
NET ASSETS			
Unrestricted	$2,176,267	$0	$0
quasi-endowment	$948,649	$0	$0
Unrestricted, invested in property and equi	$2,540,607	$0	$0
subtotal net assets	$5,665,522	$0	$0
Temporarily restricted		$291,644	
Permanently restricted			$2,121,687
TOTAL NET ASSETS	$5,665,522	$291,644	$2,121,687

equipment and vehicles owner by the organization less the amount depreciated through the years.

The liability portion of the balance sheet consists of financial obligations that the PCWA has to individuals and organizations. The accounts payable line item covers bills that are due but not paid. Accrued expenses are items that the PCWA owes but no invoice exists and the payment due date is often unknown. As an example, many PCWAs employees may accrue vacation time that the agency pays when employment ends. Deferred compensation is what the agency owes to resigning staff. A common item not part of this fictional sample balance sheet is debt. For PCWAs, this may include a conventional mortgage, a municipal bond for a large project or a line of credit drawdown

The Commitment and contingency section of the balance sheet determines the net assets by subtracting the total liabilities from the total assets. This section apprises the reader about the designation of surplus funds into temporarily restricted accounts. Many PCWA will designate net cash assets to different purposes to convey to the reader that there is intent to deploy net assets for specific purposes. In this balance sheet there are five categories: 1) unrestricted and immediately available to spend, 2) unrestricted but designated for specific purposes such as a quasi-endowment or future building projects 3) unrestricted but expended on property and equipment 4) temporarily restricted and held to implement a specific purpose or 5) permanently restricted to pay for specified purposes determined by the donor. Of these classifications, all but the temporarily and permanently restricted assets are available to meet PCWA operational costs.

Communicating Financial Information

The chair or member of the finance committee reports to the BOD on the financial statements, and the treasurer reports on investments and deposits as well as the cash, and investment positions at each meeting of the BOD. Some people believe that the staff finance director presents the financial statement information to the BOD, because this staff member needs to "own the numbers" as they and their staffs prepare the financial statements. The independent auditor verifies the authenticity of any financial information annually, or perhaps by a customer or regulatory agency doing an independent audit.

Program directors and senior managers review income and expense statements, and employ the reports to monitor program operations. As discussed above the income and expense reports document which programs are doing well financially and which are not. A plan to improve poor program financial performance becomes part of the agenda when executives meet with program managers. The managers know the issues related to poor financial performance and develop plans for improvement.

The existence of a realistic recovery plan, the length of time of the loss, and the dollar amount involved determines the type and timing of action. Act more quickly when money-losing programs have no, or an unrealistic financial plan, or cause overall agency losses. However, if the amount is small and not having much of an impact taking more time to make improvements is fine. Incremental reductions are the responsibility of the program director and the vice president. If closing a program is on the horizon than a more formal process involving a written analysis by the president and a BOD review occurs. Conduct training sessions with program directors so they understand each of the line items in their financial statements. This includes direct and indirect costs, the classifying of costs, and depreciation expenses. Program directors work with finance staff to review general ledger entries when they are unclear about the reason for an expense

Budget Planning

Most agencies use experience-based budgeting, combined with projections, and special assumptions as needed. The process from beginning to end usually takes three or four months. Typically, the first eight months of actual income and expenses and four months of projections program reductions based on the initial budget projections. For example, if the licensing division of the state child welfare agency has adopted new standards for overhead sprinkler systems than you include the costs in the capital budget. Finance staff with input from program staff develops the first draft budget. The process is useful in identifying special issues that will have financial implications. Also, consider market trends that are relevant to program services. For instance, for residential programs falling or rising energy prices influence budget planning for utility costs.

The biggest factor in budgeting income is accurately estimating the likely range of service purchases. Pay Attention to trends in the types and volume of services purchased, and federal, state, and local, budget processes. If United Way supports your PCWA, consider their campaign success. Budget planning involves judgement and guesswork. The rule of thumb is to be cautious about unfunded expenditures although there are exceptions when something important will occur because of the expenditure.

Budgeting for startup programs can be tricky. You run the risk of a deficit if you underestimate the costs of scaling up. Estimating a scale up entails how quickly and at what volume customers will purchase new services. My repeated experience is that even when customers have approached the PCWA to provide the service that startup is very slow. Between the time, it takes the GCWA staff to integrate the new service into their selection process, and the time it takes for youth to be available to use the service, ramping up to break-even service usage levels takes a year or two.

External factors help or hurt the bottom line. Less government, funding was available following the recession in 2008. Even in light of a recovering economy, rate increases were hard to come by. Organizations with endowments benefitted from the long bull stock market.

Department Staffing

PCWA's pay finance department directors well compared with their program side peers. They can move more easily between the business and nonprofit sectors. The salary difference between the business and nonprofit sector for lead financial staff is very large for PCWAs. The gap is also substantial between hospitals and PCWAs. My own experience is that recruiting and keeping finance directors is a challenge.

The finance director position at a PCWA is stressful. Finance directors have unhappy conversations with program leaders who are more attentive to their staff and consumers than the bottom line. Finance directors have a heavy workload. In addition to doing the final reconciliations on the monthly financial statements they lead the hunt when things do not reconcile properly, frustrating work when the item(s) involved are difficult to find. In addition to assuring that staff completes the work for the auditor for the agency audit they are the lead staff member in the A-133 audit and often have to make repeated requests to state and county staff to submit the federal program funding information. They also work with the auditors on the 401(k)-audit work. They are the primary staff for the BOD finance committee, 401(k) committee, and track the investment results. In addition, the annual 990-tax filing became more complex, entailing new routines between the finance department and the development department on donation reporting.

The general level of increased accountability required by government causes a growth in the finance departments' work. Income diversity and volume, reporting requirements, organizational size, and external accountability are factors that influence the size and structure of the organization's finance department.

The accounts payable staff usually issue non-payroll checks, and sometimes payroll checks as well if the organization is small. The more common practice is to have the payroll service provided externally. With an external payroll service provider, check to see what they offer by way of benefits self-management software, and timesheet software. Automation in these areas reduce administrative personnel cost. There is a minimum of one account receivable position if the routine is monthly billing to customers and federal grant drawdowns. If there is a sizeable fee for service billing for Medical Assistance or a managed care company, then several positions exist due to the volume.

The financial statement is a time intensive staff assignment. Staff involved with statement preparation also has other duties that they complete when they do not work on the financials. Assure continuity of the accounts payable and receivable staff by good compensation for the positions. There are good software programs that facilitate billing and allows for clinical record keeping systems that make financial departments more efficient. Supervision in the financial field tends to be issue specific. To keep everyone informed, and encourage cohesion monthly staff meetings are worthwhile.

CHAPTER 18 PURCHASING PROCESS, INDEPENDENT, AND IRS AUDITS, AND MEDICAID FRAUD POLICY

Purchasing Policy and Process

Start by doing some research before the agency makes important purchases, whether it is a copier or a firm to audit the financial transactions. This will help staff to think through the features desired and related products and services. These include, delivery of office supplies, learning who the sellers of particular items are in the agency market, and if the amount budgeted for the purchase is sufficient. Preliminary research is two pronged. Read about the product or service line through both product reviews and company websites. Consumer Reports is a good source for evaluating automobiles and broad range of household equipment. Both the ratings and product descriptions are useful. The annual subscription price is modest. You may also want to meet with a sales person or two. Also, a preliminary meeting with professional providers such as computer consultants or an independent auditor gets your oriented to the services these types of firms offer. This research will be of use when you send out a letter inviting bids or review price books, and go to shop at stores. The intention of the procurement policy provision specified below is to conform to federal government requirements which are in CFR 45 74.40-74.48. The reader can review them at https://www.govinfo.gov/app/details/CFR-1996-title45-vol1/CFR-1996-title45-vol1-sec74-40

On equipment and vehicle purchases, start by performing a brief purchase versus lease analysis. If the lease is more advantageous to the federal government, and there is not a substantial reason not to lease the federal regulations indicate that leasing is preferable to buying. Real estate purchases or products under control of a single seller, or items bid within a year are exempt from competitive bidding.

The purpose of a purchasing policy is to assure that everyone associated with the organization is clear on the practices associated with non - personnel expenditures. Without a policy, staff will be unsure of their authority, procedures, and important purchasing principles. If there are sound policies and practices in place, the managers will not have to fear a funding source's audit, since presumably an auditor will find documentation of processes that meet standards. If there are no policies in place, and the agency purchases a nifty but pricey copier from a BOD member's husband who said the price was low, so no comparison-shopping is done there is a risk of a cost disallowance caused by a conflict of interest if you have an external customer audit.

All goods and services purchased with government grant funds are subject to the federal guidelines. In addition, many state and local government contracts utilize federal funds so there is a good chance that state and local fiscal standards will reflect elements of the federal standards. Establish a file system that contains all of the paperwork discussed below for each service, line of supplies, and equipment that you put out to bid.

Purchase Authorization PCWA authorize purchases in a number of ways, as part of the budget adoption process, by BOD resolution, and by management authorization. The budget line item amounts are the upper limit of all purchases in a category. If the budget contains $2,500 for office supplies than there is no need for any further authorization for the expenditure unless, it alone, or combined with other expenditures exceeds the category maximum or falls under the large purchase policy. There is no allowance for the purchase of unnecessary items under federal regulations. Construct a schedule of competitively bid items and the frequency you seek bids (annually, every three years etc.). This includes office supplies, audit services, computer consultation services, banking services, etc. Ideally bid out each item out once every three to five years, though there are no government requirements on how often you bid out purchases and services.

Purchasing Process Staff involved in purchasing need to meet two standards. First, their behavior conforms to the business ethics policy. Business ethics policies address forbidden employee behavior such as taking kickbacks, compensation, etc. and the need for impartiality. The policy states that those involved in purchasing may not accept gifts from actual or potential suppliers, although small gifts worth less than $25.00 are acceptable. The employees or BOD members involved in approving purchases customarily do not have a financial interest in the business involved. If they do the agency conflict of interest policy is applicable.

For each item bid, create a specification form. Self-education regarding the item is important prior to beginning the specification process. Specification forms list the item(s) or work described in detail. Some details include product capability, or service standards and warranty type and duration. As applicable, ask bidders to address delivery, installation, and the availability of annual service maintenance agreements. The requirements vary by the type of purchase or service. Some components are product or service specific, and some are specific to the PCWA. For example, committee members bid out the purchase of a van to transport youth. Naturally, staff knows the passenger capacity. Will the agency be satisfied with a three-year 36,000-mile power train warranty or want a longer more comprehensive warranty?

The specification sheet includes necessary characteristics of the seller including years in business, professional references, location, ability to service and repair equipment, conformance with mandated laws and regulations, bonding, insurance requirements, and expertise. Also, ask the bidders, if within the last three years, did they settle any lawsuits? Is there other litigation pending or in process? Ask about any fines, criminal convictions, suspensions of license, or debarment by a federal or state agency during the last three years.

Bidders, Companies, Purchasing Resources

Always aim to have three or more bids. If you get only two bids, personally call three other companies that received an invitation to bid but did not respond and invite them to bid. Find out if a due date, time extension would allow them to bid. Document if there were other reasons, they did not submit a bid. If you extend the due date, you must inform all of the businesses initially invited to bid. Only consider extending a due date or taking other actions when you receive fewer than three bids.

The goal is that free and open competition among suppliers characterizes the purchasing process. This means that companies who are involved in illegal price fixing arrangements or practices that stifle competition are not bidders. Debarment from competing for business on government-funded purchases is not always easy to discover. Some government agencies such as Medical Assistance do a better job than other government agencies in maintaining accessible lists of debarred companies. Some of the background checks you might want to undertake are: 1) search the federal register (http://www.sam.gov/portal/SAM#1), 2) Google companies you are considering as bidders and see what comes up, and 3) check the state government website to learn if vendors you are considering have current licenses. Require companies to certify that they are not debarred as part of the contracting process, have no pending, litigation or lawsuits that they have settled in the last two years.

The invitation to bid package includes the specification form. At a minimum, the letter to potential vendors describes the project or item, the due date for submission of quotes, dates when the site is accessible to inspection (as needed), and the required components of the bid. The cover letter includes the statement "the agency is free to select a bidder of its choosing based on price, quality, and other relevant considerations". The letter also states that unsuccessful bidders receive a status notification, but the selection process is not open for discussion. Finally, the notice lists a preliminary decision date.

Create a price and bid evaluation form. The form lists the name of the item you plan to purchase, or work involved; the amount the agency budgets for the item or service, the names of the businesses you invite to submit bids, and the names of sellers that submit proposals. List the dates the PCWA opened the bids, each company and their bid prices, and the decision date. Summarize important differences between the bids. State the bidder selected and the important ways the winning bid is superior to the other bids.

Comparison-shopping without bidding is an acceptable means for selecting a supplier when detailed item descriptions and prices are publicly available. This means that in catalogs, advertisements or by going from store to store, comparative prices and product information are available. For example, when deciding upon a vendor for food for the residents or office supplies a representative of the decision-making committee makes a list of the fifteen most commonly purchased items. Specify the quantity of each item e.g. a quart of whole milk and then visit three or more markets during the same week and record the prices for the fifteen items the agency purchases most frequently. Call all of the stores and ask if they offer a discount to charities or a discount on gift card purchases. Ask if the store accept the bank credit card the agency hast. Ask if they have a store credit card. Ask if loading and delivery is available and if they bill on a monthly basis. Record this information in the file with the comparison-shopping data, and considering everything – prices, the discount, the quality of the store, and the distance traveled and any other relevant factors, such as if a store delivers, then decide. Document in a memorandum to file the decision-making process, and the advantages of the selected merchant compared with the other available merchants.

Selection of a Goods or Service Provider

The policy needs a provision establishing purchasing decision criteria. Select the supplier bid that is most advantageous to the agency in regards to price, quality, and other relevant factors. The preference is to select the low-price bidder. When the committee members do not choose the low price, the bid evaluation file contains a clear explanation of the superior characteristics of the bid selected compared to the low-price bid.

An Ad Hoc committee of a minimum of three people makes any purchasing decision where the annual value of the purchase is between$5,000 and $40,000. The program director selects the initial committee members as well as replacement members. The committee elects a member as chairperson. The committee consists of employees that are not key employees, and will include one member that holds the job title of supervisor or program director. Committee members and their families have no financial interest in a company that is a potential bidder. Select committee members for their expertise about the product or service. For example, if selecting a supermarket for group home food purchases, one of the committee members will be the staff member who does the weekly food shopping. Other members might include a staff member from the finance department, another shelter staff person, or staff that oversees meal preparation.

For items, costing $40,000 or more the appropriate standing committee of the BOD acts as the purchasing committee. For instance, the BOD finance committee is a good choice to handle bids involving banking business, retirement plans, or other financial products. Similarly, the BOD information technology committee is a good choice to handle purchases of computer hardware, software, and Information Technology consultation services. Directors who identify a conflict of interest exclude themselves from meeting participation when there is a discussion about the purchase and do not discuss the potential purchase with any agency staff member or director.

As is appropriate, usual, and customary a written agreement or contract exists regarding the service or item purchased. The agreement includes remedies available to the agency when there is a performance failure including contract cancellation.

The Audit

The PCWA arranges for a single audit by a qualified CPA firm when the funds you receive from the federal government directly, plus the portion of federal funds you receive through state and local contracts exceeds $750,000. The auditors are independent in that the CPA firm is a contractor not an employee. Their responsibility is to the BOD or audit or finance committee of the BOD and not to the management or finance department staff.

Purpose

The primary purpose of the audit is to confirm the accuracy of the financial statements issued by the agency. The question for an agency operating on a calendar year basis is: Does the December statement summarizing income, expenses, assets, and liabilities for the year fairly state the organization's actual financial condition? The auditor will review a sample of the transactions to determine if the appropriate documentation exists and if the staff journal entry is correct. They ask questions such as: Does the amount recorded in the organizational financial records match other evidence such as invoices, time sheets, etc.? Is the transaction in the appropriate general ledger account? They will also see if bank records reconcile with organizational records.

The other purpose of the audit is to determine if the organization's business standards are in conformance with the generally accepted accounting principles of the Financial Accounting Standards Board (FASB) as well as applicable government rules. Most standards apply to both for profit and nonprofit organizations, and some apply only to each organizational form. For nonprofit organizations there are standards regarding accounting for contributions. In addition, there are rules for categorizing cash balances as restricted or unrestricted. FASB regularly updates the standards. For example, in 2016 FASB updated its standards on endowments to require charities to fairly value endowments that have lost substantial value (sunken endowments).

In reaching conclusions about financial statement accuracy, the auditors pay special attention to the issue of materiality. The type of financial problem facing the organization and its magnitude determines materiality. If someone steals $200.00 out of petty cash and the auditors find there is no report of the theft, this suggests a lapse in financial procedures. If the organization has an annual budget of $750,000 though the theft is not material because of the small amount involved and because it is, a onetime rather than a repeated problem related to a lack of fiscal controls. It would be a very serious matter, however, if the organization with the small petty cash theft also had an unrecorded managed care audit finding that disallowed $100,000 as the result of many instances of improper service claims. The seriousness has to do with the frequency of the disallowed billings that indicates a lack of financial controls, and deficiency in the existing billing policies. This also has a significant impact on the accuracy of the presentation of the balance sheet, due to the amount that the managed care company will subtract from future payments. In general, if a problem, such as disallowed billings or employee theft is 5% or more of the agency annual revenue the matter is material and the audit firm report it in the opinion letter.

The Engagement Meeting

The BOD audit committee and management staff meets with the audit firm staff to plan the audit process (engagement). The outcomes of the meeting include approximate fieldwork dates, the date the draft audit report is due, and a list of materials that the PCWA staff will prepare for the CPA's field audit staff. In addition, there is a discussion of any new accounting pronouncements and any existing or potential conflicts of interest. The audit engagement letter describes the audit services, the agency responsibilities, fees, and the completion date. This letter is a lack of warranty letter. It limits the auditor's responsibility and places the responsibility for anything that goes wrong on the agency, as the firm examines financial statement that the PCWA prepares. Outline important dates and information in the meeting minutes. Email a copy of the minutes to the lead partner for the engagement as well as all agency participants.

The Audit Field Work

The audit fieldwork site is the agency building that contains the financial records and business papers of the organization. The agency provides a space in the building where the auditors can review the needed records and store them during the period the auditors complete the fieldwork. They will also need access to a copier. Lock the room when the audit staff is not using it. The audit firm sends an auditor or a team of auditors depending on the scope of the work. Often, they will work onsite for between two and five days.

During that time, the finance staff needs to be available to provide additional information answer questions, and participate in discussions with the audit staff. There is a large variety of materials. The fieldwork includes an examination of a sample of agency financial transactions, records, and accounting policies to determine the accuracy of the financial statements, the sufficiency of financial controls, and the methods to reduce the risk of fraud through the separation of employee duties. The field audit staff examines organizational records, accounting methods, the chart of accounts, etc. to assess the extent to which they conform to the Financial Accounting Standard Board's rules. The audit process also examines the extent to which the organization conforms to governmental financial management rules. The auditor will review all of the BOD meeting minutes for the year covered by the audit. PCWA financial staff prepares substantial information for the auditor to review. The basis for some of the audit is what the auditor discovers in reviewing the information supplied by the staff.

Audits are not fraud detection instruments. However, many CPA firms use analytic software that interfaces with the PCWA financial software making an in-depth review of financial records possible. The auditors spend the majority of the fieldwork time examining financial records, organizational policies, and perhaps case files. The process includes an interview with the president that addresses the existence of required policies and fraud issues. This interview is also an opportunity to question the auditor about their thinking on the strengths and weaknesses of the fiscal department and fiscal management. The auditor will interview selected finance departmental staff and ask the finance director questions about information reviewed. The audit prep and fieldwork period are stressful and time consuming for the agency fiscal staff involved in the audit.

The Audit Report

To repeat myself, the primary purpose of the audit report is to confirm the veracity of the monthly financial statements results. The formatting for the balance sheet statement is consistent across charities. The audit balance sheet and income and expense statement list current year and last year amounts. Of all of the financial material prepared and reviewed during the year this is the only one which readily allows comparisons between two years, on a line by line basis.

The balance sheet numbers should match the internal end of year financial statement numbers. There can be some adjustments due to a need to close the books for December promptly, to prepare invoices, and prepare the records for the auditor to examine. Also, sometimes the auditor decides to reclassify items in management's income and expense statements. If there were some late unexpected income or expense items, deferrals, or reclassifications these would affect the consistency between the audit and the end of year management prepared financial statement. For board and staff that regularly review the monthly numbers the audit balance sheet report allows for a comparison of the changes between the two years. Have the accounts receivables changed? Have liabilities increased due to a loan? Has the amount of cash changed? Is the amount of any permanently restricted funds increased or decreased? The important question is if the net asset number has changed significantly and if so, what is the reason?

Next are the annual income and expense statements. In as much as the audit provides a detailed list of expenses by program in a separate section of the audit, on the income and expense page only a few categories of expenses appear - administration, fundraising, and program. Donors and charity watchdog groups are interested in how much money is going to help consumers as opposed to going to administrative and fundraising costs, with the goal of keeping these costs low. Administrative staff self-reports the administration and fundraising expense numbers. Parts of the administrative expenses are program costs, as the administrative costs are for agency wide work. The amounts listed as fundraising or administrative expenses will be less than the total compensation of the administrative staff. The reporting design of these numbers is open to manipulation by clever managers who want to minimize them.

There is flexibility in listing income. One approach would be to separately list each government contract and grant when they exceed 5% or more of the total income. This gives the interested reader more information on customers by size than grouping everything together. However, others like to keep it simple and use only four- or five-income categories. The cash flow statements for the current and past year show the change in organization cash position and the significant items that contribute to it such as operating expenditures, receivables, payables etc. When the available cash has increased substantially managers should be mindful of the possibility of using lines of credit. There should not be much that is new in the balance sheet, income and expense statement, and cash flow report if staff reviews the internal financial statements carefully. The exception is the breakout of administrative and fundraising expenses.

Next, are the expenses for each program side by side - organized by budget expense category. Differences in the amount of categorical expenses across programs are of interest. For example: Why does one residential program spend less for food than another group home?

The last section consists of various footnotes. There is information in the notes that do not appear in the monthly financial statements or other internal reports. The notes begin with a description of the programs. When you have added a new program review the draft audit for its inclusion and the accuracy of the description. Next is a discussion of organizational accounting practices. This section is important to review to note any new accounting pronouncements. The section on practices also covers other organizational accounting policies such as the handling of depreciation, and income taxes. Additionally, the notes contain details on investments. The listing allows for a quick risk analysis in that that the reader sees the bank deposit amounts that are more than FDIC insurance limits. In addition, the market value of stocks, bonds, (by bond rating) are in the notes. There is further detail on property values, and depreciation taken. The notes also list funds obligated for future purposes, such as deferred compensation plans, retirement plans, mortgage and other loan amounts, multi-year leases, payment schedules, and organizational transactions involving BOD members. The notes also contain detailed schedules on the endowment, listing pledges, and they give an estimate if the assumptions for uncollectable pledges are on target.

The Audit Opinion

After the fieldwork, the auditor issues an opinion regarding the fairness (accuracy) of the organizational financial statements. An unqualified opinion means that the auditor finds that the financial statements are accurate, and there is no indication of failure to follow the FASB standards. A qualified opinion indicates that overall things are running smoothly but the charity does not follow selected standards or always follow them. A finding of material misstatement means significant deficiencies of a material nature that result in distortions to the presentation of the financial condition, or there are government rule violations, or fiscal controls or record keeping, is significantly deficient. The auditor does not give an opinion when the available information is insufficient.

Risks of negative findings are higher when there is a new auditor or a new agency finance director. If the deficiencies are significant, it raises questions about the competence of the finance department staff. This is a difficult issue in the private nonprofit organization as the finance director usually reports to a president or vice president who often has no financial training. The president and chair of the audit committee should discuss any negative findings with the finance director, and evaluate their explanation. The quality and acceptability of the finance director's corrective action plan is determined. The president and the audit committee must ensure that the corrective action plan implementation is prompt, and meets standards within four months of the plan's issuance. If the explanation, the plan, or its implementation does not inspire a feeling that things are back on track one possibility is to make staffing changes, but it could be more efficient and effective to contract out some portions of the finance functions to a firm with greater expertise as opposed to doing everything internally. The auditor will also issue a management letter that repeats any of the findings in the report, and adds suggestions to improve agency accounting practices as well as efficiency. For the most part, the charity must send both the audit and management letter to all government customers. In a cover letter to the government customers, assure them that you will correct audit exceptions promptly and include the plan of correction. Depending on the nature of exceptions, you may want to provide other information in the cover letter.

The Audit Committee

The subjects of financial stewardship and the monitoring responsibility of BOD members receive attention in the chapter on the boards of directors. The audit process is the most important annual event that occurs that documents the BOD and staff success in the financial stewardship role. A committee of the BOD or the BOD as a whole leads the audit process within the organization. The gold standard is to have a separate audit committee, but the finance committee can serve both functions if the members have the right qualifications. Two committee members should possess the Certified Public Accountant credential, and one or two should have a history in finance. I recommend against the entire BOD monitoring the audit process because of the time, effort, workload, and number of meetings. The index contains a discussion of the purpose and responsibilities of the audit committee. Briefly, the committee engages and annually evaluates the auditor. The committee reviews the draft audit, and presents it to the BOD for approval. The auditor reports to the audit committee of the BOD not to agency management.

Bidding out the Audit Work

There are several good reasons to periodically bid out the audit work, every five years, and one drawback. On the positive side, the bidding process assures the reasonableness of fees, as with all agency service contracts. There is a school of thought that agency and audit staff develop close relationships over time and consequently the auditor may go easy on the agency. Although this sounds appealing to people loyal to the agency, if the auditor does not let the agency know that there is a problem area that needs attention, and there is a subsequent customer audit, public embarrassment, fines, and repayments are a risk. Some audit firms and PCWAs deal with the coziness issue by periodically rotating the accounting firm's lead partner performing the audit.

The most important reason to bid out the work is if the audit committee members do not like the quality of the work of the audit firm. An advantage to having CPAs on the committee is that they are good judges of quality. When there is a difference of opinion about a finding, the auditor will give special consideration to the opinion of a peer.

The committee may not retain an audit firm in two other situations. The first is when there is financial wrongdoing discovered. Most of the situations that I have heard about involve a bookkeeper or another PCWA finance staff member stealing money over a number of years. Prior to the engagement auditors have you sign a letter of understanding that the audit is not a fraud detector, however, BOD members and others wonder how this kind of situation could go on for several years without the auditor discovering it. They also feel that if they switch auditors that they are demonstrating good financial stewardship.

The third reason that agencies drop an audit firm is that the staff and audit committee think the findings are overly harsh or unfair. In as much as the distribution of the management letter and audit includes government customers, management, and BOD members get concerned about making a bad impression on their customers. Finance department staff can get defensive when there is criticism of their work. Audit committee members ought to meet with the auditor to discuss the findings and engage in discussion about whether some findings can be recommendations instead. Never fire the present auditor, though until you have composed a plan of correction, and you get the current auditor's feedback and agreement to the plan. A new auditor will have access to a former auditor's staff, reports, and working papers. They will also review the accomplishment of the plan of correction that the charity adopts no matter which firm does the work.

The fourth reason for dissatisfaction is that the audit firm is late in the submission of the draft audit report. You decide on the due date for the completion of a draft audit report during the audit engagement meeting. To facilitate a review of the draft, choose a date that fits with the audit committee-meeting schedule. Agency purchase of service agreements usually has audit submission date requirements. Sometimes you need the audit reports for distribution at the organizational annual meeting.

However, the partner that reviews the audit may be late in getting the work done. If the auditor has a high volume of business, a bottleneck may occur at the review stage for the audit. It is a good practice to contact the partner assigned to the audit, two weeks before the specified draft audit due date, and inquire if the submission will be on time. If they say there will be a delay negotiate a new due date that is firm. Leaving the date open is not a good idea because other organizations waiting to get their reports will also be pressing the firm to get their audit to them as soon as possible.

Unless you are a small agency or have other constraints against paying reasonable fees, it is not a good idea to engage a sole practitioner. If the auditor becomes ill, dies, or goes out of business, you could have to quickly engage another one. In these situations, sometimes there are problems about transferring audit files if you use a sole practitioner.

Unless you are not a happy customer, invite the present firm to bid. They will sometimes lower their current price to retain you as a customer. The biggest advantage to bringing in a new auditor is that a new broom sweeps clean. There will likely be some recommendations and findings during the first year or two. Whatever the findings of the new auditor bearing the pain are usually better than the ignorance is bliss attitude. Making needed changes will strengthen the organization. However, the learning curve of the new firm is likely to be steep. The staff from the new firm will require education from the PCWA staff. It will likely take a year or two for the new firm to become familiar with the agency operations.

Review the purchasing policy material in this chapter to get a general idea how to proceed with the actual bidding out process. Limit the search to midsize or large firms having experience and expertise in nonprofit auditing. One of the bidding qualifications might be that the firm has two or more CPA's that have several years of nonprofit auditing experience. Non-profit auditing is a specialty; therefore, using a general practitioner maybe a mistake because they often lack knowledge of the FASB rules that are particular to non-profit organizations. The request for bid letter indicates the scope of the work, which could include the financial compilation review, the annual single audit, the annual 401(k) plan audit, preparing the 990-tax filing, and preparing the retirement plan annual tax filing 5620.

Indicate the agency income and expenses, number of funding sources, and describe the principal types of income and expenses encountered. In the invitation to bid letter ask for a written proposal that includes: 1) a background statement on the firm, 2) A discussion of the firms experience with nonprofit agencies, 3) a description of the experience and accomplishments of the lead partner for the account. 4) Three references from nonprofit customers, 5) the firm's nonprofit customer list, and 6) their last external quality control report (peer review) and a price quote. Compose a proposal ranking sheet, rating each proposal submitted, using criteria which includes nonprofit experience, the background of the lead partner, and the proposed fee, as well as other criteria important to the charity. Based on the audit committee review the proposals meet with staff of the top-ranking firms. Sometimes a firm will send a person who specializes in sales. However, as part of the selection process meet with the proposed lead partner for the engagement as well as the lead staff doing fieldwork.

The agency interview team should include the president, members of the audit committee, and the finance director. To ascertain a sense of their knowledge base, you might want to ask questions about government financial rules. The committee members will likely have their own relevant questions to ask, as will the finance director. It will also be important to explore if there are any conflicts of interest regarding dual relationships with any agency staff or BOD members. After the interview, evaluate the goodness of fit between the lead staff of the auditing firm and the agency's audit committee and finance staff. Ask for a fixed price, three-year contract. If the group is too uncertain about the new firm to do this, stay with the present auditor, if possible.

The Case of Dim County or No Good Deed Goes Unpunished

The Dim County Drug and Alcohol Division operates on a July to June fiscal year. At the beginning of May, Cindy Chance, the Division Director learns from her fiscal staff that the Drug and Alcohol Division has underspent their state allocation in the area of prevention. Ms. Chance calls Peter Pauper Director of Anything for a Buck Children's Services (ABCS) and tells Mr. Pauper that Dim County would like to increase ABCS contract for the current fiscal year, by $15,000 but the deadline for the expenditures is June 30th. Mr. Pauper tells her that because the school year will end soon, he doubts that he can schedule many more class room prevention education sessions. He asks if she would like to have ABCS buy a drunken driving simulator. Several providers have rented a simulator and it is a big hit with the students, teachers, and police departments. He thinks that as a drunk driving prevention strategy that the simulator is *worth the investment. Mr. Pauper says that if he buys a simulator than ABCS will not have to pay the hefty daily rental fee in the future. Ms. Chance loves this idea because she also has received very positive feedback from several school districts on the simulator. Ms. Chance and Mr. Pauper end the conversation saying that Mr. Pauper will explore prices for the simulator and call Ms. Chance back. Mr. Pauper visits several internet sites and finds that a simulator and trailer to move the simulator to different schools will cost about $15,000. ABCS will have to outfit one of their vans with a hitch, and also incur the mileage cost of bringing the simulator to different schools, estimating that mileage costs t will be about $500.00. A company offering the brand of simulator that ABCS has rented in the past bills can bill ABCS in May and deliver the unit by the end of the month. Mr. Pauper calls Ms. Chance back and they decide that ABCS should proceed with the purchase. Ms. Chance sends Mr. Pauper a contract amendment raising the maximum amount the ABCS contract by $17,000, but the amendment does not specify the purpose of the funds. ABCS buys the simulator in the middle of May, bills Dim County early in June for the prevention education sessions provided in May, the simulator, trailer, and associated expenses. The simulator goes on line in mid-October because most of the students will not be attending school during the summer vacation period, and school-based prevention services do not start at the beginning of the school year. A year later, the state audits the Dim county Drug and Alcohol program. The scope of the audit includes a review of vendor invoices. The auditor uses both Federal and State regulations in conducting the audit because the drug prevention funds allocated to the counties include both federal funds and state matching funds. The auditor discovers possible irregularities on several vendor invoices. ABCS billed the simulator as a program expense and the county division has paid the invoice. A review of the contract between ABCS and Dim county indicates it is a purchase of service agreement, with services delivered billed after the provider renders the services. There is nothing in the agreement about equipment purchases. The auditor visits the ABCS office and reviews the ABCS purchasing process documentation, the large item purchase policy, and interviews Mr. Pauper. The review indicates that ABCS did not consider the option of leasing the simulator instead of buying it. In addition, although Mr. Pauper states that he visited several websites prior to selecting a vendor there is no paperwork that shows Mr. Pauper sought competitive bids for the simulator, or engaged in competitive shopping demonstrating that the simulator purchased provided the best value for ABCS. ABCS billed the county for the entire cost of the simulator rather than only the portion of the asset's value that it expensed on an annual basis. ABCS billed Dim County three months before ABCS starting using*

Internal Revenue Service Audits

I was scared, the two times in my career, when I received letters from the Internal Revenue Service, informing me that they were going to audit VYH's books. Primarily I was frightened that there was something wrong with the organizational financial operations that would come out during these audits. One of the disadvantages of being a social worker running a business, and having little financial training is I always felt weak in my ability to supervise financial staff and know for certain if things were up to snuff. In addition, although the organization had independent audits done annually, I wondered that since we paid the auditors were, they less tough than the IRS examiners. Both times, we got a white glove pass from the IRS in the exit interview. The examiner said our accounting systems were in good shape. In addition, the IRS examiner invited me to contact her if I had questions. I did this on one occasion and she was very helpful. One of the lessons that I have taken away from the process is the value of keeping the records in good order. In as much as good record keeping is not a moneymaker for the charity, and does not help children, it is easy to let things slip.

According to their website, the IRS notification letter for an audit of the 990 filing for a particular year is likely to include the following:

"--Initial discussion between organization representative and Internal Revenue Agent

--Tour of the organization's facilities, in order to ensure that the organizational test is still met

--Governing instruments (Articles of Incorporation, Trust Indenture, By-laws, Code of Regulations, etc.) including any subsequent amendments

--Copy of letter granting exemption from income tax received from Internal Revenue Service

--List of names & addresses of all officers, directors & trustees to include compensation, if paid

In order to verify that the activities are exempt activities:

--Minute books showing any recorded meetings of the governing body (Officers, Directors, or Trustees) including committees

--Copies of newspapers, newsletters, brochures, magazines, pamphlets and other literature printed

--Any contracts, leases or agreements to which the organization was a party to in the year under examination

In order to verify the correctness of income, gross receipts, deductions and credits and to reconcile the return to the books:

--Books of account including general ledger, general journal, cash receipts and cash disbursements journal, accounts payable and accounts receivable journal plus subsidiary ledgers and a chart of accounts

--Auditor's financial statements, yearend audit and any work papers and/or schedules necessary to reconcile the return to the books

In order to determine whether the organization has properly filed all applicable return/forms for which it may be liable:

--federal employment tax returns, Form 940 and Form 941, plus employee earnings records

--Form W-2 and Form W-4. In addition, any Form 1099 issued for the year

--Pension plan information such as latest IRS approval letter plus Form 5500 series filed during the year under examination, and deferred compensation plans or tax sheltered annuities in effect during the year

--Copies of reports made to other federal agencies

--Copies of prior and subsequent year return

--Correspondence file, if any, with IRS"

(Internal Revenue Service, 2015)

When you get a letter from the IRS, you begin to wonder why me? A nonprofit consulting firm, Chapel York offers the following:

"The IRS has many ways of selecting returns for audits. It uses a computerized system called RICS to select many nonprofit returns for audit. No one outside the IRS knows exactly how this mysterious system works, the IRS simply says that "RICS applies the criteria selected by the Planning and Program Group to identify returns and line items for potential examination" ...

(Chappel and York 2015)

An advantage to having CPAs on the committee is that they are good judges of quality. When there is a difference of opinion about a finding, the auditor will give special consideration to the opinion of a peer.

Another easier to understand reason is that the IRS pays close attention to media reports regarding questionable behavior by nonprofits. Therefore, not only can negative news stories result in public embarrassment, they may prompt an audit as well (so much for the old saying, "There's no such thing as bad publicity").

The IRS has even created a special form that members of the public can fill out to report inappropriate activities by nonprofits — Form 13909, Tax-Exempt Organization Complaint (Referral) Form.

In addition, the IRS commonly targets certain types of nonprofits for special scrutiny. As mentioned before hospitals, colleges and universities are potential targets. In addition, the selection risk may be higher for the following types of organizations:

"nonprofits that conduct gambling fundraisers, nonprofits engaged in joint ventures with for profit companies, nonprofits that sponsor travel tours, nonprofits with donor advised funds, nonprofits engaging in political activities, student loan organizations, and nonprofits that fail to file IRS returns"

(Chapel and York, 2015)

However, recent stepped up nonprofit auditing rates have received press attention from Fox News:

"... the IRS audited an average of 6,205 returns of tax-exempt organizations per year from 2001 to 2008. From 2009 to 2011, however, the number of audited returns spiked to an average of 11,111 per year.

This finding is even more surprising when one considers that fewer tax-exempt organizations have filed IRS returns under Mr. Obama than did under Mr. Bush. From 2009 to 2011, the IRS received an average of 819,417 tax returns per year. Yet from 2001 to 2008, tax-exempt organizations filed a larger average of 847,898 returns per year.

What's going on here? Why is the Obama administration draining precious resources and time from charitable organizations to lawyer up and endure the long, hard slog of an IRS audit? [Full disclosure: I am the president of an organization currently under IRSconsideration for 501 (c)(3) status.]

One thing is for sure: the IRS's motivation isn't money. After all, audits of tax-exempt groups do not yield big revenues, if any.

Indeed, the IRS under Mr. Obama seems to have developed a penchant for poaching low yield auditing fruit. For example, for every hour the IRS spends interrogating small or medium-sized businesses, it would have 1,207% more than had it audited a large corporation ($702 versus $9,173). And yet from 2009 to 2011, the coverage rate (number of audits as a percentage of total returns filed) for smaller companies with assets between $10 million and $50 million was 32 percent. In the same way, the Obama administration's decision to ratchet up IRS scrutiny of charities by placing them in the auditing crosshairs will not boost revenues. So why is it happening?

The president's supporters are likely to say that the bulk of the tax-exempt organizations undergoing audits are "front" political groups, not social welfare charities like the Salvation Army and Red Cross that feed and assist the poor. But the IRS does not itemize tax-exempt audits by type, and even if they did, the IRS has designated educational groups as charities. Period.

For the president's opponent's, the increase in charity audit rates is further evidence of a politically-driven White House that leverages power to achieve its ends. Last month, for example, the Obama administration raised ire and eyebrows when it assembled a group of charitable officials at the White House and pressured them to support president Obama's proposed tax hikes -- or else"

(Schweitzer, 2013)

In most situations, either the examiner gives the reason for audit selection or the focus of the questions and materials reviewed suggests a rationale. Those reporting on their experience with the audit process agree that management should expect that the agent is very thorough in reviewing the audit materials referenced above. Their manner will be business like with some variation of friendliness based on the individual personality of the examiner. One does not get a sense though of the examiner "being out to get you". However, there is always the human factor and if department transfers an examiner and they are still learning 501(c3) work things may go less smoothly as they are still becoming acclimated. The IRS describes the audit closing process as follows:

(Zimmerman 2013)

<u>IRS Closing Conference Possibilities</u>

Revenue Agent Proposal	Conference Topics
Accept Returns as Filed (no change)	Discuss agent finding and recommendations
Accept returns and recommend changes to improve compliance (no changes with advisory)	Discuss agent findings and recommendations
Adjust tax-exempt status or tax Liability	Deliver report of examination and explain changes
Allow or disallow a claim for refund or a request for abatement	Deliver report of examination and explain disallowances

The IRS also performs compliance checks, which involve examination of material they request, and the agency submits. At the conclusion of a compliance check, the organization receives a closing letter; there is not a closing conference or call. A compliance check questionnaire may involve onlythe initial contact if all requested information is in order (so there is no follow-up contact no closing letter is sent). (Internal Revenue Service, 2015)

Medical Assistance Fraud Waste, and Abuse Policy

Many children involved in public child welfare services have Medical Assistance Health Coverage. Behavioral health coverage offered through managed care companies is common for many of these children. Often managed care company's contract with PCWAs child mental health organizations and family orient service providers to offer these services. Medical Assistance through MCO's is sometimes aggressive in enforcement regarding provider activities that are clearly fraudulent as well as services that are unnecessary, and services that exceed what is usual and customary. Provider audits may result in significant claw backs of previously paid claims. Providers need to understand and conform with the MCO case note and record keeping requirements, back up evidence for service billings, and the standard for what the MCO considers to be usual and customary services.

Fraudulent activities by direct service personnel aim at increasing income usually through submitting invoices for services not provided. This is easily discoverable in outpatient programs through reconciling staff billings with the front desk appointment book. Verifying fraud for home-based services only happens if there is regular verification with consumers regarding both the legitimacy of the consumer signature on the consumer encounter forms, and verification that the worker made the visit. If the consumer (parent) is uncertain, about staff visitation dates during a telephone verification call, then follow up by mailing the consumer encounter form(s) with a letter asking the parent to call the office to verify that the signature is authentic. These situations are a "double loss" for the agency in that managers pay the staff before they detect the fraud. The agency then needs to repay the MCO and try to recover the money paid to the staff person.

Administrative fraud occurs both in situations where the agency is in financial trouble and generates excess bills to keep the doors open. In addition, there are cases of greed where owners develop schemes to derive additional income. For example, clinic owners direct a psychiatrist to reduce the length of sessions and see additional patients in order to increase billings. MCO's also reclaim money for what they view as excessive services to what is customary and usual in terms of quantity. Accordingly, the agency should request from the MCO the criteria for customary and usual service volume.

To prevent Medical Assistance claw backs, have agency middle management meet with MCO audit staff, and review MCO written material to learn:

Guidelines for customary and usual services including:

- ➢ Frequency of service,
- ➢ Length of service episode
- ➢ Type of services allowable under different licenses
- ➢ Session Case Notes:
- ➢ Format
- ➢ Content

--Instances where additional document is required
--Allowability of Case Planning billing
--Allowability of time spent in constructing homework
  assignments for consumer

PCWA Medical Assistance fraud waste and abuse policies define the type of activities that constitute fraud, waste, and abuse. The definitions include the activities of direct service providers, agency managers, and administrators. The policy describes the agency program to prevent, detect, and manage fraud, waste, and abuse. It describes who has the authority and responsibility for policy over sight and plan monitoring activities and describes the monitoring activities. For a direct service behavioral health staff, program managers, and key employees the following list, although not exhaustive, gives a good idea of how federal law and regulation defines fraud waste and abuse.

- ➢ Billing for a service you did not provide.
- ➢ Billing a falsified claim
- ➢ Billing more than once for the same service encounter.
- ➢ Billing for more services than is usual and customary.
- ➢ Falsification of a child's record.
- ➢ Use of a more highly paid service code than the service you provide
- ➢ Billing policies that result in higher charges than when you use less expensive billing methods
- ➢ Services provided by a staff member that does not have the required education and experience credentials
- ➢ Paying people for referrals
- ➢ Billing for unnecessary services
- ➢ Misrepresenting facts related to a bill
- ➢ Supervisors approving false claims
- ➢ Employing debarred staff

Agency policy includes the appointment of an agency compliance officer and compliance committee. They perform the following duties:

- ➢ Review program statistical and financial reports, noting any areas of concerns or irregularities.

- ➤ Conduct an internal investigation when there is an allegation of fraud, abuse, or waste and conclude the investigation within 20 days of the complaint.
- ➤ Arranges for annual audits of each program's clinical records, claims, and staff invoices
- ➤ Reports the results of each audit to the president
- ➤ Makes repayment recommendations to the president when appropriate.
- ➤ Publicizes the need to report fraud, waste, and abuse through staff education programs.
- ➤ Educates managers about the prohibition against retaliation for making a report. There are several training methods: staff meeting presentations, through making the policy part of the program operations manual, through posting notices, and during staff supervision sessions.
- ➤ Assure each program supervisor audits a percentage of the program charts and claims submitted annually to ascertain if any fraud waste or abuse is in evidence. An audit includes the conformance of record keeping with established standards, the type and frequency of services within the context of the treatment plan and what is customary and usual for the diagnosis and program type.
- ➤ Committee members contact a percentage of program staff to ascertain if they understand   what fraud, waste, and abuse are and how to report it.

There is an administrative review to assure that managers screen all staff candidates through federal websites listing debarred providers. Committee members act a as consultant for staff investigating complaints. The compliance officer notifies the president of investigations that result in any monies returned due to a claim characterized by fraud, waste, and abuse. The president notifies the organization's audit committee when any claim or claims repaid exceeds $10,000.

Chapter 19 – Treasury, Investment, And Related Financial Policies

Treasury Policy

A treasury policy is one of the basic PCWA financial instruments. Its purpose is to ensure that the financial instruments used to invest cash used for everyday operating purposes 1) are safe, 2) meet organizational needs for accessibility, 3) have a low risk of loss of principal, and 4) earn the maximum interest rate.

The policy specifies:

- The types of accounts
- The position titles that decide on individual deposit instruments and institutions
- A maximum maturity time for an instrument
- A method for regularly checking on the bankruptcy risk of the banks used as deposits may exceed the FDIC deposit insurance limit
- The position titles that have check signing authority
- The goal amount for operating cash. A common goal is three months of expenses
- The credit card policy for staff
- Lines of credit and the purchase of banking products

For operating funds, the policy specifies some or all of the following types of accounts as allowable choices: checking accounts (one for payroll and one for other payables) and money market accounts. The PCWA can purchase certificates of deposits offered by FDIC insured banks, U.S. Treasury instruments or mutual funds restricted to AA or better-rated government bonds. The maturity of these latter instruments is customarily not greater than six months to a year. Money needed for operations during the maturity period of any certificate of deposit or bond will be available in the checking or money market accounts.

Unless a bank offers a very high interest rate, consider the history and prospects for charitable support, for the organization, as one criterion for the selection of banking institutions. Because deposits may exceed FDIC deposit insurance coverage amounts, finance department staff review the composite rating report on each bank monthly (available at bankrate.com). Each bank has a score between one (strongest) and five (weakest). The policy states a rank below which you move the deposits, perhaps 3.

Also, consider using two or three banks to deal with the FDIC insurance limit. Checking could be with one institution and saving accounts and CD's with another. However, when the regular checking and payroll accounts are at separate institutions it creates extra work for the finance staff.

The policy provides authorization for the purchase of financial products. The list of products could include direct deposit of payroll, positive pay, account reconciliation, zero-balance accounts, and computer-based banking, as well as new products.

There are several methods of choosing particular investment vehicles. Within the confines of the policy, compare rates. If a six-month CD is maturing, check rates to ensure that the treasurer and finance director are satisfied with the renewal rate. Also, if the staff wants to keep a CD with the present bank, but the rate offered is subpar, ask the bank to match the best comparable rate More often than not, they will seriously consider the request, in order to maintain a good customer relationship with you.

Because these decisions come up regularly do not make the decision group too large, perhaps one or two people unless the deposit amount is very high. The finance director in consultation with the president can make the decision once there is a common understanding about goals. If the BOD desires more control, the two people can be the finance director and the BOD treasurer.

The opposite is true regarding who signs checks, due to the possibility of needing a check in unanticipated circumstances, and the lack of availability of regular signers. The policy should specify the position title of the person who regularly signs checks for under a specified amount, perhaps up to $2,500. The policy also designates the position titleof the person who acts as second signer for checks above this amount. The policy then indicates the authorized signers by titles and three other signers who sign checks in the absence of the two regular signers. The executive vice presidents, BOD chair and vice chair can be additional authorized signers.

Draw on a line of credit when there is not enough cash to pay bills. It is advisable to get two separate lines of credit from two different banks and that the annual renewal date for each line is six months apart; The BOD adopts resolutions authorizing the creation of the lines of credit. In the resolution, specify a borrowing limit, perhaps six months of operating cash, and who authorizes a drawdown. Two members of the BOD the chairperson, vice chairperson, treasurer, or finance committee chair makes the decision to draw on a line of credit.

Check Signing

The finance director signs all checks under a certain amount ($2,500 limit could be appropriate) and the president signs along with the director for checks over that amount. Who signs checks, and the amounts will vary by organization. In smaller organizations, the president signs all checks and the BOD treasurer also signs large checks. Appropriate backup paperwork including invoices, purchase authorizations etc. exist for each check.

Credit Cards

The organization will probably need to have a corporate credit card program for employees. This portion of the treasury policy specifies an aggregate organization wide amount for the program and who has the authority to raise the ceiling. It specifies who decides on individual employee credit card limit amounts and how an employee is able to become a cardholder. Credit card limits for direct service staff may be higher than for managers' depending on their specific duties. For example, a shelter childcare worker who pays for the weekly food shopping may need a higher limit than a manager who does little purchasing. One approach is to set a rather low general limit ($500 or less) and then make exceptions for staff that do purchasing on a regular basis. The policy specifies situations in which an employee loses credit card privileges such as, use of the card for personal purchases, repeated failure to submit payment authorizations, or receipts.

Financial Policy Associated with the Treasury Policy

Spending Authority Limits A written policy lists the spending authority limits for each position, including the president and treasurer. The amount increases for each higher position. When an expense exceeds the limit of a direct service staff person, the person's supervisor approves the expenditure. Similarly, the supervisor's program director, the program director's vice president, and president make expenditure approval decisions as needed. The treasurer approves expenditures that are larger than the president authorizes and asks the BOD to approve expenditures above the treasurer's authorization level. Take care not to make the spending limits too restrictive to avoid the problem of excessive requests but not so large that it defeats the control objective of the policy, Specific spending limits will vary by organizational size.

Competitive Bidding Use competitive bidding for all purchases in excess of an amount you determine, perhaps $10,000. However, if you purchase like items within 12 months of the first purchase, do not rebid them given the vendor's price, service, and quality are good. Rebid certain services, i.e. audit, consultants, every three to five years. I re-bid life insurance and disability policies every two or three years because I think they are especially susceptible to rate creep. An exception to this is the 401 (k) plans because of the work entailed in switching companies; however, make the change if the fees become exorbitant or there is dissatisfaction with the service.

Purchase Documentation All purchases must include a receipt, bill, or written price quote from the seller. The staff member making the purchase signs the request form and the supervisor approves it. Before approving the check, the finance staff reviews each request to see that it conforms to requirements.

Restricted Funds Temporarily restricted fund accounts hold funds that are not immediately available for operations, and have a specific future purpose. There are temporarily restricted fund accounts that can hold money you receive during the year, but do not spend during the same year. Sometimes these accounts have transfers in / out of the operating accounts during the same year. A vacation accrual account is an example of this. Management makes additions to this fund to pay for earned unused vacation leave. Usually agencies have policies that limit the number of vacation leave days that staff can accumulate in order to avoid a large future payable. Another common type of restricted fund holds monies received for a grant program where the income in a year exceeds the expenses. For example, a foundation makes a grant towards the operating costs of a new shelter program. Due to an unexpected denial of a zoning exception, the opening date of the shelter is six months late because the PCWA successfully pursues a court appeal. The shelter opens eight months later than planned. The organization can begin to transfer the restricted money into the operating fund once there are shelter expenses to match the foundation's funds.

The BOD creates a second type of restricted fund for a specified future purpose. By resolution, they create restricted funds and may dissolve these funds, commonly known as Board restricted funds. They may vote to make deposits to these funds or transfer monies from a temporarily restricted fund to the operating fund. The BOD restricted funds are money that the organization has available to spend but chooses to put aside for an explicit future use. Accounting rules dictate that money in board created restricted funds is available cash for audit purposes. An important function of these funds is to indicate that the BOD has thought through future organizational needs and circumstances, and have set aside money to fund them. Rainy day, building, and endowment funds are common. A rainy-day fund exists to pay for unanticipated and unbudgeted events and expenses. The amount needed for an adequate rainy-day fund is subjective, but a sum that is between three and six months of operating expenses is customary, although higher fund balances are common. Building funds are for a specific building project, such as replacing an existing building, for a new adventure center, repairs, and renovations to a building. The goal for a BOD quasi-endowment fund is to maintain the principal of the fund, and use the annual earnings on principal pay for operational costs. There are also several other types of board restricted funds that are less common. These include a tail end insurance funds, to pay premiums on insurance policies for a period following a change in insurers, or if the agency closes. The amount devoted to this type of fund is the amount needed to cover the insurance premium, for a time period after you switch policies in which a claim is possible as determined by state laws. Often this is two years. Insurance deductible funds have a balance equal to the deductible on the officers, and directors and malpractice insurance policies that are sizable if the PCWA pays several claims paid during the past five years.

Investment Policy

Goal - The investment policy prescribes the management of funds not covered by the treasury policy. These are monies not needed for every day operations. There are usually two sources of funds that are subject to long-term investments, donor determined endowments and BOD determined fund accounts, such as a building fund or a board created quasi-endowment fund financed from operational surpluses. In addition, the investment policy may direct other accumulating funds such as a nonqualified executive 457(f) compensation plan. The goal of the investment policy is to preserve the principal, and reinvest gains to grow an endowment or BOD designated fund or to fund a drawdown of a specified amount of the principal or earnings to pay for capital expenses or operating costs

Risk - The issue of risk is important in considering the contents of an investment policy because the finance committee will be considering two contradictory expectations. The first is the preservation of capital. The goal of safety - the investments are not speculative in nature and the risk taken is not excessive. The second goal is to maximize returns through using investment vehicles offering a higher rate of return than offered by banking and Treasury bond products.

You are, or in the future will be dealing with endowments for a specific purpose, so the preservation of capital is important to carry out the endowment purposes. If you lose part of the principal of a building endowment there will be less money to make property repairs or purchases. If the agency gets involved in fraudulent investment schemes, the group supervising the investments is open to the accusation that they have not fulfilled the financial stewardship role.

On the other hand, the second goal is maximizing earnings. It is no longer good stewardship practice to keep all organizational funds in safe, very low paying instruments such as certificates of deposit. To the contrary, there is a responsibility to maximize earnings to increase the organization's ability to fulfill the mission.

Asset Allocation

One major task associated with planning the investment strategy is to decide upon an asset mix. As the BOD function in a stewardship role, they need to feel comfortable with the allocation plan the finance committee chooses. This choice is somewhat subjective depending on the risk tolerance of the group making the decision. If there is a BOD finance committee with the right skill set, they will probably have the knowledge to decide on an asset mix. However, in addition to the knowledge they have, they need to embody the sense of the BOD regarding risk. Put the subject of adopting an investment policy on a BOD meeting agenda initially for input and discussion and later on for approval.

An investment policy that gives both a target and range regarding asset classes provides both specific guidance and allows some discretion on the part of the investment manager. Choose a target and a range for each class of assets to give the investment manager both structure and flexibility. For example, a target for investments in large cap stocks might be 50% and the range 40%-60% of the total monies invested. The benchmark indicator is the Standard and Poor 500 index. If the committee is interested in external input regarding the design of an allocation plan, call the two largest foundations and the United Way in the community and ask what their investment allocation plans call for. An early decision is the allocation of invested funds between equities and bonds. In selecting an allocation plan, keep in mind any obligation to provide income, as periodically there will be a serious market downturn. If history is a good predictor of the future, the market will recover from a down turn within two to four years. An issue in selecting investments is the availability of funds. Financial instruments such as stocks and bonds as well as mutual funds and exchange-traded funds are liquid meaning the PCWA can buy or sell them daily. Investments in real estate are not liquid. The idea is to have enough of a position in cash and bonds to meet income obligations without having to sell a portion of equities when the price is low. For example, the PCWA owns a thousand shares of Intel stock. Intel manufactures computer chips. China creates a multibillion fund to develop computer chips that are superior to those sold by Intel. On this news, Intel's stock price drops by 10%. The roof on a group home is leaking and after inspection, there is a decision to replace it. You either use cash, or the PCWA or the line of credit to pay for the repair if you do not want to immediately sell the Intel shares.

Acceptable and Disallowed Investments Another task associated with deciding upon asset classes is the types of assets to disallow as investment choices due to their risk level. Instruments that some judge to be high risk are unregistered stock, venture capital partnerships, stock options, futures trading, derivative instruments, margin trading, commodities, short positions, foreign currency, and securities issued as part of an initial public offering. Again, this is a subjective decision. The prudent person rule and BOD risk tolerance guide the formulation of excluded financial products.

The investment policy might include a list of what constitutes acceptable investments. Types of investments could include deposit accounts at an FDIC insured bank, money market funds, U.S. Government and U.S. Government agency bonds and corporate Bonds of U.S. companies that are rated 'A' or better, large, mid-cap, and small cap equities that are traded on NYSE or NASDAQ and mutual funds with a capitalization of at least $1 billion. For equity investment, the policy specifies some percentage allocated to U.S. companies and foreign companies. In addition, place a limit on the percent a single equity or bond holding can comprise of the total portfolio in each area.

Management of Investments The next decision is who should manage the specific investments. Organizations usually make one of four choices: 1) the BOD finance committee manages the investments. This is feasible when the amounts involved are modest and the committee possesses the expertise. 2) Hire an outside investment manager. Often organizations choose the wealth management division of a bank with which the organization already does business. The advantage is that the management is professional; there are not additional vendors to deal with, and there is a better chance that the bank will increase their annual gift. Wealth management organization often charge a flat annual fee One percent of the funds invested is common. Fees usually decrease as the amount of money managed increases. In addition, there are trading fees charges if the strategy used entails investing in individual bonds and equities. Some wealth advisory services and investment companies invest in mutual funds instead of stocks and bonds and then one way or the other you also pay the annual fees associated with the fund. For some mutual funds, there are front or back end load fees. My experience with wealth management organizations is that the service is excellent but they usually meet or slightly underperform compared to the benchmark. 3) Use a stockbroker. The main advantage of this choice is the possibility of superior returns, but this depends on the skills of the broker in selecting investments. Depending on whether the holdings are individual equities or families of mutual fund there are trading and monthly account management fees. 4) Have the investment managed by a low fee mutual fund family. The advantage is that the cost of the advisory service and mutual fund fees will be substantially lower than the other options. The investment strategy is index funds that achieve the average return of the benchmark. Because these organizations operate on a low fee basis, the amount of individual attention your account receives is minimal and may involve more work for agency financial staff to translate statements into a format that the committee wants. Also compared with brokerage services or wealth management services there is little chance that the low-cost mutual fund company will contribute to the agency. There is a debate about the index fund strategy. One of the companies using it has grown to be the largest mutual fund company in the U.S. but the research is mixed. There are companies and investment advisors that outperform the index benchmark in any given year but by definition, the majority does not.

One strategy that organizations with sizable funds to invest use is to divide the monies in half or thirds and compare the performance of different managers. Once you choose an investment management method it is the job of agency finance staff and the members of the BOD finance committee to do the necessary monitoring. One method is to review the monthly or quarterly reports and meet with the managers once or twice a year. Negotiate the benchmarks and content of the report before signing an agreement with a management company.

Selection of Investment Managers To select an outside investment manager, issue a request for proposal to 7 to 10 organizations in various categories, with the idea that five may respond. There will be questions from potential vendors, and the BOD finance committee will need to review and score the proposals according to some agreed upon criterion. In reviewing proposals, consider the experience of the staff that will manage the account, the quality and costs of the products along with a three or five-year performance history of the investments relative to appropriate benchmarks. Morningstar is one good tool to use to obtain this information. Also, review the offeror's statement frequency and format. Ask potential vendors to 1) review and comment on the investment policy, 2) state their willingness to work within its context, and 3) talk to you about any suggestions they have for changing it. The firm you select will have to abide by the agency conflict of interest policy. Many companies send out a sales team to make a onetime presentation but it is a better idea to meet with the staff who will be managing the investments.

In general, the expectation of the investment manager is that they equal or surpass the market returns for a similarly balanced portfolio when measured on an annual basis. Use the investment policy benchmarks to determine this. The finance committee makes recommendations to the BOD

regarding retaining or replacing the investment management firm(s). These types of decisions consider performance and service. Any vendor can have a bad year. A comprehensive investment policy example, that also does a good job of describing committee responsibilities is issued by New York State Council of Nonprofits located at:
https://www.councilofnonprofits.org/tools-resources/investment-policies-nonprofits

Managing Endowment Gifts

The donor generally creates an endowment. The BOD can also create a fund when donors contribute to an endowment campaign. Unlike the management of other monies, the job here is to follow the donor's wishes in terms of the purpose of the gift, the disbursement of money, and any additional requirements in the endowment document. When the spirit or letter of the endowment document is not honored the agency risks contributor dissatisfaction. Some givers use litigation to get their donations repaid.

Gifts include perpetual endowments where the goal is to preserve the capital portion of the gift and disburse the earnings. Sometimes a patron wishes to increase the size of the gift. They add part of the earnings to the principal. Disbursements always conform to the terms and purpose of the bequest as stated in the endowment document. The donor may require specific investments and it may be necessary to keep a separate set of accounts to track the endowment investment results. Other endowments are time limited, for example, for twenty years with the disbursement of both principal and earnings during the life of the endowment. Acceptance of the endowment gift is at the discretion of the agency. Some organizations as part of their fundraising literature develop a gift acceptance policy, and if so, this would be the appropriate place to discuss endowment gift acceptance criteria.

Gifts of Property

Gifts of property can be complicated. For example, a BOD member's elderly father dies. The father's house is part of the estate The BOD member who is the sole beneficiary of the estate wants to donate the house to the agency as a place where boys who are participating in the independent living program can live during the period of their program participation. The BOD member knows that from time to time that the house will need repairs and wishes to make an endowment gift of $150,000 with the principal to remain unspent, and any earnings spent toward the upkeep of the house. The head of the agency maintenance staff makes a cursory inspection and reports that the ceilings show signs of water damage and the oil burner is 35 years old.

The windows are original to the house and there is a draft around the window frames. The house has enough space to house four residents and a resident advisor. The zoning code indicates small group homes are an allowed use. The home is located on a block of single-family dwellings in a middle-class neighborhood. The staff thinks some of the residents would not be happy to have four teenage boys as neighbors. The agency has operated the independent living program for ten years and it will likely continue to do so in the future. However, the GCWA staff is talking about state funding cuts and government support for the operating costs will stay the same or be lower. At 6%, earning per year the endowment will generate $9,000. There will be about $50,000 in repairs needed in the next three years. In addition, the maintenance crew needs to paint the home and make several minor repairs including the replacement of carpeting. The agency will not renew the lease on one apartment, a savings of $11,000 a year, if it accepts the gift. There is concern about alienating the BOD member by refusing the generous gift. In this situation and others like it, there are advantages and disadvantages to the gift that need evaluation, usually by the BOD finance committee.

Chapter 20 -The Mysterious 990 Tax Filing

My purpose in this chapter is to review the information that the IRS requires, as well as the voluntary standards discussed in the 990 instructions rather than deliver a line-by-line review of the form. I try to provide enough information about the filing so that leaders have a good idea of the major content areas, particularly those relevant to PCWAs. In addition, leaders will learn about the policies required and suggested by the IRS.

There is a lot of detail to the 990 instructions that may address issues particular to your PCWA that I do not cover. For instance, there is information in the instructions on what to do if your charity has not received their IRS letter of determination. Also, there is instruction concerning PCWAs that due to being new or ceasing operations filing the 990 for a short accounting period. The main instructions are 102 pages There are additional and separate instructions for the schedules, some of which many charities will need to file The instructions for the 990 are at the following URL: https://www.irs.gov/pub/irs-pdf/i990.pdf. The instructions do not have a search function. Unless you want to or need to go it alone it is more efficient to ask your PCWA's CPA firm the questions you have. If you really need to go it alone the IRS has a searchable data base for charities. The URL is: https://www.irs.gov/charities-non-profits/charitable-organizations/life-cycle-of-a-public-charity. Also, the IRS provides a resources and tools website for charitable filers. The website is: https://www.irs .gov/charities-non-profits/form-990-resources-and-tools

Some of the 990 tax form questions have the goal of, having tax-exempt organizations follow some of the policy requirements that the Sarbanes-Oxley Act imposed on public companies, and in addition lay out IRS opinion on policies that further 501©3 good governance standards.

History of the 990 Filing

The 1943 990 legislation..." requires that tax-exempt organizations file an information return with the IRS as currently codified in section 6033 of the Internal Revenue Code. When it enacted the original version...Congress was concerned that nonprofit entities were using their privileged tax status to gain an unfair advantage in competition with for-profit enterprises. Noting that it was without sufficient data to act intelligently" on the issue because tax-exempt corporations were not required to file any reports with the IRS and ""the congressional committee thus had no data on the extent of such abuses," the House bill required that tax-exempt entities begin filing returns "stating specifically the items of gross income, receipts, and disbursements and such other information, and keep such records, as the Commissioner of Internal Revenue may prescribe." [32 Revenue Act of 1943, H.R. 3687, 78th Cong. § 117(a) (1943)].

...Significantly, the Revenue Act of 1950 also required, for the first time, that in the belief that increased publicity would encourage compliance with the law..." that exempt organization information returns be made available to the public." This amendment was added by the Senate Finance Committee, and it also expanded the scope of information that exempt organizations were required to disclose, ..."mandating more extensive details on their sources of revenue, accumulation of income, expenses, and disbursements. The Senate delegated to the IRS the task of determining the manner in which this information would be made available to the public.... The final version of the bill passed by both houses included a penalty for the willful failure to furnish information required.... " Klien (1972)

"One of the best-publicized scandals that precipitated the current version of the 990 occurred in 1992 when William Aramony was the president of the United Way of America. In addition to having a $463,000 salary, he stole money for himself and to pay for gifts for his young girlfriend. The revelations had a snowball effect that resulted in a number of media reports on excess executive compensation around the country. Subsequent congressional hearings revealed excess compensation and loans at hundreds of charities (Montgue, 2013).

The resulting current tax filing first used in 2008 require nonprofits to report more extensively on finances, fundraising, and governance. Since 2008 there have been many changes to the 990.The changes to the reporting requirements have several implications.

First, they will provide data to inform the discussion about continuing the tax-exempt status for some or all charities. Morally questionable and illegal behavior for personal financial gain at PCWA do not seem widespread from what I have observed. However, I have observed, in the news, as well as through situations that have come to my attention in other ways that it does happen.

In 2016 media reports appeared about the Clinton's accepting large foundation gifts aimed at buying influence and members of the Trump families used money raised on behalf of charities to provide business income.

Second, the amount of information available to interested donors and potential donors has increased substantially. Organizations seeking funding are aware that the sophisticated individual donors, foundations, and government agency will easily be able to find out extensive detailed information about any registered charity.

Third, the task of competitor research is easier. The reader interested in child welfare organizations that offer competing services has access to important information. It is time consuming, but easy to find out some key characteristics such as business volume, asset base, executive compensation, business level by program, income share by type, and types of fundraising in which agencies are involved. You will be able to see the financial characteristics of other PCWA's golf tournament compared to your own event. You can find out if they use professional fundraising counsel.

Fourth, this information can help with organizational planning and development. For the charity that wishes to grow, they will learn about charities that are larger, and get ideas of things to do to get their organization to the next level.

Last, this information will help in determining the appropriateness of compensation for executive staff through comparison.

The returns of all of the charities that file a 990-tax return are public information and easily obtainable online at the Guidestar website (https://www.guidestar.org/search) Registration for access to some information that is free. The registered user may view the most recent 990 returns of any charity by entering the charity's name and location. In addition, previous year's returns are also available along with other information. Guidestar also offers several fee-based services, which depending on the scope of your research is worthwhile. The size of their database makes the Guidestar salary and compensation report, which you can purchase through their website, a superior resource in considering executive level staff compensation. A second source to view 990 returns is through the Charity Navigator website (https://www.charitynavigator.org/) that makes the returns available through a partnership with The Foundation Center.

The Urban Institute's National Center on Nonprofit Organizations website provides the financial data as well as data on BOD size and compensation, staff size, and other 990 data items for a large group of organizations free. However, research experience, and the time commitment to learn to use the Institute's data files, is necessary. Staff member needs to use Excel data organizing functions to get to the four organizational IRS classification types categories for private charitable child welfare funding. (children and youth, foster care, adoption, and congregate care facilities.). I suspect that family service agencies, which are in several additional categories also are substantial providers of private child welfare services. Additionally, the researcher needs to select child welfare organizations from these categories, as these classifications include many organizations, with other missions such as day care, substance abuse services, and services for people with developmental disabilities. Using the resource requires a lot of work, but is a way of pinpointing a large number of peer agencies. Get started by using the following link: (http://nccs.urban.org/NCCS-Databases-and-Tools.cfm).

Filing Completion and Approval

Filing Rules - Charitable PCWAs with income less than $50,000 complete 990N, those with more than $50,000 but less than $200,000 in income and assets of less than $500,000 complete form 990EZ and PCWAs with more than $200,000 in income or $500,000 in assets file federal Form 990, Return of Organization Exempt from Income Tax. The forms and instructions are available at: https://www.irs.gov/charities-non-profits/form-990-series-which-forms-do-exempt-organizations-file-filing-phase-in

There are special filing rules for foreign PCWAs and the possibility of group filing for PCWAs that have wholly owned subsidiary agencies or those that have an affiliation with a national or parent organization. Organizations can file the return on either a calendar year basis or the organizations' fiscal year. The filing deadline is the 15th day of the 5th month after the organization's accounting period ends. However, if your PCWA changes its accounting period you need to submit the 990 covering the short term (less than a year) file form 1128. See page 5 of the 2018 990 instructions for further instructions. Send the return to Department of the Treasury Internal Revenue Service Center Ogden, UT 84201-0027. However, if your PCWA sends out more than 250 tax forms a year (1099s + 1040's + all other federal forms) you need to file the 990 electronically. The following website provides a list of IRS approved organization to use for electronic filing. https://www.irs.gov/e-file-providers/tax-year-2018-exempt-organizations-efile-providers. Any charity can get an automatic 3-month extension of the deadline date to file by using IRS form 8868. To obtain an additional extension of time to file, (not automatic) the organization must show reasonable cause for the additional time requested. See the instructions for IRS Form 8868. All of the above applies to the Federal 990 filing, but each state has its own rule regarding submitting the 990 filing with a state agency as well. Hurwit and Associates specialize in nonprofit law. See their website for each state's 990 filing requirements. The URL is: https://www.hurwitassociates. com/states-reporting-requirements

To be complete the submitted 990 needs to have parts I- XII completed along with any required schedules completed as a result of responses in part IV. Make sure there are no blanks. Write zero in any financial item in which your organizations do not have any income, expense, asset or liability. Round numbers to the dollar. In general, record additional narrative information on schedule O.

Organizations with annual gross receipts exceeding $1,046,500 million are subject to a penalty of $100 for each day a failure to file continues (with a maximum penalty for any one return of $52,000). Penalties are lower for charities with a smaller budget. You may be able to avoid penalties with a good cause explanation of the failure to file promptly. An automatic revocation of the organization's 501© 3 status is the consequence for not filing for three consecutiveyears.

Do not put anybody's social security number anywhere on the forms, schedules, or attachments. Since this material is available to the public, do not compromise anyone's personal security.

Have the president sign the form if possible. If not have the highest-ranking employee sign. Note that the IRS gives notice that management has the responsibility to make available to the signer, and preparer, all relevant information. The organization chooses whether to give IRS staff authorization to talk with the audit firm or other preparer of the 990. If the relationship between the PCWA and the preparer is only for the preparation of completing the 990 return, and you check the box, you may need to pay the preparer for their additional time if the IRS contacts them. Do not grant permission if for any reason you do not want to have further dealings with the preparer following the filing of the return.

The Process of Completing the 990

For PCWAs that have an independent auditor, it makes sense to have staff from the firm complete the 990.There is three reasons for this. Audit firms with a nonprofit customer base regularly do this and therefore possess the expertise to do it well. The 990 has many schedules for the preparer to complete and the knowledge to do the work takes time and effort to acquire. If the organization does it in house, there is a steep learning curve, a probability of mistakes, and many staff hours devoted to the task. Last because ofthe relationship between the BOD and staff with the auditor there will be an ease of communication, as questions and suggestions from the president, finance director, andtreasurer arise.

If the organization files a 990 and does not complete an external independent audit, due to the expertise required to complete the form engage a CPA firm, or use a service that does this work regularly. Compare prices and services of people in the community and online and check their references before selecting a provider.

For smaller PCWA's filing the 990EZ the decision of whether to engage an independent audit firm or other service to complete the form depends on many factors. If the PCWA has an annual independent audit, unless management determines the fee to complete the 990EZ is excessive than have the audit firm complete the form. If there is no ongoing relationship with an audit firm and the year-end financials are internal then the staff and board member(s) with the best financial knowledge review the form and decide to complete it internally or not. Also, explore the fees of a local CPA who does this work or consider the use of an online service. A review of a few websites indicates that the fee is between $500-$1,000. This presumes the PCWA management distributes the completed 990EZ to the board and manages the BOD approval process internally. In addition, there are companies that provide the organization with the form and schedules that the preparer populates.

For the smallest PCWA filing the 990N, someone needs to first register with the IRS and then complete an eight-item electronic post card. There is no need for an external professional service to do this.

990 Approval Process

The IRS wants to know about the organization's process for reviewing the 990 prior to filing it. The IRS inquires about a charity's 990 approval process, but a formal process is not an IRS requirement. I like the idea of the president, and finance director doing a line-by-line review and then have the auditor or other preparer respond to their questions, and suggestions for modification. Next, these managers, transmit a copy of the 990 to the members of the finance committee, and then review it verbally with them at a finance committee meeting. Once the finance committee completes their review, the other BOD members receive the entire 990 packages. Many of the directors will not read the entire filing due to their busy schedules. If for some reason the president sends the BOD members a redacted version indicate this. Administrative staff coordinates the meeting dates and assures they occur so as to precede the 990-due date. If this method is, too cumbersome it is more than enough to transmit the filing to the BOD and have them approve the submission.

You need to be aware of state 990 filing requirements as they vary by state, and the responsible state agency also varies. If there is a lack of clarity about the state requirements, The Multistate Filter Project provides a state-by-state list on their Unified Registration Statement web page: http://multistatefiling.org/n_appendix.htm. Putting a copy of the 990 or the audit on the website tells visitors about a commitment to transparency, and is a step toward meeting one IRS public disclosure requirement

What the IRS Wants to Know About the Organization

Part One – This part summarizes your charity's income and expenses, assets and liabilities. Part II is the signature block. See information above regarding 990 preparation for information on completing this. In part 3 describe the mission, and the three largest programs and their total income and expenses. Supply the activities, number of consumers served and quantities of services rendered. Inform the IRS of changes in the programs including new programs and a reduction of 25% or more in program size. Use schedule O to report on other programs. This information serves to confirm that the organizational activities meet the IRS exempt purpose that qualifies the PCWA as a 501(c) 3.

"The exempt purposes set forth in section 501(c) (3) are charitable, religious, educational, scientific, literary, testing for public safety, fostering national or international amateur sports competition, and preventing cruelty to children or animals. The term *charitable* is used in its generally accepted legal sense and includes relief of the poor, the distressed, or the underprivileged; advancement of religion; advancement of education or science; erecting or maintaining public buildings, monuments, or works; lessening the burdens of government; lessening neighborhood tensions; eliminating prejudice and discrimination; defending human and civil rights secured by law; and combating community deterioration and juvenile delinquency"

(Internal revenue Service, 2015).

Part 4

Part 4 consists of 21 questions, some with sub parts which address characteristics of your organization. Yes, answers to any of these questions either requires the submission of a schedule or an
explanation recorded on Schedule O. I highlight some of the areas covered in part four, but also do not address several questions which will be applicable to some but not most PCWA.

Lobbying - The IRS general rule is that a charity may engage in some lobbying, which is any attempt to influence legislation including writing a

Measuring Lobbying Activity: Expenditure Test

If the amount of exempt	Lobbying nontaxable amount is:
Less than or equal to $500,000	20% of the exempt purpose expenditure
More than $500,000 but less than or equal to $1,000,000	$100,000 plus 15% of the excess of exempt purpose expenditures over $500,000
More than $1,000,000 but less than or equal to $1,500,000	$175,000 plus 10% of the excess of exempt purpose expenditures over $1,000,000
More than $1,500,000 but less than or equal to $17,000,000	$225,000 plus 5% of the exempt purpose expenditures over $1,500,000

letter to a state senator to support a new child abuse bill. Lobbying also encompasses trying to influence public referendums or political appointments to office. How much lobbying is too much? It all depends on the budget of the PCWA (See table   below). Unless the lobbying efforts are deminimus the organization needs to fill out Schedule C of the 990 and make lobbying intentions known to the IRS by filing IRS form 5768 if the organization uses the expenditure method to measure lobbying. There is also another method to document lobbying activity. For more information see: https://www.irs.gov/pub/irs-pdf/i990sc.pdf.

Be mindful of any lobbying pledges you made to the federal government in connection with a federal grant or contract, or any provisions of state or local child welfare contracts regarding lobbying. An alternative to the above methods is listed at the following URL:
https://www.irs.gov/charities-non-profits/measuring-lobbying-activity-expenditure-test. Complete supplemental schedules if the charity operates a basic education program and has a license to conduct a school program
Indicate If the agency operates an inpatient psychiatric hospital unit. Report scholarships, holiday and birthday gifts, and unreimbursed clothing

expenses of more than $5,000 made to clients or others. Provide details in schedule O.

Financial Information - Complete the 33/13% support test. This means the PCWA receives at least a third of its revenue from government and or individual donors

Report both the income and expenses, and assets and liabilities from the audit. Otherwise, use internal financial statements. None of this information should be much of a surprise to people in the organization if they have been attentive to the auditing process in terms of giving the audit and the accompanying notes a thorough reading. For social service agencies, government grants, government contracts, and private fundraising will form most of the income unless some wonderful ancestor established a generous endowment Expenses include the portion devoted to program, management and fundraising. Personnel cost will be the big-ticket item on the expense side. The main conclusions for agency leaders to draw from the review of numbers are principally strategic. They are: Is income matching or exceeding expenses? What have been the trends for the past few years? Is the cash portion of the assets sufficient to protect against a rainy day, or help with start- up a new project?

Report unrelated business income. This is receipts unrelated to the charitable mission and programs. Unrelated business income is not related to the sources of payment i.e. grants, donations, and fees for services garnered in connection with the mission. The classification of revenue as unrelated business income depends on how closely the activity relates to the mission and programs. Unrelated business income can include income from commercial enterprises, not related to the mission, proceeds from renting out part of a building to a business operated that seeks a profit, and there is no reasonable connection to the mission. The classification of income between related and unrelated classes can be a bit tricky. When you are uncertain about how to classify proceeds consult, your audit firm. For example, if the organization offers a program that provides housing assistance to families and also rents out part of the building to families not involved in the program there may not be a need to list the emolument as unrelated business income because part of the mission is to provide housing for families. If a business does not employ program youth or their families, does not provide skill development training for them, or use facilities to raise money to support the charity, there is more of a chance that income from the ventures are unrelated business income. However, if program youth make wooden pallets or the business exists to provide work readiness, and skills training there is less of a chance that proceeds from the venture is unrelated business income. Furthermore, if none of the youth served, or agency staff is involved with the wood pallet business even if the net income supports the agency work, it probably is unrelated business income.

The IRS also wants to learn if the PCWA staff sends the appropriate tax forms such as the 1099 to contractors and if there are withholding taxes set aside from paychecks when the payee does not supply a social security or employer identification number.

Compensation of BOD Members and Executive Staff

Report the names and compensation for BOD members, staff in leadership positions, highly paid employees and highly paid independent contractors. List current members of the BOD and the amount of compensation they receive. Write $0 for any director who does not receive compensation.

List all BOD members who served within the last 5 years, if they received compensation in excess of $10,000. List the compensation amount for anyone who is an officer of the corporation. This includes the president, finance director, and executive vice president, and any other staff member who has authority over 10% or more of the operations List the incumbents and compensation for these positions even if they do not meet the compensation minimums indicated in the instructions. In these cases, classify them as key employees rather than highly compensated employees. Also list all key employees and officers earning $150,000 or more and additionally list the top five employees whom are not officers or key employees but earn more than $100,000. If on the other hand the number of BOD members, officers and staff whose compensation is at least $150,000 add to 20 or more people, list only the 20 people with the highest compensation. Keep in mind that compensation includes everything listed as earning on the W-2 form. Also, enter information about contractors paid in excess of $100,000 per year. For social service agencies, these are most likely to be psychiatrists or physicians and the occasional management company

The PCWA provides an enormous amount of detail regarding related organizations, management companies, and foreign entities. There are several pages of instructions on the subject of executive compensation that I suspect will not apply to most social service organizations.

Organizational Structure

Report if there is a relationship between the PCWA and another organization, such as a foundation, subsidiary, or parent organization. Report situations where one organization has several entities, perhaps an operational entity that provides the service, and an administrative entity that maintains ownership of organizational assets and charges fair market value rent to the operational component. Often in the arrangements one organization provides management services to an organization that provides youth services. In other cases, there is a foundation that hold the organization 's assets.

Fundraising and Donations

The IRS wants to know if the PCWA holds donor or BOD created endowment funds or if you held funds in a temporary or permanently restricted account to benefit a specific project.

Also, report if the PCWA paid a person who is not an employee to raise money for a capital project or for operations. For instance, you hire a fund raiser or firm to organize your capital campaign for a new group home report it here. Be mindful of how you responded to the state charitable registration questionnaire so that the information between the two is consistent. If there is not consistent, be ready to explain if either the IRS of state charitable commission examines the other's filings for the organization. You supply information about receipt of substantial non-cash gifts and about specific types of non-cash gifts including art and historical treasures Also report on financial instruments such as donated life insurance policies when the agency pays the premium. For example, Ms. Generous buys a whole life insurance policy for $200,000 and names the PCWA as the beneficiary, but when she turns 65, she no longer wishes to pay the premium and asks if the charity wants to pay it rather than have the policy lapse. If it is, worthwhile to take over the premium payments, report it in on the 990. If there is bond financing on a capital project in excess of $100,000 also report it here. If you funded a capital improvement through a municipal bond offering report it here.

Wrongdoing -Excess Benefit Transactions and Theft

An excess benefit transaction is one in which a board member or leadership staff receive monies, or a benefit that has a value (i.e. car, boat, etc.) that is in excess of the value received by the PCWA from the disqualified person. If you correct the transactions in the same year it occurs, meaning you recover the funds involved plus interest than IRS can levy a 25% excise tax on the person receiving the excess benefit as measured by the value of the benefit. If another manager representing the agency's interest is involved in facilitating an excess benefit transaction, they are also subject to penalties. If more than a year passes from the time the benefit inures before there is a report than the excise tax can be 200% of the value of the excess benefit received

If someone discovers an excess benefit transaction and reports it to the IRS, I suspect it will raise a red flag. That is, it is best to rectify the excess benefit transaction as soon as it you discover it. I also think you should discuss the situation with counsel who is knowledgeable about excess benefit transactions and get their recommendations on how to handle the matter. The certainty of knowledge about the facts is important because of the risk of a slander suit against the organization, if there is a finding that no excess benefit transaction occurred.

Use the prudent person standard discussed in chapter eight. If you discover an excess benefit transaction, some issues to think about are: What steps does the BOD take to avoid future excess benefit transactions from occurring? How does the BOD assure there is no loss to the organization? This includes repayment of the excess benefit plus interest. What provisions do government contracts and government grants have about the management of excess benefit transactions? What is the appropriate discipline for the involved individuals in the situation? The IRS levies an excise tax for the beneficiary. Should the organization fail to act, it raises questions for the IRS and the public about the ability of those who govern to carry out their responsibilities. The IRS and others will have a positive view of the organization that manages the situation compared to one that does not. This also brings up the question of whether on a preemptive basis if the organization should adopt an excess benefit transaction policy.

Fraud, Embezzlement or Theft -To be reportable to the IRS, the diversion or theft of funds is equal to or greater than 5% the annual gross revenues, or 5% of the organizational assets. This is the same percentage that the American Accounting Standards Board uses to establish materiality. This percentage test affects the majority of PCWAs that have modest budgets much more than the larger PCWA. For example, in 2012 there were 2214 PCWAs in the IRS p30 classification for organization providing multiple child welfare programs. Of these, 114 organizations or about 5% of the total had $10,000,000 or larger annual budgets. For these organizations, a theft would have to be quite egregious to meet the 5% reporting level requirement; a theft of $500,000 or more. On the other hand, 50% of the charities in the p30 classification have budgets of $250,000 or less. (Urban Institute 2012). The reporting level for the smaller organizations is a theft of $12,500 or less. $500,000 versus $12,500 as a reporting criterion gives larger agencies much more room not to report wrongdoing in their organizations.

Often when theft or embezzlement takes place, organizations out of a sense of embarrassment, try to keep things quiet. Disclosure of the diversion of funds in the 990 makes the theft public information, and thereby raises the question of how the organization handles the theft. Is there a record of a police report? Was the money returned? Was the insurance company and auditor notified? Did the BOD handle the event within the context of the employee dishonesty policy, if one exists? If not, is it time the organization to adopt one? The overall question is: Did the BOD fulfill its role as fiduciary in handling the theft?

Governance and Conflicts of Interest

The IRS has the goal of widespread implementation of best practices regarding governance. The IRS does not mandate particular elements of governance. However, if the IRS audits, and the examiner discovers an excess benefit transaction, or there is theft, embezzlements or a conflict of interest situation adopting the IRS governance items demonstrates that the BOD made a proactive effort to prevent and manage these types of problems. The organization lists on the 990 the number of members on the entire BOD, but there is more interest in the officers, their role within the charity and the scope of their power. Report business transactions in which any member of the BOD, any organizational key or highly paid employees or their family members are involved in business transactions with each other or with the charitable organization. Add to this list, private grant makers, grant recipients, and donors who make gifts of $5,000 or more. The IRS views these people as having the ability to influence organizational decision-making. The bottom line is that the IRS is interested to know if key organizational people were involved with excess benefit transactions, loans, grants, or other business transactions with the organization. Also, for private grant-makers there is an interest it they have any family, or business connection with grant recipients. The IRS is interested if any of the above people, were involved in any of the cited activities and if the organization made reasonable efforts to find out the particulars of the situation and deal with the situations appropriately. These requirements are subject to a five-year lookback period. Report these situations on the 990. Only independent BOD members should be involved in situations where there is a conflict of interest.

An independent a BOD member meets four requirements:
1. The PCWA does not pay the member as an officer or employee of the PCWA
2. The member did not get payments of more than $10,000 during the organization's tax year as reimbursement for expenses incurred as a director or other than reasonable compensation for services provided in the capacity as a member but not an officer of the BOD
3. The director, or any family member of the BOD member did not have a transaction with the organization.
4. The member, or any family member did not have a transaction with a taxable or tax-exempt related organization

Consider a BOD member to be independent even if:
1. They are a donor to the charity
2. The member has taken a vow of poverty and receives compensation as an agent of a religious order
3. They receive financial benefits from the organization solely in the capacity of being a member of the charitable group served by the organization in the PCWA

The 990 Conflict of Interest Policy Question asks if the organization has a conflict of interest policy. If the PCWA does not have one, answer no. I recommend that your PCWA write and adopt a policy. See chapter 11 for a discussion of the conflict of interest policy. The policy goal here is to discourage people who have the ability to influence organizational operations, and benefit from organizational business transactions from doing so. For organizations that do have a conflict of interest policy the IRS asks if each key employee and member of the BOD makes an annual declaration of any possible conflicts listing the business involved. If there are none this should also be on the annual declaration form. The declaration form includes the individual's name, signature, and the date signed. The charity indicates on the conflict of interest form that the person with the conflict does not participate in any purchasing, affiliation, joint venture, or partnership discussion about the company named on the declaration question.

The IRS is also interested in the details of the conflict of interest monitoring process. Regarding monitoring, include the conflict of interest policy in the BOD orientation materials and require BOD members to sign that they received the policy. See chapter eleven for

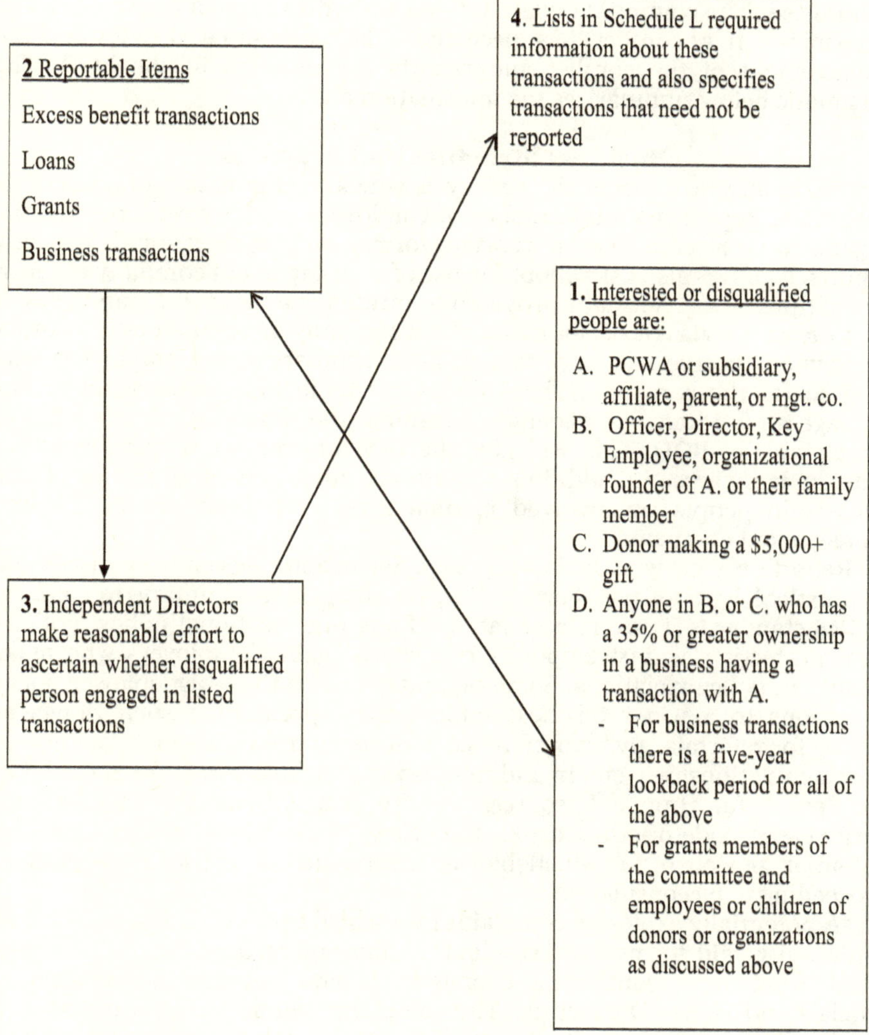
2 Reportable Items
Excess benefit transactions
Loans
Grants
Business transactions

4. Lists in Schedule L required information about these transactions and also specifies transactions that need not be reported

1. Interested or disqualified people are:
A. PCWA or subsidiary, affiliate, parent, or mgt. co.
B. Officer, Director, Key Employee, organizational founder of A. or their family member
C. Donor making a $5,000+ gift
D. Anyone in B. or C. who has a 35% or greater ownership in a business having a transaction with A.
- For business transactions there is a five-year lookback period for all of the above
- For grants members of the committee and employees or children of donors or organizations as discussed above

3. Independent Directors make reasonable effort to ascertain whether disqualified person engaged in listed transactions

monitoring activities

Another policy component could require any employee or director who becomes aware of a possible conflict reports it to the chair of the audit committee. The committee chair follows up with the people involved and determines if a conflict has occurred. The committee decides on the management of the conflict and reports the decision to the BOD. The schematic below summarizes the information above.

Business Structure and Practices

There are questions about the agency closing and elimination of parts of its programs. Report the total number of employees, and certification that the organization submits the appropriate forms, such as W-2's and quarterly reports. The IRS also asks about the use of a management company to supply any of the services normally provided by internal management employees. If so, there are questions about the name of the company or companies, the duties performed and the names of current BOD members or key employees who worked for the company. These duties might include supervision of key managers, fundraising leadership, issuing the financial statements, or managing the BOD. This will give the IRS information about the use of outside managers, in addition to internal managers and if any of the leadership people are involved in dual roles with both the PCWA and management company.

Report on your whistleblower policy. See chapter eleven for a discussion of whistleblower policies. For a policy, which again is voluntary, to conform to IRS standards it covers a violation of any organizational policy. Policies offer protection against employer retaliation against employees who make reports of policy violations. Some organizations tie the whistleblower policy provisions to a wider business ethics policy, prohibiting such things as paying for referrals, giving preference in decision-making based on previously existing relationships, etc. In addition, review the business ethics model is at the Society for Human Resources website. https://www.shrm.org/ about-shrm/Pages/code-of-ethics.aspx. the New York times reports on the potential power of a whistleblower complaint to cause impeachment proceeding to be considered.

"A potentially explosive complaint by a whistle-blower in the intelligence community said to involve President Trump emerged on Thursday as the latest front in a continuing oversight dispute between administration officials and House Democrats...The complaint, submitted by a member of the intelligence community to its inspector general, renewed questions about how the president handles delicate matters."

(Barnes et. al. 2019)

The IRS is interested to learn of changes to the organizational documents used to create the agency including by-laws, articles of incorporation, or association, and organizational constitution (if applicable). It is possible, that the president but not the finance director will be involved in this area. Two procedures are important. First, the governing board minutes note changes in organizational by-laws or other founding organizational documents. The IRS does not obligate the PCWA to report changes in these areas, if they do not involve amending the sovereign documents. The type of modifications the IRS is interested in is wide-ranging and listed below:

"Document or by-laws include changes to: The organization's exempt purposes or mission;

The organization's name (see also the instructions for *Specific Instructions, Heading,* Item B);

The number, composition, qualifications, authority, or duties of the governing BOD's voting members;

The number, composition, qualifications, authority, or duties of the organization's officers or key employees;

The role of the stockholders or membership in governance;

The distribution of assets upon dissolution by-laws;

The quorum, voting rights, or voting approval requirements of the governing BOD members or the organization's stockholders or membership;

The policies or procedures contained within the organizing documents or by-laws regarding compensation of officers, directors, trustees, or key employees, conflicts of interest, whistleblowers, or document retention and destruction; and

The composition or procedures contained within the organizing document or by-laws of an audit committee. "

(Internal Revenue Service, 2016)

For example, if an organization is unable to achieve the 70%-member attendance required in the by-laws as the necessary quorum to conduct business and the BOD amends the by-laws to require only 51% attendance for a quorum, report this on the 990. It is interesting to note that if at a BOD meeting you decide on a record retention policy, but the policy is not part of the by-laws then you do not report it. In addition, it is a bit curious to see compensation for key employees on the list of by-law matters in that as far as I know compensation is not commonly part of the by-laws.

There are questions about BOD meeting minutes. It is usual and customary for someone attending BOD meetings to take minutes. In addition, keep careful written minutes for committees that perform duties delegated to them by the board as well. These might include an executive compensation committee, or 401(k) committee. Because of the intermediate sanctions, associated with unjustified executive pay. Executive compensation committee minutes, in particular are impeccable, and use the format of the minutes described in the committee description appendix. In the BOD and BOD committee minutes record the members attending and not attending, as well as the start time and meeting place. List all motions made verbatim followed by the name of the members who proposed and seconded the motion, and the adoption vote whether unanimous or by simple majority. List the time and place of the meeting. Indicate who prepared the minutes and the date you distribute the minutes. BOD meeting minutes, and minutes of committees performing BOD delegated duties are part of the permanent organizational records.

As per the record retention policy addressed in chapter 11 the IRS seems primarily interested in business as opposed to clinical records. Clinical record retention varies by field, consumer age and other dimensions. Regarding business records retention, either adopt a version of the policy in chapter 11 or talk with the independent auditor, who will be knowledgeable about state laws and well as the American Accounting Standards Board provisions.

The IRS wants to confirm that any subsidiaries policy manual includes the organizational charitable purpose and is consistent with the parent organization's manual provisions.

The IRS also is interested if the charity makes organizational documents such as the bylaws that traditionally are internal documents available to the public. With current right to know laws in many states, except for proprietary information, interested parties can acquire a very substantial amount of information about government-funded organizations. However, considering the amount of information that is available through the 990 and contract documents I do not recommend making the by-laws and other internal documents available to the public.

Reporting information from Third Parties

Some 990 questions request information that the organization may need to obtain from a related third-party organization. These can include parent and subsidiary companies, management companies, foundations that exist solely to benefit the PCWA. if the organization is a wholly owned subsidiary. The information includes compensation paid by related organizations; family and business relationships between officers, members of the BOD of directors, trustees, key employees, and certain businesses they own or control; the organization's share of the income and assets of a partnership or joint venture in which a PCWA has an ownership interest; and certain transactions between the organization and disqualified persons.

State Charitable Commissions

The states have charitable giving statutes with the purpose of providing the public with information on charities operating in their states, preventing and prosecuting fraud by criminals using charitable solicitation as a means of theft, and regulating the operations of professional fundraisers. Private nonprofit fundraising has become a big business, in part, because of the growth in the number of charities during the last twenty years. State laws are different but some of the information that state charitable commissions are sometimes interested in is each charity's mission, and programs and the income, expenses, assets and liabilities of the charity. They gather information on the fundraising expenses and the amounts paid to fundraising firms for a capital campaign or other fundraising work. The commissions may specify required provisions of agreements between charities and fundraising firms, and they gather information about fundraising firm ownership and employees. There is a special interest in blood and marital relations between people affiliated with the firms and the charity. There is an annual registration process for both the charities and the fundraising firms. For the charities, this entails supplying basic information and completing a questionnaire annually. Each charity's annual audit and 990 filings are possible submission attachments. The size and type of staff employed in the state's charitable commission agency will give some idea of the number of audits they perform. In addition, the commissions receive and investigate complaints made against charities and fundraisers by the public.

Chapter 21 - Untangling Insurance Policies and the Insurance

Purchasing Process

an attempt to establish liability on the part of the driver of the car, the counselor driving the van, and the PCWA. A lot depends on the relationship of the youths with their parents. If there is a relationship with them, the parent(s) may begin litigation so that the child and parent can recover monies spent on current and future medical care, as well as pain and suffering. Sometimes parents who have not been in contact with their children for a long time will come forward to file a claim with the hope of financial gain.

If the state has terminated parental rights, if the parent is in prison, or if the relationship between the child and parent is distant the claim amounts paid could be lower. This happens when the parents decide not to or cannot litigate. The GCWA will assure the provision of medical and rehabilitation care but the GCWA does not usually litigate when children are accidentally injured. The PCWA attorney may recommend offering the youths a small settlement in exchange for the youth and the GCWA signing a release of claims document to protect the PCWA against future claims. If there is no release of claims by the youth, then they or their parents can sue up until the time specified in the state statute of limitations legislation, usually two or three years.

The settlement negotiations between the insurance companies involved consider the seriousness of the injuries and the determination of the percent of responsibility each driver has for the accident. The driver of the van has a legitimate worker's compensation case. The process for claim management varies by state, as each state operates its own workers compensation program. Many states require employers to buy workers compensation insurance but some states have a government program. Worker's compensation policies cover medical expenses and disability payments to the counselor. If the counselor want compensation for pain and suffering, they file a personal liability action. The counselor may hire an attorney to represent them. If a company insures the PCWA they manage the claim for the agency because they are responsible for paying the costs. The contributory impact of the previous back injury and the accident to the counselor's back pain will be the subject of medical evaluation. Also, the insurance company and perhaps subsequently the workers compensation board will decide whether the violation of traffic law precludes or reduces the payment to the counselor. Some states offer mediation service. If the claimant and insurance company cannot come to an agreement the state workers compensation board hearing officer decides on claim amounts.

There will a fixed amount paid to the family of the young person who died by the insurance company based on what is usual and customary. The costs for the insurance company of handling a death claim when a child or elderly person is the victim is often lower than for an adult who is responsible for the support of their family. Insurance payouts may be higher to pay for the costs of caring for an injured person depending on the need for long-term care and hospitalization expenses.

Depending on the seriousness of injuries to the children, and the number of injured children the PCWA will be at risk of serious financial consequences. This is based to some extent on the amount of the employee's personal auto insurance coverage, and the PCWA auto insurance coverage and umbrella insurance coverage. The agency personnel policies clearly state that staff must obey all traffic laws and drive safely while transporting youth. Because an illegal act is involved the PCWA insurance company may refuse to defend the driver, but will still defend the agency. In settling accident claims, the PCWA will take the position that the counselor acted against agency policy, if they are at fault in an accident situation and a violation of the law is involved. The agency will emphasize the training provided, driving record check, and personnel policy. The attorneys for the youth or parents know from their research and experience that counselor's personal car insurance coverage, which is primary in paying claims, will not come close to paying the costs for medical care for seriously disabled accident victims. They will also quickly figure out if the PCWA has substantial insurance coverage, property, and cash assets. The PCWA is often "the deep pocket". There can be multiple attorneys for the different youth. They will make the argument that the main issue is that the counselor acted in their capacity as an agency employee in transporting the youth. The PCWA lawyer will likely try to settle the case because of the sympathy the youths will get from a jury. If the agency does not have substantial cash assets or own much property, plaintiff counsel will evaluate the claim paying ability of the agency insurance coverage. For agencies with substantial assets, the auto coverage offers a first line of protection with umbrella insurance providing a second level of coverage. The real risk to the agency is losses that exceed insurance coverage amounts and involve a diversion of assets to settle the claims. This threat to the continued existence of the agency is the ultimate argument for adequate insurance coverage. On the other hand, if the agency has few assets it may be less likely to be the subject of litigation.

As the above plays out PCWA staff uses time coordinating efforts with insurance company claim settlement staff. If there is litigation than the counselor driving the van, and administrative staff work with the attorney appointed by the insurance company. Staff offer support to the parents of the child who died as well as the other children hurt in the accident.

The Insurance Application and Types of Coverage

The Application

Most insurers require the PCWA to complete an application for each policy. The application will include questions about organizational stability including year founded, anticipated mergers, bankruptcy filings, and the past three years income and expenses. There is a great deal of interest in employees. These questions include the number of employees, number of layoffs, and number of firings. There are questions about the employee exit process including severance packages There are questions about internal consultation with the human resources department or a labor lawyer when there is a discharge. There are a number of questions about written policies regarding the management of employee complaints, employment at will, EEOC, and sexual harassment policies. Application questions will concern the size and training of the HR department, public complaint management, and the existence of written personnel policies. The PCWA also reports insurance claims and settlement amounts, or court findings during the last three years. The application asks the agency to submit their written program descriptions and may ask if the agency has certain other policies in place. A PCWA offering equestrian, swimming, and adventure programing should emphasize their consumer safety practices in the program application. Rates will be higher for these kinds of activities than standard counseling programs. The company reviews the credentials of staff and rates are likely to be higher when some of the staff is physicians. The types of insurance policies PCWA purchases and their purposes follow.

General Liability Insurance

General liability insurance covers people the agency helps, and others who visit agency offices and residences. It also covers slip and fall claims for people walking on the sidewalks that are part of the PCWA premises. If the injury takes place on agency property, the policies often include payment of the medical expenses of the injured person, funeral expenses, settlement costs, and legal expenses for litigation brought against the agency by the injured person. **Also covered are actions, on the part of the employees or volunteers, which contribute to the circumstances that created the injury.** Special riders to extend the insurance to locations where the agency holds onetime special events such as conferences or fund raisers are available. General liability insurance policies may also cover copyright infringement, other violations of intellectual property law, and cases of libel or slander. Check your organization's policy to see if it includes these protections. Many PCWAs have a risk committee. The group tours the PCWA agency facilities to make sure that there are no fire risks, or features of a building, such as a broken step that pose liability risks. Ask your insurance agent to provide a safety checklist and to meet with the committee one time to review the most common reasons for liability claims, and examples of good risk management programs at organizations like yours. Call someone at another PCWA to find out about their risk management program.

Property Insurance

Property insurance covers buildings and their contents if fire or selected other causes damage or destroy a building. However, the policy may not cover certain events such as terrorist attacks, or floods. The policy may offer limited coverage of equipment such as computers, and depending on the gap between the replacement costs and insured amounts, a separate office equipment policy may be worthwhile. Alternatively, you can designate an appropriate amount of agency surplus funds to an equipment replacement fund. As is true with homeowner's insurance, the agency will have a choice to insure for the replacement cost either of the building or for a fixed dollar amount of coverage. Even if the agency and the main locations are insured, rental location addresses, such as consumer apartments or storage facilities are on the policy to insure their contents. Managers design policies that prohibit the storage of flammable materials inside buildings. Inspect buildings and apartments annually to check for fire risks such as trash accumulations, electrical systems that obviously are old, and need repair or replacement. Prohibit smoking in buildings, particularly in bedrooms.

Auto Insurance

There is an auto liability policy if the staff or volunteers use cars, vans, and/or trucks for agency purposes. States may set minimum coverage amount. Organizations will need one policy for employee and volunteer owned vehicles and a second one for PCWA owned vehicles. The insurance will pay for injuries a driver causes to other people or property while carrying out the agency work. Many states also mandate personal injury protection and uninsured / underinsured motorist coverage. When employees drive their own car, their personal insurance is primary and the agency insurance is secondary. Agency requirements for employee insurance coverage vary. Some agencies do not have requirements beyond what the state required minimums. Other agencies require higher coverage amounts to limit the costs of their own policies. Equity is one consideration in requiring higher coverage in light of employee compensation. Worker's compensation insurance is primary when the counselor is driving in connection with agency business.

An automobile prevention program can include:

➢ Pre- employment checks of applicant driving records, repeated every three years for current employees.
➢ Participation of employees in a driver's safety program
➢ A program to have agency vehicles well maintained
➢ Written policies regarding driving behavior exist as part of the personnel policies

Directors and Officers Insurance

A lawsuit against the nonprofit alleging fraud or financial mismanagement can name individual BOD members and volunteers. Directors and Officers (D&O) insurance cover the cost of defending the BOD and officers, and pay, any resulting monetary damages. D&O insurance is protection against a breach of "duty" by the directors and officers. The policy pays for actual or alleged wrong decisions and acts of omission. The policy also covers neglect. As with any insurance coverage, it is important to understand what the D and O policy covers and does not cover. Typical exclusions include damages arising from criminal or fraudulent behavior and claims brought by one member of the BOD against another. It is vital that the policy covers employment-related claims. Most of these start as EEOC claims. The BOD reduces the risk of lawsuits against them by:

> Having an employee complaint officer.
> Having regular attendance at BOD meetings
> Using the prudent person rule in deliberation
> Assuring financial management policies exist
> Assuring the by-laws are up to date and knowing their contents
> Assuring a conflict of interest policy exists
> Assuring a whistleblower policy exists
> Assuring that the review of all policies and practices occurs at regular intervals
> Keeping accurate and complete BOD minutes
> Assuring that a policy exists prohibiting excess compensation for leaders exist.
> Member understand their responsibility to act to further the best interests of the organization and their duty of loyalty to the PCWA

Professional Liability Insurance

Similar to D&O coverage, professional liability coverage (also sometimes called malpractice insurance) protects direct service staff and their manager against liabilities resulting from errors and misbehavior. Some claims involve sexual misconduct. Husbands and fathers sue if counselors have sexual relationships with their wives or daughters. Lack of supervision that leads to harm to or death of a client is another type of claim. The drowning death of a child in residential care is an example. The death of a child due to the use of physical restraint is also the basis of a malpractice claim. Agency policies regarding child discipline limits, and prohibitions against personal relationships with clients help prevent malpractice claims. The insurance policy covers defense and settlement costs in connection with lawsuits brought by consumers against the agency and employees for acts of malpractice. The agency minimizes its risks by having a clear ethics policy and a professional performance standards policy as part of the personnel policies. Agencies without these policies and well-written job descriptions are open to claims from consumer attorneys, that the agency has a higher level of liability because it did not specify the wrongdoing as prohibited. The policy will cover each individual named as a defendant if there is no criminal wrongdoing Named defendants may include the counselor, the counselor's supervisor, the program director, and president depending on the circumstances. The insurance company will not cover employees who commit criminal acts.

Workers Compensation Insurance

States require all organizations to have this insurance. It covers on the job injuries sustained by employees. The costs depend on the job classifications of the employees and state program rules. Rates are often higher for PCWAs that offer substantial residential services compared to PCWAs in which home-based work is prevalent. Depending on the organizational claim experience and the types of injuries incurred by the workforce, you may want to do a quick study to identify injury patterns. The insurance carrier and agent will usually work to design a generic risk management program that identifies the most frequents type of worker injury, and an injury prevention program. The federal employee safety agency the Occupational Safety and Health Administration (OHSA)offers a wide range of safety training programs. Descriptions are available at the OSHA website: https://www.osha.gov/dte/library/. In addition, your PCWA may want to contract with a hospital or physician's practice to perform the physical examinations of injured employees. Write a section on work place injuries in the personnel policies. When an injury occurs, a physician examines the employee immediately. Hang a poster in each agency building instructing employees to report immediately any work place injuries. Often PCWAs purchase posters covering EEOC, work injuries and other topics.

Unemployment Insurance

All organization pays some minimum to the state for this coverage which provides time limited payments to employees who are victims of a reduction in force. Many organizations participate in the state unemployment system that can be costly depending on the overall unemployment level in the state, as well as the unemployment rates in the applicable occupational group. Each state operates its own unemployment insurance program, which determines program rules including payments to those determined eligible to collect benefits. Each state program also determines the length of eligibility. In times of high unemployment, the Federal government payments to the states serve to extend the period that beneficiaries get payments. Most often employees that an employer lays off are eligible to collect benefits, and employees that quit voluntarily generally not. When employees quit, or employers terminate employment for cause employees may or may not be eligible to collect depending on the facts and circumstances of each situation. Financial liability for payments is with the most recent employer, or split between employers depending on the length of employment with each liable employer. The state unemployment agency arbitrates disputes between the employer and their former employee. Unemployment hearing transcripts are available to both parties in the case of subsequent litigation in some states.

It is a good idea to consider an insurance trust, for unemployment insurance, unless you are paying for many claims. Insurance trusts are as an alternative to the state system for handling premium collections and disbursements to cover claims. You make an initial deposit into the trust based on industry standards and the number of employees. You continue to make payments correlated to the quarterly employee counts, wages and claims experience. The state continues to process all claims and adjudicate contested unemployment claims. The fund pays claims from the deposits. Eventually PCWAs with low unemployment claims may build up a large balance in the fund to pay for claims. Then the quarterly payments are lower until claims rise. Unlike the state unemployment insurance system, the trust returns the account balance to the agency if participation ends. The auditor will decide whether these funds are an asset.

Umbrella Insurance

Umbrella insurance covers claim cost greater than the other insurance policy limits cover. For instance, if you have $1,000,000 in malpractice insurance and it costs more than a $1,000,000 to pay the claim umbrella insurance covers the difference in costs. Umbrella insurance carriers will specify the amount of coverage you need in existing policies before they will pay claims. An alternative to umbrella insurance is excess liability insurance. Excess liability insurance pays excess claims limited to what the existing policies cover. Umbrella policies often provide broader coverage than the existing policies and will sometimes pay all costs of an event that existing policies do not cover at all. Policy costs are often modest. As always, know what the policy you buy covers and what it excludes.

Buying Insurance

Purchasing insurance for charities is different from purchasing insurance for individuals. As an individual, there are companies that you can contact through the Internet or you can get bids from an insurance broker. Some brokers represent one company, and some seek bids from a larger pool of companies to meet consumer needs. In the not for profit world, PCWAs purchase insurance through a broker. You work directly with a broker or with an association broker through an agency's affiliation with a professional association.

Once you select a broker, the broker seeks quotes based on the type of organization you are and the type of policies needed. Among companies that offer malpractice insurance, some do not wish to insure certain types of risk. The insurance companies and not the policyholder pay the insurance broker. The earnings of the broker for procuring the agency as a customer for the insurance company are invisible to the typical nonprofit. The idea of competitive bidding based on broker fees is not feasible. You will know the bids the broker gets for the coverage, and the prices offered and you can easily find out the financial strength of the insurance companies and what their policies cover and exclude.

The tough part in comparing prices is to know what you are getting for the premium payment. The key issue is what does the policy cover and what does the policy not cover. Are there limitations on coverage amounts for some items? What are the policy deductibles? For those untrained in insurance policy content answering some questions is easy, others not so much. Very few executives will take the time to read and understand the contents of the agency insurance policies.

Start out with a broker, other than your own, who is interested in your business. Choose among local brokers who have at least three PCWAs as customers. There are also national brokers who specialize in nonprofit insurance. Ask the broker you choose to review the present policies and let you know what changes they suggest. The positive outcome of this kind of review is that it positions you to improve the quality of the insurance coverage. For example, it is better to know the present policy excludes staff sexual misbehavior (some policies do) before something occurs rather than after an incident happens. In addition, get the potential new broker's thinking on coverages and coverage amounts. The consultation that the broker offers will give you some ideas about either staying the course or changing coverage limits, adding coverage, or dropping a policy. The broker that does the analysis deserves the opportunity to be first to the starting line if you feel they have done a good job for you, and the current broker has left the agency exposed to serious risks, or the cost of current policies is excessive compared to what the potential broker can offer. Being first at the starting line has an important advantage to any broker when several brokers are seeking your insurance business. This is because the insurance companies will only quote to one broker. If the broker is knowledgeable, they will approach the companies offering the best value. These companies offer low cost but high-quality insurance policies. The other brokers will get bids from companies that are not as competitive on price or coverage, because of the one quote standard so the second broker is at a disadvantage. If the current insurance policies pass muster for coverage and cost, stay with the current broker. However, as with all purchasing, periodically, (every three to five years) ask another broker or two to provide quotes. An important element in making your decision about a broker is what their references have to say about the quality and timeliness of service. If you decide to allow the potential broker to be first in line invite at least two other brokers to get quotes to maintain competitive bidding. Also, keep in mind that some brokers with a regional or national base may offer you attractive rates by applying part of their payment from the insurance companies to reduce the premium but save money through having a small staff and service may suffer.

What amount of coverage does the policy provide per claim? What is the total amount of protection offered for all claims during the policy period? If there are several claims, how likely is it that the total claims will exceed the coverage limits? Consider if you need a higher coverage amount.

Most policies include covering the cost of attorney's fees for defending a claim. In determining coverage amounts, legal fees, expenses, and settlement amounts are all included. Check that the policy does not provide for denying a claim based on the insurance company' assertion the coverage amount is inadequate or the type of policy purchased is incorrect. Check the wrongful acts and malpractice definitions in the professional liability, directors, and officer's policies. Is the definition broad or is it limited to specific acts, and excludes coverage for other acts?

The Timing of Claims

Most liability insurance policies pay for events that occur during the time the policy is in force. For example, a general liability policy will pay for a consumer injury claim during the policy period. Other policies pay based on the date of the claim; not when the precipitating event occurs. State law allows a window of time for people to file a claim, usually two or three years. The time between the event and the claim can be considerable. If you change, insurers and have a claims made policy the former insurance company will not accept responsibility for the claim made after the policy expiration date. To avoid this situation, purchase tail end policies. They cover claims for events, which happened before the policy expiration date, but the filing of a claim occurred after the policy expiration date.

When someone files a claim, leaders consider several elements. These are: 1) Ethical considerations – PCWA stakeholders believe in social justice. What constitutes social justice is a difficult question for both the person bringing the claim as well as for the consumers of the agency whose services suffer anytime the agency spends time or money on items that do not advance the mission. 2) Economic costs - What are the various types of costs present and future, entailed in the handling of the claim? What is the usual settlement range for the type of claim made? 3) An analysis of the claim based on the facts and circumstances, and the harm claimed. 4) The "60-Minutes Perspective". This is a media view of the complaint. Ask yourself what the story would look like if a news organization covered it as a news story. What would be the headline? What would be the content of the story? This kind of analysis will give managers some idea of what outsiders including investigators, and claim adjusters will think when they review the facts of the situation.

The PCWA and insurance company have specific obligations in the management of a claim. These include the agency notification responsibility, the responsibilities of the insurance company to defend the agency, and the acceptance by the agency of the insurance company decision-making authority in the settlement of the claim. The answers to three questions are uppermost in the minds of the insurance company staff. They are: What is the settlement amount acceptable to the complainant? What will be the cost to the insurance company of defending the case in court? What is the chance that the litigant will win a sizable court award?

For its part, the PCWA needs to think through the organizational management of the event. This includes deciding the roles of the president, employee complaint officer, and the staff member accused. An important consideration is who will function as the agency staff liaison with the insurance company and the attorney defending the agency. A staff member also needs to be responsible for gathering information including anything contained in agency records, and information that different staff has about the accusation. Peers of the complainant and others also have a role in clarifying the facts and circumstances.

> *Case Example: Management of an Employment*
> *Sex Discrimination Insurance Claim*
>
> *Initial Story Mr. Grady, a childcare worker for Caring Children's Services, telephones the administrative assistant to the agency's president to schedule an appointment to meet with Ms. Cheston. Ms. Cheston is a bit mystified when she sees the appointment on her calendar because she does not know Mr. Grady very well although he is a long-term employee. She cannot imagine why he wants to meet with her. She keeps an open-door policy and is willing to meet with any employee who asks for to see her. When they meet, Ms. Cheston thinks that Mr. Grady looks tired and distracted. Mr. Grady discloses that Ms. Middleton, his supervisor, is harassing him and verbally abusing him because he is a man. He states he has worked on other units in the past and has never had problems with a supervisor. He has a history of good performance evaluations. The last year and half that he has worked in the Deerfield Cottage supervised by Ms. Middleton have been a "living hell". He reports that on one occasion she told him he was stupid and a few weeks before that she stated, in a group staff meeting, that he really did not know what was going on in the unit. On another occasion, she made an unannounced visit to the group home when he was on a break and reading the newspaper. She commented to him that he is late in submitting consumer case notes and that he is to*

attend to them promptly. On another occasion, he called her to report that there was a bat in the group home. She told him to take care of it himself although he was obviously frightened. He felt her failure to act put the children in danger. Moreover, she pressures him to come into cover for other staff that calls in sick more than she asks the female staff to do this. He says he is the only male counselor on the unit. He does not see Ms. Middleton making these negative remarks to anyone else and thinks she is singling him out because he is a man. He will not continue to work for Ms. Middleton. He wants to leave his job. Ms. Middleton's treatment of him has taken away his confidence and energy. He needs a rest. Ms. Cheston is attentive as Mr. Grady talks to her. She then says she is sorry to hear he has such a negative relationship with his supervisor. She asks him if he has contacted the employee complaint officer about his situation. He says he has not and that he came to see her because she has a reputation as a caring leader. He feels that although Ms. Middleton has discriminated against him and harassed him that Caring Children's Services is a worthwhile organization and he does not want to bring a lawsuit against the agency if he can help it. He says that he is "burned out" from Ms. Middleton's persecution, and is going to seek a job in another type of work. He proudly says he has been a loyal employee for a decade. Considering his service and his treatment by Ms. Middleton, he wants six month's severance pay and a written guarantee from her that the agency will not oppose his application to collect unemployment insurance. Ms. Cheston tells him she is concerned about his accusations and will have Ms. Jarvis the employee complaint officer contacts him and speak with Ms. Middleton as well. Following the interview, Ms. Cheston writes up the contents of the meeting and asks her administrative assistant to witness the date she wrote the note.

Ms. Jarvis contacts Mr. Grady and he repeats his account to her. She asks him if he is feeling well. He says no, and that as the harassment from Ms. Middleton continued over time, he has been seeing a psychologist because he feels depressed. Additionally, his family doctor has prescribed him antidepressant medication. When she interviews Ms. Middleton, she states that Mr. Grady's performance is poor and that he takes excessive sick time. When she comes into the Deerfield Cottage unannounced, she has found him reading the newspaper more than once. The second time this happened she told him it looked terrible to find him reading the newspaper rather than completing his assignments. At a staff meeting, she asked him about an incident involving one of the boys. Even though he was present when the boy had a temper outburst, he was unable to discuss the facts of the situation although it had happened only two days before the meeting. She said she did comment to him at the staff meeting that he did not seem to know much about what had happened. She said she did tell him to contact the maintenance department about the bat rather than handling it herself and Mr. Grady understands this is the protocol. She said she never called him stupid and that all unit staff rotates on-call coverage when someone calls in sick. Ms. Jarvis contacts two male staff members who now work in other cottages, but formerly worked in Ms. Middleton's cottage Ms. Jarvis asks them about their working relationship with her. They both reported it was fine, about the same as with their present supervisor. She also contacts other people who attended the staff meeting at which the group talked about the resident's temper outburst. They confirmed that Ms. Middleton did seem surprised that Mr. Grady was unable to discuss what happened. When asked about their own reaction they stated that it did seem odd to them that Mr. Grady did not know about the case. When asked if they observed Ms. Middleton giving Mr. Grady a hard time on a regular basis, they said they did not. They did say however, that during the last six months Mr. Grady seemed withdrawn while at work. Ms. Jarvis also reviews Mr. Grady's personnel file. The review substantiates his statement that he has a record of good performance reviews and substantiates his use of sick time is excessive.

Ms. Jarvis and Ms. Cheston discuss the results of Ms. Jarvis's complaint investigation. Ms. Cheston asks Ms. Jarvis to make sure that she is careful in the preparation of her interview notes. Next, Ms. Cheston calls the agency labor attorney Mr. Smithfield. They have a brief discussion about the case and the lawyer says he wants to examine the written material. He comments that in discrimination complaints the first step is for the employee to file an EEOC complaint with the federal Agency. It is not unusual that employees also file complaints with state and local governmental agencies as well, where laws offer protection against discrimination. He states that either the EEOC will dismiss the complaint, at which point Mr. Grady can litigate, or EEOC may investigate and try to resolve the complaint. He states that she should indicate her preference to have their firm represent the agency to the insurance company. He will call Ms. Cheston back after reviewing the materials.

Ms. Cheston asks Ms. Jarvis to send Mr. Grady a memo saying that the agency is continuing to investigate his complaint and she will be in contact with him again within 15 business days to communicate the outcome of the investigation. She also asks her to forward the requested information to Mr. Smithfield.

Ten days later Mr. Smithfield calls Ms. Cheston. The crux of the complaint is that Mr. Grady is unable to continue employment because of Ms. Middleton's verbal harassment. In addition, due to the discriminatory harassment he has become depressed enough to require medical attention. Last, he is claiming he is unable to continue to work in the field any longer due to this situation, and he needs to get other kind of work. Mr. Grady believes that what he requests is fair compensation in light of the damage done and the challenges he faces.

Ms. Cheston tells Mr. Smithfield that the investigation does not provide strong support for Mr. Grady's claim of sex discrimination. Mr. Smithfield responds that the psychologist and family physician may well see themselves as advocates and contend that Mr. Grady is depressed because of his feelings about the work situation. In addition, the observation of fellow workers that he is withdrawn adds credibility to his claim of being depressed while working. Mr. Smithfield suggests that one response, considering Mr. Grady's tenure and employment record as well as the potential cost, time, and effort on the part of management in disputing the claim is to grant Mr. Grady's request. In this scenario, Ms. Cheston makes a counter offer to Mr. Grady. Ms. Cheston and Mr. Grady negotiate a settlement amount. Mr. Smithfield then prepares a settlement agreement and a release of claims document that both Mr. Grady and Ms. Cheston sign. The settlement agreement states the amount of the settlement, and that Caring Children's services will not dispute any truthful assertions that Mr. Grady makes in the course of pursing unemployment insurance payments. Furthermore, neither party will discuss the settlement terms, nor make disparaging remarks about the other party. Mr. Grady agrees not to seek employment with Caring Children's Services in the future. The release of claims document provides that Mr. Mr. Grady will not seek additional compensation, to the settlement agreement amount or file complaints against Caring Children's Services. or initiate litigation against the agency. The agreement provides that Mr. Grady must return the cash if he violates the terms of the agreement. After both parties sign the agreement, Caring Children's services issues a check to Mr. Grady.

An alternative response the attorney suggests is to inform Mr. Grady that the investigation concludes discrimination did not take place, however in light of Mr. Grady's, years of service and the poor relationship with Ms. Middleton that he is being offered a transfer and a reasonable accommodation will be offered to him related to his depression.

Ms. Cheston thinks about all of this and she has several thoughts, which suggest different actions. She believes that Ms. Middleton, although having a poor relationship with Mr. Grady, did not discriminate against him based on sex. She accepts that Mr. Grady wants to change fields of work, and he no longer feels good about his job. Several factors suggest he is depressed. Many staff enter social work in part due to a traumatic past. The agency has a contract with an employee assistance program that is a resource to help staff with either personal or professional issues. There is no precedent at the agency for this kind of payout to settle a complaint. She is uncertain about Mr. Grady's authenticity, and wonders if he just wants financial help while making a career change. There have been two employee complaints during the last three years involving insurance claims. The policy deductible did increase once and another claim will bring another increase. Sometimes employees threaten to make complaints but do not follow through. She wants to discourage this kind of request from others.

Ms. Cheston asks Ms. Jarvis to send Mr. Grady a memorandum saying that the investigation into his complaint is complete and the finding is that Ms. Middleton did not engage in sex discrimination against him. He has negative feelings about his relationship with her, and has better relationships with past supervisors. Caring Children' Services welcomes him to continue his employment. Ms. Cheston regards him as an employee in good standing. He will be eligible for transfer to another cottage to fill the next vacancy. In addition, upon submission of a doctor's s note, CCS will make a scheduling accommodation so he can keep doctor's appointments and he can he can have a change in his work schedule if he is having difficulty in waking up on time to get to work. He is to notify Ms. Jarvis if he wants the agency to consider any other accommodation. He is also welcome to use the employee assistance program. If he chooses not to remain employed at the agency, the organization will provide a positive employment reference but not grant his request for severance pay and uncontested unemployment insurance payments due to a lack of precedent, and the importance of equal treatment for all employees.

Mr. Grady submits a letter of resignation three days later. His letter describes in detail the conversation he had with Ms. Cheston regarding his discrimination claim. Two weeks later Ms. Cheston gets a letter from Mr. Simmons informing her that his law firm is representing Mr. Grady regarding a complaint of discrimination against Caring Children's Services. The letter states that due to the irrevocable damage done to Mr. Grady and his debilitation caused by Ms. Middleton's discriminatory behavior, and his job loss that he is demanding $150,000 to settle the complaint. The letter also states that Mr. Grady has filed a sex discrimination complaint with the EEOC and the state human relations agency.

First Annotation Ethical Issues Discrimination complaints are troubling events for social service agencies. These organizations exist to promote social justice and discrimination complaints raise the possibility that in some situations they have done the opposite. As in all ethical situations, there are multiple competing claims. First, the agency wants to know that either the agency did not discriminate against the complainant, or if a staff member did discriminate then the PCWA rectifies the situation. There is a need to expend agency funds wisely to benefit consumers. Excess compensation whether to an executive or an unhappy employee is undesirable. In addition, it is important for the president to support the management staff when possible. On the other hand, the president will want the direct service staff to know that if they complain, there will not be reprisals, and the response will be fair. In this situation, the employee complaints officer investigates the complaint. The employee can transfer to another cottage, and the employer offers a reasonable accommodation. In addition, the president meets with Ms. Middleton to both express her support and to advise her of the importance of empathy in implementing her staff supervision responsibilities.

Analysis of the Complaint An employee makes a sex discrimination complaint against his supervisor. The complaint does not involve a significant action on the part of the employer. Significant discriminatory employer actions include firing, demotion, loss of pay, or benefits or other employer behavior such employee job relocation to a distant location, or an unreasonable work schedule that an employee views as burden. There are three aspects to Mr. Grady's complaint. The first is that Ms. Middleton's harassment has caused him to contract a medical condition covered by the American with Disabilities act. Second Ms. Middleton's behavior toward him is so egregious that she has created a hostile work environment that is so odious that he cannot his employment. These two elements are the most important parts of the complaint because they are associated with employment ending which causes economic harm to Mr. Grady. Third; by asking him to cover on call shifts when the supervisor did not ask female employees to cover shifts the employer creates discrimination because the supervisor required additional duties of Mr. Grady even though he and the female staff have the same job description

Ms. Jarvis's memo makes it clear he is an employee is good standing and he can transfer to another cottage and another supervisor. This attempt by the employer to resolve the complaint will put them in a good light.

Several facts suggest that the employee is seeking funds to help transition to a new career. These include his on the job behavior including withdrawal and inattention to his duties. In addition, he chooses not to use the employee assistance program to deal with his depression. Also, he makes his termination compensation request directly to the president rather than using the employee complaint process. This also tells of his understanding of organization power. Finally, his decision to resign and seek counsel confirms his goals of ending employment and receiving compensation.

Management of the Complaint The "he said, she said" nature of these situations makes it important to verify facts as much as possible. Interviewing others present during the time the complainant alleges certain behaviors occurred, and a review of employment records will help to supplement the information given by the accused and the complainant. It is common that these additional interviews and record reviews yield supportive material for both sides. In addition, the analysis needs to consider the different versions of the same events.

Although Mr. Grady makes his request to her directly, Ms. Cheston delegates the management of his complaint to the employee complaint *officer.* There are several reasons for this. First, the president should spend as little time as possible on this kind of matter. Interviews with lawyers, testimony at the unemployment hearing, and possible depositions, all take valuable time. In addition, the president should not leave herself open to negative publicity that can result from employee litigation. Most important the employee complaint officer has the training and experience to conduct a proper investigation of the matter.

Economic Costs From an economic perspective, the Directors and Officers policy deductible amount makes a difference in the cost benefit analysis of the situation. If this is an initial claim than the insurance deductible the agency will have to pay is likely to be modest. This will also be true if the last claim was in the distant past. If there has been more than one complaint filed within the last two years, it is likely that there will be an increase in the deductible perhaps to $25,000. If the agency files another claim within the same two-year period, it is likely that there will be another increase perhaps up to $50,000. This is important because it represents a potentially large agency expense if there is another claim. So, from an economic perspective, if the child care worker earns $35,000 a year plus benefits, it may be best to pay the six months' salary. Another economic issue is the opportunity costs of Ms. Cheston, Ms. Jarvis, and Ms. Middleton due to the time and effort to respond to an EEOC investigation. On the other hand, the EEOC dismisses many complaints. In addition, because attorneys representing employees in discrimination matters receive all or part of their compensation through receiving a portion of the settlement amount Mr. Grady will need to locate an attorney who feels there is enough merit to the case to agree to represent him.

Following Insurance Policy Procedures In considering other factors, the decision is not to settle with Mr. Grady. Ms. Cheston receives a notification of Mr. Grady's intent to file an EEOC complaint, and there is a settlement amount demand. At this point, the president needs to notify the insurance company providing the officers and directors policy of the claim. The agency cover letter informs the insurance company of the claim. The letter from Mr. Grady's attorney, a brief summary of the complaint, and complaint investigation materials are attachments to the letter. Ms. Cheston requests that their labor attorney represent the agency. She identifies the contact person for the agency as Ms. Middletown. Be clear that the notification to the insurance company occurs as soon as there is substantial knowledge of the claim. Do not wait until the EEOC complaint proceeds. Do not have Mr. Smithfield proceed with any work until you receive authorization from the insurance company. There are two reasons for this. The insurance company may not pay attorney's fees to Mr. Smithfield, if they decide not to engage him to handle the case. Second, the attorney who does help may want to proceed in a different direction than Mr. Smithfield pursues.

Working with the Insurance Company In about two weeks, the insurance claim manager contacts the president or their designee. The claim manager may inform you that the company will appoint counsel or you may use the labor attorney. The insurance company has a range of fees they pay and a group of attorneys they regularly use based on the attorney's, specialization and fees, and the particulars of the claim. The claim manager may not want to decide about counsel until they review the situation. Whoever oversees the claim for the PCWA will likely be involved in giving testimony and coordination of others at the agency. The agency liaison responds to information requests and questions from counsel. During the initial telephone conversation with the insurance company representative, discuss the management of the unemployment insurance claim process. Depending on the state, the proceedings from unemployment insurance hearings are admissible at trial and the insurance company usually wants the agency represented at the hearing. The company may have services that they use that are different from the attorney services that handle the insurance claim.

Story - Part II In a month's time, Ms. Cheston receives a letter from EEOC notifying the agency that Mr. Grady filed a complaint two weeks ago. By this time, the insurance company has named counsel. They decided not to use Mr. Smithfield, the agency attorney, but give no reason for this. They have appointed Mr. Martins. Ms. Jarvis had an initial contact with him. He is professional and business like, but not overly friendly or supportive.

Sometimes the EEOC letter informs the agency that they have dismissed and the EEOC has issued a right to sue letter to the complainant. This can happen if the EEOC judges that the complaint involves a law outside their jurisdiction, or the complaint appears to be without merit. In addition, the EEOC has limited resources and chooses not to investigate complaints that have merit but are not significant.

In the case of Mr. Grady's complaint, the EEOC asks the agency to send a respondent's position statement. The agency is to submit a response within 30 days that addresses each specific charge of discrimination in the complaint along with supporting attachments. These include Mr. Grady's job description, and any disciplinary actions. Also, EEOC asks for investigation materials, and affidavits of employees having knowledge that supports the agency position. Ms. Jarvis supplies the dates of events relating to the complaint. She indicates the resolution to the complaint that the agency offered Mr. Grady following her investigation. She includes her complaint investigation report. She writes about the materials that the agency wants the investigator to consider confidential. Confidential materials include sensitive medical information, trade secrets or confidential financial information, personal information about witnesses and other items. Medical information about Mr. Grady's depression is not confidential both because he has already shared it with Ms. Jarvis and shared it with EEOC as part of his claim. The EEOC releases the complaint to the employer, and the employer position statement to the employee. However, EEOC ultimately decides which material is confidential and does not release this information.

EEOC in the letter offers a mediation service. In addition, the EEOC investigator includes a list of questions. In evaluating the merits of Mr. Grady's complaint EEOC wants to know the number of male and female employees and a list of the names and addresses of all male employees. They ask for a copy of the cottage schedule for a range of dates. In addition, without informing the agency they contact a list of employees given by Mr. Grady along with a list of questions. Ms. Jarvis continues to do the lion's share of the work, and reviews the submission with the insurance company lawyer, Mr. Martins. Ms. Jarvis informs Ms. Cheston that she is developing a lot of compensatory time due to this assignment. As Ms. Cheston can see the amount of effort required, she feels frustrated in using so much staff time on the matter. Ms. Jarvis asks EEOC for and gets a 5-day extension to submit an affidavit because the employee is returning from a Family and Medical Act Leave. Ms. Jarvis submits the rest of the material within the 30-day time limit.

Two months pass and Ms. Jarvis receive a letter stating the EEOC complaint process is complete and that Mr. Grady will receive a right to sue letter. This means the complaint is without merit. In certain situations, EEOC assesses financial damages. Upper limits of damages vary by agency size (number of employees) and can be between $50,000 and $300,000. Where there are serious legal violations, the EEOC may refer the case to the Department of Justice.

Mr. Grady's lawyer, Mr. Simmons, writes to inform Ms. Cheston that his client has received a right to sue notice from EEOC and a he has filed a lawsuit seeking a $150,000. Ms. Jarvis supplies Mr. Simmons with the name and address of agency counsel.

About a month later, the insurance company claims manager contacts Ms. Cheston to get the agency's concurrence in settling the lawsuit for $20,000. She reluctantly acquiesces since the insurance company will not pay legal fees or any settlement costs if she does not. However, she continues to feel negatively about the cash settlement, both because both the internal and EEOC investigation found that no discrimination took place, and also because of the precedent this will create. A written settlement agreement is prepared and Ms. Cheston signs off on it. In the agreement, both parties agree that the settlement is confidential and Mr. Grady agrees not to seek employment with the agency.

Second Annotation Ethical Issues Ms. Cheston does not want to make any settlement offer to Mr. Grady. However, if she does not agree to the insurance company proposal then the agency handles the case on its own.

The insurance company will not pay legal fees or any settlement costs. She reluctantly agrees. Her initial ethical framework included the ideas that she did not believe Mr. Grady was the object of discrimination, that she did not wish to encourage this kind of behavior among other employees and the PCWA had no history of making exit payments to departing employees. As the situation evolves the EEOC ruling confirms her belief about the lack of discrimination, but she is frustrated by the staff time spent on this matter, and that she has the choice of approving an insurance company settlement or going it alone. She still feels agreeing to the settlement is wrong. She considers the alternative and recognizes that legal and staff costs may be high if she does not agree. Furthermore, she feels spending agency money and time on a quagmire is taking energy away from advancing the agency mission. Ethical decision-making involves choices. As the complaint process develops, her choices are different from when Mr. Grady made the complaint.

Analysis of the Claim The EEOC asks for substantial information and conducts an initial investigation before dismissing the claim. The EEOC investigator and Ms. Jarvis who conducted the Caring Children's Services investigation came to the same conclusion, finding no merit in Mr. Grady's claim. This exoneration is good news for the agency, and strengthens the position of the insurance company in negotiating with Mr. Simmons.

Economic Costs Caring Children's services has a $50,000 deductible on their directors and officer's insurance policy due to filing two prior claims during the last two years, in which there were modest settlements. Because of the high deductible, the agency pays for the settlement costs. In addition, Ms. Jarvis will be taking a long vacation due to the compensatory time she earned in managing the case. It is likely that the insurance company will raise the policy deductible again, so additional cost to handle any future claim is possible. Of the settlement, Mr. Grady gets a bit more than $13,000 and Mr. Simmons gets about $6,500. Mr. Simmons and Mr. Grady stipulated when Mr. Simmons agreed to represent Mr. Grady that Mr. Simmons would get 1/3 of any monies awarded to Mr. Grady. This kind of contingency fee arrangement is common. In this arrangement, the attorney does not get a fee if there is no award to their client. The insurance company regards this as a nuisance case settlement. These low settlement amounts are common in cases of limited merit. It protects the insurance company against litigation. The insurance company avoids the considerable costs of defending the case in court and still worse the possibility of a considerable judgement. The settlement amount is a small price to pay for this kind of protection.

Conformity to Insurance Company Requirements Even though the agency leadership thought it was wrong to settle this case, they did so because the insurance company, which bears the payout risk of defense and settlement costs, judged it a reasonable settlement. The insurance company controls the decision-making in settlement decisions, unless the agency wishes to assume the risk of an alternative approach.

Conclusion

The cost to the agency to settle Mr. Grady's claim is about the same as his initial payment request. The insurance company pays for the time it took to manage the claim and legal costs. The agency pays the settlement cost, and has opportunity costs in the time staff spent on the claim. The attorneys gain income. It would have been more convenient and less expensive to negotiate to pay Mr. Grady 15 to 20 week's salary not as severance pay, but to settle the complaint. PCWAs sometimes offer severance packages on a voluntary basis when firing a long-time employee who has some years of good service, which the agency wants to recognize and avoid litigation. This amounts to internal claim management to avoid an increase in the insurance deductible, paying the claim and spending a significant amount of time on the claim. The agency staff time involved in managing the claim is not productive in that it does not advance the mission. It is better to file a claim with the insurance company when the risk for a high payout is substantial. Determining the range of payouts for claims is a judgement call, and a labor attorney can help in deciding. Settlement of the employee's initial demand is never a good idea if the ethical objections are strong. However, leaders need to be mindful that the available choices change

Acknowledgments

I have learned from many people and this is especially important in my role of growing Valley Youth House as my actions reflect the ideas and opinions of many members of the board of directors, the staff, as well as my peers in the community. I name a few people here and apologize in advance to those who I should acknowledge but do not. I thank Gary Stone Valley Youth House's first president who hired me to supervise operations. He is a kind and supportive leader.

Dayton Prior, and Eleanor Workman expressed their confidence in my ability to lead the fledgling organization although I had no financial or business experience. Without Anne Shire developing the board of directors we could not have attracted the interest of the high-level community leaders that have made such a difference in organizational success.

My friend Charlie Versaggi the longest serving board member has a big heart but a hard head in business. Current Air Products leaders can take pride in the role Charlie, Hayward Bell, Hap Wagner, Dayton Pryor, Don Shire and many others played in the success achieved. My chief mentors in finance were Neil Glickstein, retired CFO, of Binney and Smith and Jon Durn, Managing Director at Deloitte. They educated me in accounting, the key components of the nonprofit audit process, and managing investments, Father Daniel Gambet, OFCS, President Emeritus, DeSales University was my fundraising mentor and volunteer fundraising counsel.

Another board president Rob Weinberg, Senior Vice President at Lutron moved us from paper to cloud-based BOD communications. John Hayes, Vice President, SolarTech a past president, follows Charlie in tenure and leadership of our fundraising, and marketing programs. His loyalty and dependability taught me about the importance of being an even constant presence at the youth house.

Bob Robertson, Executive Vice President was our clinical leader developing the clinical program at Camp Fowler, and most notably the Independent Living Program. Also, of importance was his leadership at the group home for sexually reactive boys. Pat McGarry, head of our out-client and home-based services defined good people. Her clinical acumen, devotion to quality, and love for people provided a moral compass for me. Anne Adams our chief of prevention services, is a hard worker, established firm relationships with community customers, and had the best eye for detail among the group. When I was in a rush, she reminded me that slow and steady win the race.

Bill Motsavage, Lisa Weingartner, Allison Moore, Linda and Jeff Rolley and Michele Engler, were responsible for growing the independent living program. Sandra Molnar a great clinician, also supported quality of services at the youth house. Lorrie Reddie who headed all of the group home services always amazed me by minimizing bad behavior at three group homes that served hundreds of youth a year. Kathi Krablin, another very hard worker, and the agency grant writer, was the chief Valley Youth House cheerleader as well as raising millions of dollars each year through the grants she wrote. Diane Stadler, a quiet, effective and efficient administrative assistant kept me organized and allowed me to focus on my work. Nancy Haley and Kevin, Dolan both of Northampton County's Division of Children and Youth Services encouraged Valley Youth's growth through three decades. Lynn Rainey played the same role in Bucks County. Most important is the love and support of my wife Elizabeth Gilgoff, also the leader of an area charity, and my three boys, Ben, Dan, and Josh and my sister Mary Beth.

Works Cited

Administration for Children, Youth and Families. (2015). *Basic Center Program FOA*. Washington: Health and Human Services. Retrieved from: http://www.grants.gov/web/grants/search-grants.html

Association of Social Work Boards. (2013). *Social Work Practice and Related Definitions*. Culpepper, Va., ASWB. Retrieved from: https://www.datapathdesign.com/ASWB/Laws/Prod/cgi-bin/LawWebRpts2DLL.dll/1ny3aok0amtj7o17zmgpu0k9xjm6/$

Barnes, et. al. (2019) *Whistle-Blower Complaint Sets Off a Battle Involving Trump New York Times, September 19, 2019 Retrieved from:* https://www.nytimes.com/2019/09/19/us /politics/ intelligence -whistle-blower-complaint- Trump.html?action=click& module=Top%20Stories&pgtype=Homepage

BibleInfo (2019) Ten Commandments: King James Version Retrieved from: https://www.bibleinfo.com/en/topics/ten-commandments-list#

Caro, R. (1975) The Power Broker, VintageBooks, NY

Child Welfare Information Gateway. (2012). *State versus County Administration of child Welfare services*. Washington, D.C.: U.S. Department of Health and Human Services, Children's Bureau. Retrieved from: https://www.childwelfare.gov /pubs/factsheets /services/

Children's Bureau. (2015). *Reports and Results of the Child and Family Service Review*. Washington: Administration for Children Youth and Families. Retrieved from: https://library. childwelfare.gov/cwig/ws/cwmd/docs/cb_web/SearchForm

Children's Bureau. (2016, 12 7). *Worker Turnover*. Washington: Administration for Children Youth and Families. Retrieved from: https:// www.childwelfare.gov /topics/management/ workforce/retention /workforce-retention/turnover/

Children's Bureau. (2017). *Child Welfare Policy Manual.* Washington, D.C.: Department of Health and Human Services. Retieved from: https://www.acf.hhs.gov/cwpm/ public_html/programs /cb/laws/_policies /laws/cwpm/index.jsp

EEOC (2019) Laws Enforced by EEOC Retrieved from: https://www .eeoc.gov/laws/ statutes/index.cfm

Fidelity Charitable (2019) *Will tax reform affect your charitable deduction? What you need to know.* Retrieved from: (https://www. fidelitycharitable.org/articles/will-tax-reform-affect-your-charitable-deduction.html

Giving USA. (2016). *How Well Do Human Services Organizations Do at Fundraising, Compared to Other Charities.* Retrieved from: https://givingusa.org/how-well-do-human-services-organizations-do-at-fundraising-compared-to-other-charities/

Guidestar. (2014). *Guidestar Nonrofit Compensation Report.* Williamsburg: Guidestar USA. Retrieved from: http://www.guidestar.org/ downloadable-files/2014CompREeport-sample.pdfgeographic proximity

Internal Revene Service (2008) *Governance and Related Topics - 501(c)(3) Organizations* Retrieved from: https://www.irs.gov/pub/irs-tege/governance_practices.pdf

Internal revenue Service. (2015). *Exempt Purposes - Internal Revenue Code Section 501(c)(3).* Washington: Department of the Treasury. Retrieved from https://www.irs.gov/Charities-&-Non-Profits/Charitable-Organizations/Exempt-Purposes-Internal-Revenue-Code-Section-501%28c%29%283%29

Internal Revenue Service. (2016). *2016 Instructions for Form 990 Return of Organization Exempt From Income Tax.* Washinginton: Department of Treasury. Retrieved from: https://www.irs.gov/pub/irs-prior/i990ez--2016.pdf

Internal Revenue Service (2018)Compliance Guide for for 501© 3 Public Charities   IRS Tax Exempt and Government Entities IRS Exempt Organizations   Publication   4221-PC   Retrieved   from: https://www.irs.gov/pub/irs-pdf/p4221pc.pdf

IRS (2019) *Required Discloses* Retrieved from:
https://www.stayexempt.irs.gov/se/files/downloads/Required_
Disclosures_Print.pdf

Kelly, T. (1999, 10 2). *In Quiet Fields, Father Ritter Found His Exile; After Scandal, Covenant House Founder Had a Simple, Solitary Life Upstate.* Retrieved from: New York Times: http://www.nytimes.com/ 1999/10/22/nyregion/quiet-fields-father-ritter-found-his-exile-after-scandal-covenant-house-founder.html

Amy Kosanovich, A. and R. Joseph (2005). *Child Welfare Consent Decrees.* Child League of American and American Bar Association. Retrieved from: https://thehill.com/sites/default/files/ consentdecrees _0.pdf

Mckeever, B. (2015). *The Nonprofit Center in Brief.* Urban Institute. Retrieved from http://www.urban.org/research /publication/nonprofit-sector-brief-2015-public-charities-giving-and-volunteering

Montgue, J. (2013). *The Law and Financial Transpareny in Churches Reconsidering the Form 990.* Washington: Cardoza Law Review. Retrieved from: https://papers.ssrn.com/sol3/papers .cfm?abstract_id=2349093

NASW Center for Workforce Studies and Social Work Practices (2011). (2011). *Social Workers in Social Service Agencies: Occupational Profiles.* Washington: National Association of Social Workers. Retrieved from: http://workforce.socialworkers.org /studies/profiles/Social%20 Services.pdf

Nonprofit Research Alliance. (2015). *Winter 2015 NonProfit Fundraising Survey.* NonProfit Reawarch Alliance. Retrieved from: https://www.urban.org/sites/default/files/publication/49731/2000202-Winter-2015-Nonprofit-Fundraising-Study.pdf

Nonprofit Times. (2014). *2014 Nonprofit Organization Salary Report.* Morris Plains: NPT Publishing Group. Retrieved from: from http://www.shopthenonprofittimes.com/2014 Salary Report

Pennsylvania Department of Human Services (2019), Pennsylvania Child Protective Services 2018 Annual Report; Retrieved from: http://www.dhs.pa.gov /cs/groups/webcontent/documents/ document/c_289620.pdf

Pennsylvania Department of Human Services (2017), Pennsylvania Child Protective Services 2016 Annual Report Retrieved from:http://www.dhs.pa.gov/cs /groups/webcontent/documents /report/c_260865.pdf

Sage Works. (2015). *Industry- P30 Children and Youth Services*. Sage Works.

Stotzfus, E. (2017). *Child Welfare: An Overview of Federal Programs and their Current Fundng*. Congressonal Research Service. Retrieved from: https://fas.org/sgp/crs/misc/R43458.pdf

Thomson, M. (2013). State Revenue Collection Through The Great Depression. *Indiana Busiess Review*, v88 X3.   Retrieved from: https://www.ibrc.indiana.edu/ibr/2013/fall/article2.html

Urban Institute. (2015). *NCSS Core File (Public Charities)*. Washington: National   Center   for   Charitable   Statistics.   Retrieved   from http://nccsweb.urban.org

U. S. Coastguard (2019) *Diversity Policy Statement* , The Com mandment of the United States Coastguard, Washington D.C. Retreived from:
 https://www.dcms.uscg.mil/Portals/10/CG-1/Civilian/docs/dps.pdf ?ver=2017-05-01-150641-110

Watkins-Uiberal. (2013). *2013 Non Profit Compensation Survey*. Memphis: Watkins-Ubiberal. Retrieved   from http://www.cnm.org/ Documents 2012-Watkins-Uiberall-NFP Survey.pdf

Appendix
BOD Committee Descriptions

Following are examples of general committee descriptions. If the BOD is small, combine or eliminate some of the committees and tasks listed. Another option is to stagger the accomplishment of projects. For instance, the development committee is responsible for running one fundraising event every two years rather than multiple annual events. As necessary prioritize committee duties, enlist people who are not BOD members to help, or expand the size of the BOD.

Finance and Property Committee
The committee purpose is to create and periodically review financial policy, to monitor income and expenses, and investment results. The committee presents the annual budgets, 990-tax filing, and other documents as is necessary to the board of directors. In addition, the committee assures that the physical facilities of the agency meet existing and future needs. At least five members of the BOD, the president, and the finance director staff the committee. Community members with special expertise can serve as nonvoting members with the approval of the BOD chairperson. Senior management staff participating in succession training may also staff the committee. Only elected directors participate in voting.

The committee:

> - Verifies that a written set of financial policies and procedures exists which assures that the financial operations and financial records of the organization meet applicable American Accounting Board standards.
> - Adopts and assures the implementation of both an organizational treasury policy and an organizational investment policy for operating cash, endowment funds, and investment funds
> - Assures, that using a competitive bidding process, that two firms are engaged to manage investment and endowment funds. The committee reviews quarterly reports from these firms and meets with their representatives annually. The retention or replacement of ae current firm is a committee decision.
> - Reviews and Recommends to the BOD for approval, the annual 990-tax filing.

➢ Reviews and recommends to the BOD two annual budgets one for operations and one for capital projects. The committee assures the proposed operating budget is in balance, includes input from the appropriate program personnel, and is experience based.

➢ Assures the annual operating budget for the year ahead includes a general cost of living percent, and allowance for a percent for staff salary increases. The personnel committee recommends a percentage for staff salary increases and the finance committee approves it.

➢ Assures the appropriate vice president has the chief of maintenance inspect every property owned by the organization annually and that the capital budget for the year includes all anticipated repairs and replacement items more than $5,000. The annual capital budget total does not exceed the annual depreciation amount.

➢ Reviews and discusses each monthly (quarterly) financial statement, raising questions and hearing staff plans to manage any program deficit where expenses exceed income by more than 5%, or in situations in which the overall agency income and expenses are in deficit.

➢ The president has the vice president, who supervises the agency property and maintenance function attend the committee meetings when there are property and maintenance agenda items.

➢ Reviews and approves capital acquisition business plans submitted by the president and recommends them to the BOD. These recommendations include making motions before the BOD for the property acquisition and application for any mortgages or borrowing involved.

➢ Annually reviews and recommends to the board of directors the 990-tax filing for approval and submission. Reviews bids involved in construction projects where the project size exceeds $100,000.

➢ Meets with and provides feedback to the president on candidates for the finance director position

Audit committee

The audit committee selects and collaborates with an outside audit firm responsible for performing an annual audit of the PCWA financial statements and fiscal operations. The committee assesses organizational risks. The committee investigates any alleged wrong- doing. or conflict of interest by executive staff or members of the board of directors. The committee examines any financial, business and clinical records, buildings and personnel as necessary to investigate alleged wrongdoing.

At least five members of the BOD of directors, the president, and the finance director staff the committee. Community members with special expertise can serve as nonvoting members with the approval of the BOD chairperson. Only elected directors participate in voting Members of the committee do not have relationships that interfere with their independence and they are financially literate. The duties of the committee are:

> Recommend to the BOD independent auditors to undertake an annual audit of organizational financial statements.
> Evaluate the auditor's performance and fees.
> Discuss the strength and characteristics of the audit process and study the audit reports. The chairperson of the committee is available to the auditors.
> Ascertain that the auditors have no relationships that compromise their independence.
> Assures a discussion involving committee members, and the auditors occurs annually regarding the sufficiency of accounting policies, financial presentation formats, estimates, reserves and accruals, existing financial controls, fraud, excess benefit transactions and business transaction involving conflicts of interest as well as observations about financial risk.
> Review the annual management letter and any findings, and approve a plan submitted by the president and finance director to address recommendations and findings
> Review with staff significant risks faced by the organization and the steps staff has taken to mitigate such risks. The areas of risk covered will include, staff turnover, insurance coverage and uncovered risks, litigation, operational problems, and any other matters that could have an impact on the financial position of the organization.
> Receives and investigates complaints of wrongdoing or conflicts of interest involving members or the BOD, key employees, and anyone holding the position of service director, vice president, or president. Informs the executive committee of the BOD of the results of each complaint investigation.

Program Committee

The purpose of the program committee is to assure that service programs fulfil the agency mission and are operational, sufficiently utilized, and precipitate positive outcomes among participants. The committee recommends program adoption and discontinuation to the BOD. The committee assures that programs operate efficiently and effectively. At least five members of the BOD of directors, the president, and the lead clinical officer staff the committee. Community members with special expertise may serve with the approval of the BOD chairperson. Senior management staff participating in succession planning may also staff the committee. Only elected directors participate in voting. The committee:

> Recommends the adoption of new programs to the BOD. As part of this process, the committee reviews the business plan of the president to assure an appropriate need assessment, and program implementation plan exists. The committee receives input from the finance committee on the financial portion of the business plan. The committee considers the new program development criteria (covered in chapter 9).

> Using written criteria (also covered in chapter 9) recommends discontinuation of current programs to the BOD.

> Reviews the format for program annual reports and makes necessary modification to the format as needed.

> Following the program director's presentation of their annual report to the BOD, members review the report and make recommendations or comments to the president regarding service levels, outcomes, and program goals.

> Periodically adopts a strategic plan (covered in chapter 12). In every year that there is not a new plan, the committee reviews the current strategic plan and makes recommendations to the BOD for any substantial alterations.

> As part of the strategic planning process, the committee decides upon the nature of the participation from the BOD of directors, all customers responsible for 5% or more of agency income, school personnel, consumers, and staff including vice presidents and program directors, supervisors and selected direct service staff.

> The committee decides upon the planning method, report format and time span.

> The chairperson presents a plan to the BOD for adoption.

Development and Nominations

The purpose of the development and nominations committee is to lead and provide oversight of the organizational private fund-raising efforts and manage all aspects of BOD membership. At least seven members of the BOD serve on the committee. The president, and the director of development staff the committee. Community members with special expertise, or good community contacts can serve as nonvoting members with the approval of the BOD chairperson. Senior management staff participating in succession training may also staff the committee. Only elected directors participate in voting. The committee:

- ➤ Adopts an annual fundraising goal and specifies the financial results of each segment of the fund-raising program (i.e. events, foundation grants, large donor gifts, etc.).
- ➤ Reviews the development report monthly. The report indicates by category current month's results, year to date results, the annual goal, and last year's results.
- ➤ Decides on the number and type of annual fundraising events. The committee provides oversight and support to the committees implementing events. One member of each event committee is a member of the BOD level committee
- ➤ Reviews donor prospect lists, and prioritizes them. Each committee member, based on their relationships, contacts two prospects each year, meeting with them and the president, preferably at one of the program sites
- ➤ Presents donor prospect lists at BOD meetings and enlists other BOD members in donor cultivation, soliciting gifts and assisting with other aspects of the development effort.
- ➤ Contacts or arranges for others to contact foundation BOD members to support agency applications for grants.
- ➤ Recommends capital campaigns and other major fund drive initiatives to the BOD
- ➤ Designates a member to solicit the BOD members for an annual gift at the October meeting of the BOD, and assures follow-up to the solicitation with the goal of getting 100% participation in the campaign
- ➤ Reviews potential BOD member nominees.
- ➤ Assures that at any time two directors are youth under 21 years of age and that a parent of a service user is a member
- ➤ Considers the need for particular skills, gaining representation from major companies in the community, achieving a diversified BOD of directors, and the ability of the person to advance fundraising efforts when reviewing nominees
- ➤ Arranges for an annual meeting of the BOD and assures the president makes a report containing the financial information specified in the bylaws.
- ➤ As they deem appropriate brings the names of current directors whose two-year terms are expiring into nomination for additional terms.
- ➤ The committee decides upon, and presents at the annual meeting, the officers for the year ahead and members at large of the executive committee.

Personnel Committee

The purpose of the personnel committee is to assure the adequacy of the organizational personnel policies, and to make compensation and benefit recommendations to the BOD for non-executive level staff. The vice president for programs staffs the committee. Community members with special expertise, or good community contacts can serve as nonvoting members with the approval of the BOD chairperson. Senior management staff participating in succession training may also staff the committee. Only elected directors participate in voting. The committee:

> ➢ Annually reviews the organizational personnel policies
> ➢ Ensures the policies change in response to new legislation
> ➢ Periodically learns about local industry compensation patterns
> ➢ Recommends a salary pool amount for staff raises as part of the annual budgeting process.
> ➢ Monitors implementation of the staff succession policy.

Information Technology Committee

The committee 1) assures staff maximize the IT function to support agency programs and operations, 2) reviews hardware, interface, and communication infrastructure, 3) analyzes software needs including software that customers require, and its implication for hardware requirements, internal software development, software purchases and using externally owned software on a licensing basis. 4) Reviews annual hardware and software budget line items in the capital budget, 5) assures the IT staff implement work station replacement as per schedule., and 6) every other year reviews written IT policies, protocols, routines, and standards. The committee consists of at least three BOD members and may include, in an advisory capacity, current outside IT service providers, and persons with IT expertise who are not BOD members. At least three of the members will have sufficient technical knowledge to evaluate and make recommendation regarding committee agenda items.

The committee:

> ➢ Provides feedback to staff on the planned annual capital IT expenditures, including equipment, software, and personnel.
> ➢ Brings before the BOD any proposed policy related to the organization's IT program.
> ➢ Reviews biannually all written IT policy and practices including the employee IT manual biannually
> ➢ Evaluates and monitors agreements with external IT vendors. Bids out IT purchases and services and reviews bid submissions for purchases of items and services if the annual cost in the aggregate exceeds $100,000.

> Reviews the sufficiency of hardware, interface, and communication infrastructure annually
> Reviews a summary of the IT staff service logs annually
> Reviews the functionality and needs for replacement and / or upgrades to clinical and financial software
>

Executive Compensation Committee

The purpose of the committee is to determine compensation for the president, to review, and approve compensation for other highly compensated executives. The committee assures the organization conforms to IRS safe harbor provisions regarding executive compensation, protecting the organization from IRS Intermediate Sanctions. The committee performs responsibilities regarding the organizational deferred compensation plan. The committee monitors, and in concert with the Audit committee manages excess benefit transactions.

Membership

Annually the chairperson of the BOD appoints or reappoints a committee chair person and committee members. All voting members are members of the BOD. Non-voting members attend with the authorization of the chair of the BOD. The chairperson may not appoint disqualified BOD members or non-BOD members to serve. A disqualified person has more than a 34% ownership interest in a business that receives more than deminimus compensation from the agency, a family member of a disqualified person, or a person having a business relationship with a disqualified member of the BOD. The committee:

Executes those duties listed in the 457f plan, and brings plan amendments to the BOD for approval and also:

> Recommends annually to the BOD the compensation amount for the president, the finance director, and up to eighteen other employees defined as highly paid by the IRS
> Annually reviews independent comparative compensation information for all of the employees in positions listed in item 2.
> Keeps written meeting minutes that document the committee's recommendations and decisions. The minutes also include: the meeting date, time and place; the members present and absent, that a review the minutes of the last meeting occurred, and that the committee reviewed IRS executive compensation rules. The minutes state each motion, who made it, who seconded it, and if it passes unanimously. If not, the written record states the yeas and nays.
> Assures the necessary steps to have any person discovered to be the recipient of an excess benefit transaction return the money plus interest in the same tax period in which the recipient gets the payment.

> Annually undertakes a review of the current IRS intermediate sanction rules and any proposed rulemaking. Reviews PCWA policies for conformance with any changes in IRS rules and amends the committee charter as appropriate.
> Annually reviews the committee charter.
> Reviews recent competitive market comparability survey data at any meeting in which the committee makes decisions about executive compensation. Discusses recommendations from the president concerning management team compensation.
> Meets without the CEO to discuss any compensation adjustments for the president.

401(k) Committee

The purpose of the 401(k) Retirement Plan committee is to implement the duties of the administrative fiduciary of the agency 401(k) plan, and as such, be generally responsible for the management, interpretation, and administration of the plan. The plan provides a vehicle for retirement savings for eligible employees of the agency. The plan is a participant-directed defined contribution retirement plan subject to the provisions of the Employee Retirement Income Security Act of 1974 (ERISA), and all subsequent amendments

The plan offers multiple investment options. The fund options choices provide participants with a variety of choices that cover the major asset classes within the bond and equity markets. The choices also provide participants with a variety of risk profiles, from conservative to aggressive allowing a participant to create a portfolio of funds that best meets his/her unique return/risk profile.

The committee will consist of the chair people of the finance and personnel committees of the agency BOD or their designees, the president the executive vice president, and the director of finance. No person shall serve as a member of the committee convicted of, robbery, bribery, extortion, embezzlement, fraud or any other crime or violation as provided in Section 411(a) of ERISA

No person will serve as a member of the committee who is an employee, owner, or family member of an employee of any organization that manages plan assets or audits the plan.

The committee:
> Has general responsibility for the management, interpretation and administration of the plan
> Manages the administration of the plan in accordance with the agency 401(k) plan document.
> Resolves questions of participant eligibility and vesting Interprets plan provisions

- ➤ Approves or denies participant appeals for benefits
- ➤ Recommends to the agency BOD changes to the committee charter
- ➤ Has authority with respect to the investment of Plan assets, including: Direction to the trustee as to the investment of any plan assets, that are not participant directed. Initially all undirected deposits go into a cash management fund. At any subsequent time, these employees may redirect their investments to other plan investment choices.
- ➤ Recommends appointment or removal of an investment manager to the BOD.
- ➤ Selects investment advisors or consultants, as the committee may deem advisable or necessary from time to time
- ➤ Assures that the investment vehicle has a reasonable cost.
- ➤ Reviews a semi-annual analysis report of current and available investment funds, investment, performance, and investment fees.
- ➤ Makes an annual evaluation of the performance of each fund in the context of an appropriate benchmark
- ➤ Prior to making a recommendation to terminate a fund from the plan, the finance director may recommend to the committee that an investment fund be subject to "watch" status
- ➤ Will meet at least two (2) times per plan year
- ➤ Will take no action as a fiduciary of the Plan unless the committee determines that such action is consistent with the terms of the plan. Actions will be solely in the best interest of the plan and the participants.
- ➤ May allocate or delegate its powers and responsibility, as it may from time to time deem advisable to one or more persons, whether or not such persons are members of the committee or employees. Any such allocation or delegation is in the written records of the committee.
- ➤ Members who are also plan participants will have no authority with respect to any matter especially affecting his or her individual interest in the plan

Index